HOLLYWOOD EXILES IN EUROPE

NEW DIRECTIONS IN INTERNATIONAL STUDIES

Patrice Petro, Series Editor

The New Directions in International Studies series focuses on transculturalism, technology, media, and representation, and features the innovative work of scholars who explore various components and consequences of globalization, such as the increasing flow of peoples, ideas, images, information, and capital across borders. Under the direction of Patrice Petro, the series is sponsored by the Center for International Education at the University of Wisconsin–Milwaukee. The center seeks to foster interdisciplinary and collaborative research that probes the political, economic, artistic, and social processes and practices of our time.

Niki Akhavan
Electronic Iran: The Cultural Politics of an Online Evolution
A. Aneesh, Lane Hall, and Patrice Petro, eds.
Beyond Globalization: Making New Worlds in Media, Art, and Social Practices
Dora Apel
War Culture and the Contest of Images
Daniel Leonard Bernardi, Pauline Hope Cheong, Chris Lundry, and Scott W. Ruston
Narrative Landmines: Rumors, Islamist Extremism, and the Struggle for Strategic Influence
Mark Philip Bradley and Patrice Petro, eds.
Truth Claims: Representation and Human Rights
Melissa A. Fitch
Side Dishes: Latina American Women, Sex, and Cultural Production
Elizabeth Swanson Goldberg
Beyond Terror: Gender, Narrative, Human Rights
Linda Krause, ed.
Sustaining Cities: Urban Policies, Practices, and Perceptions
Linda Krause and Patrice Petro, eds.
Global Cities: Cinema, Architecture, and Urbanism in a Digital Age
Andrew Martin and Patrice Petro, eds.
Rethinking Global Security: Media, Popular Culture, and the "War on Terror"
Tasha G. Oren and Patrice Petro, eds.
Global Currents: Media and Technology Now
Peter Paik and Marcus Bullock, eds.
Aftermaths: Exile, Migration, and Diaspora Reconsidered
Rebecca Prime
Hollywood Exiles in Europe: The Blacklist and Cold War Film Culture
Freya Schiwy
Indianizing Film: Decolonization, the Andes, and the Question of Technology
Cristina Venegas
Digital Dilemmas: The State, the Individual, and Digital Media in Cuba

HOLLYWOOD EXILES IN EUROPE

The Blacklist and Cold War Film Culture

REBECCA PRIME

RUTGERS UNIVERSITY PRESS
New Brunswick, New Jersey and London

Library of Congress Cataloging-in-Publication Data
Prime, Rebecca, 1974–
Hollywood exiles in Europe : the blacklist and cold war film culture / Rebecca Prime.
pages cm. — (New directions in international studies)
Includes bibliographical references and index.
ISBN 978–0–8135–6262–9 (hardback) — ISBN 978–0–8135–6261–2 (pbk.) — ISBN 978–0–8135–6263–6 (e-book)
1. Expatriate motion picture producers and directors—Europe—History—20th century. 2. Motion picture actors and actresses—United States—History—20th century. 3. Motion picture industry—Political aspects—Europe—History—20th century. 4. Motion picture industry—Political aspects—California—Los Angeles—History—20th century. 5. Blacklisting of entertainers—United States—History—20th century. 6. Blacklisting of authors—United States—History—20th century. 7. Cold War—Influence. I. Title.
PN1993.5.E8P65 2014
302.2'34309409045—dc23 2013013406

A British Cataloging-in-Publication record for this book is available from the British Library.

Visit our website: http://rutgerspress.rutgers.edu

Manufactured in the United States of America

In memory of my father

CONTENTS

ACKNOWLEDGMENTS

This book has benefitted from the assistance of many individuals and institutions over the long years of its making. At UCLA I had the good fortune to discuss different aspects of my research with Steve Mamber, Steve Ricci, Dominic Thomas, and Peter Wollen. Vivian Sobchack was instrumental in guiding the book's development and has remained a source of support and inspiration. I am also very grateful for the excellent feedback offered by my wonderful cohort and writing group members, with special thanks to Chiara Ferrari, Ali Hoffman-Han, and Sachiko Mizuno.

My understanding of the blacklist and exile has been immeasurably enriched by the generosity of the many members of the blacklisted community and former émigrés who spoke with me about their experiences. Norma Barzman welcomed me into her life and proved to be the most charming of interlocutors. Rosemary Chodorov, Sylvia Jarrico, and Jean Rouverol Butler likewise shared their memories with me and inspired me with their wit, intelligence, and powers of endurance. In Los Angeles, I also benefitted from conversations with Mickey Knox and Norman Lloyd, while Walter Bernstein spoke with me in New York. During the year I spent researching this book in London and Paris, I met with many friends and family members of the blacklisted, who offered important new insights. In London, I am grateful to George Coulouris, Robin Dalton, Maureen Endfield, Alice and Zachary Leader, Herbert Lom, Michael Seifert, and David Vorhaus. In Paris, I was the recipient of Ellie Boris's memories (and a fabulous pair of green shoes!); I also extend my thanks to Denis and Jan Berry, Luli Barzman, Pip Chodorov, Richelle Dassin, Jacques Nahum, Pierre Rissient, Bertrand Tavernier, and Joe Warfield. Donald Ogden Stewart Jr. and Erik Tarloff also contributed their memories of their families' experiences during these years. Sadly, my heartfelt thanks must be extended posthumously to a number of the blacklisted community who passed away during the writing of this book: Betsy Blair, Jules Dassin, Bernard Gordon, and Joan LaCour Scott. Alain Bernheim, who was a gracious host and correspondent, also passed away in 2009.

I am fortunate to have met or corresponded with many of the scholars whose knowledge and insights inform the book. Thom Andersen and Lary May discussed my research with me in its early stages, and Paul Buhle, Patrick McGilligan, and David Wagner offered helpful clarifications. Brian Neve and Alastair Phillips have likewise provided assistance at important junctures. During my time in Paris and London, my research benefitted from conversations with Pierre

Billard, Geoffrey Nowell-Smith, Gérard Dessère, and Reynold Humphries. I am indebted to my dear friend Kevin Brownlow for numerous contacts, news clippings, coffees, and fascinating conversations.

The original archival research that provides the foundation for *Hollywood Exiles in Europe* could not have been possible without the assistance of numerous knowledgeable archivists. At the Margaret Herrick Library of the Academy of Motion Picture Arts and Sciences, Barbara Hall offered invaluable support; I am also grateful for Faye Thompson's skillful photo research. Lauren Buisson was an able guide through the many riches of UCLA's special collections, while Janet Moat helped ensure that my time at the British Film Institute was well spent. Haden Guest and Peter Lev were also kind enough to share with me their knowledge of relevant archival holdings. My research at archives in France and England was made possible by a Fulbright Fellowship, while the writing of the book was supported by a Board of Associates McCardell Professional Development Grant from Hood College. Portions of the book have been presented at conferences in North America and the United Kingdom; I am grateful to Dennis Broe, Giuliana Muscio, Joanna Rapf, and Daniel Steinhart for their comments and feedback on these occasions. I would also like to thank Frank Krutnik and Daniel Leab for their intelligent editing of the articles drawn from the book that they shepherded to publication. At Rutgers, Leslie Mitchner has been an enthusiastic (and patient!) guide and supporter.

My family has also offered assistance in numerous forms over the years. My aunt Janet Post copyedited an earlier version of this book. My parents were characteristically unstinting in their love and encouragement. From my love of film to my love of language, I owe them so very much. My in-laws, Bob and Nancy Bloch, and sister-in-law Lisa Bloch, have also provided support and assistance, from kind words to childcare. I would also like to thank Judy Elofson for her heroic efforts scanning reams of documents in preparation for my time abroad.

There are a few individuals without whom the writing of this book would have been infinitely harder and lonelier. My interest in this subject was initially developed in Janet Bergstrom's seminar on the French crime film, and Janet has remained the project's most dedicated advisor and a most valued friend. My scholarship has been indelibly influenced by her high standards and meticulous approach to archival research. Emily Carman has likewise been a constructive sounding board and sympathetic confidante during the book's long gestation, in addition to coming to my rescue with some last-minute photo research. Finally, I feel the deepest gratitude toward my exceptional husband, David Bloch, who not only found a way to accompany me to Paris but also read multiple drafts of the manuscript with a scrupulous eye. Next time, I'll try for Rome.

HOLLYWOOD EXILES IN EUROPE

INTRODUCTION

> Of course, none of us was really aware of how fragmented McCarthy would cause our lives to be. Now no matter what we've left bits and pieces in various places, perhaps too many places.
>
> —Ben Barzman

THIS BOOK OWES ITS existence to a chance meeting. On a spring afternoon in Paris, I bumped into an acquaintance from New York who invited me to join her at her favorite tea room, nearby on the rue Royale. Over rainbow-colored macarons, I listened as Suzo Barzman, daughter of the blacklisted screenwriters and Hollywood exiles Ben and Norma Barzman, recounted her expatriate childhood in Paris, where her parents had settled in the early 1950s. I had of course heard of the Hollywood blacklist, but I had no inkling of the exodus of Hollywood directors, screenwriters, and actors to Europe that the House Un-American Activities Committee's investigations into communism had prompted.

My conversation with Suzo lodged itself in my head for years. Eventually, as a graduate student in film studies, I began the process of discovery that has culminated in this book. Starting with the Barzmans, I began to populate the Paris exile community, its extension in the south of France, the small group in Rome, and the large colony of blacklisted Americans in London. To my astonishment, my own expatriate childhood in London turned out to have been spent in the shadow of the blacklisted émigrés, a number of whom had lived around the corner from my family's house.

A serendipitous personal connection thus led to a commitment to documenting the neglected history of the blacklisted exiles in Europe. In piecing together what Suzo Barzman's father called the "bits and pieces" left by those whose lives were disrupted by the HUAC investigations and 1950s Cold War politics, this book has several goals. On the most fundamental level, it aims to tell the tale of a group of people whose lives were driven in unimagined directions as a result of the anticommunist sentiment that pervaded American postwar culture: a tale not previously told, but with significant implications for our understanding of an important era in American and European cultural history and film culture.

Despite the voluminous and ever-growing scholarly literature on the blacklist, very little attention has been paid to the blacklisted diaspora and its members' important contributions to postwar European cinema.[1] My study's scope extends far beyond Hollywood and challenges the periodization and resolutely domestic terms in which the blacklist is usually—and categorically—discussed.[2] By calling attention to the Hollywood blacklist's important and understudied transnational dimensions, I argue that the history of the blacklisted exiles in Europe is significant to our understanding of postwar American and European cinema for a range of reasons. The professional triumphs of the blacklisted community in Europe played a direct role in hastening the end of the blacklist in America, while the inconsistencies in the blacklist's enforcement overseas reflected the complex interplay and negotiations—between Cold War cultural policy, the Hollywood studios, conservative pressure groups, and the blacklisted themselves—that characterized the blacklist's slow demise over the course of the 1950s and 1960s.

Analyzing the experience of the blacklisted in Europe also allows us to reconsider the development of postwar European cinema and its changing relationship with Hollywood during this era. Was the presence of the blacklisted Americans in Europe at a time when European cinema's prestige was growing and Hollywood's was diminishing an ironic coincidence, or did the blacklisted play a more catalytic role in shifting Hollywood's attention toward Europe? How did the exiles' contradictory status as Hollywood communists and American political refugees complicate European concern with preserving their national cinemas from Hollywood's powerful influence? As these questions suggest, the role of the American blacklisted community in Europe in the postwar shift from national to "transnational" cinema has not been fully considered until now.

The practical challenges of reconstructing the history of the blacklisted community in Europe have undoubtedly contributed to its absence from film history. None of the key exiled filmmakers is still living. (Three passed away during the writing of this book: Bernard Gordon in May 2006, Jules Dassin in March 2008, and Betsy Blair in March 2009.) There are few secondary sources devoted to the subject, or even closely related ones, such as the rise of Hollywood "runaway production" in Europe beginning in the late 1940s or studies of the relationship between the Cold War and transatlantic film culture.[3] A number of important archival collections, including the records of the House Un-American Activities Committee, were unavailable until recently.[4] Many of the exiles' European films are hard to find or are available only in poor-quality copies with no current distribution.

In considering this lacuna in an otherwise richly considered subject, a comparison with the experiences of the earlier generation of European émigrés to

Hollywood is illuminating. That the role of European filmmakers in Hollywood has been a popular subject of study is not surprising, corresponding as it does with America's deeply rooted self-image as a bastion of liberty and land of opportunity.[5] This correspondence facilitates the appropriation of the tremendous contributions of émigré filmmakers such as Fritz Lang and Billy Wilder to the development of classical Hollywood cinema. In contrast, the conception of Hollywood as a locus of politically motivated persecution runs counter to the vision of America as an inclusive society that places constitutional value on freedom of expression—for films no less than other forms of protected speech. The experience of the blacklisted community in Europe exposed the fragility of democratic ideals in the face of a climate of fear, much as the fact of their exile contradicted CIA-sponsored Cold War cultural propaganda.[6]

Interpreting the history of the blacklisted diaspora as a Cold War "counterhistory"—one that challenges and opens up the dominant narrative of American ideological supremacy after World War II—provides *Hollywood Exiles* with its third thematic thread and historiographic focus. If, as Richard Maltby has claimed, no "adequate history of the Cold War in America can be written without reference to the blacklist and other agencies of cultural repression that were generated by those encounters," why has the blacklist featured only minimally in accounts of the cultural Cold War in Europe? Why has the impressive transnational cultural production that the blacklist (and by extension, the Cold War) inadvertently encouraged been overlooked?[7] I suggest the answer to this question is that the blacklisted exiles in Europe, as American political refugees with Hollywood associations, occupied a paradoxical position in the heated debates provoked by America's economic and cultural presence in Europe in the years following World War II. Their experience thus provides an alternative perspective to more traditionally delineated histories that frame postwar transatlantic relations in terms of American economic and cultural imperialism and European protectionism.[8] Due to their interstitial position vis-à-vis Hollywood and Europe, the experiences of the blacklisted exiles produce "the frisson of the anecdotal rupture, the flash of the undiscernable real" that destabilizes conventional histories of U.S.-European cultural relations during the Cold War era.[9]

To account for the complexity of the experiences of the blacklisted diaspora in Europe, *Hollywood Exiles* takes a multifaceted methodological approach that incorporates social and cultural history with industrial and aesthetic analysis. It emphasizes the ways in which the experiences of the American exiles were mediated through the various political and cultural discourses—particularly those prevalent in contemporary film criticism—shaping the perception of America in Europe.

As film history, *Hollywood Exiles* also reflects a broad engagement with new historicism and questions of historiography. As historical subjects, the blacklisted exiles in Europe were outliers whose lives defied prevailing cultural norms; as such, their voices—presented here through a patchwork of anecdote, quotation, and cinematic suggestion—have not been reflected in standard accounts of the period. A revisionist approach also suits this study inasmuch as the Hollywood blacklist was an event whose charged and contested historiography reflects the ways in which our understanding of the past and its subsequent "re-presentations" is shaped by tendentious narratives ranging from the political to the psychological.[10]

In using the evidentiary fragments of the blacklist to tell us something valuable about its history and legacy, *Hollywood Exiles* draws largely on extensive, original primary research, encompassing archival collections, government files, legal and financial records, and contemporary periodicals and trade journals. As these sources are mediated no less than any other, my interviews with surviving members of the blacklist and their family, friends, and associates provide a different perspective, one that often also differs from that presented in the émigrés' official memoirs and published interviews.[11] To illuminate the mix of admiration and resentment embedded in European attitudes toward Hollywood at the time, I use numerous production histories as case studies. These histories provide a means of assessing the degree of integration between the blacklisted and European film communities along with the exiles' differing abilities to adapt to European modes of production and film culture.

My perception of the blacklisted diaspora in Europe as, among other things, an "oppositional cultural formation" reflects my book's debt to Rebecca Schreiber's *Cold War Exiles in Mexico: U.S. Dissidents and the Culture of Critical Resistance.* In this history of the community of radical American artists in Mexico during the 1950s, Schreiber convincingly argues that "the Cold War culture of political exile made possible a space of critique for left-wing U.S. artists, writers, and filmmakers in Mexico," the significance of which has been "minimized or omitted within scholarship on U.S. Cold War culture."[12] Among the questions *Hollywood Exiles* poses is whether exile in Europe likewise fostered a critique of Cold War America through the cultural production of those blacklisted. And in its consistent underscoring of the transnational dimensions of the exiles' creative output, *Hollywood Exiles* situates itself in relation both to Schreiber's work and the growing body of recent scholarship devoted to the complex cultural exchanges that resulted from the geopolitical and economic realignments of the postwar period.[13]

Definitions and Parameters

Hollywood Exiles focuses on the experiences of the blacklisted in Europe because, in contrast to the colonies of blacklisted filmmakers in New York and Mexico, they alone as an exile community produced a significant body of film work during the blacklist era. During the 1950s and early 1960s, these Hollywood exiles directed, wrote, or starred in almost 100 European productions, their contributions ranging from crime film masterpieces like *Du rififi chez les hommes* (dir. Jules Dassin, 1955) to international blockbusters such as *The Bridge on the River Kwai* (scr. Carl Foreman and Michael Wilson, 1957) to acclaimed art films like *The Servant* (dir. Joseph Losey, 1963). London was home to the largest group of blacklisted Americans (over twenty at the community's peak), including three of Hollywood's most talented screenwriters—Carl Foreman (*High Noon*, 1952), Howard Koch (*Casablanca*, 1942), and Donald Ogden Stewart (*The Philadelphia Story*, 1940).[14] The directors Cy Endfield, Joseph Losey, and Bernard Vorhaus; the screenwriters Lester Cole, Ian McLellan Hunter, and Frank Tarloff; the writer/producer Adrian Scott and his wife (the television writer Joan LaCour Scott); the producer Bob Roberts; the actors Phil Brown and Sam Wanamaker; and the composer Larry Adler also established themselves in London during the 1950s and early 1960s. Although she was not blacklisted herself, the television producer Hannah Weinstein was an important figure within the blacklisted community in London and a close friend of many of the exiles, whom she frequently employed.

The Parisian community was smaller and more tightly integrated. At its core were the screenwriters Ben and Norma Barzman, Lee and Tammy Gold, Paul Jarrico, and Michael Wilson; the directors Jules Dassin and John Berry; and the actress Betsy Blair. A satellite community formed in the south of France in the late 1950s and included the Barzmans, the distinguished screenwriter/producer Sidney Buchman, his brother and fellow screenwriter Harold Buchman, and the screenwriter Edward Chodorov. By the early 1960s, Paris was also the base of operations for the screenwriter/producer Philip Yordan's "script factory," where blacklisted screenwriters, including Bernard Gordon and Arnaud d'Usseau, churned out scripts for the Russian American producer Samuel Bronston's Spanish-made sword-and-sandal spectacles.[15]

The blacklisted community in Rome was more fluid and included at various points the screenwriters Leonardo Bercovici, Hugo Butler, Ring Lardner Jr., Dalton Trumbo, and Julian Zimet. The playwright and screenwriter Lillian Hellman lived in Rome for much of 1953 while working on a screenplay for the Hungarian-born British producer Alexander Korda. Although never home to significant numbers of exiles, Rome was a frequent work destination largely due to the presence of the producer Dino de Laurentiis, who used blacklisted screenwriters (Michael Wilson being a particular favorite) for numerous projects. During the early 1960s, Madrid also hosted a small colony of blacklisted Americans, all of whom were screenwriters employed by Samuel Bronston. Ben Barzman, Arnaud d'Usseau, and Bernard Gordon temporarily relocated there from Paris, while Julian Zimet and Guy Endore came over from Rome.

Of the estimated 300 individuals whose careers in Hollywood were ended by the blacklist, only a small percentage chose to go into exile abroad. Those who left did so not in a mass exodus, but in a trickle, their timing based on individual circumstances and opportunities. Bound by friendship, shared experience, and professional ties, the blacklisted in Europe formed a diaspora. Hopscotching between European capitals on the trail of work, they were uniquely positioned to contribute to three key developments in postwar European cinema: Hollywood "runaway production," the European co-production, and the international blockbuster. Through case studies of films including *Night and the City* (dir. Jules Dassin, 1950) and *The Bridge on the River Kwai*, I examine the American exiles' influence on these major trends along with how their participation intervened in the charged discourse of national cinema. And in documenting the negotiations that shaped these films, I use these case studies to suggest how the creative work of the U.S. exiles in Europe represented a distinctly transnational mode of cultural production.

Although they never propounded a coherent aesthetic manifesto, the blacklisted Americans did share a conception of social cinema that reflected the radical education they received in the New York theater and Hollywood during the 1930s and 1940s. To what degree did this vision endure during their years of exile? Thom Andersen has argued that the 1950s British films of Cy Endfield and Joseph Losey represent a continuation of *film gris*—his term for the small outpouring of socially conscious noirs produced by members of the Hollywood Left including Berry, Dassin, Endfield, and Losey during the period between the 1947 and 1951 HUAC hearings.[16] Taking Andersen's claim as a starting point, my book examines whether working in Europe satisfied the exiles' yen for a more political and socially meaningful mode of filmmaking. The effect of exile on the émigrés' social realist aspirations, and on their creative potential more generally, provides one of *Hollywood Exiles*'s principal lines of inquiry.

The influence of the Hollywood blacklist on the exile communities and the European film industries more generally is another of the book's central concerns. What obstacles did the blacklist put in the way of the émigrés' attempts to relaunch their careers? What influence did it exert over European film production? The blacklist would linger longer in Britain than in France, where government support for the film industry allowed producers and distributors greater independence from Hollywood and rendered the blacklist comparatively irrelevant to their decisions. In Britain, on the other hand, the greater involvement of the Hollywood studios in Britain's domestic industry meant that the blacklist continued to be an issue for the exiles until the early 1960s. In addressing these questions, I argue for a reconsideration of the blacklist as a phenomenon with international—not merely domestic—ramifications.

My historical parameters closely mirror what Larry Ceplair and Steven Englund refer to as "The Blacklist Era" (1947–1960), although I end my study later, in 1964.[17] Encouraged by reports of the blacklist's demise, some of the exiles returned to America that year. At the same time, others cemented their reputations in Europe with commercial and critical hits. With its members embracing different professional and personal paths, the blacklisted community in Europe began to fracture and disperse.

Throughout this book, I consistently use a number of terms to refer to the blacklisted filmmakers working in Europe and the nature of their experiences abroad. Although they tended not to refer to themselves as "exiles," and in some cases explicitly rejected the appellation (on the grounds that it implied victimhood as opposed to volition), I nonetheless employ it. The exiles were indeed not exiles in the formal sense—they had not been legally banished from their native countries and retained the option to return home—but they had been driven from their professions and fled abroad, in many cases to escape subpoenas.[18] The experience of exile thus defined them as a community, not least in the eyes of others, and forced them to rely on each other (in varying degrees at different times) for professional and emotional support. In their accounts of the period, the blacklisted frequently described the extraordinary feelings of camaraderie and community that sustained them through these difficult times.[19] Their status as blacklisted exiles also defined them in the eyes of their European hosts, who offered personal sympathy, if not always professional opportunity. Finally, I also refer to the exiles as "refugees," the political connotations of which are appropriate to their circumstances, and by the more neutral term "émigré."

With regard to the professional realm in which they operated and the distinctive characteristics of the work they produced, I use the terms "transnational," "international," "transatlantic," and "cosmopolitan" somewhat interchangeably, with distinctions of nuance. "Transnational," as a means of referring to the circulation of individuals or ideas across national boundaries, suits discussion of the cross-cultural production of the blacklisted in Europe (on the level of industry, genre, etc.). "International" in turn refers to a historical mode of production or experience that encompasses more than one country, but does not necessarily entail the cross-border circulation implied by "transnational." "Transatlantic" focuses the book's geographic and intellectual terrain on issues pertaining to Euro-American cultural exchange.[20] Finally, "cosmopolitan" describes an individual, film, or other cultural formation that looks beyond the limitations of any single nation in its self-definition.

Structure and Organization

Hollywood Exiles begins with an overview of Hollywood's radical community in order to better understand the political perspectives, professional experiences, and social connections that shaped the exiles prior to their departure for Europe. Chapter 1 explores the contradictions of Hollywood communism, which contributed to the future exiles' sense of being outsiders within Hollywood. It also addresses the question of communist propaganda, which played such a central role in the HUAC show trials, through introducing one of the book's principal lines of investigation: whether the blacklisted exiles formed an artistic community. While the blacklisted did their best to address the same issues of social justice (racism, antisemitism, poverty, etc.) on screen as they did in their offscreen political activism, the structural checks and balances built into the Hollywood studio system minimized the possibility of unsanctioned, direct political propaganda. In discussing the role of the screenwriter and director in relation to the industrial changes occurring in postwar Hollywood (such as the growth of independent production), this chapter also provides a measure of comparison for the consideration of the European modes of production to follow.

Chapter 2 situates the exiles' early experiences in Europe amid the tense backdrop of U.S.-European relations during the early years of the Cold War. To what degree did the exiles' radical politics and status as refugees from *le Maccarthyisme* insulate them from the anti-American sentiment elicited by America's economic, military, and cultural presence in postwar Europe? Conversely, what obstacles did the blacklist put in the way of the émigrés' attempts to relaunch their careers overseas? As illustrated by events such as *l'affaire Dassin* (in which Jules Dassin was summarily fired from a French production on account of having been blacklisted), the blacklist's reach extended across the Atlantic and provides a measure of postwar European cinema's complicated relationship with Hollywood. The anxiety surrounding notions of national cinema surfaces in this chapter's discussion of the heated debates provoked in France by the bilingual Franco-American co-productions that provided a number of the exiles with their first European employment. The chapter closes with a comparison (vis-à-vis France) of the different political and professional environments that the exiles encountered in Britain.

My next chapter articulates the relationship between the blacklist and the industrial trend of Hollywood "runaway production," which exploded in Europe during the 1950s. If, as some scholars have suggested, the blacklist was primarily an economic strategy for the studios, enabling them to rid themselves of costly talent at a time when their business was dramatically retrenching, it was a poorly conceived strategy that ultimately backfired.[21] By creating a critical mass of Hollywood-trained talent in Europe, the blacklist had the unanticipated effect of invigorating both indigenous and international film production in Europe and diminishing Hollywood's competitive advantage. This chapter examines the ways in which blacklisted participation in the range of American overseas production—from studio to independent to "international"—reveals the complex and often contradictory interplay between Hollywood's conservative elements and increasingly international orientation. The experiences of the screenwriter Michael Wilson and the writer/producer Carl Foreman working for high-profile, independent producers such as Dino de Laurentiis, Sam Spiegel, and Darryl F. Zanuck provide the opportunity to examine the rise of the big-budget, U.S.-European co-production. However, the widespread practice of "clearance"—whereby a blacklisted filmmaker could "clear" his name with Hollywood by submitting a letter recanting his past communist affiliation (but, significantly, *not* naming names)—indicates that politics had yet to be eclipsed by economics in the discourse and practice surrounding runaway production and Hollywood's "runaway" filmmakers.

During their first years in Europe, those American exiles who succeeded in finding film work were limited primarily to the film noir or crime film genres. This restriction reflected the strong association between those genres and the Hollywood cinema in which the filmmakers were trained—an association that in turn makes the European noirs of the blacklisted intriguing examples of transnational filmmaking. As hybrid texts reflecting the complex negotiations between American and European cinematic traditions, films such as *Du rififi chez les hommes*, *Je suis un sentimental* (dir. John Berry, 1955), *Hell Drivers* (dir. Cy Endfield, 1957), and *Blind Date* (dir. Joseph Losey, 1959) adapt and manipulate the restrictions of genre to the filmmakers' personal experience of the blacklist and exile. Through close textual readings, chapter 4 calls attention to the continuities between the experience of exile and film noir's emphasis on transient spaces and emotions of alienation and estrangement.

The changes the exile community underwent during the latter half of the 1950s reflect the broader social trends and developments within the film industry in Europe and America that I discuss in my next two chapters. Hollywood's growing fascination with European cinema proved complicated for the exiles, increasing their cachet even as it extended their struggles with the blacklist, at least in some cases, due to the larger financial presence of the U.S. studios in Europe—especially in the United Kingdom. Chapter 5 queries the effect that the more crowded and competitive expatriate scene of the late 1950s and early 1960s had on the blacklisted exiles, both in terms of the professional opportunities available to them and to their continued coherence as a community. It also examines whether their status as exiles and their expatriate experience created a space for the blacklisted to express a more critical perspective on America's Cold War culture. Did the blacklisted make films in Europe that, whether on account of a "transnational" or "cosmopolitan" vision that rejected an explicitly chauvinistic framework or as a result of their allegiance to a resolutely pre–Cold War vision of the social cinema, could be considered a "counter-canon" to 1950s Hollywood domestic production, with its implicit attempt to win over hearts and minds to the "American way of life"?

Chapter 6 focuses on the career trajectories of the émigré directors—particularly Jules Dassin, John Berry, and Joseph Losey—in relation to three key developments in European cinema in the 1950s and early 1960s: the European co-production, the emergence of the Free Cinema movement in Britain and the New Wave in France, and the ascendance of the concept of the *auteur*. Dramatic changes in film criticism in England and France (as well as in the United States, although in a more diluted fashion) meant that by the beginning of the 1960s, Dassin and Losey found themselves on opposite ends of critical favor due to the growing influence of a new generation of film critics. The chapter closes with a comparison of Dassin's and Losey's critical reputations in America at this time, an exercise that reveals not only the evolution in attitudes toward the blacklist but also significant transatlantic differences in the perception of the European art film and its relationship to national cinema. By highlighting the stature granted to European art cinema by U.S. film culture in this period, this consideration of the exiles' American reception also illuminates the degree to which the strong association between European filmmaking and a certain type of intellectual, personal cinema further distanced the exiles' from the blacklist—albeit at the high price of their nationality.

The end of the blacklist, a subject on which most studies of the period do not linger, is discussed at some length in my final chapter. By the end of the 1950s, a number of the blacklisted were enjoying successful careers in Europe, careers that called attention to the apparent irrelevance of the blacklist (and by extension, Hollywood) to an increasingly international and Eurocentric film industry. At the same time, the ambiguity surrounding the blacklist's demise—when and how it finally ended—hastened the disintegration of the European blacklisted communities. The public's taste for red-baiting waned after the televised Army-McCarthy hearings of 1954, when Senator Joseph McCarthy's belligerent performance prompted the Army's attorney Joseph Welch to famously query the senator's sense of decency. By the late 1950s, the blacklist, whose existence was never officially acknowledged, posed a public relations quandary for the studios, which responded with caprice. Why were some of the exiles able to begin working under their own names while others could not? The recently declassified HUAC files of the director Cy Endfield, who testified before the committee in March 1960 (the year commonly cited as the end of the blacklist), provide an extreme example of how the shared experience of the blacklist had now become a source of division among the exiles.

In its conclusion, *Hollywood Exiles* returns to the theme of community. Were the blacklisted in Europe able to sustain the legacy of the radical community that

HUAC had extinguished in Hollywood? As a means of measuring of the community's fault lines, the treatment of informers by the blacklisted in Europe is also considered. The feelings of the blacklisted regarding the effect of exile on their creative output—and personal lives—provide a coda to my summation of their contributions to postwar European cinema. Finally, I explore how the experiences of the blacklisted in Europe challenged and disrupted strict perceptions of national identity and national cinema and, in doing so, foreshadowed the film industry's nascent cosmopolitanism.

1 • THE RADICAL COMMUNITY IN HOLLYWOOD

HOLLYWOOD IN THE 1940S was still a relatively small community, with roughly 50,000 people employed by the film industry.[1] During the tumultuous course of the 1930s—marked by the Depression, the struggles of the talent guilds for recognition, and the enthusiastic embrace of antifascist causes—it had also become a highly politicized community that supported a remarkable number of left-wing political organizations and charitable groups. Not surprisingly, considering Hollywood's moderate size and politically oriented social life, left-leaning film industry professionals—a group that encompassed both radicals (communists and fellow travelers) and liberals (noncommunist antifascists)—tended to know each other. Connections made at professional schools such as the League of American Writers' (LAW) School for Writers and political organizations such as the Hollywood Independent Citizens Committee of the Arts, Sciences, and Professions (HICCASP) were solidified at Schwab's Drugstore and the Black Watch Delicatessen on Sunset Boulevard, as well as at private cocktail parties, which often doubled as fund-raisers or even Communist Party branch meetings.[2]

Social connections intersected with numerous professional associations and collaborations. A glance at the films written and produced by future targets of the blacklist shows a high degree of creative cross-pollination, with films such as *The Prowler* (directed by Joseph Losey from a script by Hugo Butler and Dalton Trumbo), *He Ran All the Way* (directed by John Berry, also from a script by Butler and Trumbo, and starring John Garfield), and *The Boy with Green Hair* (directed by Losey from a script by Ben Barzman) boasting impeccable left-wing pedigrees.[3] William Morris agent and Communist Party organizer John Weber represented many left-wing writers and directors, including Ben Barzman, Bernard Gordon, Julian Zimet, Ring Lardner Jr., Joseph Losey, Vladimir Pozner,

Jean Rouverol Butler, and Bernard Vorhaus. The Hollywood radical community was also bound by ties of sentiment. Hugo Butler was introduced to his wife, the actress and screenwriter Jean Rouverol, by his roommate, screenwriter Waldo Salt. Producer Dore Schary was the best man at their wedding. Aspiring novelist Michael Wilson was convinced to give Hollywood a try by his future brother-in-law, screenwriter Paul Jarrico. Norma Barzman met her husband Ben at a Russian War Relief party hosted by the writer and director Robert Rossen.[4]

The question of community merits particular consideration in relation to Hollywood in the 1940s on account of the focused attack to which the Hollywood Left was subjected as the decade wore on. The tactics of the House Un-American Activities Committee were designed to fracture and divide the Hollywood community through the emphasis placed on informing, or naming names. In his investigation of the moral dimensions of the blacklist, Victor Navasky highlights the destructive effect of the investigations on the Hollywood community, noting that "the informer's particular contribution was to pollute the public well, to poison social life in general, to destroy the very possibility of a community; for the informer operates on the principle of betrayal and a community survives on the principle of trust."[5] Screenwriter Howard Koch's description of the noxious effect of the blacklist on Hollywood supports Navasky's analysis: "Hollywood had changed. . . . It was like a pall that fell over. People began to be suspicious of each other. Should you go and see a Russian movie, or would they take your license plate and send it in to the FBI? Suddenly fear enveloped the atmosphere of Hollywood. . . . All the idealism had evaporated and, now, fear had taken its place."[6] A sense of loss pervades personal accounts of the blacklist: loss of income, loss of friendships, loss of community, and, perhaps most of all, loss of a remarkable moment in history, a time when faith in the possibility of changing society for the better brought people together in a shared sense of purpose. The radical movement invested Hollywood in the 1940s with a "ferment of ideas" that, in Koch's opinion, rivaled the intellectual excitement of Greenwich Village of the 1910s and 1920s. For screenwriter and director Abraham Polonsky, politics was *the* defining feature of postwar Hollywood. "You can't write about it [the blacklist] unless you also represent the excitement, the political excitement, of the radical movement. . . . Because if you miss that, you don't know what a great place this town was. . . . There was so much going on."[7]

This chapter attempts to chart just *what* was going on in Hollywood in the 1940s in order to better understand the political perspectives, professional experiences, and social connections that shaped the exiles prior to their departure for Europe. Many of the exiles formed close friendships during this period, friendships that proved instrumental to the choices they made in the wake of the blacklist. These friendships were forged in the variety of contexts already mentioned: social gatherings, political organizations, the studios, professional schools, and, for a significant number, the radical New York theater scene of the 1930s. The common thread uniting the individuals in these different milieus was their shared commitment to a set of issues (labor rights, the fight against fascism, racism, and antisemitism) and values (social equity) for which membership in the Communist Party—or in one of the broad alliance of communist and liberal antifascist Popular Front organizations that formed during the late 1930s—provided the most direct means of expression. Whether as radical Communist Party members or sympathetic fellow travelers, the future exiles shared a general political orientation that gave shape not only to their lives in Hollywood but also, more fundamentally, to their sense of identity and their perspective on the world. The 1940s were also an important period of professional development for all the future exiles, many of whom arrived in Hollywood in the early 1940s and were hitting their stride professionally toward the end of the decade. Their work in Hollywood during this period would affect the course of their subsequent careers in Europe, in some cases providing a degree of professional recognition that would ease their entrée into the European film industry.

Mapping the network of relations between the future exiles allows a number of themes to emerge, the most significant of which is that of the radical community's paradoxical relationship with Hollywood. With few exceptions, the relationship between the Hollywood Left and the studios was structurally antagonistic, with the conservative leanings of the studios pitted against the political and artistic impulses of their radical employees. This tense *pas de deux* would take center stage in the HUAC investigations; as a number of studio production heads noted, the committee's central accusation—that radical directors and screenwriters were using motion pictures as vehicles for communist propaganda—implied that the studios were not fulfilling their self-ascribed function as gatekeepers and protectors of the public interest.[8] My interest in the charged dynamic that existed between the studios and the blacklisted exiles has less to do with probing the veracity of the committee's claim—which derives its bite from a misapprehension of what it meant to be a communist in Hollywood in the 1940s—than with understanding the complex, often contradictory relationship between the Hollywood Left and . . . Hollywood. To what degree did the Hollywood radicals identify with "Hollywood," the capitalist dream factory? How did they reconcile their left-wing politics with Hollywood's material excess? The radical community functioned as a bulwark against the sense of artistic frustration and spiritual compromise shared by many of its members, and shored up their self-image as Hollywood outsiders.

New York Social Theater

The New York social theater of the 1930s provides important background for understanding the Hollywood experience and political and artistic beliefs of many members of the radical community. Directors Jules Dassin, John Berry, Joseph Losey, Cy Endfield, Elia Kazan, and Nicholas Ray; screenwriters John Howard Lawson, Albert Maltz, and George Sklar; and actor John Garfield, along with his Group Theatre colleagues Franchot Tone, J. Edward Bromberg, and Roman Bohnen, all got their start in the radical New York theater world. Jules Dassin worked with Elia Kazan on the Federal Theatre's production of *The Revolt of the Beavers,* a children's play labeled "Mother Goose Marx" by *New York Times* theater critic Brooks Atkinson.[9] John Berry found work as an extra with Orson Welles's Mercury Theatre. Joseph Losey directed a production of *Hymn to the Rising Sun* for the Theatre Union, a radical collective whose members included Albert Maltz, George Sklar, and John Howard Lawson. Losey also directed Kazan in an agit-prop play called *Newsboy* and worked with Nicholas Ray and Norman Lloyd on the Federal Theatre's "Living Newspaper" productions; as he put it when asked about those members of the New York theater scene who would go on to make a name for themselves in Hollywood, "We all knew each other."[10]

The New York social theater movement also sparked the political consciousness of those involved. Numerous workers' theaters, including the Yiddish Artef and the Theatre of Action, staged agit-prop productions that addressed labor issues or unemployment and aimed to stimulate the audience to political action. As the decade progressed, the movement's emphasis shifted toward social issues, with the Group Theatre depicting proletarian themes in a context of greater aesthetic realism. More politically engaged than the Group Theatre, the Federal Theatre staged a wide variety of plays, ranging from Shakespeare revivals to contemporary dramas by Eugene O'Neill, but its greatest success was the radically and theatrically innovative "Living Newspaper" plays. With audience participation encouraged through elements of agit-prop, the "Living Newspaper" plays were too subversive for the newly formed HUAC, whose criticism led to the withdrawal of federal funding in 1939.[11]

The closure of the Federal Theatre was followed by that of the Group Theatre the following year. Having never developed a strong financial base, the social theaters were particularly vulnerable to shifts in the political climate. The Left resisted the demise of the radical theaters, seeing their loss as emblematic of changing times. For Dassin, the Federal Theatre was "a magnificent promise for the cultural life of the country. . . . When that was assassinated—demolished—there was anger and protest. . . . We were just devastated when it was undercut."[12] With their hopes crushed and jobs gone, the talent fostered by the social theater movement began its reluctant westward migration.

Jules Dassin as Oakleaf (holding flag) in *The Revolt of the Beavers* (National Archives, Records of the Work Projects Administration)

The social and professional connections forged in New York in the 1930s provided a ready-made network of contacts in Hollywood in the 1940s. The Group Theatre was reborn in the form of the Actors' Lab. John Berry got his first Hollywood job thanks to the recommendation of John Houseman, Orson Welles's partner at the Mercury (the job was to replace former Group Theatre director Harold Clurman as the director of *Miss Susie Slagle's*). In addition to a fledgling community, the Hollywood Left's experiences in New York's radical theater movement instilled in them a profound ambivalence toward Hollywood. Jules Dassin articulates the sense of artistic and political compromise that haunted the new arrivals: "When we all went to Hollywood—we went out there feeling that we were betraying the theater. We were ashamed. We were idiots."[13] Dassin's strong feelings suggest the significance of New York's social theater for his generation, for whom it provided a foundry for their political beliefs and hopes for social change.

A Hollywood Education

By 1945, Dassin and Losey were both under contract at MGM, both rather unhappily. Asked in an interview why a conservative studio like MGM would employ left-wing filmmakers like Losey and himself, Dassin responded with an anecdote: "I can't remember if it was Mayer or Warner, but one of them said: 'These kids, they're Reds, communists. Why do we keep them around? Because they're talented.' That's how cynical it was." Dassin, who joined MGM in 1942 following the accidental success of his short film adaptation of Edgar Allen Poe's *The Tell-Tale Heart*, fought back at the studio by going "on strike" following a conflict over the reshoots he had been promised on *The Canterville Ghost*. For the next fourteen months, he spent his days reading at the beach and collected his paycheck once a week, until his desperation to work forced him back into the studio. During his time at MGM, Dassin was so miserable that he "wanted to go back to New York forever."[14]

Losey found his experience at MGM similarly demoralizing. Although his contract was for features, Losey was coerced into doing a short with the threat of his contract being dropped. The film—made in three days "with a very bad script and a very bad cameraman"—was pronounced "uncuttable" by the head of the shorts department. Fearing for his job, Losey begged to be allowed to cut the film himself, becoming so emotional that he burst into tears. "I felt thoroughly ashamed of myself. The result of it, which was not at all calculated, was that I was allowed to cut it." The short, *A Gun in His Hand*, went on to be nominated for an Academy Award. Describing the studio to a friend as "a great factory operating in a vacuum," Losey left MGM as soon as he could, joining Dore Schary, a friend and fellow transplant from the New York theater world, at RKO in April 1947.[15]

Individual frustrations aside, the studios provided a site of contact for the left-wing community in Hollywood. Losey describes meeting "writers who were absolutely staggering (they included Donald Ogden Stewart and [William] Faulkner) and directors who were also beginning, like [Fred] Zinnemann, Dassin, and [Vincente] Minnelli" while at MGM. "We all had offices in the same buildings, so I saw them all the time."[16] Cy Endfield, who directed his first short films for MGM in 1942, remembers meeting Carl Foreman there.[17] Abraham Polonsky overlapped with John Berry at Paramount. However, the studios were first and foremost a source of employment, not a viable outlet for artistic ambition or social concerns. To fulfill these other needs, the Hollywood Left could choose from an array of "extracurricular activities," many of which bore either a direct or indirect relation to the Communist Party.

Screenwriter Ring Lardner Jr.'s description of his Hollywood years gives a sense of the time and energy the Hollywood Left devoted to their political beliefs:

> Besides marriage, children, and career, my principal activities in the years before the United States entered WWII involved left-wing politics, mostly of the CP kind. . . . Being a communist was time-consuming. I attended events of one sort or another four or five nights a week. There were separate organizational and educational gatherings of my branch, and "fraction" meetings of Communists and close sympathizers within the Screen Writer's Guild. Meanwhile, as a representative of

> the younger writers, I had been elected to the Guild's executive board, which had all-too-frequent meetings of its own. In addition, there were the various Guild committees and similar groups like the Hollywood Anti-Nazi League, the Motion Picture Artists Committee for Spanish Democracy and, during the war years, the Hollywood Writers Mobilization and Russian War Relief. Silvia [his wife] practically had to join the party so that we could see each other.[18]

When Lardner joined the Communist Party in 1936, there were only about two dozen Party members in Hollywood. Five years later, that number had risen to over 200. A number of factors contributed to this growth. Party leaders, acknowledging Hollywood's potential for delivering candy-coated communism to a mass audience, started directing resources toward the movie industry section of the CPUSA. In 1936, the Party began dispatching experienced East Coast organizers to California with the task of organizing the growing number of film industry members into branches.[19] While the organizing principle may have varied ("Once it would be on a neighborhood basis; once it would be on a studio basis; once it would be on a craft basis," screenwriter Maurice Rapf recalls), each branch remained small, never numbering more than a dozen members.[20] One reason for the small branch size was the need for secrecy; it was generally understood that membership in the CPUSA could come at the cost of employment and even personal safety.

Despite these risks, or perhaps because of them, the CPUSA quickly made inroads into the Hollywood studios, largely facilitated by the Party's support for the formation of a Popular Front against fascism. As a result, the CPUSA retreated from its more revolutionary ideas and moved closer to the liberal and progressive mainstream. For a brief window of years between 1935 and 1939, the CPUSA—with its strong track record of defending liberal *causes célèbres* (as in the case of the Scottsboro Boys) and proven skill at worker organization—represented to Hollywood's radicals such as Albert Maltz "that force in the United States—and internationally—which was the best hope of humanity."[21] Carl Foreman, who joined the Party shortly after his arrival in Hollywood in the early 1940s, explains its appeal in terms of the context of the times: "I was very much affected by [the Depression] and by the phenomena of the thirties—the rise of Fascism, the Depression here at home, the steel massacre in Chicago, labor disputes, Spain, Germany—you know. I still feel that the American Communist Party performed a very worthwhile function in the thirties, both in the field of labor, in terms of union recognition etc., and in agitating against the rise of fascism in Europe."[22] As Foreman's comments suggest, the Communist Party's antifascist position garnered it much support in Hollywood, where concern with Nazi aggression ran high. Opposition to fascism was seen as justification enough for joining the CPUSA; as screenwriter Budd Schulberg explains, "The feeling in those days was extremely broad, that any man of good will opposed to fascism could join the Party."[23] American communism, shorn of its revolutionary edge, approached the liberal mainstream, converging with the progressive ideals stimulated by Roosevelt's New Deal. By 1937, the Party adopted a new slogan (coined by CPUSA general secretary Earl Browder) that reflected the new mood of cooperation: "Communism is Twentieth Century Americanism."[24]

Communism's allure in Hollywood can also be understood as a reaction against Hollywood itself, against its material excess and spiritual emptiness. The Party represented a prophylactic or a penance, a way of preserving the soul from corruption or of purging it of decadence. For Donald Ogden Stewart, one of Hollywood's leading screenwriters throughout the 1930s, communism's appeal was clearly tied to the feeling that "something was missing" from his privileged, pampered life. Describing his political awakening, he explains: "Deep within me had been growing the disquieting realization that my childhood gods had played me false, that my quest for security through social and financial success had let me up the garden path—a very pleasant path but one which had come to a dead end. The jackpot had brought security but no inner satisfaction." Stewart's romantic conception of communism (or socialism; by his own admission, he didn't know there was a difference at the time) was directly tied to his experiences in Hollywood. "The essence, to me, was the freedom of the individual, and I somehow associated it with the freedom I had surrendered . . . to Louis B. Mayer." Stewart became one of the Hollywood Left's most active and eloquent spokesmen.[25]

Communism thus offered a salve for the sense of moral compromise, of having sold out their talent and their beliefs for a price, that plagued many of those working in Hollywood. In Budd Schulberg's opinion, joining the CPUSA gave people "a sense that they were doing something more serious and more socially useful, which would compensate for the waste of so much of their talent. Dialectical materialism by the pool . . . some of it was hilarious."[26] Schulberg's feelings are echoed by Joseph Losey, who joined the Communist Party in 1946 as a response to his sense of living in a "cultural vacuum." "It was there [in Hollywood] that I became a party member because I felt useless. . . . It was a kind of guilt that let me into that kind of commitment."[27] Paul Jarrico also points to the guilt and sense of hypocrisy shared by many Hollywood communists: "There was a feeling that here we were, living middle-class lives, enjoying a higher standard of living than most people, being paid higher amounts of money for our work than most people get paid for their work, yet identifying ourselves with the oppressed and the poor."[28] Joining the Communist Party offered a way of assuaging these feelings through actions and by becoming part of a community of like-minded people.

In addition to intellectual dedication, the Party expected active service from its members. Between attending branch meetings, selling the Party's newspapers, and trying to recruit new members from minority communities, "I was busy all the time," recalls Norma Barzman.[29] Party membership also guaranteed a ready-made social

Donald Ogden Stewart at work in Hollywood (From the collections of the Margaret Herrick Library)

life; "You never had to go out by yourself," explains Abraham Polonsky. "There were dinners, parties, meetings, causes." For some, Polonsky suggests, these social benefits came to predominate, obscuring any real dedication to Marxist ideals. "The Party was a kind of social club here. A lot of people talking about Marxism were certainly not Marxists."[30] Whatever their degree of political commitment, the Hollywood communists didn't rush to trade in their dinner jackets for hair shirts. "Mostly we gave parties to raise money for causes," Barzman explains. "After all, it was Hollywood."[31]

Hollywood's Popular Front

While the CPUSA may have been the instigating force behind the growth of the Left in Hollywood, it was through the numerous Popular Front organizations it helped spawn during the late 1930s that the Hollywood radical community really began to coalesce. In addition to providing educational opportunities—not to mention an excuse for cocktails—the CPUSA taught Hollywood how to organize.[32] The Hollywood Anti-Nazi League (HANL), formed in 1936 by Dorothy Parker and Oscar Hammerstein II, hosted star-studded fundraising events that made it a focal point of Hollywood social life and served to boost its membership to close to 5,000 people. Reflecting the strong opposition to fascism throughout the film community, the HANL's list of sponsors was politically inclusive, ranging from radical writers such as John Howard Lawson and John Bright to liberal producers such as Dore Schary and Walter Wanger to a future friendly witness, studio mogul Jack Warner.[33]

With the outbreak of the Spanish Civil War in July 1936, Hollywood's efforts to combat fascism expanded to include groups such as the Spanish Refugee Committee, the Writers' and Artists' Committee for Medical Aid to Spain, the Joint Anti-Fascist Refugee Committee (JAFRC), and the Motion Picture Artists Committee (MPAC), whose membership grew to over 15,000 at its peak and included studio executives and producers. Because of its broad political appeal, anti-fascist causes attracted a much larger membership than the Communist Party ever achieved in Hollywood, with approximately 25 percent of the film community active in some sort of Popular Front organization at various points during the late 1930s.[34]

The Nazi-Soviet Pact of 24 August 1939 destroyed the alliance between communists and liberals (and even some conservatives) that had sustained the Front. With the Soviet Union now allied with a fascist regime, the Popular Front organizations of the 1930s were dissolved or discredited. When the pact ended two years later after Germany invaded the Soviet Union, the Hollywood radicals were thrilled to be rid of the ideological conflict it had created. Donald Ogden Stewart remembers weeping with "joy and relief. I was once more on the 'right' side, the side of all my old friends."[35] After America entered the war following the bombing of Pearl Harbor, the Communist Party USA would enter what Nancy Lynn Schwartz describes as a "honeymoon" period: "For the first time in its history, the CP's aims were in concert with the American political consensus."[36] Communist Party membership grew rapidly nationwide during the early 1940s, reaching an all-time high of 80,000 by 1944.[37]

The Life of the Party: Hollywood Screenwriters and the Question of Propaganda

The presence of the Communist Party in Hollywood had a significant effect not only on the political education and organization of the Hollywood radicals, but also on their professional development and sense of belonging to an artistic community. The CPUSA exerted a particularly strong attraction for screenwriters, who accounted for over half the total party membership in the Hollywood branches by the middle of World War II.[38] Not coincidentally, the CPUSA was also behind the only opportunities to study screenwriting in a serious, theoretically informed way. In 1940, the League of American Writers, a nationwide Popular Front organization, established a School for Writers, drawing its instructors from its roster of over 100 screenwriting members (including Donald Ogden Stewart, John Howard Lawson, Albert Maltz, Alvah Bessie, John Bright, and Paul Jarrico). While the League's members were not exclusively communist, the LAW school operated on the fringes of the Party, serving as a point of entry into the world of Hollywood left-wing politics. Among those who enrolled at the LAW school were Carl Foreman and Norma Barzman, who recalls taking classes in screenwriting with Gordon Kahn and script-reading with Al Levitt, in addition to John Howard Lawson's American literature course. If she was aware of the school's communist affiliation, it did not worry her. "Shortly after I arrived [in Hollywood]," she explains, "I came to understand that all the progressive people I liked and who were politically active were communists." Both Barzman and Foreman would later become Party members, an experience whose educational value was not limited to Marxist theory, as this comment by Foreman suggests: "I don't know if it was at the LAW schools or in the Party discussions, but I was learning about form and content."[39] The LAW School and the Party were both interested in the same goal: encouraging Hollywood screenwriters to infuse their films with "the revolutionary spirit."[40]

In early 1942, the CPUSA made its focus on screenwriters even more explicit when it organized the Writer's Clinic, an informal workshop headed by George Sklar. Coinciding with the demise of the LAW School toward the end of 1943, the People's Education Center (PEC) emerged as yet another educational organization where the Hollywood Left convened to hone their craft. Screenwriting instructor Robert Lees, who had also taught at the LAW School, felt the PEC to be the more Marxist of the two organizations. "I taught that you have to have a political consciousness," he recalls.[41] The school's political orientation soon caught the attention of California state senator Jack Tenney, chairman of the Joint Fact-Finding Committee on Un-American Activities of the California Legislature, who made the school a target of attack. Ben Barzman, an instructor at the school, recalls being followed into the parking lot. Years later, while living in exile in Paris, he was told that his U.S. passport had been confiscated on account of his having worked at the PEC.[42]

Was the aim of these schools to produce students who would then go out and infiltrate the film industry, leaving subtle but insidious instances of communist propaganda in their wake? This, of course, was the central charge of the HUAC investigations, a charge that most radicals with any studio experience found ludicrous. With a few exceptions, studio producers—concerned with finding the broadest possible audience for any given film—exerted a conservative influence over the final shape and content of their productions. Because of this, "scripts that combated the system were rare, and they were due only to very tough struggles on the part of specific individuals," according to Jules Dassin.[43] Joseph Losey goes even farther than Dassin in his negative assessment of progressive filmmaking in Hollywood, finding HUAC's charge of propaganda "quite absurd because there were no films made in Hollywood that had any real left-wing impact at all—with the possible exception of *The Grapes of Wrath*."[44] Carl Foreman concurs, asserting that the investigations "only served to prove conclusively that Hollywood was very far from being a propaganda medium for anything; in terms of content, we've never really been able to be really proud of our little industry."[45]

Others took a less extreme view, finding pleasure in small victories. Paul Jarrico recalls his experience working on an RKO production called *Beauty for the Asking* (1939), in which Lucille Ball played a woman who is unlucky in love but successful in business, inventing a line of beauty products. "A minor element in the plot was some sort of exposé about cosmetics that sell for a high price because of the packaging and advertising, but really the ingredients cost very little. It wasn't much of a social point. But I remember feeling kind of pleased about having got that in."[46] Most radicals, however, found the notion that they simply sneaked bits of left-leaning dialogue or visual commentary into their films reductive. Albert Maltz emphasizes the distinction between a writer consciously inserting political messages into his films and a film written by a politically conscious writer. "I never considered that I was going to try and use films to express my political attitudes. Certainly they reflected attitudes that I had, and these were manifested in the way my characters spoke and what they thought about and so forth. This has to be borne in mind in reference to any film, or any piece of writing: the minds of the people who have worked on it are reflected by what they say or what they don't say."[47] Abraham Polonsky shares Maltz's view that the social content of many Hollywood films of the 1940s should be understood as a reflection of the zeitgeist. As he explains, Hollywood in the 1940s was home to "a generalized political awareness existing in a number of people who were trying to make films that reflected this awareness in one way or another when they had an opportunity to do so. But that opportunity in Hollywood is very limited."[48]

Yet the question of propaganda cannot be diminished in accounts of the blacklist given its role in the HUAC investigations. The string of pro-Soviet films produced by Hollywood following the dissolution of the Nazi-Soviet Pact in 1941 provided HUAC with its key exhibits, despite the fact that they were in line with government policy seeking to raise public support for America's new ally.[49] Films such as *Mission to Moscow* (dir. Michael Curtiz, scr. Howard Koch, 1943), *The North Star* (dir. Lewis Milestone, scr. Lillian Hellman, 1943), and *Song of Russia* (dir. Gregory Ratoff, scr. Paul Jarrico, 1944), produced by Warner

Bros., Samuel Goldwyn, and MGM, respectively, reflected the studios' interest in making "topical" films that took advantage of the wartime public's desire to understand current events. That all three were written by either committed communists (Paul Jarrico and Richard Collins) or liberal sympathizers (Howard Koch and Lillian Hellman) says more about the pervasiveness and acceptance of left-wing politics in Hollywood at the time than it does about the films' value as propaganda, whether for the CPUSA or for American government policy. In each instance, studio executives were careful to avoid explicit political commentary; Collins recalls being instructed to remove references to collective farms, while Hellman was so enraged by the changes made to her script for *The North Star* that she bought back her contract from Goldwyn for $30,000.[50] To the extent that the films cast too rosy a light on life in Soviet Russia—in her friendly testimony before HUAC, Ayn Rand criticized *Song of Russia* for showing peasant women wearing pretty clothes and lipstick—these "improvements" would seem to have as much to do with the aesthetics of classical Hollywood as with politics.

The question of propaganda is further complicated by the dramatic cultural and political transformation that occurred in Hollywood in the aftermath of World War II. While Steven Ross notes that the "postwar climate of fear had its roots in wartime Hollywood's anti-Communist movement," as reflected in the Motion Picture Alliance for the Preservation of American Ideals' (MPA) organized opposition to the Hollywood Left, factors such as the bitter labor disputes of 1945–1947 played a significant role in cementing Hollywood's postwar turn toward the right.[51] With the coming of the Cold War, communism no longer had any purchase on its claim of being "twentieth-century Americanism," and phrases such as "share and share alike" uttered by Ginger Rogers's "Rosie the Riveter" character in *Tender Comrade* (dir. Edward Dmytryk, 1943) assumed dangerous connotations, at least in the opinion of the committee.

While many of the Hollywood Left were communists, what this meant to them differed dramatically from the Cold War stereotypes of spies, conspirators, and violent revolutionaries. Instead, it manifested itself in the "generalized political awareness" referred to by Abraham Polonsky and which did find expression in numerous films from the 1940s, as the Hollywood radicals tried to address through film some of the same pressing social issues they tackled through their political activism. Just as the Left had raised awareness of Los Angeles's racial problems through their organized response to the Sleepy Lagoon Case (in which twenty-four Mexican American youths were indicted for the murder of José Diaz) in 1942 and the Zoot Suit riots (in which small altercations between Mexican Americans and white sailors escalated into a full-on attack on the youths of the barrio by thousands of whites) in 1943, films such as Losey's *The Lawless* (1950) and the underground blacklisted production *Salt of the Earth* (dir. Herbert Biberman, 1954) called attention to the Chicano experience.

Just as the Left had sided with the workers in their acrimonious struggles with the studios in the mid-1940s, so films such as *From This Day Forward* (dir. John Berry, 1946), *Body and Soul* (dir. Robert Rossen, 1947), *Force of Evil* (dir. Abraham Polonsky, 1948), *Thieves' Highway* (dir. Jules Dassin, 1949), and *The Sound of Fury* (dir. Cy Endfield, 1951) place their sympathies squarely with an American working class ill served by capitalism. And just as the Hollywood Left had come together in the fight against fascism, so Edward Dmytryk, Adrian Scott, and Elia Kazan addressed what they saw as a growing problem of intolerance and specifically antisemitism in America in *Crossfire* (dir. Dmytryk, prod. Scott, 1947) and *Gentleman's Agreement* (dir. Kazan, 1947).[52]

Whatever sense of futility the Hollywood Left may have felt regarding its ability to influence motion pictures, it did not prevent the relationship between politics and art from being highly divisive. In February 1946, Albert Maltz voiced his dissatisfaction with communist literary doctrine, which he felt placed undue restrictions on an artist's freedom of expression, in an article entitled "What Shall We Ask of Writers?" published in the prominent Marxist magazine *New Masses*. Specifically, Maltz took issue with the concept of art as a weapon, which he felt had been "converted from a profound analytic, historical insight into a vulgar slogan" used to dismiss all art that did not serve "immediate political ends." Maltz's article sparked months of heated debate, with the influential communist literary critic Mike Gold castigating Maltz for allowing "the luxury and phony atmosphere of Hollywood to at last poison him."[53] With this charge, Gold struck not only at Maltz but at the Achilles' heel of all the Hollywood communists who struggled to reconcile their political beliefs with the material comfort of their Hollywood lifestyle. By stirring up these fears, Gold effectively swung opinion away from Maltz, who publicly recanted and thanked the Party for its edifying critique in articles published in the *New Masses* and the *Daily Worker*.

A Social Film Movement?

In an article written in 1970, Abraham Polonsky responds to a question he is frequently asked: "Was there really a social film movement going on among certain writers and directors that was cut off by the McCarthy movement?" He answers yes, but clarifies that "it wasn't an aesthetic movement, in the sense of surrealism is an aesthetic movement." In other words, the social film movement in Hollywood did not articulate a specific aesthetic doctrine.[54] Nonetheless, while the Hollywood Left may have focused on politics over aesthetics, the two realms converged in a general interest in social realism that extended to both film content and film style.

John Berry sees *From This Day Forward*, his 1946 drama about the struggles of a young, working-class couple in New York, as having more in common with the films of the Italian neorealists than with Hollywood films of the period. "I tried to convey my personal experience of New York, the streets where I grew up, my first impressions." He shot the film on location and in the studio in New York and stripped his lead actress, Joan Fontaine, of her usual Hollywood glamour. "It was the first time anyone had tried to do this sort of thing in America," he explains, "and people didn't understand it."[55] While Berry's comments do not indicate whether he had already seen *Rome, Open City* (1945) when he was working on *From This Day Forward*, the influence of the Italian neorealists on the Hollywood Left is certain.[56] For Jules Dassin, Roberto Rossellini's film showed him a way to combine his interest in documentary aesthetics with narrative form, something he hoped to do in *The Naked City*. "When I saw *Rome, Open City*," he recalls, "I said 'that's the way we have to go.' To use the documentary form to bring a city to life, to bring a thought to life, using what existed or what could exist."[57] Joseph Losey likewise acknowledges the profound impact of Italian neorealism: "Of course I was influenced. Enormously by Rossellini, and also by De Sica. I thought *Open City* and *Paisà* were absolute revelations, and I was enormously impressed by *Shoeshine*."[58]

Along with Italian neorealism, a new awareness of the documentary also exerted a significant influence on postwar filmmaking in Hollywood. During World War II, many film personnel were assigned to work on government

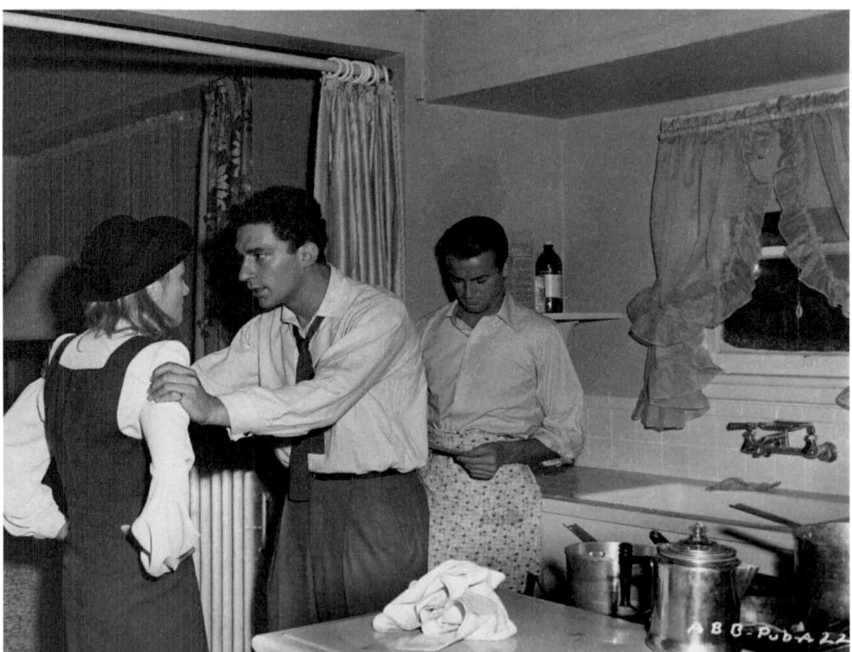

John Berry directing Joan Fontaine in *From This Day Forward* (From the collections of the Margaret Herrick Library)

documentaries, an experience that provided many young filmmakers and technicians with their first exposure to the documentary form.[59] The war also had the effect, at least according to one contemporary analysis, of changing public taste. Noting Hollywood's bent toward stylistic and psychological "realism," *Los Angeles Times* film critic Philip Scheuer suggests that "the late war swept aside sham . . . and taught us to respect direct action and plain speaking."[60]

The director Cy Endfield suggests that it was this shift in the general public that the studios recognized and responded to by (briefly) throwing their weight behind the so-called "social problem" film. After the war, "picture makers, including the people who were approving the pictures, became aware of an audience that wanted to be given the material with which they could make evaluations of themselves. They wanted to look at the more subtle crosscurrents and forces within people, at what can make them warriors and killers of their brothers."[61]

Whether or not for these reasons, a number of top Hollywood producers supported the postwar vogue for realism, as long as it remained commercial. Before he was ousted by Howard Hughes, who took control of the studio midway through 1948, RKO chief of production Dore Schary had planned to make a series of low-budget films addressing social issues.[62] The influential Warner Bros. producer Jerry Wald harbored similar ambitions, stating in an internal memo his view that "the screen isn't a pulpit, but you still can do something that is important and constructive in peoples' lives and make it entertainment that will sell at the box office."[63] At Twentieth Century–Fox, Darryl Zanuck helped launch the cycle of semi-documentary police procedural films that would briefly flourish between 1945 and 1950. However, despite the grit of realism imparted by its use of documentary aesthetics, the semi-documentary was conceived, at least by Zanuck, primarily as entertainment, not as a vehicle for any sustained form of social critique.[64]

Independent Production

By offering progressive filmmakers greater autonomy, the growing field of independent production also made significant contributions to postwar social cinema.[65] Shortly after he had finally freed himself from his seven-year contract at MGM, Jules Dassin received a call from Mark Hellinger, an independent producer with a deal at Universal. Dassin would go on to make two films with Hellinger, *Brute Force* (1947) and *The Naked City* (1948), and credits Hellinger with giving him the freedom and protection he needed to grow professionally. Dassin describes Hellinger's approach as very hands-off. "His attitude was 'You're the director—go make the film.'"[66] Hellinger's respect for Dassin is likewise evident in his decision to let Dassin have a say in the casting of *Brute Force*

Cy Endfield instructs Frank Lovejoy on the "correct way" to strangle a victim for his anti-lynching drama *The Sound of Fury* (From the collections of the Margaret Herrick Library)

and to grant him the right to approve the final screenplay for *The Naked City*, a rare privilege for a director at the time.[67] Joseph Losey, whose last four films in Hollywood were independent productions, found working with independent producer Sam Spiegel on *The Prowler* (1951) to be a similarly positive experience. "[Spiegel's] attitude was, 'You're right for this, but you're not very experienced. I'll give you the best cameraman in Hollywood, the best technicians, the best first assistant. I don't care what I pay, and you do it any way you want to.' This was extraordinary. I owe him a great deal, because I know nobody else in Hollywood at that time who could or would have given me that kind of freedom and implementation."[68]

Abraham Polonsky's Hollywood career is closely tied to that of the independent Enterprise Studios, which allowed him to make the transition from writer (*Body and Soul*, 1947) to director (*Force of Evil*, 1948) very rapidly. During its brief heyday, Enterprise attracted a coterie of radical or liberal artists, including—in addition to Polonsky—the writer Arnold Manoff, the actor John Garfield, and the directors Robert Rossen, Robert Aldrich (at the time an assistant director), and John Berry.[69] Aldrich praises the positive "esprit de corps" the company fostered through its enlightened attitude toward labor relations. All company employees received a life insurance policy and guaranteed vacation—in addition to free doughnuts and coffee—none of which was standard within the industry at the time. Technicians were paid at top rates and directors were given creative and financial support. "Enterprise embodied a really brilliant idea of a communal way to make films," Aldrich recalls. "It was a brand new departure, the first time I can remember that independent filmmakers had all the money they needed."[70] By seeming to present a viable alternative to the studios, the independents offered the Hollywood Left a much-needed outlet for their professional aspirations, in addition to providing another important point of contact for the radical community.[71]

As the blacklist set in and Hollywood turned toward the right, independent productions also provided a much-needed source of employment for blacklisted writers. Dalton Trumbo collaborated clandestinely with Hugo Butler (who would not be blacklisted until 1951) on the screenplays for *He Ran All the Way* (1951)—directed by John Berry, starring John Garfield, and produced by Garfield's independent production company, Roberts Productions—and *The Prowler* (1951), directed by Joseph Losey. Another member of the Hollywood Ten, Ring Lardner Jr., took over from Butler on the script for Losey's *The Big Night* after Butler was blacklisted and left for Mexico; Lardner's wife Frances, an accomplished stage and radio actress, helped coach the film's teenage star, John Barrymore Jr.[72]

While independent productions did present Hollywood's radical filmmakers with greater opportunities for self-expression than studio productions, they were still ultimately commercial enterprises in which the producers—not the writers or directors—had the last word. Independent production gave writers and directors the ability to decline to work on a particular project, a choice they were denied under the studio system, but it rarely gave them the opportunity to select their own material. Whether because of commercial concerns or an instilled sense of self-censorship, independent producers also acted as gatekeepers, monitoring their productions for potentially offensive content. Carl Foreman recalls how Stanley Kramer, his partner in the Kramer Company, excised any scene he felt was too political from *Home of the Brave* (1949), a film depicting the racism suffered by a black G.I. in World War II. Jules Dassin, who had made a point of emphasizing the stark contrast between New York's extremes of wealth and poverty in *The Naked City*, was so upset by Universal's edited version that he walked out of the film's premiere in tears. Joseph Losey complains that the producers of *The Lawless*, which deals with the plight of migrant Mexican farm workers, imposed a "completely banal" score over the film that reduced many sequences to melodrama in opposition to his intentions.[73] Despite these compromised visions, independent productions provided the Hollywood radicals with an important opportunity to make films they found meaningful during a period when the Hollywood establishment was growing increasingly hostile to progressive politics.

The cognitive dissonance created by the dramatic shift in Hollywood's political climate between 1945 and 1950 is reflected in the statistics gathered by Dorothy Jones in her 1957 study. Having monitored Hollywood's wartime production for the Office of War Information, Jones was skeptical of HUAC's investigations, which she suspected were motivated by the fear that Hollywood films were "beginning to devote themselves seriously to an exploration of some of the social, economic, and political problems of our time." The results of her analysis of 159 films produced between 1929 and 1949 are telling. During the first half of 1947, 21 percent fit the Production Code Administration's "social problem" category; this was the first time this genre was represented in significant numbers. By 1950, only 9.5 percent of Hollywood's productions addressed social issues; this percentage would remain the average for the first half of the 1950s.[74] This decline suggests the efficacy of the committee's strategy: by conflating any form of social critique with communism, it was able not only to rid Hollywood of its radical element, but also to scare the establishment away from its more liberal impulses.

The Blacklist Comes to Hollywood

As the circumstances surrounding the instigation and imposition of the Hollywood blacklist is thoroughly recounted elsewhere, I will focus my account on the immediate impact of the blacklist on Hollywood's radical community.[75] When HUAC issued its initial round of forty-three subpoenas in September 1947, the Hollywood Left quickly rallied to support the nineteen left-wingers included in the group. The Progressive Citizens of America (PCA), a communist-dominated political action group, published a daily newsletter to provide an alternative to the accounts put forth in Los Angeles's right-leaning media outlets. The PCA also sponsored a protest meeting held in downtown Los Angeles at the Shrine Auditorium and organized by Joseph Losey. Norma Barzman, who helped Losey in his efforts, remembers the event "at which the massive audience sang 'The Bill of Rights' set to music."[76] The most high profile organization involved in the defense of the Hollywood Nineteen was the Committee for the First Amendment (CFA), founded by screenwriter Philip Dunne and directors William Wyler and John Huston. Concerned "with the assault on civil liberties, what looked to us like the persecution of the so-called 'unfriendly' witnesses, and the reputations of hundreds of others who were being slandered," Dunne and fellow liberals Wyler and Huston attracted a wide swath of Hollywood to the CFA's first meeting, held at Ira Gershwin's home. Abraham Polonsky recalls the standing-room only crowd: "You could not get into the place. The excitement was intense. The town was full of enthusiasm because they all felt they were going to win. Every star was there."[77] Because of this star power (and its resources), the CFA was able to garner national attention for its efforts in support of the Nineteen. In addition to organizing two national radio broadcasts, it flew a planeload of Hollywood celebrities, including Humphrey Bogart, Lauren Bacall, and Katharine Hepburn, to Washington, D.C., to support the Nineteen during their testimony in front of HUAC.

However, Hollywood's enthusiasm for defending civil liberties quickly evaporated once the hearings got under way in Washington on 20 October 1947. Up until the afternoon of his appearance on 27 October, Eric Johnston, head of the Motion Picture Producer's Association (MPPA), had lent visible support to the Nineteen, reprinting letters he had written to Congress criticizing HUAC in ads placed in the *New York Times* and the *Washington Post*. In his testimony in front of the committee, however, Johnston defended the film industry but not the Nineteen. Arguing that Hollywood's producers used every means at their disposal to keep their films free of communist propaganda, Johnston expressed his support for the committee's mission, going so far as to tell the committee that Hollywood welcomed their investigations.[78] Ceplair and Englund attribute Johnston's volte-face to John Howard Lawson's combative performance before the committee that morning. The first of the "unfriendly" witnesses to be called, Lawson had been repeatedly gaveled into silence when he tried to read from his prepared statement. His feisty refusal to bow to the committee's narrow line of questioning ended in his being cited for contempt of Congress and forcibly "escorted" from the courtroom.[79] With Lawson and, by extension, the rest of the unfriendly witnesses refusing to publicly dissociate themselves from communism, Hollywood's producers could no longer risk defending them.

By the end of November, this position had become policy. During a two-day meeting held at New York's Waldorf-Astoria Hotel, Hollywood studio heads and executives agreed to fire or refuse to employ the ten unfriendly witnesses who had been called to testify. And although the studios would consistently deny the existence of an industry-wide blacklist, the language of the Waldorf Statement, issued to the Guilds on 3 December, is unequivocal: "On the broader issue of alleged subversive and disloyal elements in Hollywood, our members are likewise prepared to take positive action. We will not knowingly employ a Communist or a member of any party or group which advocates the overthrow of the Government of the United States by force or illegal or unconstitutional methods." Ironically, the statement concludes by warning against the dangers of creating an atmosphere of fear and of the need to "safeguard free speech and a free screen."[80]

Henceforward, support for the unfriendly witnesses who became known as the "Hollywood Ten" came primarily from the radical, communist core of the Hollywood Left as opposed to Hollywood's sizable liberal community. Under pressure from the studios, the stars who had lent visibility to the CFA quickly withdrew their support from the cause. Humphrey Bogart went so far as to issue a public apology in the form of a feature article published in *Photoplay* fan magazine with the unambiguous title, "I'm No Communist." The PCA and HICCASP were still active in their defense of the Ten, but, lacking members from the much larger community of Hollywood liberals, these organizations had limited reach. Although groups such as the PCA-sponsored Freedom from Fear Committee and the Hollywood Ten Defense Committee managed to raise over $150,000 toward the Ten's legal expenses, fewer and fewer donors were willing to put their name on a check in support of the cause. Edward Biberman, whose brother Herbert was among the Ten, recalls that "the state of fear and terror in those months was such that anyone who even offered anonymous cash gifts seemed courageous."[81]

Yet the sense of being under siege did have the effect of strengthening the ties within the radical community, which was bound together in its conviction that the Ten—who were for the most part friends and often close friends—would triumph. Sylvia Jarrico describes the passion that supported the radicals in their efforts: "We thought the Ten would win at every stage of their trial and appeals. Our community held together really well during this struggle. The issues were so clear-cut that I felt I made a point every time I opened my mouth."[82] Norma Barzman echoes Jarrico's certainty in her description of the fund-raiser "New Year's Eve with the Hollywood Ten" at Lucy's restaurant, an industry hangout on Melrose Avenue, opposite Paramount Studios: "It was mostly Party people, few of the old liberal friends. Nevertheless, that night we managed to raise several thousand dollars. Like Adrian [Scott], everyone was certain we'd win in the courts. We toasted 1948 with champagne."[83] The Ten even produced a film, titled simply *The Hollywood Ten* and directed by John Berry, intended to raise funds for their defense and awareness of their cause. No American exhibitors, however, would risk showing it, and pressure from the U.S. government, acting in concert with the MPPA, prevented the film from finding any sort of foreign release. In the absence of commercial assistance, the wives and friends of the Ten distributed the film themselves and organized screenings in venues ranging from meeting halls to living rooms.

The mood of Hollywood's radical community was evolving rapidly as anger and disbelief faded into despair. Many on the Left put off acknowledging the changing political climate for as long as possible. "I never really felt any fear in

1946," recalls Sylvia Jarrico, "so I guess I underestimated the dangers."[84] Her husband Paul explains that while he understood the ramifications of the case of the Ten in theory: "I didn't see it as applying to myself. . . . Sure, I understood that there was more involved than merely the fate of these ten people, that the cold war had started and that the witch-hunt was not probably going to stop with the Ten in Hollywood. But nevertheless, I felt quite secure professionally and was rather surprised when my contract was not renewed, or when the option for my services was not picked up, for my continued services."[85] With the benefit of hindsight, Norma Barzman marvels at her naïveté: "Ben and I hadn't believed such a thing could happen [the issuing of subpoenas to the Nineteen]. Even when it did happen, we couldn't imagine the catastrophic events that lay in wait for all of us."[86]

Yet by the fall of 1948, the Barzmans were switching houses with their friend, the director Bernard Vorhaus, in an attempt to confuse the "slim jims" sent to deliver their subpoenas (the ruse worked).[87] Betsy Blair describes "suitcases packed for emergency flight," while Jean Butler recalls being "terribly paranoid; afraid to use phones."[88]

The radical community began to buckle under the stress created by the witch hunts and the blacklist. "People began to avoid everyone except close friends," explains Betsy Blair, while Sylvia Jarrico remembers "the constant sense of being hunted."[89] Joseph Losey provides a particularly vivid inventory of the blacklist's destructive effects on both individual lives and the culture at large: "It became so terrifying. . . . I know of suicides, deaths from heart attacks, talented writers who had to get jobs as waiters or in shops. . . . Marriages were destroyed, children destroyed . . . but the most serious thing was that the right of the American people to say what they thought with freedom and to protest against what they thought was wrong, was destroyed."[90] Within the course of a decade, the sense of shared political commitment and comradeship that had defined Hollywood's creative community for many in the film industry had been replaced by an atmosphere of fear.

In an interview given in 1947, Jules Dassin describes the plot of a play he wanted to write depicting the transformation of the "$500 a week writer who promises himself if he can afford it, to refuse to compromise," into a producer who "justifies the trivia he is making on the grounds that he has to cushion himself for the time when honesty may not pay off."[91] Clearly intended as a parable illustrating the corrupting influence of Hollywood, Dassin's story is indicative of the acrimonious relationship with the film industry experienced by many of the future exiles. While the flirtation between Hollywood and the Left flourished for a time during the late 1930s and early 1940s, it was a relationship riddled with contradictions. Communism allowed the Hollywood radicals to be simultaneously of and apart from Hollywood, to be insider outsiders. It offered a way of preserving their integrity, of warding off the corruption Dassin warns against in his play, yet at the same time it presented a way to belong in Hollywood, to be a part of the large community of politically engaged writers, directors, and actors.

The spiritual protection communism seemed to offer, however, was not without its price, as the charged debates provoked by the Albert Maltz affair revealed. Life in Hollywood may have been politically fulfilling, but neither the studios nor the Party offered filmmakers much chance of artistic fulfillment, although for very different reasons. As a result, many of the future émigrés worked increasingly within the realm of independent production toward the end of their Hollywood careers. Frequently working with the same key set of creative personnel, they experienced a foretaste of the sort of artisanal approach to production and greater autonomy they would find in Europe. A number of these independent productions were written under pseudonyms by blacklisted writers such as Dalton Trumbo, Hugo Butler, and Ring Lardner; that directors such as Joseph Losey and John Berry were willing to take on additional risk by working with these men foreshadows the way the radical community would work together, sharing both jobs and, in some circumstances, incomes, while overseas. To what degree life in Europe would offer a solution to the personal and professional disjunctures experienced by the progressive community in Hollywood is explored in the following chapters. Once again, the Hollywood radicals would find themselves negotiating a contradictory space as insider outsiders, only under very different terms.

2 • LIFE ON THE BLACKLIST

Production and Politics in Postwar Europe

BY DECEMBER 1954, Joseph Losey had been away from Hollywood for more than three years. On tour in Dublin, he evokes the weight of his exile in a letter to Ring Lardner Jr.: "I have had a rather tough few months with a play which I am afraid is not worth the trouble. It is making money on the road. I am dubious about it for London. In all other respects, the struggle goes on—only differences of detail. It is extremely lonely here and often seems pointless and wasted and the temptation to return is great. There is very little peace of mind or heart in my life."[1] For most of the blacklisted community in Europe, these were dark, lean years. Dassin recalls playing cards with the other Americans in Paris to pass the time, "but nobody had any money to lose, so we just redistributed the pot all over again."[2] Not only were the majority of the exiles struggling to get by financially, but they still lived with the sense of dread and anxiety they had hoped to leave behind in California. As Norma Barzman sums up the situation, "From 1951 through 1956, we were frightened most of the time, felt that our own country was spying on us, and never knew if our next job was our last."[3] The exiles' FBI files confirm that their suspicions of surveillance were justified; a review of her own file prompted Betsy Blair to conclude in her memoir that "there were informers everywhere."[4] Underscoring these feelings of insecurity was the genuine precariousness of their legal status within their host countries. Many of the exiles had their passports confiscated by the U.S. government, an outcome that not only limited their ability to travel (and consequently, the work opportunities available to them), but that could also jeopardize the validity of their residence permits.

Despite these difficulties, for some blacklist victims exile in Europe offered a renewed sense of professional and personal freedom. In numerous interviews, John Berry describes the wonder and relief he experienced upon his arrival in Paris. "For someone who had grown up in the Bronx, seeing Paris for the first time was a stunning moment, a moment of incredible discovery. When the

French officer stamped my passport at the airport and welcomed me to France, I felt free for the first time after the months of pressure and being on the run."[5] Similarly, Carl Foreman recalls feeling "suddenly . . . completely liberated" upon his arrival in London in 1952. "I have never felt like that before or after. I felt free, and I know now what it must mean to come out of prison, because that's what it was like, and not only to come out of prison, but to come home."[6] Others responded to their circumstances with measured pragmatism. Donald Ogden Stewart had not planned to start a new life in London as an exile, but found himself trapped there when the U.S. government refused to renew his passport. However, according to his son, Stewart "was never reluctant about having to reside in England. He figured he could get film work there; he had a hope of getting one or more of his stage plays on."[7]

A glance at the exiles' filmographies during these early years in Europe suggests the challenges they faced finding work. Between 1949 and 1954, blacklisted Americans contributed to only seventeen European productions, whereas they would go on to direct, write, or perform in more than forty-four films between 1955 and 1960. Cy Endfield was able to stay employed by directing two low-budget British B-movies: *The Limping Man* (1953) and *Impulse* (1954). Joseph Losey returned to the theater and directed two plays in London's West End. Most everyone picked up ad hoc television work. For the Parisian community, dubbing provided another welcome source of income. Having run through his savings during his first year in France, John Berry recalls getting by thanks to small dubbing jobs that paid 35 francs a day.[8] In both England and France, the exiles found people eager to help them. Losey recalls surviving this unhappy period "with a little help from my friends . . . mostly English people who were outraged by the political situation and who really fought," while Norma Barzman remembers Picasso welcoming her as a fellow exile in Paris.[9]

Of the Hollywood radicals who decided to give Europe a try in the late 1940s and early 1950s, many proved reluctant exiles and returned to America for a variety of reasons. Adrian Scott was compelled by his feelings of loyalty toward the rest of the Hollywood Ten. "I had friends in England and France who said I was foolish to go back then, because I knew by this time that I was going to stand trial for Contempt of Congress. . . . They said they'd hide me out and then fix it up with the government. I was tempted. It could have been arranged. But nine of us couldn't go to court with the tenth on the lam. That would have made it impossible for the rest who were left."[10] Jules Dassin likewise was compelled by a sense of duty (and egotism) to return to the United States temporarily. Upon learning that he had been named, he immediately left France—where he had been attending the Cannes Film Festival—for New York. "I really wanted to be questioned. I had all the heroic answers ready. I was going to be a hero."[11] After spending the summer of 1952 scrounging for work in London, Losey returned to

New York for more prosaic financial reasons. "I didn't stay in England very long because I didn't see how I could live," he explains, but his prospects in New York proved no brighter and he returned to London.[12] The screenwriters Marguerite Roberts and her husband John Sanford also returned to the United States in 1952, having failed to find any work during their four-month stay in England.[13] Others consciously rejected a life of exile. Abraham Polonsky, who had moved to the south of France in 1948 to write a novel, returned to California in 1950 despite the worsening political climate, unable to make "the self-exiled group's long-term commitment abroad."[14]

Much as the previous chapter established the professional, political, and personal ties that connected the radical community in Hollywood, along with the circumstances of its dissolution, this chapter picks up the thematic threads of film, politics, and community in the context of the Hollywood radicals' early years of European exile. How did the friendships and professional experiences discussed in the last chapter affect their attempts to restart their careers in Europe? What obstacles did their blacklisted status put in the way of the opportunities available to them in Europe's film industries? How did postwar geopolitics, both in terms of European reconstruction and the escalating Cold War, influence the reception granted the exiles in France and Britain? Examining the broader political and cultural context in which the exiles found themselves upon their arrival in Europe provides insight into the European perception of the Hollywood blacklist and the conservative politics of the McCarthy era and, in doing so, suggests the degree to which the blacklist was not an exclusively domestic phenomenon, but one with hitherto overlooked transnational dimensions.

"U.S. GO HOME"

The American political exiles arrived in Europe during an important transitional moment in U.S.-European relations. The United States was anxious to consolidate its political and economic influence in Western Europe and to reinforce its Cold War agenda through cultural means, with Hollywood serving as its most reliable and effective ambassador. In turn, European concerns about American cultural imperialism were felt particularly acutely as America's prominent role in the reconstruction of Europe facilitated an unprecedented degree of involvement—or interference—in European domestic affairs. The massive economic assistance provided by the Marshall Plan (1948–1951), while enabling Western Europe's phenomenal economic growth during the 1950s and 1960s, came at the price of a reduced political bargaining power on the part of the European recipients. While certainly adding new fuel to the established discourse of anti-Americanism, the U.S. presence in postwar Europe evoked sentiments that were on the whole more complex and contradictory. For, after years of wartime deprivation, American movies and consumer goods—two of the most visible symbols of American cultural imperialism—were also intensely desired by Europeans. As Jean-Pierre Jeancolas writes in the context of France, "to be able to watch American films was seen as a sign that the country was free again."[15]

Despite such sentiments, by the early 1950s America's relations with France were at a particularly low ebb. Some sectors of the Parisian Left, especially communists and "neutralists"—as those who rejected the East–West dichotomy of the Cold War were known—perceived the Marshall Plan as a rigged game that allotted France necessary aid but in exchange for the imposition of American culture and values. After the signing of the NATO treaty in 1949, America began rebuilding its military presence in France. With American G.I.s once again a common sight, the graffiti "U.S. GO HOME" appeared on walls throughout the country.[16] The slogan became a war cry in the "Ridgeway Riots"—named after General Matthew Ridgeway, the recently appointed commander of NATO forces—of May 1952, during which 20,000 protesters marched through the streets of Paris carrying banners reading "Go Home" and "Americans belong in America." Angered by the government's decision to ban a march planned by the peace movement, the Parti Communiste Français (PCF) organized a protest demonstration that was anything but peaceful. Clashes with the police left over 200 people wounded and one demonstrator dead, and led to the arrest of several hundred others. The execution of the Rosenbergs in June 1953 likewise fueled anti-American sentiment both in the press and on the streets. When President Dwight D. Eisenhower ruled against clemency, the PCF organized a vigil outside the American Embassy that resulted in over 800 arrests and one shooting.[17]

The combination of America's presence in France—whether in the form of its military or its consumer goods—and news of American political repression at home triggered a popular anti-Americanism that tapped into France's anxieties concerning its diminished political and economic position in the postwar world order. In the context of the film industry, these geopolitical and ideological tensions coalesced in the response to the 1946 Blum-Byrnes agreement, which, in allocating only four weeks out of every thirteen for the exclusive exhibition of French films, was seen as a triumph for Hollywood.[18] As Colin Crisp notes, the agreement "mobilized the French film industry in a concerted political campaign as no other cause was to do in the postwar era," inspiring the formation of the Comité de défense du cinéma français in June 1946.[19] In January 1948, the committee organized a protest demonstration that attracted over 10,000 members of the film industry. As a result, the government raised the quota of screen time reserved for French films to five weeks when it revised the agreement in July 1948. However, the vehement opposition to the Blum-Byrnes agreement was restricted primarily to the film community and did not affect the popularity of American films with the French public during these years. "It's not just coincidence," observes Pierre Billard, "that the French box office peaked in 1947, the year that marked the [postwar] return of Hollywood cinema to French screens."[20]

Hollywood's "Other Face"

Arriving in France at a time when the influence of the French Communist Party was at its peak, the exiles found that their status as leftist political exiles provided them with some protection from anti-American sentiment along with a sense of belonging to a broader community.[21] Although no longer Party members, "we continued to feel like Communists," Norma Barzman recalls. "And since we were in a country where the Communist Party was a mass party, winning a large bloc of votes, we felt part of the mainstream." Vladimir Pozner, the French novelist and screenwriter who had spent the war years working in Hollywood, served as the exiles' bridge to the French Left. Pozner was a close friend of the radical director Louis Daquin, a frequent contributor to *L'Ecran français* and an active member of the Comité de défense du cinéma français and the Fédération du Spectacle Confédération générale du travail (CGT).[22] "Socially we inhabited a Communist milieu," Norma Barzman recalls, a milieu that included Pierre and Irène Joliot-Curie, Jacques and Pierre Prévert, and Yves Montand and Simone Signoret, in addition to Pozner and Daquin.[23]

At a time when the majority of those involved in the French film industry were Communist Party members, or at least sympathizers, the exiles found themselves warmly welcomed by their French colleagues.[24] Their refusal to capitulate to HUAC provided them with a certain cachet; "it was very fashionable to greet the refugee Americans," remembers John Berry.[25] Although HUAC's activities received relatively limited coverage outside the left-wing and communist press, at least until about 1953, readers of *Ce Soir, Combat, Le Franc-Tireur, L'Humanité, Libération,* and especially *L'Ecran français* would have been well aware of *la chasse aux sorcières* (the witch-hunt) taking place in the United States.[26] *L'Ecran français* kept its readers apprised of the "*sinistre comédie*" unfolding in Hollywood by publishing numerous articles about the Hollywood Ten and organizing a letter-writing campaign in their defense.[27] Demonstrating its awareness of the political divisions within Hollywood, it distinguished between those stars on the right and those on the left, referring to the latter as "Hollywood's other face."[28] Georges Sadoul, the influential film critic for the communist journal *Les Lettres Françaises,* whose attitude toward Hollywood was one of unbridled disdain, likewise made an exception for the films of the Hollywood Ten. Sadoul's reputation as the communist conscience of the French film industry meant that his embrace of the blacklisted exiles set the standard for the rest of the industry to follow.[29]

The American exiles welcomed the opportunity to set themselves apart from Hollywood and give voice to the creative frustrations that had dogged their Hollywood careers. Asked why he had decided to stay in Europe after starring in *Christ in Concrete* (dir. Edward Dmytryk, 1949), Sam Wanamaker launched into an impassioned critique of the Hollywood "dream factory." "Despite the financial difficulties that you encounter over here, at least you're free from Hollywood's stranglehold. Here you can make films that say something about our times, that address what is happening in the world today. Because it's not true that people only go to the movies to forget."[30] While Wanamaker's assessment would prove optimistic, it is nonetheless representative of the perception of Hollywood as a site of capitalist oppression and Europe as a haven for artistic freedom that the French Left and the blacklisted Americans shared and mutually reinforced.

The strong social support they received from the French film community did not result in an abundance of professional opportunities for the exiles. "You couldn't just fall into work," John Berry recalls; "you had to go out and meet producers."[31] In contrast to Hollywood, the structure of the French film industry was fragmented or "artisanal." In the absence of an oligarchy of large studios, small production companies proliferated; during the early 1950s, France had somewhere between 150 and 500 small-to-medium-sized firms producing an average of one film a year. Lacking a network of industry contacts, in addition to proficiency in the French language, the exiles were at a disadvantage in such an unfamiliar and diffuse production environment. Their careers were also hurt by the fact that the French film industry was highly unionized and required that for every non-union member employed on a film, a union member must also be hired. Therefore, hiring an American required hiring an additional crew member and thereby increased production costs.[32]

Pardon My French: Dual-Language Co-Production

One important source of employment for the exiles during the early 1950s was the dual-language Franco-American co-production. The short-lived vogue for this type of production is closely tied both to the industrial context of postwar French cinema and the political context of Franco-American relations in the immediate postwar era. In an effort to stimulate both its film industry and the domestic economy, France established incentives to encourage American companies to reinvest their frozen currency in domestic film production, raising financing toward this end through levies placed on cinema admissions and the importation of foreign films. As long as a production received no more than 50 percent of its funding from American sources, employed a French-based crew, and included a French-language version, it could apply for government assistance through the newly created Centre national de la cinématographie (CNC).[33]

At the end of 1949, the Benagoss-Union générale cinématographique (UGC) agreement created support for a minimum of three Franco-American feature films per year, to be made in France. In addition to these economic motivations, which included production costs that compared favorably with those in the United States, where crew salaries were much higher, American producers were also attracted by the opportunity to distinguish their films through the use of real European locations. Between 1948 and 1952, a handful of Franco-American or Franco-Anglo-American productions were made in France, typically with international casts and plot lines that justified the presence of Americans in Paris.[34]

The blacklisted exiles made two contributions to this cycle: *Dans la vie tout s'arrange / Pardon My French* (1951) and *C'est arrivé à Paris / It Happened in Paris* (1952). Directed by Bernard Vorhaus in English and Marcel Cravenne in French, *Pardon My French*'s origins lay with Edward Dmytryk's ex-wife, Madeleine, and Adrian Scott, who had sold the original story to the French producer André Sarrut before returning to the United States in the fall of 1949.[35] According to Vorhaus, it was not much of a story, and the comedy writer Ronald Kibbee was brought in to do a rewrite.[36]

Starring Merle Oberon as Elizabeth Rockwell, a Boston schoolteacher who inherits a chateau in the south of France and falls in love with Paul Rancour (Paul Henreid), the bohemian musician who has been using the property as a makeshift orphanage, *Pardon My French* shares the superficial cross-cultural orientation of most of these Franco-American productions with regard to both its cast and content. The film's producers, as quoted in the *New York Times*, worked from the "theory that the swift American brand of 'romantic comedy' may be enhanced when it is set against, and makes use of, a genuine French provincial background."[37] The romance between Elizabeth and Paul plays out mainly in terms of cultural clichés: Elizabeth is depicted as an uptight (albeit impoverished, much to the surprise of the French) New England schoolmarm who finds her innate Puritanism no match for Paul's Gallic *joie de vivre.*

Yet since stereotypes bear a relationship to reality, albeit a distorted one, *Pardon My French* illuminates certain aspects of postwar Franco-American cultural relations. Being clean, and possessing products that promoted proper hygiene, were values associated with modernity and, for the French, epitomized by the United States.[38] In light of the cultural significance of cleanliness in postwar France (Roland Barthes devotes one of his essays in *Mythologies* to the soap powder Omo), Elizabeth's obsession with hygiene in *Pardon My French* merits consideration.[39] She is shocked by the sight of a group of French women contentedly washing their clothes in a communal bathing pool; given the absence of modern domestic appliances in Europe at the time, her response was calibrated to evoke the association between America and such technological improvements.[40] Yet rather than rejecting the Old World, Elizabeth ultimately embraces its simpler pleasures and the life rich in beauty, wine, and music that Paul represents. At the film's conclusion, she tells Paul, "I no longer want the things I dreamed of."

Perhaps to a surprising degree given the film's hasty development and the practical impetus behind its production, *Pardon My French* succeeds in presenting a Franco-American perspective within the limitations of its light romantic comedy genre. Its celebration of the French *môde de vie* taps into the romantic vision of France that has exerted its pull on Americans, particularly those of an artistic bent, since the late nineteenth century. Yet in setting the action within an abandoned chateau serving as an orphanage, the film comments on the social disruption and acute housing shortage created by the devastation of World War II. This grounding of the plot in France's immediate postwar context can be seen as a reflection of its American participants' continued commitment to socially relevant filmmaking; the film's implicit rejection of the sterile materialism of American culture is consistent with Scott's and Vorhaus's politics. By promoting an alternative set of values to those of capitalist consumption, *Pardon My French* speaks to the anxieties created by the increased presence of America in France, whether in terms of the economic assistance offered by the Marshall Plan or the flood of Hollywood films on French movie screens.

Bernard Vorhaus (center) on the set of *Pardon My French* (From the collections of the Margaret Herrick Library)

That *It Happened in Paris* also focuses on an American heiress in France suggests the cultural sway of *le mythe américain*: the perception of America as a land of possibility and plenty.[41] But whereas *Pardon My French* challenged the economic dimensions of this stereotype, *It Happened in Paris* allows its heiress to be extremely wealthy. To gain the audience's sympathy, Ben Barzman makes some token gestures meant to suggest that Patricia Moran (Evelyn Keyes) is in fact just a normal girl, eager for romance and independence (she refuses to stay in a fancy, Right Bank hotel and instead books herself into one on the "bohemian" Left Bank).[42] She soon becomes involved with Vladimir, who presents himself as an impoverished Russian prince but is really a scam artist. When Patricia's father learns of her relationship, he cuts off her funds, but by this time Vladimir has fallen in love with Patricia and the pair decide to elope. Vladimir's cronies try to blackmail Patricia's father, demanding five million francs to break up the relationship, but their plan fails and Vladimir and Patricia ride off into the sunset (with the five million).

It Happened in Paris was Ben Barzman and director John Berry's first film project since their arrival in France, and the insecurity of their situation, along with their financial desperation (as least on Berry's part), could help explain the feeling that they were simply churning out a film that they thought would appeal to their French producer, Henri Lavorel.[43] They had originally pitched Lavorel a "sketch picture" based on three of Barzman's short stories,

It Happened in Paris, publicity still (Cinémathèque française – Iconothèque)

but after Gérard Philippe—who was to play the lead in the first sketch—was forced to drop out, the decision was made to extend the second sketch into a feature.

As with *Pardon My French, It Happened in Paris* was filmed in both French and English in order to qualify for government assistance, with Lavorel and Berry each directing his native-language version. The production had its share of difficulties. The French and American actors struggled with the linguistic challenge of acting in two languages, many having to resort to learning their lines phonetically. Michel Audiard, the screenwriter hired for the French version, was overcommitted and delayed the production by failing to meet his deadline. Other problems were more specifically related to Barzman and Berry's blacklisted status. Concerned about unwanted publicity, the production hired a press agent for the express purposes of keeping publicity *away* from the film. The agent failed to grasp her assignment, however, and a crew from *Life* magazine and the Hollywood gossip columnist Louella Parsons both paid unwelcome visits to the set. John Berry recalls the subterfuge he had to go through when Parsons arrived to do an interview: "I told my assistant to keep working as though he were the director. I went upstairs—it was in the train station of the Gare de Lyon—to the restaurant, which has a balcony. I stood in the balcony and watched them set things up and shoot without my being there. Jacques, my assistant, would sneak up and ask me, 'What else? Good, no good?' Then they would shoot the scene again. All the time Louella was down there doing interviews on the set."[44]

Despite the advance press, *It Happened in Paris* was never released in America. In France, the reviews were highly critical, particularly of the film's clichéd plot and use of national stereotypes. *Le Figaro* described the screenplay as childish and unworthy of the director's attention, adding that Evelyn Keyes needed to work on her French accent. *Le Monde* wondered why Lavorel had bothered with the story in the first place, kindly suggesting that only a director with the experience of Ernst Lubitsch or Frank Capra could have done anything with the hackneyed plot.[45]

It Happened in Paris's poor reception is of a piece with that of many of the other Franco-American, or Franco-American-themed, productions of the early 1950s. Michel Fourré-Cormeray, the director of the Centre Nationale de la Cinématographie, suggested that the problem was intrinsic to the nature of the Franco-American co-production, in that "the effort to appeal to audiences in both countries often results in bland, colorless films."[46] Fourré-Cormeray's comments are mild in comparison to the ire provoked by Franco-American co-productions in other sectors of the film industry. The Fédération du Spectacle CGT, the communist-dominated film industry trade union, opposed the Benagoss-UGC agreement on the grounds that the UGC, as the only French production company under government control, should show its support for indigenous production instead of joining forces with an American company like Benagoss. In January 1950, the French screen actors union presented a manifesto on the subject of co-productions, expressing concern about French films becoming the vehicle for foreign ideas. This fear of a loss of national identity is a constant presence in contemporary discussions of the topic. More specific critiques were that while French-American co-productions monopolized limited studio space, they failed to enlarge the market for French films since only the English-language versions were exported; similarly, by using film stocks that often had to be developed abroad (France lacked the capacity to develop Technicolor, for instance), these French-American co-productions deprived French laboratories of work.

Attitudes toward Franco-Italian co-productions provide a revealing measure of comparison. In a protectionist move intended to support their local film industries in the face of intense competition from Hollywood, the French and Italian governments signed a co-production agreement in 1949. The agreement established strict controls regulating the percentages of each country's financial and artistic contributions to any given production and worked upon the principle of reciprocity; a Franco-Italian production made in France, to which France contributed 70 percent of the financing and Italy 30 percent, would have to be balanced by a Franco-Italian production filmed in Italy with Italy contributing 70 percent of the financing and France 30 percent. Although not without controversy—the nationality of technicians or of studios used were constant subjects of discord between the French and Italian unions—the Franco-Italian agreements did not elicit anything near the degree of rancor evoked by the Franco-American co-productions. A series of articles published in the noncommunist but leftist *Combat* in April 1950 set out to explore this paradox, noting that "while Franco-Italian co-productions have never been the subject of much discussion, Franco-American co-productions have provoked debates that assume the tone of electoral polemics."[47] Without exception, the articles—representing a diversity of perspectives, from the French syndicates to the Motion Picture Association of America (MPAA)—make no mention of Franco-Italian co-productions, a silence that speaks volumes. As Patricia Hubert-Lacombe notes, the more favorable reception of Franco-Italian (and, after 1951, Franco-German) co-productions reflects the influence of the communist-dominated trade unions and communist press, which analyzed the situation as a shared battle by two small, pacifist European nations against the militant, capitalist Hollywood Goliath. *L'Ecran français* promulgated this perspective: "It is comforting that two European countries forced to fight to defend their national cinema against the Hollywood invasion know to collaborate on the basis of complete equality, with mutual respect for the rights and qualities that are unique to each nation. . . . Two countries whose people want to live, and *to live in peace*, should be able to express this desire through their cinema. This international agreement [between France and Italy] that helps them to do so deserves our close attention."[48]

Supporters of the Franco-American co-production, such as *Pardon My French*'s producer André Sarrut, put forward a line of argumentation that, while not contradicting that of the Left, shows the other side of the coin. Sarrut puts it bluntly: the French film industry must make co-productions or die. Comparing France's political authority to that of Andorra, Sarrut argues that the French should not expect audiences in other countries to flock to see their films. Yet in order to amortize their costs, French films need access to the vast American market, and their "only hope of penetrating the American market is through [English-language] co-productions."[49] Sarrut's comments demonstrate a certain weariness with the nationalist discourse that had dominated the French film industry since the end of World War II and also indicate one of the reasons the American exiles succeeded in finding work in France, despite the film industry's anti-American bias. While their Hollywood training enhanced their appeal to French producers, their left-wing politics immunized them to a large degree from the rancorous discourse surrounding the American film industry.

L'Affaire Dassin

The situation of the blacklisted exiles became something of a cause célèbre in May 1953, when the French press learned of Jules Dassin's last-minute dismissal from *L'Ennemi public no. 1* as a result of American pressure. "L'Affaire Dassin," as the event was dubbed in the French trades, outraged the French film community, for whom it provided further proof of America's desire to control their industry.[50] For Dassin, the incident was at once a rude introduction to the overseas reach of the blacklist and a surprising entrée into his new life in France. After his contract with Fox was cancelled early in 1951, Dassin accepted an offer to direct the French comic actor Fernandel in an Italian production based on Giovanni Guareschi's novel *The Little World of Don Camillo*. However, unable to reach an agreement with the producer regarding the screenplay, Dassin abandoned the project and left Italy for France. Upon learning he had been named by Edward Dmytryk, he returned to New York and spent the next year developing a number of theater projects while waiting to be called to testify.[51] In September 1952, he began preparing a revue with Bette Davis, whom he remembers as one of the few stars still willing to thumb her nose at the blacklist. During rehearsals that fall, he was served with a subpoena only to be informed that the hearings were canceled before he was able to get to Washington.[52] He was then offered the job of directing *L'Ennemi public no. 1* in France for producer Jacques Bar's Cité Films.

Another comedy featuring Fernandel, this time as a nearsighted store clerk who is mistaken for a gangster, the film was envisioned as a send-up of American film noir and mobilized all the clichés of the genre, including the hard-boiled gangster's moll, here played by Zsa Zsa Gabor. As a Hollywood director of a number of acclaimed noirs (*Brute Force, The Naked City, Thieves' Highway,* and *Night and the City* were all highly regarded in France) and whose location shooting in New York (where part of the film was to be shot) in *The Naked City* was much admired, Dassin seemed the ideal choice to Bar.[53] Bar changed his mind, however, when the head of the International Alliance of Theatrical Stage Employees (IATSE), Roy Brewer, threatened an American boycott of not only this film, but any others the producer would go on to make. On 20 April 1953, less than forty-eight hours before filming was to begin, Bar fired Dassin, stating that "for personal reasons, [Dassin] was unable to fulfill his professional obligations."[54]

Prominent left-wing members of the French film community quickly rallied to Dassin's cause. Claude Autant-Lara, Louis Daquin, Jean Grémillon, and Vladimir Pozner were among those who signed an open letter to the Cannes Film Festival protesting "the interference of the House Committee on Un-American Activities in the French film industry."[55] Dassin was stunned by the level of support he received.[56] "They were very angry about what happened to me. . . . Many people in French film came to my hotel and said this was awful and asked what they could do. There was big solidarity. They immediately declared me a member of the French director's union. The French were wonderful. But nevertheless . . ." Contained in that ellipsis are the disappointments that followed, the numerous projects that fell through on account of Dassin's blacklisted status, a situation that repeated itself "with different variations for over five years," as Dassin notes.[57] What "l'affaire Dassin" reveals is the French film industry's relative impotence in the face of pressure from Hollywood. No matter the amount of fiery anti-American rhetoric issuing from the cafés of Saint-Germain, the threat of being barred from the elusive and lucrative American market was enough to persuade many French producers to toe the Hollywood line.

(Un)Americans in Paris

By the end of 1953, the small colony of blacklisted filmmakers in Paris included the screenwriters Lee and Tammy Gold and the producer Hannah Weinstein—known to many of the Hollywood progressives through her work for Henry Wallace's 1948 presidential campaign—in addition to the Barzmans, John Weber, and John Berry. The American exiles quickly banded together.

Berry's daughter, Jan, recalls the weekend baseball games in the Bois de Boulogne and the holiday dinners at the Golds. Her father describes the important emotional and financial function the group served during his early years in France. "There was a profound, extremely rewarding, and secure connection among those people, among all of us, and it was something absolutely marvelous

Norma Barzman with Bernard Vorhaus's daughter Gwyn, on vacation in the Alps (Personal collection of David Vorhaus)

in terms of human relations. We could all count on each other. If you were broke or in trouble, you always had someone to call up. If your personal life was stressful and you needed someone to share your grief, you had somebody day and night."[58] Since most of the exiles had trouble making ends meet, they put the maxim "from each according to his ability, to each according to his need" into action, pooling their financial resources and reallocating these funds according to individual circumstances. Norma Barzman recalls voting to raise the stipend allotted to the Golds to allow them enough money to start a family. The exiles would also meet to discuss issues of importance to the community, such as problems with their U.S. passports or French residency permits. The political life in which they had all been active back in Hollywood had accustomed them to making decisions by consensus and to seeing themselves as members of a larger social group. The particular circumstances of their exile provided the opportunity to take their beliefs one step further, to replace Hollywood's cocktail party communism with a more direct and intimate Parisian version.

Within the privacy of the group, politics continued to be of critical importance. Jan Berry recalls her mother, Gladys, feeling left out because she did not share the communist orientation that was such a central part of the identity of the other blacklist victims. However, their precarious legal status meant that the exiles generally chose to restrict their public political activities. "Our French political life was limited to going to French ciné-clubs, such as Ciné Action, that were Communist-oriented," Norma Barzman recalls.[59] "Every time there was a *manifestation*—demonstration—we had to ask ourselves whether we could afford to participate."[60] Although John Berry reports attending a *manifestation* for Julius and Ethel Rosenberg to no ill effect, the Barzmans' caution is understandable in light of the U.S. State Department's efforts to make life difficult for the blacklisted in Europe. Without exception, the exiles—or, for that matter, any left-leaning American in Paris—found themselves faced with a choice when they tried to renew their passports at an American embassy. They could either sign an affidavit swearing that they had never been a member of the Communist Party, or they could have their passports confiscated and marked "valid for return passage only." Even children were not exempt; Jan Berry recalls that she and her brother, Denis, ages ten and eight, were forced to sign.[61]

In Britain, France, and Italy, the U.S. government's network of informants kept tabs on the blacklisted, reporting their changes of address, their means of employment, even the loudness of their parties.[62] These "confidential sources" took a variety of guises.[63] Joseph Losey recalls how John Barrymore Jr., the young actor he had directed in *The Big Night*, came to visit him in London during this period. Barrymore had money to burn, and Losey was happy to help him spend it in London's bars and clubs. Years later, Barrymore confessed to Losey that his trip had been at the behest of the FBI.[64]

For Ellie (Pine) Boris, an American actress in Paris, the paranoia of the blacklisted community was not "so much of a surprise as a growing realization of what they must have lived through." The day after her arrival in Paris, she met the Barzmans for breakfast at La Coupole. "I was speaking in my natural voice and they shushed me, convinced that a spy could be hiding behind a newspaper at the next table. It was the first time I'd felt this sort of fear."[65] The exiles followed events in America closely, gathering together to "weep and suffer for every friend who succumbed" to the committee, according to Jules Dassin's recollection.[66] Nor did they know whom to trust in Paris. As Jan Berry offers by way of explanation, "There were always people who somehow had money, but whose sources of income were unclear."[67]

The Blacklisted Community in London

The blacklisted exiles who settled in Britain encountered a distinctly different dynamic with regard to their political circumstances. Britain was America's partner in the Cold War, with its own fears of espionage and double agents and even internal purges of its media industries.[68] Carl Foreman recalls receiving a less-than-warm welcome when he arrived at the port of Southampton.

> I remember my first entrance into England was very discouraging in view of what came about later because when the immigration man said to me, "Why are you here, Mr. Foreman?," I said, "I'm here to study the British film industry. I'm a writer and producer and I want to look at Britain and see if it's possible to make films here," and all that. Well, I thought he would greet me with open arms; instead, he gave me thirty days, which I thought was not very gracious, and it wasn't, because every thirty days for six months I had to go in and get my goddamned thing renewed for another thirty days with the police. It was terrible.[69]

Joseph Losey describes a similarly restrictive stance on the part of the British authorities, who required him to report to Immigration every week and refused to issue a permit for more than thirty days.[70] As in France, the U.S. government did its best to interfere with the lives of its blacklisted subjects in England, most frequently through depriving them of their passports. Having gone to the American embassy to renew his passport, Donald Ogden Stewart instead watched as it was added to a pile on a shelf behind the passport official. As word of the embassy's tactics made the rounds, the blacklisted community reacted by applying for renewals at provincial consulates that were less likely to have received the latest State Department updates.[71] The embassy also sent out letters to the blacklisted requesting that they turn in their passports; Carl Foreman delights in the irony of receiving one such letter on 4 July 1953 while watching an American

Armed Forces football game.[72] Although Foreman reports being able to get his U.K. residence permit renewed without a valid passport, apparently through the intervention of a sympathetic civil servant, Losey did not have similar luck. Having been informed that his residency permit would be extended only if his passport were revalidated, in May 1956, he went to the U.S. Embassy in London and signed an affidavit stating that he had joined the CPUSA in 1946 and left in 1947 or 1948. His passport was subsequently renewed.[73] HUAC went so far as to organize several "fishing trips" to England to drum up friendly witnesses and even issued subpoenas to Americans living in England.[74]

Recently declassified MI5 files reveal that the British government not only turned a blind eye to HUAC's extraterritorial maneuvers, but directly assisted the U.S. embassy's efforts to keep tabs on known "subversives" living in the United Kingdom. Sam Wanamaker was placed under surveillance by British security services shortly after his arrival in London, and details about his activities and whereabouts were routinely passed on to American officials.[75] Nonetheless, many of the blacklisted found ardent supporters within the ranks of British politicians; the screenwriter Howard Koch recalls that "several Liberal members of Parliament took a special interest in their blacklisted American guests."[76] Koch and his wife, Anne, became close with the Labour MP Elwyn Jones; Carl Foreman lists the Welsh socialist Aneurin Bevan and the future Labour Party head Michael Foot as friends, while Joseph Losey frequently sought assistance from Sir Leslie Plummer, a Conservative MP and firm believer in individual freedom.[77] In Losey's view, the English respect for civil liberties was largely responsible for the "generous, warm, cordial, helpful community" he found in England. For while the British reputation for reserve may be true, "if you are in trouble, particularly in something that's an infringement of personal liberty, of Civil Rights there's an astonishing amount of support."[78]

At the time, London was home to a large community of political dissidents, including anti-apartheid protesters from South Africa and Canadians fleeing their country's own anticommunist investigations. Erik Tarloff, whose father—the director Frank Tarloff—came to London in 1956, offers the reminder that the blacklisted Americans were "part of a larger left-wing expat community that included Canadians, South Africans—Mordecai Richler was there, Doris Lessing."[79] The Sunday afternoon open houses held by Donald Ogden Stewart and his wife, Ella Winter, at their Hampstead home brought together an eclectic mix of left-leaning Londoners or adopted Londoners. Their son, Donald Ogden Stewart Jr., recalls, "One never knew whom one would meet going up there; Graham Greene, Kenneth Tynan. Doris Lessing came a couple of times with [the British actor] Miles Malleson." Other visitors included the "brightest of the English left"—among others, the scientist J. D. Bernal and the barrister D. N. Pritt—and fellow Americans in London such as the writers Sally Belfrage, James Thurber, and Edmund Wilson. Stewart Jr., who frequently visited his father in London during these years, emphasizes that these open houses maintained a political dimension: "The Sunday socializing at 103 Frognal was more than a pleasant way of getting through a non-working day; it was focused on urging people to do something about something," be it through bidding in the fund-raising auctions Ella Winter would organize or through showing support for activists such as W.E.B. Du Bois or Paul Robeson, both of whom visited on occasion.[80]

The British Film Industry and the Blacklist

The blacklisted Americans presented British producers with a dilemma: although their Hollywood experience would increase a production's prestige and perhaps its chances of commercial success, their blacklisted status could jeopardize the film's chances of U.S. distribution. Access to the U.S. market was more essential to British producers than to their French counterparts, who could rely on government aid and audience preferences to sustain the French domestic market.[81] The centralized nature of the British industry, which was dominated by a small number of vertically integrated studios such as Rank and Associated British Picture Corporation (ABPC), not only limited the options for the blacklisted community in London, but also meant that the few remaining alternatives were more susceptible to pressure from Hollywood. And while American financing was not yet the deluge it would become in the 1960s, it nonetheless provided backing for over a third of British films by 1956, further strengthening the ties between the two industries.[82] Historically, the British and American film industries were also more closely interwoven, with the presence of American studios in Britain and of British stars in Hollywood creating a greater sense of interdependence and competition than that which existed between France and America.

Although the London exiles seemed to have had no trouble finding agents—both Joseph Losey and Howard Koch were quickly signed by the prestigious Christopher Mann agency—finding credited feature film work was a different matter. Ealing Studios's interest in hiring Donald Ogden Stewart cooled once it realized the implications of his blacklisted status; Rank canceled its contract with Carl Foreman for similar reasons.[83] In light of the studios' squeamishness, it is not surprising that most of the exiles' initial films in Britain were low-budget independent productions, whose producers were drawn to the value the exiles represented. As Joseph Losey recalls: "The English market wanted to employ me because first, they knew that I knew my job; second, they got me very cheaply; third, they thought I would make pictures for the American market; fourth, they thought I would attract American stars; and fifth, in some strange way they thought they could keep it all secret."[84]

Despite their professed enthusiasm, even independent producers drew the line at giving the blacklisted credit for their work. Cy Endfield directed (and in some instances wrote) his first five British films using the pseudonyms Charles de La Tour, Hugh Raker, and C. Raker Endfield; Joseph Losey was Victor Hanbury and Joseph Walton for his first two productions.[85] Through the intervention of his close friend Katharine Hepburn, Donald Ogden Stewart was hired to polish the script for *Summertime* (dir. David Lean, 1955) but received no credit for his work. For *Escapade* (dir. Philip Leacock, 1955), Stewart used a pseudonym at the insistence of the film's distributors.[86] In December 1955, the *Picture Post*—Britain's version of *Life* magazine—devoted a feature article to the predicament of the blacklisted exiles, asking, "How is it that the British film industry, which desperately needs these men, often dare not employ them—or, if it does use them, dare not let them work under their own names?" The article cites "one of the most famous British producers" on the subject: "'If we could use some of those writers, British films would sweep the board.' I asked him if I could quote him. 'Yes,' he said, 'but don't use my name.'"[87]

The genesis of Losey's first British feature, *The Sleeping Tiger* (1954), provides further insight into the industry's view of the blacklisted. Carl Foreman recalls that "there was an English producer who was anxious to work with me at any price. He wanted to hire an American writer-director to increase his production's prestige."[88] Despite his professed enthusiasm, the producer, Nat Cohen, required that Foreman and his co-screenwriter, Harold Buchman, use the pseudonym Derek Frye, while Losey directed the film under the name Victor Hanbury. Nonetheless, Losey does not include Cohen among those who exploited him during these early years of exile. "He was prepared to employ me and it was essential for me to work—absolutely essential."[89]

Just as the blacklist extended all the way to England through the threats of American distributors (themselves responding to pressure from right-wing groups such as the American Legion and the AFL Film Council), so did the black market for scripts by blacklisted screenwriters. Carl Foreman's lawyer and close friend Sidney Cohn recalls fielding multiple offers for his client from major studios; among the films he says Foreman wrote "under the table" are *The Man Who Loved Redheads* (dir. Harold French, 1955) and *Heaven Knows, Mr. Allison* (dir. John Huston, 1957).[90] Foreman's contacts in the British film industry no doubt helped procure him such assignments. In 1954, Foreman had begun working as a script reader and executive assistant for Alexander Korda's London Films, which produced *The Man Who Loved Redheads*; he also had close associations with Joe Moscowitz and Buddy Adler, executives at Twentieth Century–Fox's U.K. subsidiary, which produced *Heaven Knows, Mr. Allison.*[91]

Another obstacle to entry faced by the exiles in Britain came from the industry trade unions. As in France, the trade unions in Britain were communist-dominated and, consequently, generally sympathetic to the situation of the American exiles. The Association of Cine Technicians (ACT) "bent over backwards to help the blacklistees," recalls Michael Seifert, whose father, Sigmund, was a prominent left-wing solicitor and legal advisor to many in the blacklisted community.[92] George Elvin and Ralph Bond, the ACT's general secretary and vice president, respectively, were frequent guests at the Seiferts' weekend gatherings, which were also attended by many of the Americans in London, including Bernard Vorhaus and Hannah Weinstein.[93] The director Anthony Asquith, president of the ACT since 1937, made a point of befriending Joseph Losey soon after his arrival in Britain; in a letter to Elvin years later, Losey recalled the "extraordinary lengths" Asquith went to in order to assist him.[94] Nonetheless, despite such ties of sentiment, gaining membership in a closed-shop union such as ACT was a challenge at a time when the unions were seeking to restrict the number of foreign directors working in the British industry. "There was immense pressure on the unions not to include me . . . because no major company wanted me. The majors wanted their own directors to work," Losey explains.[95] Losey received his union credentials one year later, in October 1954, thanks to a special dispensation extended to him through the efforts of George Elvin and others precisely on account of his political status.[96]

On the other hand, the absence of linguistic barriers created additional employment options for the London exiles, particularly in the theater. The blacklisted actor Phil Brown directed Donald Ogden Stewart's play *The Kidders* at the Arts Theatre in London's West End in November 1957. Cy Endfield directed the famous British character actor Roger Livesey in *The Teddy Bear* in 1955 and adapted his film, *The Secret,* for the stage the following year.[97] Joseph Losey also returned to the theater for the first time since his 1947 production of Bertolt Brecht's *Galileo,* but without great success. His first production, *The Wooden Dish,* closed after a seven-week run in the fall of 1954, while his follow-up effort, *Night of the Ball,* fared little better, opening to mediocre reviews in January 1955 despite a cast that included Wendy Hiller and Jill Bennett.[98] In 1952, Sam Wanamaker began his very successful career in the British theater when he directed and starred in the London premiere of Clifford Odets's *Winter Journey.* In addition to his frequent stage appearances, which included his performance as Iago opposite Paul Robeson's Othello in the 1959 Royal Shakespeare Company production of the eponymous play, Wanamaker ran the New Shakespeare Theatre in Liverpool from 1957 to 1960 and would later be the driving force behind the reconstruction of Shakespeare's Globe Theatre in the early 1990s.

Television to the Rescue

Given the challenge of finding work in feature films, the blacklisted in both Paris and London often relied on television to keep them afloat during their early years of exile. Attracted by lower production costs and the allure provided by authentic European settings, in 1951 a young American television writer named Sheldon Reynolds began producing television series in Europe intended for the U.S. market. His formula proved so successful that by 1955 American television companies occupied sound stages at three of the main Parisian-area studios.[99] Reynolds's first European series, *Foreign Intrigue*, ran from 1951 through 1955, in three permutations: *Dateline Europe* (1951–1953, 78 episodes), *Overseas Adventure* (1953–1954, 39 episodes), and *Cross Current* (1954–1955, 39 episodes). Using the concept of the American foreign correspondent in Europe as its premise, *Foreign Intrigue* won praise for its suspenseful pacing and Cold War plot lines. The irony that a series described by the *Los Angeles Times* as "decidedly anti-Communist" was being written by a bunch of blacklisted Americans in Paris remained a secret joke among the TV group, which included John Berry, Norma Barzman, and Lee and Tammy Gold. They had no direct contact with Reynolds, who preferred to let intermediaries handle all business with the blacklisted. Norma Barzman recalls receiving "phone calls from people we'd never heard of, giving us assignments."[100]

In addition to *Foreign Intrigue*, Berry, Barzman, and the Golds churned out scripts for other English-language television series being filmed in Europe, including *Orient-Express*, *Mr. Potter*, *Captain Gallant of the Foreign Legion*, and later Hannah Weinstein's *The Adventures of Robin Hood*. Financed by a generous divorce settlement, Weinstein arrived in Paris in 1951 and set about training for a new career as a television producer. Initiating a practice that would serve her well, she hired her blacklisted friends to write and direct a pilot episode for a television series called *Adventure in Paris*, set during the Resistance. Vladimir Pozner and Ben Barzman wrote a script that John Berry directed, with Weinstein learning the ropes in the process. Although she never managed to sell the series, the experience proved invaluable to Weinstein, not least for convincing her to abandon France in favor of England, where union regulations were more relaxed.[101]

Weinstein settled in London in 1952, working first as an uncredited producer on the television series *Colonel March of Scotland Yard* (1952–1954) before launching her own company, Sapphire Productions, in 1954.[102] Through mutual friends, she approached Sid Cole, an associate producer at Ealing Studios, with her ideas for making a television series either about Robin Hood or King Arthur. Cole advised her to choose the former ("the great thing about Robin Hood is that it enables you to sympathize with the outlaws") and signed on as her associate producer.[103] By the fall of 1954, preparations for *Robin Hood* were under way, with Ian McLellan Hunter and Ring Lardner Jr. writing the majority of the episodes from New York and Howard Koch revising their scripts in London.[104] The subject matter resonated with its "outlaw" writers in ways Cole could not have anticipated. Robin Hood became an ideal cipher through which the Hollywood radicals could continue to express their views on social justice, while the prevalence of plots hinging upon threats of informing and betrayal likewise shows the mark of the HUAC investigations.

Sapphire quickly hit the big time with *The Adventures of Robin Hood* (1955–1959, 143 episodes), which achieved top-ten ratings within a week of its debut in September 1955.[105] The success of the series on both sides of the Atlantic was such that "American children have exchanged their Davy Crockett hats for Robin Hood fore-and-afters," noted Lindsay Anderson, who directed five episodes for the series. In an account of his experiences published in *Sight and Sound*, Anderson makes special mention of the unusual camaraderie that existed between all levels of crew and cast on the set, along with the unusual quality of the result. "'It's only TV' is often said as a justification for shoddy workmanship, shoddy scripting, and schedules so cramped as to prevent directors and actors even attempting to do more than get the clichés onto celluloid. *Robin Hood* is made for TV, but it is made as *cinema*."[106] Sapphire's other, less successful productions included *The Adventures of Sir Lancelot* (1956–57), *The Buccaneers* (ITV, 1956–57), *The Adventures of William Tell* (ITV, 1958–59), and *Sword of Freedom* (ITV, 1958–60).[107]

Among the exiles drawn to Weinstein's elegant Chelsea home was Joseph Losey, who counted Weinstein among his closest friends during his early years in London.[108] Although not employed on any of her productions, Losey likewise relied on American-produced television work to sustain him financially during his first year or two in London. Through Carl Foreman, he met Edward and Harry Danziger, brothers who had run a dubbing studio in New York and produced a number of feature films (including *So Young, So Bad*, Bernard Vorhaus's last American production) before establishing themselves in London in 1952. Their first UK venture was the half-hour crime anthology *Calling Scotland Yard* (1953–54), for which they hired Losey as script editor. Losey also directed a number of episodes of the Danzigers' next project, a suspense series called *The Vise* (1954–55), in addition to working with Foreman on the series *The Adventures of Aggie* (1956–57). Losey worked for minimal pay and no credit, enduring conditions that were challenging at best. "Most of the time you couldn't rehearse and you had to film the whole episode in half a day. I have no fond memories of the experience, which was simply a means to an end. Financially, I needed the work; that's really all I can say about it."[109]

Transatlantic Communities

Whether fostered in the Stewart's home in Hampstead or the Golds' apartment in Montparnasse, a strong sense of community sustained the blacklisted émigrés during their difficult early years in Europe. Nora Sayre, a young writer and frequent guest at 103 Frognal, compares the blacklisted community in London to an "intimate extended family." "Over the decades, most had not only worked together, they'd spent their free time with one another, rented rooms to each other, raised their children together, and—by the time I met them—suffered together. They had their differences . . . but cohesion was based on an assumption that commitments were still shared. That gave them a continuity that seemed to be heartening in their blacklist years."[110] In addition to their professional collaborations and frequent socializing, the blacklisted community in London even lived together on occasion, with Joseph Losey subletting the top floor of the Kochs' Kensington home for a period in the mid-1950s, before relocating to Carl Foreman's for a few months in 1956.[111] Preexisting friendships seem to have played a negligible role in determining where the exiles settled, a choice that was more greatly affected by practicalities or predilection. The language difference was also certainly an issue for some. Foreman expresses his admiration for Dassin's accomplishments: "I could never have done what [he] did with *Rififi*, to write in French, I just don't think it's possible."[112] Yet for others, their choice was driven by emotional factors. Despite not speaking a word of French, John Berry was enamored of French culture, which he had been exposed to through the films of Jean Renoir and René Clair.[113]

While interconnected, the London and Paris exile communities maintained significant differences. The London community was larger in size and integrated into a broader international expatriate community, whereas the Paris group operated within the smaller circle of the French left-wing film community. In his memoirs, written in 1977, Carl Foreman articulates his perception of the distinction between the two groups: "I think if I had fallen victim to the temptation to, let's say, go to Paris and join the French group, my life would have taken a completely different turn. . . . But beyond that, to be part of a tight little group of émigrés, the incestuous nature of it. . . . In England, I moved with people from all different fields."[114] Most significant, the members of the London community never supported each other financially in any formalized way, unlike the blacklisted group in Paris.

The two exile communities also operated in very different professional environments. The absence of linguistic barriers created additional employment options for the London exiles, particularly in the theater. The British film industry was still dominated by major film conglomerates such as Associated British Picture Corporation (ABPC), Ealing Studios, and the Rank Organization, while France's system of state support encouraged the existence of numerous independent producers. The proliferation of small production companies in France, along with France's participation in European co-production agreements, created opportunities for the Parisian exile community that did not yet exist in Britain. Independent production in Britain was growing, however, thanks to new funding measures such as the NFFC and the British Film

Production Fund, and although independent producers were no more willing than the Rank Organization to give credit to a blacklisted writer or director, they were at least willing to employ the American exiles.[115] The French and British film industries voiced similar fears about Hollywood domination, but the debate was much more vigorous in France, fueled by broader concerns about American influence. And after decades of seeing their brightest stars lured to Hollywood, the French and British film communities took a certain delight in the reverse emigration prompted by HUAC.[116]

For the exiles, however, the limited opportunities available to them were a harsh introduction to life on the blacklist. Not only was it a challenge to find work, but their blacklisted status repeatedly compromised the success of their overseas ventures; Hollywood's leading role in the global film industry had yet to feel the impact of its domestic decline. Despite the generally sympathetic reception they received from their European colleagues, they were often compelled to work without credit and, time and again, experienced the vulnerability of life on the blacklist. Regardless of the production context—which ranged from independent production to studio films, from Hollywood runaway production to Franco-American ventures, and from dubbing to television—the exiles' blacklisted position left them with little recourse or ability to negotiate.[117]

3 • THE BLACKLIST AND "RUNAWAY" PRODUCTION

IN ADDITION TO THE blacklisted exiles, Europe was awash with Hollywood expatriates during the postwar years. Some, such as the directors Lewis Milestone and Nicholas Ray and the screenwriter Howard Koch, had been "graylisted."[1] The graylist was the work of powerful red-baiting organizations such as the American Legion and a private firm called American Business Consultants (ABC), and it targeted Hollywood's noncommunist liberals. These pressure groups combed through sources ranging from HUAC transcripts to back issues of the communist newspaper the *Daily Worker* for names of "subversives," whom they then included in their respective publications—the American Legion's *Firing Line* and *American Legion Magazine* and ABC's *Counterattack* and *Red Channels*, an index known as the bible of the graylist. Although the studios denied that they circulated a list (either black or gray) of names of those considered subversive, the blacklisted could at least be certain of their status, whereas the graylist was as obscure as its name suggests. As Lewis Milestone explained, "You had adversaries, but you never knew who they were, so you couldn't face them. You were a marginal citizen, unsure of where you stood."[2]

Other Americans came to Europe for economic reasons. In 1951, a new income tax ruling came into effect that excused Americans from paying taxes on income earned abroad for a period of eighteen months. Although the legislation had been intended to encourage America's titans of industry to expand internationally, it was passed at a time when Hollywood's stars were eager for a break from the high taxes of the period (for this reason, many Hollywood actors also formed their own production companies in order to be taxed on their income at the lower capital gains rate). Gene Kelly was among those who decided that an extended stay in Europe made good economic sense.

Kelly's studio, MGM, readily agreed on account of the postwar currency restrictions that froze American assets in Europe in order to help Europe's war-ravaged economies rebuild.[3] Unable to repatriate the profits made from European distribution, the studios had limited choices: they could hold the funds in European accounts, invest them in European goods or products, or use them to produce films in Europe. With domestic box office receipts rapidly declining, the studios could not afford to wait for the restrictions to be lifted. While many studios did make non-film European investments in assets ranging from real estate to wine, they primarily directed their frozen funds into industry-related ventures, establishing foreign offices, buying production and post-production facilities, and making films abroad.[4] The dollar's strength in relation to the European currencies also meant that production costs in Europe were significantly lower than in Hollywood, where the studios were obliged to pay union wages. With no language barrier and close cultural ties, Britain held particular appeal to Americans, who invested heavily in British studios and productions, one-third of which had U.S. financing by 1956. In addition to the Hollywood studios, penny-pinching independent American producers hoped to take advantage of Europe's cheap, skilled labor along with the availability of cut-rate blacklisted talent. According to one contemporary survey, American production in Europe doubled between 1950 and 1957.[5]

Not surprisingly, this trend was not welcomed by some in Hollywood, where unemployment was on the rise as the industry struggled to regain its economic footing in the wake of the Paramount decrees (which forced the studios to divest themselves of their theaters) and competition from television. Film industry labor groups such as the AFL/CIO brought attention to the ill effects of this so-called "runaway production," a term coined by the Hollywood AFL Film Council in a 1949 report and that quickly assumed negative connotations. As noted in a 1953 editorial in the *Hollywood Reporter*, "THAT TAG, 'runaway productions,' slapped on the foreign production efforts of our Hollywood producers by the IATSE [International Alliance of Theatrical and Stage Employees] is a bad smear on a most necessary effort."[6] Nor were these foreign productions always a welcome presence in their host countries. As the reaction to the Twentieth Century–Fox London production of *Night and the City*, discussed later in this chapter, demonstrates, Hollywood's overseas filmmaking was frequently perceived as a threat to indigenous production and national cinema.

Leading the charge against runaway production was the conservative labor leader Roy Brewer, IATSE's international representative and founder of the Hollywood AFL Film Council, an umbrella organization of twenty-eight AFL-CIO unions. An avid anticommunist, Brewer was particularly incensed that overseas production could benefit the blacklisted in Europe while harming American workers in Hollywood. Over the course of the 1950s, the Film Council would try repeatedly to tie its concerns about runaway production to the anticommunist crusade. It was frequently supported in its efforts by the American Legion, the veterans organization whose leadership, publications, and 3,000-plus branches exerted considerable influence over the studios in the postwar years.[7]

Despite the Hollywood AFL Film Council's numerous campaigns aimed at curbing overseas production, Hollywood's declining economic fortunes and waning concern with anticommunism ultimately rendered these efforts ineffectual. By the time the studios had largely used up their blocked funds by the early 1950s, most Western European countries had established subsidy programs that ensured the continued presence of American filmmaking interests in Europe.[8] The model of Hollywood's European production evolved accordingly, shifting away from studio to independent productions with studio distribution.

The blacklisted exiles in Europe were closely involved in each stage of the development of American overseas production during the 1950s. Examining the histories of this range of runaway production—from studio to independent to "international"—reveals the complex and often contradictory interplay between the film industry's conservative elements and increasingly international orientation. While the Film Council's increasingly unsuccessful efforts to shut down blacklisted production in Europe hold a mirror to the waning power of the blacklist, the persistence of the practice of "clearance" (described below) on the part of studios illustrates how the growing American presence in Europe's film industries ironically breathed new life into the blacklist.

A Blow against HUAC? *Christ in Concrete*

The first exile production in Europe is an early example of the appeal European film production subsidies held for American independent producers. *Christ in Concrete* (dir. Edward Dmytryk, 1949) was originally conceived as a Hollywood project for Roberto Rossellini working with his *Rome, Open City* (1945) and *Paisan* (1946) producer Rod Geiger.[9] That it entered production in England in March 1949 at J. Arthur Rank's Denham Studios, with Edward Dmytryk directing, reflects the financial and industrial considerations at the heart of runaway production. In 1949, the British government established the National Film Finance Corporation (NFFC) as a source of state funding aimed at encouraging domestic production. In addition, a certain percentage of the American studios' "blocked funds" were to be redirected toward indigenous production. Despite the American nationality of *Christ in Concrete*'s key talent, the production was nonetheless eligible for these forms of government assistance by virtue of its predominantly British crew; its religious subject matter also appealed to the NFFC's chairman, Lord Reith, who selected the film as the fledgling fund's inaugural project.[10]

A more unlikely combination of production interests—both in terms of practicalities and politics—is difficult to imagine. The story of the struggles of an Italian American bricklayer in New York during the Depression, *Christ in Concrete*'s narrative was deeply enmeshed in the specificity of its setting. Ben

Barzman, whom Edward Dmytryk persuaded to write the screenplay, remembers finding the decision to make the film in London "a bit absurd."[11] The politics of those involved in the project were also ill matched. Why would J. Arthur Rank, a devout Methodist, agree to finance a film based on a novel by Pietro di Donato, a Communist Party member, and directed by Edward Dmytryk, one of the Hollywood Ten and on every studio's blacklist? Clearly, Rank's religious beliefs did not get in the way of his professional aspirations, which focused on raising the profile of British films abroad through an ambitious postwar production program and his Eagle-Lion U.S. distribution network.[12] Rank was also no doubt attracted to Dmytryk's strong track record; *Crossfire* (1947), Dmytryk's last Hollywood film, had been a critical and commercial success that earned him an Oscar nomination for Best Director.

Shortly after Dmytryk and Barzman arrived in Britain, the production ran into financial difficulties, although accounts differ as to their cause. According to Norma Barzman, the Bank of England refused to release any production funds until her husband signed a release saying he had been paid in full (when he had not received a cent, and never would for this production). Dmytryk asserts that Barzman, along with Sam Wanamaker, the blacklisted actor who was cast as the film's lead, delayed the production through their insistence on being paid in U.S. dollars, which Geiger could get only on the black market. Geiger blamed the situation on Dmytryk's political troubles, which cast doubt over the film's prospects for an American release.[13]

Whether the production's financial difficulties actually had to do with the blacklist is unclear. While J. Arthur Rank would certainly have been abreast of the political situation in America due to his involvement in the U.S. distribution market, HUAC's investigations were not front-page news in the United Kingdom.[14] The autumn 1948 issue of *Sequence*, the influential film journal co-founded by Lindsay Anderson and Gavin Lambert, refers to this lack of coverage in the British press:

> The Hollywood Witch Hunt now seems to have taken a more sinister turn. Reports are scarce and tactfully, perhaps, absent from English papers, but what is certain is that eleven people, including three scriptwriters . . . have been sentenced to a year's imprisonment for alleged Communist sympathies and Contempt of Court. Dmytryk and Adrian Scott have been dismissed by their studio and black-listed. . . . The plight of Maltz, Trumbo, Lawson, and others, and all that it implies, should arouse indignation and disgust in liberal-minded people everywhere—at the moment, the most important thing seems that at least it should be known and recognized.[15]

British reviews of *Christ in Concrete*—or *Give Us This Day,* as it was called in Britain—suggest that awareness of the filmmakers' political troubles was limited

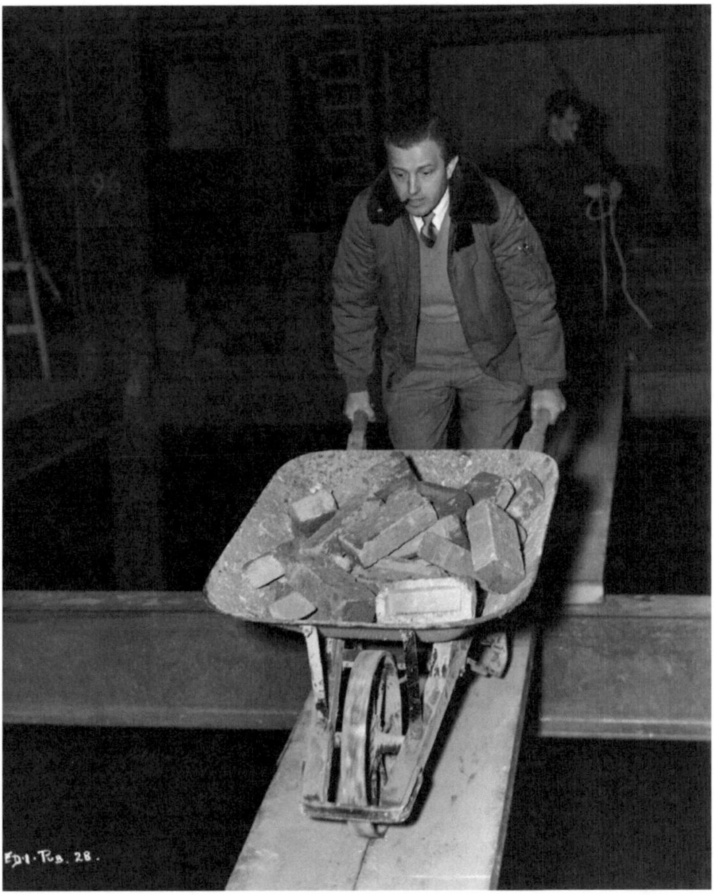

Edward Dmytryk on the set of *Christ in Concrete* (From the collections of the Margaret Herrick Library)

to those on the Left and to more serious cinéphiles.[16] The future Labour MP Joan Lester refers to her admiration for Dmytryk's stance against HUAC, and Richard Winnington, writing in *Sight and Sound,* situates his perceptive but mixed review of the film in the context of the blacklist.[17] That the film was released in the United States with Dmytryk's name in the credits is notable given the subsequent exhibition history of films by the blacklisted and speaks to the fact that the blacklist was still in its relative infancy. While a few American reviewers refer to Dmytryk's troubles (the film's release coincided with Dmytryk's incarceration for contempt of Congress), none of them calls attention to the film's politics.[18] However, despite generally positive reviews, *Christ in Concrete* had little chance to find a domestic audience due to the American Legion, which threatened a boycott of all theaters showing the film. This strategy, which would effectively exclude the European films of the blacklisted from the U.S. market throughout much of the 1950s, meant that the film was hardly the "blow against HUAC" that the Barzmans had hoped.[19]

"A Back Lot for Hollywood"? The London Production of *Night and the City*

Christ in Concrete was just one of a number of American films shot in England in 1949. The previous year, the president of the Motion Picture Association of America (MPAA), Eric Johnston, had successfully negotiated an agreement according to which the United Kingdom would remit $17 million per year to Hollywood in exchange for the U.S. studios investing their frozen earnings in production in England. Studios with their own British facilities, such as MGM, Twentieth Century–Fox, and Warner Bros., quickly ramped up production, eliciting protests from the AFL Film Council and the British press.[20] C. A. Lejeune, film critic for the *Observer,* bemoaned the fact that "the studios in and around London are becoming more and more a back lot for Hollywood," noting the American connections of almost all the major films in production at that time. Fox production chief Darryl Zanuck defended the practice of producing films overseas whenever the stories necessitated foreign locations, which was certainly the case for *Night and the City.*[21] Based on Gerald Kersh's eponymous and hard-boiled account of London's underworld, which Fox had purchased for a record $175,000, *Night and the City* depended heavily on its London setting for atmosphere and authenticity. Assigning the project to Jules Dassin, Zanuck selected a director known for his skill with extensive location shooting as demonstrated on *The Naked City,* which made headlines for its use of over 100 exteriors.[22] *Night and the City*'s underworld milieu also presented the opportunity to try to copy the success of another up-market European thriller, Carol Reed's *The Third Man,* which had performed very strongly in Britain after its March debut.

In contrast to *Christ in Concrete,* with its studio-constructed New York streets, *Night and the City* spent ten out of the production's twelve weeks of shooting on location work. Just as he never stopped scouting for additional backdrops during the production of *The Naked City,* Dassin devoted himself to getting to know London. "For every minute of screen material I found I walked an hour—getting more and more frightened all the time," he told the *New York Times.*[23] In addition to key locations in the East End and Soho, where the novel is primarily set, Dassin shot scenes in the West End, Covent Garden, and some of the grittier parts of South London. A lengthy *New York Times* profile focuses not on the film's content or stars, but on the spectacle created by the "production of a full-scale 'Hollywood' film in the streets of the city."[24] As had occurred with *The Naked City* in

New York, the circumstances of *Night and the City*'s production were themselves considered newsworthy, testimony to the relative novelty of such extensive location shooting at the time.[25]

Dassin seems to have enjoyed a degree of relative autonomy in making the film. Although Zanuck, on vacation in Antibes, kept tabs on the production through his producer Sam Engel, he never came to London during the shoot. Dassin was allowed to make most of the casting decisions on his own.[26] He also contributed to the final script, assisting screenwriter Jo Eisinger with last-minute rewrites, most notably the addition of Gene Tierney's role two weeks before shooting was scheduled to begin.[27]

Considering his involvement with locations, casting, and the script, Dassin played a role in *Night and the City*'s creation that certainly exceeded that of a standard contract director at the time and must have pleased a director with a history of bridling at Hollywood's bit. Yet Dassin's recollection of both the production and the film wavers, perhaps reflecting his ambiguous feelings toward the film noir beginnings from which he distanced himself in his later career.[28] His view of the film may also be colored by the sense of having been betrayed; without his knowledge, Twentieth Century–Fox released different versions of the film in Britain and America.[29] The two versions differ most obviously in their scores, but also in their editing and exposition of certain scenes. The hiring of British composer Benjamin Frankel may have been necessary for the production to qualify as British and therefore meet the requirements of the quota system instituted in the 1930s to protect indigenous production by placing limits on the exhibition of non-British films.[30] The British version also includes retakes that lend prominence to Gene Tierney's role and clarify the relationship between her character and the film's protagonist, Harry Fabian, played by Richard Widmark. Other, more minor changes, such as giving the narrator of the voiceover that accompanies the film's opening montage a British accent, seem to have been motivated by the desire to tailor the film to British audiences.

Despite such attempts to accommodate cultural difference, *Night and the City* was on the whole poorly received in Britain. A common complaint among the critics was that Dassin had mixed apples and oranges in applying American genre conventions to a British setting.[31] The *Times* criticized the imposition of the "fundamentally American theme" of the city after dark to "London's comparatively unromantic streets," resulting in a film that was "about as British as Sing Sing."[32] Dassin's dark vision of London was taken as an affront to British pride. The *Star*, one of the three main evening papers, complained in a headline, "This Film Insults London," while its competitor, the *Evening Standard*, joked that the film would be "a great help in sending American tourists to Paris."[33] The indignation aroused by the film suggests the degree of resentment elicited by

Hollywood's presence in the United Kingdom. While Hollywood production provided a much-needed boost to the British film industry and kept thousands of British technicians employed, it also played into the industry's ever-present fear of Hollywood domination. A London screening of *Night and the City* in June 1950 prompted protests on the part of British actors who objected to "the existing position in which the Ministry rubber-stamps applications for American stars to play British parts in films which attempt to portray the British way of life."[34]

The AFL Takes Aim: The "Runaway" Productions of Riviera Films

While *Night and the City* was part of a growing wave of Hollywood studio productions in Europe, this type of production was largely off-limits to the blacklisted exiles (despite his suggestions to the contrary, Dassin was not yet *persona non grata* in Hollywood when he made *Night and the City;* upon his return to London, his option at Fox was renewed for another year and included a pay raise).[35] Accordingly, some of the blacklisted decided to take a more entrepreneurial approach to their employment problems. In the spring of 1950, Bernard Vorhaus approached the Barzmans with the idea that they join him and the agent John Weber as partners in an independent production company that would make films in Europe. That fall, Riviera Films was formed and was soon hard at work on two projects: *A Bottle of Milk,* about an unlikely friendship between a man on the run for murder and a boy whose only crime is stealing a bottle of milk; and *Finishing School,* a coming-of-age story set in a Swiss boarding school. Weber scored a coup when he booked Paul Muni for the lead in *A Bottle of Milk.* Although Muni's star had waned considerably since the actor's heyday in the 1930s, his name still had marquee value and he could be had at a bargain price. Vorhaus set up a distribution deal with United Artists for both films, for which he and Weber had found financing in Italy. Vorhaus would direct Norma Barzman's script for *Finishing School,* while Joseph Losey signed on to direct Ben Barzman's script for *A Bottle of Milk.*[36]

The production of *A Bottle of Milk* was plagued with financial and political difficulties from the beginning. Riviera Films had struck a deal with Andrea Forzano, whose family owned a studio on the outskirts of Pisa. When Forzano ran out of money, Riviera brought in a second producer, an Italian American businessman named Albert Salvatore. In an ironic twist, both producers turned out to have had ties with Mussolini, making *A Bottle of Milk* a half-fascist, half-communist production: "a very good Italian combination," as Losey noted.[37] Weber recalls having great difficulty extracting any funds from the producers; the company's finances were so straitened that he and the rest of Riviera Films were compelled to pick up extra work dubbing Italian films into English.

To make matters worse, the Barzmans, Losey, Vorhaus, and Weber were all named in HUAC testimony over the course of the spring and summer of 1951.[38] Weber remembers the problems that ensued. "Our names appeared in *Variety.* We were red-baited in print half a dozen times. We had to explain to the Italian Department of Culture that we were kosher. It didn't matter too much to them, but it was a problem."[39] The Barzmans were unable to travel to Italy for the production, having had their passports confiscated by the American Embassy in Paris in July. When Losey arrived in Italy in August, the communist newspaper *L'Unità* brought him unwanted attention by devoting a two-page spread to him. Shortly thereafter, HUAC announced the names of those still unserved with subpoenas; Losey's was among them.[40]

Exacerbating the already difficult circumstances were the additional challenges of shooting in a foreign locale. Losey recalls his frustrations working with "Italian and French actors who couldn't speak English and were largely having to learn their lines phonetically. And of course they couldn't play—you can't play under such circumstances." The working conditions were the worst he had ever encountered. The Forzanos' Tirrenia Studios were "rickety" and some of the sound stages too small for Henri Alekan, the expert French cinematographer, to photograph properly. Alekan did not speak English and was forced to rely on his camera operator to translate Losey's requests for him. Despite these obstacles, Losey and Alekan formed a strong bond; Losey's refers to Alekan's presence as "a great gift," and Alekan describes their collaboration as "total and unreserved."

Other problems were not unique to the circumstances of filming overseas. Losey was unhappy with Ben Barzman's script, which in his opinion "suffered from the fact that Barzman was still a Hollywood-oriented writer," as well as from Barzman's absence and subsequent inability to collaborate on revisions. He also found Paul Muni's approach to acting—which emphasized the character's appearance over his inner life—antithetical to his own. In addition, Muni was "absolutely petrified at the idea that he might be associated with a Communist or somebody who was going to be blacklisted," and was additionally suspicious of Losey on account of his relationship with Joan Lorring, who played Muni's love interest in the film. The various tensions on set erupted toward the end of the production. Losey describes going on strike in solidarity with the film's crew, whose members, like himself, had yet to be paid for their services. Weber tells a different story, according to which Losey demanded more money, despite having received a salary of $40,000 while Weber was living on $125 a week. David Caute reports a falling out between Losey and Vorhaus, the latter later claiming to have had no part in the making of the film, his energies having been taken up with directing *Finishing School* at Cinecittà.[41]

Joseph Losey, flanked by Paul Muni and Henri Alekan, on location for *Stranger on the Prowl* (From the collections of the Margaret Herrick Library)

Toward the end of the film's production, the AFL Film Council submitted a letter to HUAC calling for a ban on films made overseas by known communists or fellow travelers. The letter charged that "persons who have been identified as Communist by your committee" were making films in "England, France, Mexico, Italy, and other countries." As Exhibit A, the letter singled out *A Bottle of Milk*, which had by then been rechristened *Encounter.* The letter concluded by saying that "these communist refugees must learn once and for all that they cannot get away with what they are attempting to do with *Encounter* and with the others that assuredly will follow it."[42]

The effect of the Film Council's letter was immediate. When Arthur Krim of United Artists flew to Rome to meet with Vorhaus and Weber, he went with the knowledge that the ultra-conservative screen projectionists' union—prompted by the Film Council and the American Legion—was threatening a boycott of all United Artists films if the company went ahead with its plans to distribute *Encounter.* Krim, who had taken on the task of reviving the moribund company the previous year, opted to rename the film and replace the names of its blacklisted participants with those of their Italian backers. Thus, *Encounter* became *Stranger on the Prowl,* written and directed by Andrea Forzano; *Finishing School* became *Luxury Girls,* directed by Piero Mussetta and written by Ennio Flaiano. Reedited and shortened, both films were further distorted through the marketing that United Artists devised for their very limited U.S. releases. *Luxury Girls,* which opened in October 1952, played in the seedy theaters near Times Square, where the photos of semi-nude girls that lined the marquee gave prospective patrons false expectations of what to expect inside. *Stranger on the Prowl,* released the following November, was presented as yet another bleak and gritty Italian film at a time when the vogue for neorealism had peaked.[43]

Riviera Films was a brave initiative that might have had better chances of flying under the AFL's radar were it not for another, much more high profile runaway production being filmed in Rome concurrently. *Roman Holiday* (dir. William Wyler, 1952) began production in Rome in the summer of 1952 but had been attracting the American Legion's unwanted attention for months on account of Wyler's liberal politics, the supposed communist affiliations of Wyler's associate producer, Lester Koenig, and the rumored participation of the blacklisted screenwriter Dalton Trumbo. *Roman Holiday* also sparked domestic concern about runaway production by completing not only its production but also all its post-production work abroad.[44] While Wyler's stature within the industry and support from Paramount buffered him to some degree from the AFL Film Council's ire, Riviera Films had no such protection. Vorhaus had invested his personal savings in *Finishing School* but owned only the U.S. distribution rights; he was financially ruined by the experience. He was subsequently offered a contract by another Italian producer, but his precarious political situation led to his expulsion from Italy. Unable to get a *permis de séjour* for France, Vorhaus went to England, where—having been advised by his lawyer to maintain a low profile—he began a second career as a real estate developer.[45] John Weber returned to the United States and joined his brother's dental services company.[46] Riviera Films was liquidated and the Barzmans and Losey pursued other opportunities in France and Britain, respectively.

Credits and "Clearance": The Case of Carl Foreman and Columbia

The short history of Riviera Films illustrates that for the blacklisted in Europe, credited work on independent productions was not a viable option if the production depended in any measure on the U.S. market for distribution. As noted in chapter 2, most of the exiles who found employment on independent productions in England were compelled to use pseudonyms; this was less the case in France if only because some of the low-budget productions on which the exiles worked were intended only for domestic release. The rise of the international co-production in the mid-1950s presented the blacklisted exiles with more lucrative, higher-profile work, but still on the condition of anonymity. The opportunity for fame and fortune presented by these big-budget films—usually co-produced by a U.S. studio and a European-based independent production company—significantly intensified the pressure on the blacklisted to resolve their political situation. With location shooting a central feature of the international co-production, having a valid passport (which few of the blacklisted did) was a necessary prerequisite for employment. Likewise, the involvement of the U.S. studios encouraged some among the blacklisted to pursue the option of "clearance," whereby they submitted a letter to the studios describing their political activities in Hollywood and affirming their break with the Communist Party. Unlike HUAC testimony, clearance letters did not require naming names and were therefore easier for the blacklisted to stomach; however, they did not offer the guaranteed career rehabilitation that testifying did.

The international co-production aimed to capture the international market through a formula that included international stars, universal themes, and exotic locales. Whether to accompany the crew on location or to attend script conferences with producers, participation in these productions usually required some degree of travel. Carl Foreman remembers his disappointment at having to turn down an offer to adapt *War and Peace* for Dino de Laurentiis's 1955 production due to his inability to travel to Rome, where the film was being shot.[47] In May 1956, Donald Ogden Stewart filed suit against the State Department on the grounds that its refusal to grant him a passport deprived him of the ability to make a living, stating that he had been forced to turn down offers of "gainful employment" in Italy, France, Germany, and Israel.[48]

Following a two-year legal battle, Foreman succeeded in getting his passport reinstated in January 1956.[49] Shortly afterward, he went to New York to begin work on the screenplay for a new project being produced by Sam Spiegel and Columbia: *The Bridge on the River Kwai*. Foreman had optioned the rights to Pierre Boulle's novel while working as an executive for Sir Alexander Korda. Unconvinced of the project's viability, Korda sold the rights to Spiegel, whose independent production company, Horizon Pictures, was based in London. Spiegel was willing to hire Foreman to write the screenplay without credit, but he knew that Columbia would be skittish about using a blacklisted writer. At Spiegel's suggestion, Foreman's lawyer Sidney Cohn met with a number of executives in Columbia's London office. Cohn describes a very positive reception:

> Leo [Jaffe, vice president of European production] had to be very circumspect, but he was very anxious to help in any way that he could. He wasn't going to fight the industry, but if there was any way in which he could help, or if Abe Schneider, who was his boss and head of the company at the time, could help, they gave me the feeling they would help considerably. . . . Abe and Leo made it very clear to me that they were helping Carl to break the blacklist, if possible without any expectation

> that that would automatically result in his entering into a contract with Columbia. They were doing it 'for the good of the industry,' and because they liked Carl.[50]

Cohn and Foreman were particularly keen to come to an arrangement with Columbia because Cohn had arranged for Foreman's writer's fee to be supplemented by a 22 percent profit participation.[51]

Foreman's involvement in the project, however, was to prove complicated, not because of his political situation but due to a personality conflict with the film's director, David Lean. Lean's reaction to Foreman's draft of the screenplay was sharply negative. Foreman had "reduced the story from an epic to a melodrama" in Lean's opinion, and he "showed no understanding of the British mentality." Lean continued: "I said in my first notes that the writer and the book are like oil and water. I was too polite. The book and the characters in the book have completely escaped him [Foreman]." Foreman refused to let Lean's criticism ruffle him, chalking it up to "the somewhat in-built antipathy to Americans that you find in some Britons" and to Lean's limited experience as an "art house director." With no shortage of chutzpah, he told Lean: "You have made only small British films . . . you have no experience of the international market." With Spiegel's support, Foreman stayed on the project, revising the script with Lean first in Paris and then in Sri Lanka, where the film was to be shot. After one too many disagreements, however, Lean insisted that Foreman be replaced, and in September 1956, Michael Wilson, whom Foreman had recommended for the job, arrived in Sri Lanka.[52]

Meanwhile, Foreman's lawyer Sidney Cohn had contacted the HUAC chairman, Francis E. Walter of Pennsylvania, and persuaded him to take Foreman's testimony in private executive session. Foreman flew to Washington and, on 8 August 1956, testified without invoking the Fifth Amendment and discussed his past involvement with the Communist Party without naming names. In a statement that was later expunged from the record, Congressman Walter explained his decision to forgo what had been the essential condition of HUAC testimony: "I do not think that [naming names] is important, because the thing that is important here now is the opportunity that Mr. Foreman has sought to try to let the world know what a phony, if that is the word, Communism is and the deception that was practiced on many people and is still being practiced, and the hope, as he [Foreman] expressed it to me, that he may make a contribution toward keeping people out of the movement."[53]

On 1 March 1957, Columbia announced that it had signed Foreman to a four-picture deal worth $250,000, according to the terms of which Foreman's London-based Open Road Films would produce four British pictures for Columbia over the next three years.[54] In America, news of the deal spurred the red-baiters into action: the Veterans of Foreign Wars (VFW) protested that the deal made a mockery of the anticommunist effort and, convinced that Foreman had not fully cleared himself, called for the release of the complete transcript of his testimony.[55] Although the committee did not yield to this demand, it nonetheless took the precaution of drastically editing Foreman's testimony. When Cohn and Foreman were allowed to review the transcript, they were shocked to see that the committee "had taken out whatever they wanted to take out for themselves, and changed words, and put in words that were never said."[56]

Among the blacklisted community in Europe and America, the content of Foreman's testimony was also the subject of much speculation. In a letter to his brother-in-law Michael Wilson, now part of the exile community in Paris, Paul Jarrico discussed what Foreman's deal could mean for others on the blacklist:

> There are other good signs too, but you'll accuse me of over optimism. You've heard, no doubt, that Columbia has hired Foreman, who appeared in executive session last August, without recourse to the Fifth. We have it on good authority (Foreman's lawyer) that he refused to name names . . . though it is fairly obvious that he crawled plenty. Some people around here are sore at Foreman, but clearly that's subjective on their part, they admit, for it is clearly quite a breakthrough. If stoolpigeoning is no longer the *sine qua non* for employment, looks like work ahead for others. Can you affirm or deny the report that Julie [Dassin] and Jacques [Berry] have been in New York recently in search of a similar deal?[57]

Some interpreted Foreman's move more warily. Writing from their home in Santa Barbara, the blacklisted screenwriters Marguerite Roberts and John Sanford signed off a letter to Joseph Losey by warning him to "stay off the Road, whether Open or Closed," code for not cooperating with HUAC, as they apparently believed Foreman to have done.[58] Donald Ogden Stewart Jr. remembers hearing through the grapevine that Foreman had spoken to HUAC lawyers in London in order to be removed from the blacklist.[59] Others speculated that Columbia had bribed Congressman Walter.[60] Whatever the rumors, Foreman remained close with many of the Americans in London, socializing with the Vorhauses and with Cy Endfield and his English wife, Maureen, and maintaining his personal and professional ties with Joseph Losey; it seems unlikely these relationships would have remained as strong as they did had there been a widely held sense that Foreman had become an apostate.[61]

"L'Affaire Wilson"

The experience of Michael Wilson offers a revealing counterexample to that of Carl Foreman. Both men relaunched their careers in Europe as screenwriters for international co-productions and were among the most financially successful of the blacklisted exiles. However, while Foreman negotiated with HUAC—apparently on his own terms—Wilson, who remained a committed Marxist if not a communist, refused to take this step and had a quite different career trajectory.

Wilson arrived in Paris in the midst of the ideological crisis instigated by Nikita Khrushchev's denunciation of Joseph Stalin's crimes in his "secret speech" of February 1956. Jan Berry recalls the effect of Khrushchev's revelations on the Paris blacklisted community: "I remember they were very depressed but didn't want to relinquish their ideals."[62] While some retained their belief in Marxism, if not in Stalin himself, for others, the events of 1956—a tumultuous year that culminated in the Red Army's invasion of Hungary in October—swiftly did away with any lingering feelings of loyalty to the Communist Party.[63] Wilson was among those who refused to relinquish his radical beliefs, which he considered distinct from communism as practiced by the Soviet Union. Described by his sister-in-law Sylvia Jarrico as a "genuine philosophical Marxist" who "took his activities on the Left very seriously because he really believed in socialism, at least academically," Wilson's radical credentials facilitated his acceptance by the French left-wing film community, and his social connections included the usual suspects, with Simone Signoret and Yves Montand counting among his closest friends. *Salt of the Earth* (dir. Herbert Biberman, 1954), the independent blacklisted production depicting a miners' strike in New Mexico for which Wilson had contributed the screenplay, was much admired in France. The *Cahiers du cinéma* called *Salt of the Earth* "far and away the best American film in the last ten years," and the film attracted lines around the block during its run in Paris in 1955. The following year, Wilson presented the film to a packed audience at a cinema conference in Paris.[64]

Wilson's efforts to obtain credit for his contribution to *Friendly Persuasion* was the most passionately debated topic of the 1957 Cannes Film Festival and provides another example of the solidarity between the blacklisted and the left-leaning French film industry. Dubbed *l'affaire Wilson* by the press, Wilson's plight was supported by the French Writers Guild, which was outraged that Wilson's name did not appear in the film's credits.[65] Prior to the film's screening, Wilson held a press conference in which he noted his appearance before HUAC in 1951 as an unfriendly witness: "For this reason, Mr. Wyler feared that my name would hurt the film's commercial possibilities."[66] Significantly, *Friendly Persuasion*'s chief competition for the festival's top prize came from Jules Dassin's *Celui qui doit mourir / He Who Must Die*. *Friendly Persuasion* was awarded the Palme d'Or, an outcome manipulated by the American delegation, according to some accounts.[67]

Because of his willingness to work anonymously, Wilson's radical politics did not prevent him from swiftly becoming one of the most sought-after writers of international co-productions. His rapid ascendancy to the ranks of Europe's screenwriting elite was due in part to his outstanding Hollywood credits. *A Place in the Sun* (dir. George Stevens, 1951), his adaptation of the Theodore Dreiser novel *An American Tragedy,* had earned him an Oscar for Best Screenplay; his work on *Friendly Persuasion* was nominated for the same award, although Wilson himself was not because of an Academy bylaw that made him ineligible on account of his blacklisted status.[68] For enterprising producers like Dino de Laurentiis, Carlo Ponti, and Sam Spiegel, eager to compete with Hollywood for a share of the global market, the opportunity to work with an Oscar-winning screenwriter was irresistible.

Wilson's spectacular European career also owed much to the success of *The Bridge on the River Kwai,* for which he was hired just four months after his arrival in Europe. Although he would not receive official credit for his work on the film until 1984, his contribution was the subject of much open speculation in the press and within the film industry. David Lean encapsulates the situation in a letter to Wilson from early 1958: "By now, whether you like it or not everyone knows you did it—and in fact only yesterday the Academy put it 'out' as an Oscar nomination on some grounds—which I think was that it was a European script—some such thing. They all know, Mike—and I must say I am very glad. You are in fact the top screenwriter this minute—but it's acknowledged in whispers!"[69]

As Lean's remarks suggest, Wilson experienced few of the employment and financial shortfalls that plagued the earlier wave of blacklisted émigrés. In August 1958, in a letter to his close friend Dalton Trumbo, he writes of being offered more work than he could handle, all at "thumping good prices." "My personal problem at the moment," he continues, "is how *not* to work so hard or continuously that I burn myself out, get stale, break my health, or end up earning so much in 1958 that Uncle Sam takes in surtax everything I make on a third or fourth assignment."[70] Having proved his worth to Sam Spiegel on *The Bridge on the River Kwai,* for which he was paid $10,000, Wilson accepted a contract worth $25,000 to write an original screenplay for Spiegel's Horizon Pictures. Over the course of the next year, Wilson tried unsuccessfully to interest Spiegel in a number of projects. At the same time, he developed a relationship with Dino de Laurentiis when he went to Rome to work on rewrites for *La Tempesta* (dir. Alberto Lattuada, 1958), an adaptation of a Pushkin story starring Silvana Mangano and Van Heflin.[71] Wilson remained in close contact with de Laurentiis over the next few years, but of the numerous projects they tried to develop together—including a biopic of the South American revolutionary Simón Bolívar and a film about the trial of Sacco and Vanzetti—only *Five Branded Women* (dir. Martin Ritt, 1960) was produced.

Although Wilson worked steadily throughout his eight-year stay in Europe, the improvement to his professional situation was primarily financial. Because the European projects on which he was involved were either destined for the American market or co-produced with a Hollywood studio, there was no question of Wilson's name appearing in the credits. Eager to hire Wilson for a project called *King of Paris*, the American producer and former Famous Artists agent Ray Stark contacted him in the spring of 1958 with an offer to negotiate a deal with HUAC similar to Carl Foreman's. Wilson declined, despite the lure of a higher salary held out by Stark. Describing the encounter in a letter to Trumbo, Wilson says, "I clung to the old-fashioned notion that no committee had a right to know my political beliefs or associations as the price of my right to work." The prospect of writing for credit—with no strings attached—would appear on the horizon from time to time but ultimately remained illusory. In March 1958, Otto Preminger told Wilson's agent that he didn't "give a damn what anybody says" and would give Wilson screen credit. Around the same time, the King brothers—low-budget American producers who frequently hired blacklisted screenwriters—held out a similar offer, but nothing came of either venture.[72]

Wilson's final produced project before his return to the United States at the end of 1964 was the most celebrated, if also the most contentious. In September 1959, Wilson signed a contract with Spiegel worth $100,000, plus 2.5 percent of the film's net profits. In addition to these generous terms, the contract included a clause stating that Spiegel's company (Academy Pictures Enterprises in this instance) would credit Wilson "as the writer of the screenplay on the screen" and would also "use its best efforts to secure similar credit for the writer on all exhibitions of said picture in the Western Hemisphere." The film was David Lean's *Lawrence of Arabia*. By early 1960, Wilson had completed a treatment that Spiegel used to convince T. E. Lawrence's brother to sell him the rights to *The Seven Pillars of Wisdom*. Lean was also initially thrilled with Wilson's work, cabling Wilson in Paris with his praise. "What a masterly job you are doing. Your extraordinary grasp of complex subject and character fills me with admiration and excitement."[73] Wilson worked on the screenplay all summer, much of which he spent holed up at the Palace Hotel in Burgenstock, Switzerland, with the Spiegels and the Leans. "Sam and David kept him locked up except for when there was a meeting," recalled Spiegel's wife, Betty.[74] Wilson completed his first draft by the beginning of August, but in spite of numerous rewrites over the coming months, he found himself increasingly at odds with Lean over their vision for the film. Feeling that they had arrived at an impasse, Wilson walked off the project in December 1960. As he told his successor, the playwright and screenwriter Robert Bolt, "I felt I had gone about as far as I could go, that if I lived to be a hundred I could not fully satisfy David Lean."[75]

Wilson terminated his contract with Spiegel in February 1961. While agreeing to waive his right to a percentage of the film's net profits, Wilson reminded Spiegel's attorney, Irwin Marguiles, that the settlement should have no bearing on his right to screen credit, which "will be determined after the picture is completed on the basis of my contribution to the shooting script, and in accordance with procedures established by writers' organizations in the United Kingdom and the United States for the determination of credit." In response, Marguiles reminded Wilson of a stipulation in his contract that he seemed to have overlooked. "You will recall I discussed this matter with you on the telephone last December and informed you that unless you furnished a written statement [regarding Wilson's communist past] to Mr. Spiegel, you were to get no credit in the Western Hemisphere."[76] A few weeks before the film's release in December 1962, Wilson learned that Spiegel had given a solo screenplay credit to Robert Bolt. Finally prevailing upon Spiegel to send him a copy of the final shooting script, Wilson found that while little of his dialogue remained, his structure had been preserved more or less intact. "Most of my inventions have been retained in the shooting script," he wrote to Spiegel, "inventions . . . which are not to be found in *Seven Pillars of Wisdom* or any work about Lawrence." When Spiegel refused his request for joint credit, Wilson wrote to Bolt directly, explaining his predicament through the prism of his experience of the blacklist:

> For the past eleven years I have been one of the blacklisted American writers. I have just begun to emerge from that shadowy realm, not through any abandonment of principle on my part, but because at long last I have found an American producer who has the courage to give credit to a writer he engages, and the witch hunters be damned.
>
> The men in control of LAWRENCE OF ARABIA lack that courage. If I were "clean," my name would already be alongside yours as co-author of this picture.
>
> I implore you to believe this is not a paranoid assertion . . . while martyrdom ill suits me, there are aspects of the blacklist that do fill me with mirth. If I could tell you (and if you're interested some day I shall) the enormous pressures the top brass of this production put on me to "clear myself," you would see that this is the heart of the matter.[77]

Bolt insisted that the work was his alone, but the arbitration committee of the British Writer's Guild found otherwise, ruling in December 1963 that Wilson was entitled to equal credit. Recognition from the Writer's Guild of America, however, would not be forthcoming until 1995, seventeen years after Wilson's death.

Joseph Losey's "Old Bogey"

As Michael Wilson's experience illustrates, life in Europe in the late 1950s was not by any measure free from the concerns of the blacklist. In addition to its effect on personal fortunes, the extent to which the blacklist continued to haunt the exiles also provides a measure of the changing nature of Hollywood's relationship with Europe. As the American film industry became more fragmented following the collapse of the studio system and rise of independent production, developments in Hollywood no longer had the direct effect in Europe that they did a decade earlier. For the blacklisted, however, progress at home did not necessarily translate into progress abroad. On the one hand, the move toward independent production was in part hastened by the growing internationalization of the film industry. American independent producers could not only make films more cheaply in Europe, but could earn a return on investment in Europe and other foreign markets. These developments encouraged the arrival of a second wave of American expatriate filmmakers in Europe (discussed in chapter 5) for whom the blacklist was increasingly irrelevant. However, as Hollywood continued its love affair with overseas production and became directly invested in Europe's film industries, its European subsidiaries were forced to pay greater heed to the blacklist than were their independent American counterparts.

Joseph Losey's experiences in the late 1950s illustrate the irony of this dynamic. After the extreme difficulties of his first years in London, by October 1957 Losey had reason to feel optimistic about his prospects. His most recent film, *Time Without Pity* (1957), made with a decent budget and top-drawer cast, was poised to be released in America under his own name; he had almost finished the first of three pictures for which he had signed a contract with Rank in May; and Sam Spiegel considered him "'employable' on a picture made in Europe," as he told Michael Wilson.[78] A year later, after a string of disappointments, he would view his status vis-à-vis the blacklist very differently.

Losey's relationship with Rank was not a happy one. After turning down one project after another, Losey finally agreed to do a period film, *The Gypsy and the Gentleman* (1957). Although unimpressed by the script, he liked the idea of working with Melina Mercouri, whom he cast as the gypsy. The challenge of doing a historical film also intrigued him, as he explained to Michel Ciment. "I had decided we should make an extravagant melodrama and at the same time try and present something of the real feeling of the Regency period, where there were no toilets, and people bathed once a week if they were lucky, in a tub, and the gentlemen, when they got drunk, pissed in the fireplace." The film's budget was close to $1 million, making it by far the most expensive production Losey had ever directed, but such luxurious financing came at the cost of studio interference. "I had all the usual problems that you have with big studios," Losey recalled. "There were arguments about rushes and things had to be retaken because they didn't think Melina looked pretty enough, etc. . . . I had no artistic control."[79] The film's associate producer, David Deutsch, remembers the obstacles Losey faced in re-creating the Regency period visually "within the framework of a very conventional major studio. Joe was a lonely figure there [at Rank] because they weren't used to people doing things that way."[80]

Immediately upon the film's completion, Rank informed Losey that it wished to terminate his contract; "Everybody in England knew that I had, in effect, been fired," Losey later explained.[81] What followed was another long period of unemployment, during which Losey tirelessly pitched projects to every London producer he knew. He approached Sydney Box—who had run Gainsborough Studios in the late 1940s—with a treatment he had written with Ben Barzman called *SOS Pacific*, a melodrama about the dangers of the atomic bomb. Box was interested in the idea and confident he would be able to get backing from Columbia in London. Yet when Losey approached him again months later with a finished script, Box was reticent, finally admitting that Columbia had refused to contribute any financing because of Losey's tainted political status. In a letter dated 20 August 1958 to John Collier, an English screenwriter and close friend of many of the blacklisted, Losey described his predicament: "Just a note to tell you that the old bogey has reared its ugly head again. John Woolf says he cannot get American distribution with Columbia if I do the picture and he refuses at the moment to honour my contract. Box seems to be sticking to it and there is talk of transferring the whole deal to Rank."[82] Losey's sense of frustration was all the more acute in view of the reports he was receiving of developments in Hollywood. He continued: "Adrian Scott advises that the American independents are no longer budgeting on the basis of the American market and that they estimate the black list will be quite dead within a year, so it would appear that once more the British producers are lagging well behind the times. In any case, I cannot let this one go, or I would be quite dead in England."[83] Losey held Box to his contract, to which Box responded by proposing a low-budget crime melodrama that would not require American financing. Ironically, the film that resulted would prove just how much life was still left in the blacklist.

Disliking the film's original script by Eric Ambler, Losey persuaded Box to let Ben Barzman—who had likewise been under contract for *SOS Pacific*—do the rewrite. Box assented, provided Barzman could finish the script within four weeks. The Barzmans were temporarily living in London while Ben wrote *The Ceremony* (dir. Laurence Harvey, 1963) for the Canadian producer Harry Saltzman. According to Norma Barzman, Losey insisted that Ben immediately "drop everything" to help him out. In order to meet Box's deadline, Ben Barzman agreed to divide the work with another blacklisted writer, Millard Lampell, who also happened to be in London at the time. Lampell would take the love scenes and Barzman the rest. The partnership between Losey and Barzman proved difficult, however, with Losey behaving erratically and Barzman taking to his sick bed. In one instance, no sooner had Losey delivered a letter to Barzman accusing him of arrogance and condescension than he called him up to beg him not to read it, having had a change of heart.[84] By the time the film entered production in the spring of 1959, Lampell had returned to New York and Barzman was in a state of "nervous hysteria," according to Losey. "The film goes along seemingly well," he wrote to Lampell in April 1959, "but it is hard to tell because I am so wildly out of continuity. Ben fell ill and deserted me, so I'm doing my own patchy rewrites. Never mind, it was a great contribution from you both and maybe it will turn out successful."[85]

Losey's hopes for the film were not disappointed. For the first time since his arrival in England seven years earlier, he had a hit. The British reviews were almost uniformly positive. Described by the *Guardian* as a "well-made and intriguing . . . who-dunnit," *Blind Date* also won praise from the *Financial Times* for its "assurance" and "deftness," while the *Spectator* admired its "dash and polish." More realist in style than *Time Without Pity* or the baroque *The Gypsy and the Gentlemen*, the film's careful mise-en-scène supported the theme of investigation with the clues to the mystery found in the characters' rooms and belongings. Nor did *Blind Date*'s overt class-consciousness go unnoticed. Many reviewers were prompted to compare it to other recent British "New Wave" films such as *Room at the Top* and *Look Back in Anger* in its anti-establishment critique.[86] The film's two male protagonists—Jan, the Dutch painter played by the German actor Hardy Krüger, and the Welsh Inspector Morgan, played by the Welsh actor Stanley Baker—are both working-class outsiders to British society. Their class status informs their key relationships, whether Jan's with his lover, the wealthy and sophisticated Lady Fenton (Micheline Presle), or Inspector Morgan's with his condescending English superior, Sir Brian Lewis (Robert Flemyng).

A commercial as well as critical success, *Blind Date* was in the black even before its August 1959 U.K. premiere, thanks to Sydney Box's skills as a salesman. On a trip to New York earlier that summer, he sold the U.S. distribution rights to Paramount for £140,000, exactly the cost of the film.[87] The film's success brought Paramount knocking at Losey's door, offering him a three-picture deal with complete artistic control apart from the initial choice of subject; in other words, "a dream situation," as Losey recalled.

While he was busy putting together a list of projects for Paramount, however, disaster struck. In early February 1960, the American Legion learned of *Blind Date* and the talent behind it and launched a campaign to halt the film's U.S. release. The press quickly got on the bandwagon, running stories with headlines such as "Alleged REDS, in partnership with ex-Nazi, sell BLIND DATE to Paramount" (*Variety*) and "Studio Buys Film from 'Subversives'" (*New York Times*).[88] Losey was particularly offended by the cheap shots at Hardy Krüger, who had become a close friend. Rather than having supported the Nazi war effort, Krüger, in Losey's words, had "deserted the German Army and spent a year in a prisoner-of-war camp. He was always basically *anti*-Nazi."[89] Nonetheless,

Inspector Morgan (Stanley Baker) interrogates Jan (Hardy Krüger) in *Blind Date* (Cinémathèque française – Iconothèque)

Paramount canceled Krüger's U.S. tour and temporarily shelved *Chance Meeting*, as the film had been retitled for U.S. distribution. Having struck a deal with the American Legion, Paramount quietly released the film that October with the original credits intact.[90] A number of American reviews refer to the controversy the film elicited, conveying the sense that the blacklist had become superannuated. By adopting the language of HUAC, Hollis Alpert—writing in the *Saturday*

Review—lampooned the culture of conspiracy it fostered. "I hesitate to name names," he writes, "but I think I should, if only to point out that Joseph Losey . . . and Ben Barzman . . . have made a . . . tightly constructed chiller. . . . As for social content—hardly enough for the American Legion to get concerned about." The *New York Times* likewise took indirect aim at the blacklist by paying Paramount a somewhat backhanded compliment, praising the studio's executives "who somewhat timidly released" the film.[91]

On the cusp of signing his "dream" deal with Paramount in early 1960, Losey was suddenly thrust back in time to 1953, when the American Legion led a similar campaign against his first European film, *Stranger on the Prowl.* Writing to the playwright Evan Jones in April 1960, Losey seems uncertain how to interpret the situation in America: "This is either the end of a bad period or the beginning of a worse one—nobody seems to know quite which."[92] By the following month, however, the latter view prevailed. Losey contacted Sidney Cohn, the attorney who had arranged Carl Foreman's deal with Columbia, to inquire about the possibility of drafting a statement in which he repudiated his communist past. Would this suffice to clear him with a major studio? Foreman had sponsored George Tabori, a playwright and friend of Losey's from Hollywood, to write a screenplay for Losey to direct. Columbia would put up the financing under the terms of Foreman's 1957 deal and Losey was anxious not to jeopardize the opportunity to direct what he would come to refer to as his "magnum opus."[93] By the end of September 1960, Losey had a "noncommunist" statement on file with Columbia.[94]

Runaways No More

In a statement submitted to Congress in March 1959, the Hollywood AFL Film Council finally made explicit the association it had long suggested between runaway production and the "'runaway' American producers." The resolution called on Congress to launch "a full-scale investigation of 'runaway' foreign production by American producers," charging that in most instances these productions "give employment to known Communists and thus give aid and comfort to the Communist conspiracy against the free world."[95] The resolution makes no mention of the studios, thereby implying as its target the growing ranks of American independent producers working overseas—and employing blacklisted Americans. As the examples of "clearance" discussed above make clear, Hollywood's European subsidiaries were still intimidated by the prospect of the punitive measures proposed by the Film Council and American Legion (the council's 1959 resolution threatened a boycott of all "'runaway' foreign production by American producers") and felt it necessary to make some concessions to the blacklist. However, Hollywood's increasingly cosmopolitan outlook meant that these concessions became increasingly immaterial as the decade progressed. Whereas United Artists removed the names of the blacklisted from *Stranger on the Prowl* and *Finishing School,* Paramount released *Chance Meeting* with Losey's and Barzman's names intact. Likewise, Columbia's commitment to Carl Foreman—and to the sort of "international" pictures it expected him to produce, featuring American and European stars—suggests that the economics of runaway production, along with the film industry's shift in orientation toward Europe, were beginning to trump the politics of the blacklist.

4 • THE BLACKLIST, EXILE, AND THE TRANSATLANTIC NOIR

WITH THE ARRIVAL OF the blacklist in Hollywood, many members of the radical community found themselves living under conditions not dissimilar to those of the alienated, persecuted protagonists of the film noirs they wrote or directed. While writing the script for Joseph Losey's film *The Big Night* (1951), Losey and Hugo Butler moved from one remote motel to another, like noir characters, in their attempt to stay ahead of their subpoenas.[1] Similarly, when making *The Prowler* (1951) the previous year, Losey was obliged to meet with Dalton Trumbo, his already-blacklisted screenwriter, under cover of darkness in order not to jeopardize the production.[2] Trumbo and Butler, using Guy Endore as their front, also wrote the screenplay for John Berry's last Hollywood film, *He Ran All the Way* (1951). Although Berry gives a feisty account of working conditions ("We were combative. We had a feeling we would come off. We knew things were dangerous and all that, but so what?"), he readily concedes that the ominous mood that saturates the film was a reflection of the climate in which it was produced: "It's about doom. That's not coincidental."[3]

Accounts of how the future exiles made their escape from Hollywood suggest the degree to which a sense of persecution permeated the memories of the blacklisted. Jules Dassin describes Darryl Zanuck arriving at his house late one night, shoving a book at him, and telling him to get out of the country as fast as he could.[4] In a variation on this occurrence, Joseph Losey summoned Philip Waxman, the producer of *The Big Night*, to his home in the middle of the night. Having learned that a subpoena had been issued in his name, Losey was leaving America in a few hours and wanted to tell Waxman how to cut the film.[5] John Berry's story is perhaps the most dramatic of all, becoming something of a legend within the exile community. Berry's own description indicates his awareness of the cinematic quality of the circumstances:

> One day, there was a knock at my door. I saw two men wearing hats, these polite men who wanted to see me. It was like a scene out of a film noir. . . . My father, who was a business man, had taught me how to evade the G-Men, so I started to avoid any form of encounter with these types of men. I dodged them in the street, in car chases, by escaping out windows; you would have thought I was the most wanted criminal in the world. This went on for months and still they never succeeded in serving me with the subpoena nor in proving that I was evading it! One day, after having given the idea much thought and asking the advice of certain friends, I decided to get on the plane and by doing so, realize a long-standing dream: to come to France. I thought I would be gone six months, but things didn't work out that way.[6]

Berry's account is corroborated by Betsy Blair's and Norma Barzman's recollections.[7]

It is less clear how much life imitated art in the case of Jules Dassin. Correspondence between Lew Schreiber, executive manager at Twentieth Century–Fox, and Ann Rosenthal, Dassin's agent at William Morris, clearly documents Dassin's negotiations with Fox regarding his travel arrangements to England, where *Night and the City* was to be filmed. These memos, dating from the beginning of April to the beginning of May, cast doubt on Dassin's version of events, which presumably wouldn't have permitted time to lobby for first-class travel.[8] Whether the discrepancy was deliberate or the result of a weakened memory, Dassin's story of going into exile can be seen as an indication of the psychological effect of the blacklist on his sense of self and his personal narrative.

This chapter examines the degree to which the experience of the blacklist and exile haunted not only the memories of the blacklisted, but the films they made in Europe. Accordingly, it is necessary to consider the connections between the noir genre in which most of the exiles were compelled to work upon their arrival in Europe and the Cold War culture that both led to their expatriation and dogged them overseas. My work thus extends Vincent Brook's analysis of the role of the Jewish exile experience in the construction of classical Hollywood noir to the postwar era and the development of transnational film noir.[9] While the parallels between this earlier group of political refugees to America and the blacklisted diaspora in Europe are intriguing and converge in the sense of a shared outsider status (whether as Jews, political radicals, or as artists working in Hollywood), I am less interested in attributing the latter group's affinity for noir's mood of pessimism and paranoia to their ethnic and religious heritage than to their lived experience of political persecution and exile.

In his penetrating rereading of American film noir, Jonathan Auerbach argues for a connection between the sense of alienation common to the genre and anxieties about citizenship and national belonging in mid-century America. Noting the irrational extremism of postwar American anticommunism, Auerbach suggests that its intensity reflects the anxiety surrounding the shifting definition of what it meant to be "American" and the sense of uncertain citizenship fostered by the FBI and HUAC's investigations of "subversives." The idea of a danger from within found expression in the need to "purify the republic by imagining a group of fellow citizens as illegitimate outsiders who warranted . . . some sort of expulsion or detention. . . . This perceived emergency in internal security severely tested American citizenship during the 1940s and 1950s."[10] Auerbach's insight—that the bitterness and confusion of much American film noir can be attributed to "a profound sense of dispossession corresponding closely to the Cold War's redefinition of the rights and responsibility of citizenship"—has obvious relevance to the experience of the blacklisted exiles and their European noirs, which are populated by outsiders and outcasts and are shot through with themes of informing and betrayal.[11]

As a genre (or style, or movement), noir contains within its form and, by virtue of its transatlantic and cosmopolitan heritage, a hybridity that likewise challenges the boundaries of national cinema. This chapter also explores the ways in which these films express Cold War–era anxieties about borders and belonging not only thematically, but also on the level of genre. As transnational texts reflecting the complex negotiations between American and European cinematic traditions, Jules Dassin's *Night and the City* (1950) and *Du rififi chez les hommes* (1955) provide revealing case studies. A more cursory review of John Berry's noir parodies *Ca va barder* (1954) and *Je suis un sentimental* (1955) along with Cy Endfied's and Joseph Losey's early British noirs likewise reveals the interplay between national cinema and cultural exchange in the construction and perception of genre. In addition to adapting film noir and crime film genre conventions to the filmmakers' personal experiences of the blacklist and exile, these films provide insight into the continuities between Hollywood's socially conscious noirs of the 1940s and indigenous European noir traditions such as the British spiv film and the French *policier.*

The Noir Experience

Without delving too deeply into the debates about whether film noir represents a cohesive genre, or even whether it exists at all, it is nonetheless necessary to say *something* about what film noir may or may not be, since it provides the through-line for my analysis of the films of the blacklisted exiles in this chapter. Most attempts at definition mention the influence of German expressionism evident in the form's use of chiaroscuro cinematography and canted compositions, along with its narratives drawn from the hard-boiled world of crime and detective fiction. Conceived as a primarily American phenomenon by the French critics who gave the term currency, film noir is often interpreted as a reflection of and response to the immediate postwar climate.[12] However, recent studies have expanded film noir's influences and periodization to include other genres (the gangster film, the gothic romance, the horror film) and other national traditions (French poetic realism), as well as to acknowledge that many significant noirs were made during, not after, World War II and that their style and mood have as much to do with wartime privations (not least those affecting the film industry) as with postwar anxieties.[13] James Naremore and Marc Vernet both point to the important role played by the French postwar context in the critical conceptualization of film noir, calling attention to certain political factors and philosophical traditions that predisposed the French to see *noir* as "*noir.*"[14] Possessing a sophisticated, and left-leaning, film culture strongly influenced by the heritage of surrealism and existentialism, French audiences and critics may have been more inclined to read as social critique these films that differed so starkly from the popular imagery of a secure and prosperous postwar America.[15]

Just as the context that gave birth to film noir is as much a matter of discourse as chronology, so something as seemingly indisputable as noir stylistics has come into question as an organizing principle. For while, as Paul Schrader observes, "*film noir* was first of all a style"—in the sense that it valued style above content or theme—it was a far from homogeneous one.[16] Noting that "a number of distinct '*looks*'"—ranging from baroque expressionism to documentary realism—"as well as various combinations of them, mark the *noir* canon," J. P. Telotte concludes that "the *noir* style . . . ultimately seems as curiously diverse as its subject matter, and equally inadequate for defining the form."[17]

Of course, noir itself is a retrospective label, a critical category applied to films referred to as "psychological melodramas" or "red meat crime thrillers" at the time of their production.[18] As Jules Dassin explains, "I didn't know there was a *film noir* until I heard the term in France."[19] Nonetheless, while definitions of film noir continue to prove elusive, there is no denying the historical reality of the films themselves; as Vivian Sobchack observes, even if "film noir is shown to have no clothes, its body remains." As a way around the shortcomings of both the "Zeitgest" approach to noir (in which the films provide metaphorical or allegorical readings of their contemporary historical and cultural context) or the suggestion that noir exists primarily as a discursive construct, Sobchack turns to phenomenology as a means of rooting the films in lived historical experience.[20] Restricting her analysis to American film noir, Sobchack explores the relationship between domestic anxieties surrounding the home (as an idea and a literal reality, idealized by the war and challenged by the postwar housing crisis), the homeland (made insecure by Cold War threats to national security), and postwar noir production. She offers this summary:

> Between 1945 and 1955, the years generally (if problematically) acknowledged to bracket film noir's most significant period of production and reception, themes such as the impossible return to a highly mythologized 'home front,' attempts to 'settle down,' and the desire for 'stability,' 'security,' and 'loyalty' (rather than mere loyalty oaths) resonate and mark to an extraordinary degree the lived sense of insecurity, instability, and social incoherence Americans experienced during the transitional period that began after the war and Roosevelt's death in 1945, lasted through the Truman years (1945–1952), and declined as the Eisenhower years (1952–1960) drew to a prosperous close.

Sobchack argues that this sense of insecurity manifests itself in the loss of home, which functions as a "structuring absence" in film noir filled in by a mise-en-scène that emphasizes transitory "non-places" such as motel rooms, night clubs, bars, and boarding houses.[21] Sobchack's phenomenological approach to noir resonates profoundly with the blacklisted exiles' experiences. As the opening section of this chapter illustrated, the arrival of the blacklist plunged many of Hollywood's progressive filmmakers into situations similar to those they had written or directed: secret meetings under cover of darkness, desperate flights through the night on the run from the G-men, and so on. As a result of HUAC's investigations, the Hollywood radicals would soon find themselves literally homeless and expatriated, the sense of insecurity common to the postwar era compounded by the reality of exile. Yet at the same time, and with no small degree of irony, it was their professional experience making Hollywood noirs that facilitated their *entrée* into Europe's film industries. The European perception of noir as an American genre worked in the exiles' favor, as much as the historical realities that contributed to noir's distinctive mood and tone precipitated their exile.

Night and the City and *Du rififi chez les hommes*: Jules Dassin's Metropolitan Vision

In light of the centrality of the city to noir iconography and its relevance to noir's preoccupation with notions of home and belonging, Jules Dassin's transnational noirs are a good place to begin to explore the effect of exile on the films of the blacklisted along with questions of genre and national cinema. Although most of the exiles made noirs on both sides of the Atlantic, Dassin is distinguished by his success in adapting the genre to the distinctive urban environments of London and Paris. For *Night and the City* (1950), his London noir, Dassin unleashed a full arsenal of noir themes and visuals, producing what is, for many, the quintessential film noir.[22] In *Rififi* (1954), Dassin created a film that was both criticized as too American and praised as the only authentic French film noir.[23] Although Dassin was not yet an exile when he directed *Night and the City*, its production was clearly marked by the prospect of the blacklist, just as *Rififi* was by its reality. That his vision of the "city after dark" in *Night and the City* incited criticism in equal measure to the praise that his portrait of Paris in *Rififi* garnered is revealing of the specific circumstances of their production as well as of the distinctive traditions of the British spiv film and the French *policier*.

As we saw in the last chapter, *Night and the City* was part of the wave of American "runaway productions" in Britain that began in the late 1940s as a means for Hollywood studios to access their frozen currency. Hollywood's presence within the British film industry fed into fears of American cultural domination that influenced the critical reception of *Night and the City*. Despite Dassin's extensive location shooting, most British reviewers saw nothing authentic in the film's depiction of London after dark, but rather felt that the film imposed a fundamentally American vision of the noir city onto London's comparatively sedate streets. Only one perceptive critic, Virginia Graham writing in *The Spectator*, managed to see *Night and the City* outside the box of American noir and connect it instead to a more home-grown cinematic tradition: the British spiv film.[24]

As Robert Murphy points out in his study of British cinema during the wartime era, the spiv was a "peculiar forties phenomenon . . . a generic term for someone who dressed flashily and had underworld connections."[25] Peter Wollen provides a more comprehensive definition: "Spivs were racketeers with roots in the working-class. Despite their wide-lapelled suits and flash neckties, they were an indigenous type originating . . . from the black market economy which grew up during wartime and continued growing with post-war scarcity and rationing."[26] While spivs certainly preexisted the war—acting as tactful intermediaries between various members of the underworld—what the war changed was their visibility. Unlike the classic gangster to whom he was sometimes compared, the spiv was something of a popular hero, seen as providing a service to a public fed up with shortages and restrictions.

The "spiv cycle," spanning from 1945 to 1950, was short but significant, constituting the first group of British films to be set in what was clearly a working-class milieu. In addition to spivs, the characters of these films included war veterans and petty criminals. While ranging in style from expressionism, as in Alberto Cavalcanti's *They Made Me a Fugitive*, to realism, as in Robert Hamer's *It Always Rains on Sundays* (both from 1947), spiv films shared a preoccupation with corruption, violence, and underworld activity.

As is clear from the above description, the spiv film also shares a number of narrative and formal characteristics with film noir. Like its American counterpart, the British film noir peaked in the years following World War II and emphasized the difficulties of traumatized war veterans trying to readjust to society. As in the United States, German-trained cinematographers such as Günther Krampf, Erwin Hillier, and Otto Heller contributed to noir visuals, while the influence of French poetic realism can be seen in the realist sensibility of films such as *It Always Rains on Sunday*, shot on real city streets and caught up in the everyday concerns of working-class characters.[27]

Night and the City—whether it marks the end of the spiv cycle, as Wollen suggests, or represents the ultimate synthesis of noir expression, as others claim—occupies hybrid cultural and stylistic ground. Although the source material was British and reflected author Gerald Kersh's firsthand experience of London's seedy underworld, it was adapted for the screen by an American, Jo Eisinger (best known for his work on *Gilda*), and photographed by the German cinematographer Max Greene (*né* Mutz Greenbaum). The film's cast was of a similarly transatlantic makeup. The Americans Richard Widmark and Gene Tierney were familiar from their work in noirs such as *Kiss of Death* (dir. Henry Hathaway, 1947) and *Laura* (dir. Otto Preminger, 1944), respectively, while the British actress Googie Withers had played the female lead in *It Always Rains on Sunday*. Widmark's Fabian is an English "super-spiv," constantly (and unsuccessfully) on the make.[28] In the book, Fabian's American affect marks him as a true spiv, a creation that a number of British critics considered a pale imitation of a Hollywood gangster.[29] That Fabian is actually American in the film makes the layers of imitation and exchange—between reality and representation, between national cinemas—even more intricate and convoluted.

While Dassin was most likely unfamiliar with the British spiv films mentioned above (both of which received very limited releases in America), he probably would have seen *The Third Man*, the highest-grossing British film of 1949 and the sort of up-market spiv film Darryl Zanuck had in mind when he purchased the rights to Kersh's novel.[30] *Night and the City*'s mise-en-scène gives the nod to American film noir in its interior sequences, which center on common noir settings such as nightclubs, sports arenas, and cold-water flats. However, Dassin's love of location shooting ensured that the film's exteriors were marked by the distinctive character of postwar London and, by extension, the spiv film. For all its neon lights, Piccadilly Circus is not Times Square, nor could the banks of the Thames be mistaken for the docks of San Francisco. Most strikingly, *Night and the City*'s London clearly bears the scars of the recent war. Whereas American noir could only reflect the experience of World War II indirectly, through the presence of disillusioned G.I.s or allusions to the postwar housing shortage, *Night and the City* foregrounded the war's devastating impact on London's cityscape. By showing Fabian on the run across the backdrop of the Blitz, Dassin creates an atmosphere of fatalism: just as the city could not escape the Germans' bombs and rockets, Fabian will not be able to escape his unhappy destiny.

Without abandoning the social realism present in Kersh's source material, Dassin elevated the film's emotional register through his use of an expressionistic noir style in ways that also reflected the mood of fear and paranoia fostered by the blacklist. In light of his personal circumstances and considerable input to Jo Eisinger's screenplay, *Night and the City*'s scenes of betrayal, informing, and flights through the night resonate strongly with the disregard for friendship and abandonment of moral principle that the HUAC investigations instigated in Hollywood. For example, nightclub owner Phil Nosseross (Francis L. Sullivan), in the midst of delivering Fabian to the underworld boss, Kristo (Herbert Lom), offers this cynical explanation of his actions: "There comes a time when a lad must learn the true facts of life . . . and death. Well, dear boy, your time has come." The film's conclusion articulates the lethal combination of fear, self-interest, and venality that HUAC used to destroy the Hollywood radical community. Aware that his death is inevitable, Fabian attempts to provide for his loyal and loving girlfriend Mary (Gene Tierney) by giving Kristo the impression that she betrayed him. As she walks away from him, he yells at her, in Kristo's direction: "You rat, you double-crosser, you Judas. You cut my throat for a thousand quid. All right Kristo, pay her the blood money."

Night and the City's manifest hybridity—on the level of production, narrative, and aesthetics—did not go unobserved, as attested by the negative reaction of British critics to the film. An American film noir filmed in London and drawing heavily upon elements of the British spiv film, *Night and the City* defied easy categorization on account of its transnational characteristics and thereby challenged existing associations between genre and national cinema.

Dassin's next film, *Du rififi chez les hommes,* would likewise combine elements of Hollywood and European cinematic traditions, yet its status as a transnational noir proved much less disconcerting to the French on account of the inherent hybridity of *le film policier.* The French passion for crime fiction and films has roots in the prewar era. American hard-boiled writers such as Raymond Chandler and James M. Cain were available in translation in the 1930s, with Pierre Chenal directing the first adaption of James M. Cain's *The Postman Always Rings Twice* (*Le dernier tournant*) in 1939. Indigenous thrillers were likewise adapted for the screen: Jean Renoir based *La nuit du carrefour* (1932) on a Georges Simenon novel, while Detéctive Ashelbé's account of Pépé le Moko provided the basis for Duvivier's eponymous film. While to some degree inspired by their American counterparts, these explorations of the French underworld placed greater importance on "a human *milieu* rather than crime as such," a shift in emphasis that would be a defining feature of the French noir.[31] What changed during the years following the war was the genre's prominence, in large part due to the success of the *Série Noire,* the prestigious Gallimard imprint founded by Marcel Duhamel in 1945. From its initial roster of English and American pulp fiction, the *Série Noire* soon expanded to include French authors such as Auguste Le Breton and Albert Simonin, whose debut novel *Touchez pas au grisbi* (1953) sold out its initial print run in under a month.[32] Despite the generally dismissive attitude toward the French film noir displayed in their seminal *Panorama du film noir américain: 1941–1953* (1955), Raymond Borde and Etienne Chaumeton acknowledged the importance of the *Série Noire* in French film noir's development, attributing "the appearance of a typically French gangster film" to "the works of Le Breton and Simonin."[33] What Le Breton, Simonin, and their followers achieved was the fusion of typically noir elements (crime, fatalism, eroticism) with a "number of 'French' features: the centrality of Paris, the slang, and a more permeable border between criminals and police." In doing so, they created a "new sub-genre in which Parisian gangsters took centre stage."[34]

As with the spiv film in Britain, the specific circumstances of postwar France had created a need for a more indigenous form of cinematic expression. Just as the spiv film reflected a new social arena (the black market and, more generally, the world of the working class) that emerged as a consequence—both direct and indirect—of the war, so in France, *le roman policier* and its cinematic adaptations provided a forum for dealing with France's experience of World War II.[35] Narratives foregrounding "underground activities, plotting, violence, torture, loyalty, and betrayal" provide oblique references to the trauma experienced by a country divided by the Occupation and the Resistance.[36]

Not discounting these nationally specific interpretations of French film noir, it was the strong association between *le film policier* and American film noir that proved to be Dassin's salvation. In 1954, when the producer Henri Bérard gave him a copy of Auguste Le Breton's novel *Du rififi chez les hommes* to read over a weekend, Dassin was close to the nadir of his career. The last-minute collapse of *L'ennemi public no. 1* (see chapter 2) had left him stranded in Paris, with no money and no passport.[37] Burt Bernstein, a young writer from New York, recalled meeting him most evenings at La Coupole or Le Dôme in Montparnasse, near Dassin's apartment on the Boulevard de Raspail: "Dassin was absolutely broke, despite all the money he had made in Hollywood. We were very good at making a vermouth-cassis or a beer last all evening."[38] Dassin seemed to catch a break when an Italian producer expressed interest in hiring him to direct *Maestro Don Gesauldo*, a classic of nineteenth-century Italian literature by the Sicilian writer Giovanni Verga. Dassin spent several months in Sicily and Rome scouting locations and working on the screenplay before Clare Boothe Luce, the recently appointed American ambassador to Italy and ardent anticommunist, used her powers of intimidation to shut down the project.[39]

Dassin returned to Paris "a sad man." "Those lean years were beginning to tell on me," he explained. "Sometimes I wondered if I'd ever make another picture."[40] The collapse of *Maestro Don Gesualdo*, coming on the heels of that of *L'ennemi public no. 1*, had the effect of scaring producers away from him: "French producers thought I was a liability. If they gave me a film to do, would Paris be bombed?"[41]

Dassin's stigmatized status raises the question of why Bérard would entrust him with a project by such a popular author as Le Breton. The answer lies in the political situation at the time. By 1954, the first guerilla skirmishes of the Algerian War had begun, making *Rififi*'s negative depictions of North Africans politically sensitive. By Bérard's reasoning, Dassin was well placed to resolve this conundrum by virtue of his nationality and the association between film noir and American cinema: he could make the film's ruthless gangsters not North African, but American.[42]

This anecdote leaves unsaid the other, obvious reason Bérard would have been eager to hire Dassin: he was a great bargain. *The Naked City* had earned Dassin a reputation in France as a pioneer of American neorealism, and his subsequent films (*Thieves' Highway* and *Night and the City*) had likewise received very positive reviews.[43] From Bérard's perspective, Dassin was an A-movie Hollywood director who, in light of his current circumstances, might be willing to work for peanuts on a low-budget *film policier*.[44] Indeed, Dassin's appeal was such that Bérard hired him to replace Jean-Pierre Melville despite the fact that Melville had brought the project to him in the first place.[45]

Overcoming his initial aversion to the project, Dassin signed on for a salary of four million francs, or about $11,500, along with 20 percent of the profits, terms that would prove very favorable in light of the film's eventual success.[46] Following the same approach he had used in writing *Night and the City*, Dassin found inspiration touring the city streets; "I wrote the screenplay while walking around Paris," he recalled.[47] Le Breton, along with the screenwriter Réné Wheeler, assisted Dassin with the French dialogue, but felt that his greatest contribution to the film was in helping the American director discover the underworld "*milieu*" in which the film was set. "I introduced him to [the gangster] Jo Attia, long before he died. I also took him to the funeral of Pierre Cuc, whom we used to call the arbitrator of the French underworld. These activities gave Dassin some ideas."[48]

Du rififi chez les hommes was shot between September and December 1954 and showcased the somber beauty of Paris in winter. Aiming for the effect of *tombée du jour* or dusk, Dassin refused to film in sunlight.[49] He also made extensive use of his new city, creating a vision of Paris that reflected his personal process of discovery. While well-known tourist sites such as the Place Vendôme figure prominently, so do metro stations and the less glamorous neighborhoods of Paris's northern periphery. In the film's remarkable finale, Dassin demonstrates his mastery of cinematic time and space in his depiction of the aging gangster Tony le Stéphanois's (Jean Servais) desperate attempt to deliver his godson Tonio to safety in the city. Having rescued Tonio from a rival gang's hideout on the outskirts of Paris, Tony circumnavigates the city in his convertible, allowing us fleeting glimpses of landmarks both familiar (the Place de l'Étoile and the Arc de Triomphe) and unfamiliar (Place Clichy, the elevated metro tracks along the Boulevard de Rochechouart) along the way.

The unusual specificity of place that Dassin brought to *Du rififi chez les hommes* contributed significantly to the film's enthusiastic reception by the French. Like many other critics, François Truffaut was particularly struck by the skill with which Dassin transformed a well-worn genre and a much-photographed city with his fresh vision.[50] *Le Figaro* rhapsodized over Dassin's portrait of Paris: "He depicts Paris and her hidden fauna with a vibrant realism for which the majority of French filmmakers have shown neither ability nor interest. Certain images of the area around the Place Vendôme will astonish you. It's possible to recognize certain well-known thoroughfares, but they are shown in an unfamiliar light."[51] Yet the film's showstopper was not an exterior but the extraordinarily detailed, thirty-three-minute depiction of the jewel heist that forms the crux of the plot and is all the more astonishing for the silence in which it is conducted.

Dassin in the rain on the set of *Rififi* (Cinémathèque française – Iconothèque)

While lavishly praised by most critics, the scene outraged certain audiences who saw in it the equivalent of a how-to manual for aspiring jewel thieves.[52]

Du rififi chez les hommes's ambiguous morality proved provocative even in France, despite *le film policier*'s tradition of humanizing criminals. Jean-Paul Marquet reported that certain audience members exiting a screening at the Musée Guimet in Paris declared themselves "repulsed" by the film's immorality.[53] Nor could French critics prevent themselves from interpreting this aspect of the film as some sort of mischievous response on Dassin's part to the moral hypocrisy of McCarthyism. After briefly discussing Dassin's political difficulties, Borde and Chaumeton describe *Du rififi chez les hommes* as Dassin's "temporary revenge on the imbecility of the self-righteous," while Marquet imagines that "Dassin must have been amused, even seduced by the idea that he could make his audience (and especially those right-thinking, highly principled members) sympathize with the crooks."[54]

The interpretation of *Du rififi chez les hommes* as an attack on American capitalism and hypocrisy was entirely in keeping with the French response to American film noir. Both Naremore and Vernet have called attention to the complex and often contradictory anti-Americanism that predisposed French critics, particularly those on the Left, to read American film noir as anti-bourgeois critique.[55] Dassin shared this political orientation and had demonstrated his sympathy with the working class in his earlier noirs. Nevertheless, his personal experience of exile and persecution provides the more immediate subtext for his depiction of the gangsters in *Rififi*. One of the film's minor characters, Teddy Levantine—the "fence" for the stolen jewels—wears a pair of glasses with one frosted lens modeled after those worn by Mischa Altman, a member of the blacklisted group in Paris.[56] More significant, in writing the character of César le Milanais, the safecracker who "cracks" and betrays the group, Dassin was channeling his feelings about the Hollywood blacklist: "I was thinking of all my friends who at that moment, during the McCarthy era, betrayed other friends. I was thinking of those who couldn't take the pressure."[57] In an interview given in the middle of the film's shoot, Dassin encapsulated its theme in a phrase that could just as easily describe the experiences of the blacklisted, telling the reporter that *Rififi* is about "how men retain their humanity even when they live outside the moral order."[58] And in numerous interviews conducted in conjunction with the film's rerelease in 1999, Dassin reiterated the point that "*Rififi*, for me, above all is a film about friendship," a comment that suggests that in the loyalty and mutual respect that unite the thieves Dassin found expression for his feelings toward the blacklisted community.[59]

In addition to the film's unusual evocation of Paris and Dassin's political troubles, the tradition of *le film policier* provided another crucial context for critical interpretations of *Rififi*. Almost without exception, no French reviewer failed to compare the film (for the most part favorably) to the plethora of *films policiers* that had inundated French screens in recent years. Another Le Breton adaptation, *Razzia sur la chnouf* (dir. Henri Decoin, 1955), opened just six days before *Rififi*, whose release was also sandwiched between that of the low-budget noirs *Les Pépées font la loi* (dir. Raoul André, 1955) and *Pas de souris dans le bizness* (dir. Henri Lepage, 1955). Borde and Chaumeton go so far as to hail *Rififi* as "the only 'authentic' film in the French noir series," dismissing other French noirs such as Jacques Becker's *Touchez pas au grisbi* (1954) and *Razzia sur la chnouf* as mere stylistic exercises.[60] Marquet praises the delicacy with which Dassin deals with some of the conventions of the French film noir, such as the "sacrosanct 'loi du milieu'" and "the strong ties of friendship uniting the thieves . . . in contrast with *Grisbi*'s ponderous exposition of the same themes."[61] Connecting *Rififi* more specifically to the French postwar context, Catherine Gaston-Mathé observes that, for French audiences, the film's emphasis on loyalty and solidarity would have resonated with the experience of the Resistance and the dangerous consequences of betrayal.[62]

Recent scholarship, however, has detected more distinctly "American" elements in *Rififi*. Philippe Carcassonne suggests that Dassin's clear delineation of the gang members as types (the sensual Italians, the virtuous ex-con) and overheated romanticism (evident in the film's finale) indicate that "Dassin's work in this film clearly follows the American model" of grand gestures and clichéd characterization.[63] Ginette Vincendeau also mentions two aspects of *Rififi* that hew more closely to the American noir than to the French: the concern exhibited for the social origins of criminality and a central character (Tony le Stéphanois) who is washed out and on the make at the film's inception (the haggard Jean Servais compared to the still suave Jean Gabin in *Touchez pas au grisbi* or Roger Duchesne in *Bob le Flambeur*).[64] While not entirely eschewing the portrayal of the criminal gang as a kind of bourgeois, all-male family—a common feature of French film noirs of the period, as Vincendeau observes—*Rififi* also includes scenes of family life, a concession to realism that Vincendeau associates with American film noir.[65] In its depiction of the domestic life of Jo le Suédois (Carl Möhner) and his wife and son Tonio, Rififi recalls *The Naked City* in particular, which devotes screen time to the young family of the rookie detective Jimmy Halloran (Don Taylor). However, presented through the weary perspective of Tony le Stéphanois, for whom Jo's home provides a temporary haven, the scenes are imbued with a sense of unfulfilled longing and tragic impossibility in which it is possible to see a reflection of Dassin's own experience of exile and the desire to return "home" to America.

This discussion of Dassin's transnational noir production makes evident the complexity of the cinematic form and the difficulty of parsing the lines of influence that shape the association between a country and a genre. As Vincendeau concludes in her analysis of film noir's multicultural heritage, "All this goes to show

how wary we should be of apparently neat national divisions in cinematic identities and influence."[66] Whether working in America, England, or France, Dassin had to negotiate the varied terrains of commerce, culture, and politics in his role as a director. Film noir, with its consistent iconography and malleable narratives, provided an ideal vehicle for Dassin's professional evolution during the tumultuous early years of the blacklist. On the one hand, his noir trajectory from the high expressionism of *Night and the City* to the poetic realism of *Rififi*, from the spiv film to *le film policier*, can be understood as a director's pragmatic response to his shifting cultural context. On the other hand, this stylistic variation can be seen to reflect Dassin's quest for his ideal form of cinematic expression: "This mixture of documentary with the lyrical in my films represents my humble search for cinematic truth, even when limited to thrillers or detective stories."[67] What is constant in these films is the degree to which Dassin foregrounds the city, "revealing," as Truffaut said, "Paris to the French as he revealed London to the English."[68]

As we have seen, Dassin was committed to location shooting, often acting as his own location scout. On the set of *Night and the City*, he told reporters, "I look at cities as if they were actors, and let them tell me something about themselves."[69] While it makes good copy, this comment appears somewhat disingenuous in light of the many consistencies in Dassin's depiction of London and Paris. In addition to the standard noir iconography of neon, nightclubs, and wet city streets, *Night and the City* and *Rififi* both feature dramatic final chase scenes, during which the central character's isolation is underscored by compositions that set him against the gray, forbidding urban environment and equally gray, forbidding city skies. Asked what he made of these similarities, Dassin answered: "Well, if you were brought up in New York, as I was, you know how lost and lonely a boy can feel in a vast, indifferent city. I suppose the city's stayed with me. The isolation, the crowding can have one of two effects—it can be hostile, threatening, or it can be protective in a puzzling kind of way. This may account for all that steel and granite against dimly lit skies. But I think it's more than that. I try to see a man in his background."[70] This "sociological" approach to understanding the duality of modern city life, whose anonymity could be both welcome and alienating, applied equally well to Dassin's ability to adapt film noir conventions to different national contexts and to understanding his own, often bewildering, experience of political persecution and expatriation.

John Berry's Noir Parodies: *Ca va barder* and *Je suis un sentimental*

Contributing to the enthusiastic reception of *Du rififi chez les hommes* were broader changes in French film culture. For Borde and Chaumeton, the film's exceptional feeling for detail and startling depiction of Paris were a welcome departure from the easy clichés of other recent French noirs. "At the time of writing, unadulterated rubbish goes on being churned out. The producers announce *Pas de whisky pour Callaghan* and *Les Salauds vont en l'enfer.* It's a matter of urgency to put a stop to this squandering of celluloid and to make some *serious* film noir."[71] In their dismissal of *le cinéma du samedi soir*—the popular, commercial comedies and gangster film parodies that catered to a mass audience—Borde and Chaumeton anticipate the emphasis on cinema as art that would prevail as the 1950s progressed.[72] The revival of the ciné-club movement along with the critical discourse promoted in a rash of new film journals all contributed to a shift in the public's perception of cinema from entertaining pastime to cultural necessity.[73]

Yet as Borde and Chaumeton were well aware, these popular parodies of American film noir were far more representative of French noir production in the first half of the 1950s than any *Grisbi* or *Rififi.* With their fistfights, nightclubs, and whisky-drinking, skirt-chasing private-eye protagonists, these films reflected the influence of the pulp fiction published under Gallimard's *Série Noire* imprint.[74] Borde and Chaumeton's disdain for the inauthenticity of "the noir series *à la française*" makes an exception for Dassin's fellow exile, John Berry, whom they credited with possessing "more nerve and skill than our pathetic lot of third-raters, who race through their work with one eye fixed on the cash drawer."[75] Berry's two contributions to the popular French noir, *Ca va barder* (1955) and *Je suis un sentimental* (1955), both starred Eddie Constantine, an American actor and singer already strongly associated with the genre through his performance in films such as *La Môme vert-de-gris* (dir. Bernard Borderie, 1953), *Cet homme est dangereux* (dir. Jean Sacha, 1953), and *Les Femmes s'en balancent* (dir. Bernard Borderie, 1954). In these films, based on *Série Noire* novels by the British author Peter Cheyney, Constantine plays Lemmy Caution, a hard-drinking, tough-talking undercover FBI agent operating in France. According to Pierre Billard's insightful characterization, Caution was a European reinterpretation of the American private eye, his self-mocking violence reflecting the "mix of fascination and repulsion, of envy and rejection" characteristic of France's relationship with Hollywood.[76] Constantine brought a strong physical presence to the role; he "came off the screen," in Berry's opinion.[77]

Like *Rififi, Ça va barder* was a film born of desperation. Through Dassin, John Berry had met the agent Claude Briac, who introduced him to David Medioni, a film distributor from the French provinces who had optioned a pulp novel by the popular mystery writer Maurice Dekobra.[78] The story of an Englishman who, suspecting his French wife of infidelity, sells her to a brothel in Algeria, *La Rue des bouches peintes,* was truly the bottom of the barrel for Berry, whose first reaction was to refuse. But having not directed a film since *C'est arrivé à Paris* over three years earlier, he felt compelled to accept the project: "I was in terrible financial and work need," he recalls. At his agent's urging, Berry signed a deal with Medioni for a salary he remembers as pitiful, "a hundred a week for six weeks. And I had been earning seventeen hundred a week when I left Hollywood!"[79] To compensate for the low salary, Medioni gave Berry a 10 percent interest in the film.

Since Medioni did not intend to distribute the film outside of France and therefore did not have to rely on American-owned domestic distribution circuits, he considered Berry's blacklisted status irrelevant. Berry's assistant, Jacques Nahum, explained the logic: "Here was this small-time producer. He knew that John had made great films in Hollywood and he thought it would be quite a coup if he could get this big Hollywood director who had worked with John Garfield to direct his little B-movie."[80] Nor were there problems with Berry's work status, despite the fact that he did not have a director's permit as required by the CNC and the French director's union. In order to employ foreign personnel, a French production also had to hire a French national for the same position; in this case, Jacques Nahum fit the bill.[81] Since Berry had only limited industry connections, Nahum was also responsible for assembling the crew for the nine-week shoot on the Côte d'Azur. Nine weeks turned into twelve, much to Medioni's horror, but Berry remembers the shoot fondly. "I loved making it," he recalled.[82]

The finished film bore little resemblance to Dekobra's novel. Berry and Nahum, assisted by Nahum's friend Jacques-Laurent Bost, came up with a story about arms trafficking set in Latin America; Constantine's character, Johnny Jordan, breaks up the cartel and wins back his old girlfriend while he's at it. Despite generally mediocre reviews, *Ça va barder* was a hit with the public, who warmed to Berry's humorous wink at the *Série Noire*.[83]

With the success of the film, Berry's circumstances changed overnight. "I had gone from nowhere to become a big, established figure. I bought a house, signed contracts, ran around, and was able to take care of the kids." Almost immediately, Berry began work on his next film, another Constantine vehicle. "I was eager to work with Eddie again because we really got along well. He asked me to do *Je suis un sentimental*."[84] For the screenplay, Berry brought in his former television writing partners, Lee and Tammy Gold, to collaborate on the story while working with Jacques-Laurent Bost again on the French dialogue. The result was a much more ambitious film than *Ça va barder*. While not devoid of wisecracks and action sequences, *Je suis un sentimental* also manages to incorporate a degree of class commentary (the "bad guys" represent French old money) and demonstrates a concern with corruption and justice that recalls the social cinema of late 1940s Hollywood. Humphrey Bogart and John Garfield were Berry's models for the role of Barney Morgan, the callous newspaper journalist who discovers his conscience, played by Eddie Constantine.

While some reviewers criticized the film for a lack of realism in certain passages, the majority succumbed to its mix of humor and melodrama, as did the

Eddie Constantine as Barney Morgan in *Je suis un sentimental* (Cinémathèque française – Iconothèque)

public. Yet it is indicative of the strict association between America and film noir—even in the diluted form of parody—on the part of the French that when Berry tried to capitalize on his success with *Ca va barder* and *Je suis un sentimental* by straying from the genre, his career in France never recovered.[85]

The Alienated Eye

The European conception of film noir (and, by extension, the crime film) as a particularly American mode of filmmaking is likewise evident in the professional opportunities available to Cy Endfield and Joseph Losey in Britain during the 1950s, as well as in the critical reception of their films. Like their counterparts in France, Endfield and Losey spent their early years in Britain working primarily on low-budget genre productions. In one of the few accounts of Endfield's early British films, Brian Neve calls attention to their noir elements. *The Limping Man* (1953) stars Lloyd Bridges—who had previously appeared in Endfield's *The Sound of Fury* (1950)—as Frank Prior, an American veteran returning to Britain in the hope of rekindling a wartime romance with Pauline French (Moira Lister), an actress. His plans quickly go awry when, upon disembarking the plane, a stranger is shot dead in front of him; a picture of Pauline is found in the dead man's pocket. The ensuing plot abounds in betrayals and subterfuge as circumstances force Frank to question Pauline's loyalty to him at the same time as he assists her in her flight from the authorities. By plunging Frank into what

Neve describes as the "nightmare of life in the new homeland," *The Limping Man* recalls common noir themes of disorientation and mistrust, both of which assume additional poignancy in light of Endfield's insecure status as a political refugee without a passport.[86]

Likewise, *Impulse* (1954), which Endfield co-wrote, throws its American protagonist, Alan Curtis (Arthur Kennedy), into two different worlds that are equally foreign to him: the quiet provincial life of an English village and the London underworld. A real estate agent married to an Englishwoman, Curtis readily abandons his predictable routine to come to the assistance of the attractive Lila (Constance Smith), whom he accompanies to London. Curtis soon finds himself wanted for a murder he did not commit as a result of Lila's lies and conniving. Again, the film's ending is lackluster—Curtis returns to his life in the country and to his wife, who forgives him for everything—but in its frank association of sexuality and violence (after sleeping with Lila, Curtis starts displaying his masculinity by showing off the moves he learned in the marines) and its depiction of Lila as a classically manipulative femme fatale, *Impulse* succeeds in fusing classic noir themes with "an outsider's view of the underside of polite British life."[87]

Using the pseudonym Hugh Raker, Endfield wrote and directed his next film, *The Master Plan* (1954), an espionage thriller replete with Cold War gadgetry such as miniature cameras and a cigarette lighter containing microfilm, but lacking an explicitly anticommunist message. Instead, the film "leaves us with a queasy sense that this is a crazed militarized culture in which everyone is a dupe, a spy, a paranoid schizophrenic, or some diseased combination of the same," observes Jonathan Rosenbaum.[88] *The Master Plan* once again features an American protagonist, Major Thomas Brent (Wayne Morris). Endfield's next film, *The Secret* (1955), also gave a starring role to an American actor, this time his fellow blacklisted exile Sam Wanamaker.

It was only with his discovery of the Welsh actor Stanley Baker, who would become a close friend, that Endfield began casting non-American actors in his leading roles. Baker first appeared in Endfield's *Child in the House* (1956), a drama in which a motherless child and her ne'er-do-well father disrupt the comfortable assumptions of the child's upper-middle-class relations, but it was his performance as Tom Yately in *Hell Drivers* (1957) the following year that revealed the extent of his synergy with Endfield's direction. Baker plays Tom, a Welshman and recently released ex-convict eager for a new start. He takes a job as a truck driver with a gravel haulage company, but quickly grows outraged by the dangerous conditions and corrupt management. Filmed with a brutal realism that Andrew Spicer sees as characteristic of late British noir, *Hell Drivers* also evokes certain Hollywood noirs of the 1940s, particularly *They Drive by Night* (dir. Raoul Walsh, 1940) and Jules Dassin's *Thieves' Highway*, with which *Hell Drivers* shares a working-class context and concern with capitalist exploitation.[89]

Endfield credited *Hell Drivers'* perceptive social analysis to his status as an exile. "I was still an American when I made the picture, looking with a fresh view. People should see with an alienated eye, seeing things that others saw as ordinary and therefore not worth delineating."[90] British critics were likewise inclined to attribute the film's strengths to the director's foreign nationality, but for different reasons. The *Spectator* noted that, despite the unpromising theme ("lorry drivers and a gravel pit"), *Hell Drivers* was "given a lot of punch and the edge and sharp honesty British films so seldom achieve by its American director, C. Raker Endfield."[91] The *Sunday Times* called *Hell Drivers* "a well-made, exciting, tough film with a pace and a masculine command of violent action uncommon in the British cinema," while another critic observed that "British essays in toughness are seldom convincing. If *Hell Drivers* is an exception, it may be largely because C. Raker Endfield . . . is a Yale man who worked in Hollywood before coming to England."[92] In other words, *Hell Drivers'* success was seen as a reflection of the superiority of Hollywood's thrillers and used as an opportunity to critique Britain's purportedly anodyne domestic film industry. This focus on the relationship between genre and national cinema in the film's reception obscured the social critique implicit in *Hell Drivers'* depiction

Cy Endfield with the cast of *Hell Drivers* (From the collections of the Margaret Herrick Library)

of the petty rivalries (based on differences of ethnicity or nationality) that divide the truck drivers and the desire for profit that motivates their bosses.

Joseph Losey's early career trajectory in England bears many similarities to Endfield's. Like Endfield, the only film work Losey was offered was in B-movie production, which he found as distasteful in England as he had in Hollywood.[93] His first British film, *The Sleeping Tiger* (1954), was made under conditions that contained constant reminders of his blacklisted status. Not only was Losey unable to direct under his own name, instead borrowing that of Victor Hanbury, one of the film's producers, but at one point he had to be "smuggled" out of the studio in the trunk of Dirk Bogarde's car in order to escape the notice of Ginger Rogers, whose mother Lela was a notorious red-baiter. From its opening shot of a robbery on a dark, deserted street to its narrative emphasis on psychology (Bogarde plays Frank Clemmons, a petty criminal taken in by a well-meaning psychologist, Dr. Clive Esmond, who hopes to reform him) to its jazz sound track, *The Sleeping Tiger* uses familiar noir elements and themes in its attempt to transform source material that Losey described as "bedtime reading for senile stags."[94]

Losey's next British film, *The Intimate Stranger* (1956), revealed its relationship to the director's blacklisted status and noir experience even more explicitly. Under the pseudonym Peter Howard, Howard Koch crafted an original screenplay that allegorically addressed the experiences of the blacklisted exiles. The American actor Richard Basehart plays Reggie Wilson, an American filmmaker living in England and working as a producer for his English wife's father, who happens to run a film studio. Reggie is being blackmailed by an unknown woman claiming past relations with him; she is in fact being paid to derail Reggie's marriage and career by a jealous colleague. Colin Gardner lists the "transparently obvious" connections between Reggie and Losey:

> Both are exiled from Hollywood, one for a sexual scandal, the other for politics. . . . Both men are continually haunted by the past, leading to black*mail* (Reggie) and black*list* (Losey). Each falls victim to the machinations of an impotent informer, whether in the form of Ernest Chapel [a rival producer who threatens to disclose Reggie's supposed infidelity to his boss/father-in-law] or HUAC's endless parade of broken stooges. Moreover, it is also significant that the burden of proof is placed squarely on Reggie's shoulders. . . . One of the trademark strategies of the McCarthy era was that HUAC placed the legal onus on its suspects, not on its own investigative prowess. The subpoenaed had to show good faith and prove that they were no longer Communists by naming names. In contrast, the Committee did little to provide legal evidence to prove that they were subversive.[95]

Visually, the film contains a few nods to noir, such as the dramatic concluding chase sequence that makes good use of the sound stage arc lights to isolate and

Joseph Losey directing Dirk Bogarde and Alexis Smith in *The Sleeping Tiger* (Cinémathèque française – Iconothèque)

"catch" Reggie's nemesis and rival producer, Ernest Chapel (Mervyn Johns). Evelyn Stuart (Mary Murphy), the woman Chapel hired to blackmail Reggie, accessorizes her femme fatale role with the requisite trenchcoat and cigarettes. *The Intimate Stranger*'s relationship to film noir is also reflected in the film's flashback structure and sense of fatalism and entrapment suggested by Basehart's performance as Reggie Wilson.

After his contract with Rank was cancelled following his dispiriting experience making *The Gypsy and the Gentleman* (1958), Losey found himself back in familiar territory when independent producer Sydney Box brought him the script for *Blind Date*, adapted from a novel by the British mystery writer Leigh Howard. Losey remembers the story of a love affair between a young Dutch painter and an older married French woman as "very ordinary" and a "cliché": "We felt the only justification for the film was on the one hand skill and on the other to make the characters so interesting that it had a level other than mere suspense."[96] Working from a new script by Ben Barzman and Millard Lampell, Losey succeeded on both counts. While bearing little visual or thematic relationship to film noir, *Blind Date* relates to Losey's personal experiences of exile through its central characters. Like Cy Endfield, Losey found a fitting surrogate in actor

Joseph Losey goes over the script to *Blind Date* with Micheline Presle and Hardy Krüger (From the collections of the Margaret Herrick Library)

Stanley Baker, whose working-class, Welsh (i.e., not *English*) background placed him squarely outside of the establishment and gave an unusual, aggressive edge to his talent.[97] In *Blind Date,* Losey plays up Baker's Welshness, using it to accent the class differences between his character, Inspector Morgan, and his English colleagues. Nor are the film's other main characters—the young painter played by Hardy Krüger and his sophisticated, older lover played by Micheline Presle—English, but Dutch and French, respectively, a choice that Losey supposes gave him "a little more freedom" in presenting his own, "still foreign, observations about England."[98]

In *Eve* (1962), Losey once again transformed pulp fiction source material (in this case, the eponymous thriller by the British writer James Hadley Chase) into a statement about the exile experience. Baker plays another Welsh outsider—not to England's class-bound society but to Italy's glittering expatriate milieu. Baker's character, Tyvian Jones, is a self-described "full-time exile," a stranger to himself whose life is built on false pretences (he has taken credit for a novel written by his dead brother).[99] For Losey "[*Eve*] was an intensely personal film and it was a film in which I was working out my sexual, personal relationships, but also working out my exile, which again sort of had to do with the Stanley Baker character. To be dislocated in terms of background and place to the extent that I was is to dislocate your personal relationships." Indeed, it was only after *Eve* that Losey finally began to feel more integrated into British society and, subsequently, more able to comment upon it, as he would do in *The Servant* (1963).[100]

Emigré Texts, Exile Cinema

With its transient spaces and isolated protagonists, the film noir genre in which the blacklisted émigrés often worked during the 1950s proved ideally suited to the expression of exile and estrangement. A striking number of these films feature central characters who are outsiders either by virtue of their nationality or social class. Others reflect the psychological repercussions of the blacklist through plots that feature men on the run, informers, and interrogations, and that question the meaning of friendship and community. The haunting presence of the past is a common theme in many of these films. In *Night and the City,* Harry Fabian's girlfriend Mary shows him a photograph of the two of them in happier times and asks him if he remembers these people. In *The Intimate Stranger,* Reggie complains that "the past won't leave me alone. Lately it's been coming at

Reggie Wilson (Richard Basehart) gets his eyes examined in *The Intimate Stranger* (Cinémathèque française – Iconothèque)

Stanley Baker (foreground) as the ex-convict Tom Yately in *Hell Drivers* (Cinémathèque française – Iconothèque)

me from all sides." Tom, the protagonist in *Hell Drivers,* is anxious to hide his past from his new employers since it contains a prison sentence. And in *Eve,* Tyvian tries unsuccessfully to keep his past from catching up with him and revealing the fiction of his existence. The men in these films are on the run, whether literally or metaphorically, from their histories. Norma Barzman pins the appeal of *A Bottle of Milk,* the short story that provided the basis for *Stranger on the Prowl,* on the conjunction between their personal circumstances at the time and those recounted in the story: "I think Ben loved that short story because in it, he felt there was something about what he was feeling about exile and being a little boy, afraid, but also being a man and outside society and having to run. There wasn't very much in the short story, but Ben saw it as a movie and saw that there was something he wanted to express. I think it was a way of his saying something about exile."[101]

Not only do the European noirs of the blacklisted allow us to perceive a reflection of the exiles' personal experiences of persecution and dislocation, but they offer insight into the processes by which film genres evolve and are transformed through diverse cultural and historical influences. The emigration prompted by HUAC of these Hollywood filmmakers, a number of whom had apprenticed with European émigré filmmakers in Hollywood (Jules Dassin with Alfred Hitchcock and John Berry with Billy Wilder), created a productive convergence of Hollywood and European noir filmmaking. The films of the blacklisted discussed in this chapter are exemplary transnational texts on the level of production by virtue of their cast and crew; stylistically, due to their mix of Hollywood and European noir traditions; and thematically, as a result of their often pulp-fiction source material that was filtered through their directors' (and often screenwriters') experience of the blacklist.

In his excellent monograph on *Rififi*, Alastair Phillips examines the film's "specific historical status as an émigré text" that reveals some of the "fundamental faultlines of French cinema during the 1950s" due to its transnational hybridity.[102] As we have seen, all the films discussed in this chapter could similarly be considered "émigré texts" to the extent that they are marked by the realities and experience of migration and cultural exchange. Not only do they illuminate the degree to which film noir and the crime film genre were focal points in the highly charged debates surrounding Europe's national cinemas and the issue of American influence, but they do so from a perspective that meshes neatly with a European reading of American noir as social critique. As examples of what was perceived as an American genre but made by American political exiles according to European modes of production, the European noirs of the blacklisted embodied the insider-outsider paradox that characterized the blacklisted even in Hollywood. In addition to being "émigré texts" that expose the inconsistencies of postwar European film culture's attitude toward Hollywood, these films function as "accented cinema"—to borrow Hamid Naficy's term for contemporary exilic and diasporic filmmaking—in the degree to which the filmmakers inscribe their liminal, interstitial position between Hollywood and Europe into the film text.[103]

5 • COSMOPOLITAN VISIONS, COLD WAR FEARS

A continuing shift in the center of motion-picture production, away from the familiar American facilities into the booming European studios, is a well-nigh inevitable occurrence within the next few years, if conditions continue to prevail and develop in the way they are going today. So don't say we didn't warn you if, five or so years from now, you will find that the majority of movies shown in this country have been made abroad. This is the startling conclusion your humble observer brings back from a tour of European film centers and a knowledge of conditions in Hollywood.

—Bosley Crowther, *New York Times*

THIS "HUMBLE OBSERVER," the *New York Times*' long-standing film critic Bosley Crowther, called belated attention to the film industry's new European focus in a series of dispatches filed during his travels in Europe in June 1960. Noting that of "thirty-one films being made by American companies last week, eleven of them were being shot in foreign locations and studios," he concluded, "As things stand now, the magnetism of the European centers has a strong pull and the balance is shifting in their direction. It looks bad for Hollywood."[1]

The American film industry's orientation toward Europe during the 1950s was both a reflection and a harbinger of the dramatic power shift occurring between a superannuated Hollywood and a vibrant European cinema. As European films began to perform strongly in America as well as in their home markets, the U.S. studios no longer wanted to make films in Europe simply for financial reasons—they wanted to make "European" films. This was particularly so in Britain, where the domestic and international success of films such as *Room at the Top* (dir. Jack Clayton, 1959) and *Tom Jones* (dir. Tony Richardson, 1963) convinced producers of the merit of hiring indigenous, as opposed to Hollywood, talent. Mike Frankovich, Columbia's powerful London-based chief of production, explained these changes in a 1961 interview: "[The British] go to see their own films. You have to compete with the native product."[2] The perception of a dynamic, creative British film industry also proved attractive to the ambitious, non-blacklisted American directors and screenwriters who poured into London in the late 1950s and, in doing so, deprived the exiles of their unique position as Hollywood-trained, Europe-based talent.

By 1960, the major Hollywood studios were increasingly adopting the so-called "European approach" to circumvent the blacklist. Because the Waldorf Statement's interdiction against hiring suspected subversives had generally been interpreted in relation to Hollywood productions, the studios saw a loophole that would allow them to acquire the European-made films of the blacklisted and even enter directly into production deals with blacklisted talent in Europe without violating the agreement's terms. In May 1960, Twentieth Century–Fox announced that it had signed a contract with Sidney Buchman, one of Hollywood's highest-paid writers before he was convicted of contempt of Congress in 1953. According to the terms of the deal, Buchman would write and produce films in Europe for distribution by Fox.[3] The previous March, Jules Dassin had signed a four-picture production deal with Lopert Films, a production company and foreign film distributor owned by United Artists.[4] MGM had recently purchased the distribution rights to Dassin's *La Loi* (1959), and Paramount's controversial acquisition of Losey's *Chance Meeting* (1959) was also public knowledge.[5]

That the studios were not only willing, but eager, to hire blacklisted talent in Europe reflects how dramatically the industry had changed since the exiles left Hollywood ten years earlier. With European cinema all the rage, the exiles' experience of European production made them highly attractive to Hollywood, much as their Hollywood training had initially recommended them to European producers. Likewise, the more overtly transnational structure of the film industry created new opportunities for the exiles to showcase their increasingly transnational vision. Both geographically and mentally, Hollywood had decamped to Europe to such a degree that a joint report submitted by the AFL Film Council and the Motion Picture Producers Association to the U.S. Department of Labor in 1963 forecast the "eventual destruction" of the American movie industry as a result of "foreign subsidies and quota restrictions."[6]

This chapter poses a number of questions: What impact did the more competitive professional environment of the late 1950s and early 1960s have on the way the blacklisted exiles functioned as a community? How did that environment affect the sort of work opportunities available to the blacklisted abroad? Did the weakening of the blacklist create a space for the exiles to express a more critical perspective on America's Cold War culture, one that bore the mark of their expatriate experience?[7] Did the European films of the blacklisted offer any counter-commentary to the attempt to win over hearts and minds to the "American way of life" implicit in many domestic Hollywood films?[8] To answer this last question, this chapter closes by returning to the issue of social content and the type of socially conscious filmmaking to which so many of the exiles aspired.

Hollywood Europe

In the late 1950s, London began to welcome a new crowd of American expatriate filmmakers, attracted by a favorable exchange rate and the ability to access government incentives such as the Eady Levy, which paid producers of British films a percentage of their total box office receipts.[9] This second wave of émigrés included the producers Julian Blaustein and Hal E. Chester, the director Anton Leader, and the screenwriting team Melvin Frank and Norman Panama. The blacklisted screenwriter Frank Tarloff also settled in London during this period. Despite his recent breakthrough in Hollywood as a writer on the *Dick Van Dyke* and *Andy Griffith* shows, he was eager to break out of television, a motivation he shared with a number of the recent American arrivals.[10] In Paris, Bernard Gordon joined screenwriter-producer Philip Yordan's transplanted Hollywood "script factory," where Gordon toiled alongside other blacklisted writers such as Arnaud d'Usseau on American producer Samuel Bronston's Spanish-based productions of the early 1960s.[11] During this period, Rome was also home to a number of expatriate Americans, including Nicholas Ray, and the blacklisted screenwriters Leonardo Bercovici, Hugo Butler, and Julian Zimet, not to mention Dalton Trumbo, who spent an extended period in Rome during 1963–1964 while working on the screenplay for *Dark Angel*, an ultimately unproduced project for Dino de Laurentiis.[12]

This more crowded professional scene, coupled with the uncertainty surrounding the legal and practical status of the blacklist, contributed to growing rifts within the blacklisted diaspora in Europe. Why were some able to work under their own names and others not? Why did some prosper while others continued to struggle? Yet despite personal animosities and divergent career paths, the exiles still functioned as a social and professional community during the latter half of the 1950s. After their arrival in Paris in May 1956, Michael and Zelma Wilson held regular Sunday open houses that became a fixture among the expatriate crowd.[13] Paul Jarrico and his wife, Sylvia—Zelma Wilson's sister—joined the community in Paris two years later, having finally been able to obtain their passports as a result of the Supreme Court's June 1958 ruling that a citizen's right to travel could not be denied without due process.[14] As Paul Jarrico put it, "I'm afraid that the exiled people, though we didn't use the word 'exile,' tended to hang out with each other quite a bit. In that sense, I guess we were homesick."[15]

With regard to their careers, the blacklisted community continued to develop projects together and to turn to one another for ideas, advice, and support. Hannah Weinstein, in addition to giving jobs to many blacklisted writers on her various television series, co-produced *Escapade* (dir. Philip Leacock, 1955), for which Donald Ogden Stewart provided the screen adaptation.[16] The brothers-in-law Michael Wilson and Paul Jarrico collaborated on the screenplay for *Five Branded Women* (1960), a Dino de Laurentiis production directed by the formerly blacklisted Martin Ritt, in addition to working on several other unproduced scripts together. When John Berry's career stalled after the disastrous reception of his slave melodrama *Tamango* (1958) in France, Michael Wilson tried repeatedly to drum up work for his friend, praising Berry's skills as a writer to Burt Lancaster and even going so far as offering the low-budget King brothers an original screenplay on the condition that they hire Berry to direct it.[17] The exiles constantly suggested projects to each other, and films that would start off in the hands of one director could easily migrate to those of another, as in the case of *10:30 P.M. Summer*, an adaptation of a Marguerite Duras novel that Losey had hoped to do but that was eventually directed by Dassin.[18]

The "swing away" from Hollywood to Europe observed by Bosley Crowther affected the blacklisted in terms not only of the career opportunities available to them, but also their self-perception. By the early 1960s, some members of the blacklisted community, most notably Dassin and Losey, had developed a somewhat schizophrenic relationship with Hollywood, rejecting its commercial approach if not its dollars. Whereas the shared experience of the blacklist and the difficulties of exile had initially bound them together, by 1960 their lives had assumed new dimensions that further relegated Hollywood to the past. In his notes for his autobiography, Foreman commented that the "only community of interest I had with many of the émigrés was simply the fact that we were blacklisted." Despite the resentment it fostered, he made a point of cultivating friends outside the expatriate colony. "It was necessary," he explained, because "otherwise you just sat around and talked about the same things all the time and broke up each other's marriages."[19]

In London, the Hollywood exiles interacted with a larger group that brought together the Canadian expatriate community, which included the writers Ted Allan, Reuben Ship, and Mordecai Richler and the producer Harry Saltzman, and the writers and directors associated with the new British cinema.[20] In Paris, the American expatriate community expanded to include the Russian-born Hollywood director Anatole Litvak and the writers Irwin Shaw and James Jones, whose weekend poker games were frequented by Jules Dassin and Nicholas Ray, among others.[21] Ties with the African American artists in Paris were more tenuous. With a few exceptions such as the Berrys' friendship with Richard and Ellen Wright and the Wilsons' and the Jarricos' with the actor William Marshall (who would become Sylvia Jarrico's long-time companion), contacts with the African American community were generally limited to casual encounters at the cafés and jazz clubs of St. Germain.[22]

Two of the most colorful figures among this new cast of characters were Hal E. Chester and Samuel Bronston, both of whom played significant roles in the careers of the blacklisted in Europe. Chester began his Hollywood career as a Bowery Boy, making the jump into production with *Joe Palooka, Champ* (dir. Reginald Le Borg, 1946), the first of the eleven Joe Palooka films he would produce for Monogram Pictures. Ten years later, he moved to London, producing the thriller *The Weapon* (dir. Val Guest, 1957). For his next effort, he called upon the services of an old friend from Hollywood, Cy Endfield. Chester and Endfield had collaborated on the screenplay of *Joe Palooka, Champ*, and Chester had gone on to serve as Endfield's producer for *Gentleman Joe Palooka* (1946), *Joe Palooka in the Big Fight* (1949), and *The Underworld Story* (1950). "They were very close," Maureen Endfield recalls, "but Hallie used to milk Cy for bits of writing, as on *Night of the Demon*," a Jacques Tourneur film for which Endfield received no credit for his contributions to the screenplay.[23] Chester also hired blacklisted writers for his next two projects: *The Two-Headed Spy* (dir. André de Toth, scr. Michael Wilson, 1958) and *School for Scoundrels* (dir. Robert Hamer, scr. Frank Tarloff, 1960).

Chester's interest in working with the blacklisted was motivated by financial considerations, not high-minded principles; he was "really a hustler," Frank Tarloff recalled. "[Chester] had a script for *School for Scoundrels* which he couldn't get made. He hired me for a thousand pounds, roughly eighteen hundred dollars. After I did the rewrite, he was able to get the picture made, and I stayed on it through the whole production. But I never got a credit on the screen, because he said he wanted the film for the American market, and therefore, because of the blacklist he said he had to put his own name on it." Despite this injustice, Tarloff was grateful for the opportunity to write for film. "In those days, if you were a television writer, you were a television writer."[24] It was also through Chester that Tarloff became connected with the project for which he would win an Oscar, *Father Goose* (dir. Ralph Nelson, 1964).

Chester's model of operation was similar to that of other small-scale independent producers of the time. *The Weapon, Night of the Demon*, and *The Two-Headed Spy* were all low-budget B-movies that Chester then sold for distribution (Eros distributed *The Weapon* in the United Kingdom, while Republic managed its U.S. release; Columbia handled both *Night of the Demon* and *The Two-Headed Spy*). Samuel Bronston and his right-hand man, Philip Yordan, pioneered a different model of production financing that became an industry standard: presales.[25] Before a project had even begun filming, Bronston and Yordan would sell its distribution rights to international territories; the funds thus generated could then be funneled directly into production or Bronston and Yordan could use the distribution contracts to obtain production loans from banks.[26] With these funds covering his above-the-line costs for the cast and key talent, Bronston relied upon his relationship with Pierre S. du Pont III to obtain his remaining financing.

In the mid-1950s, Bronston gathered a consortium of prominent American financiers and industrialists—including du Pont—into a limited partnership for the purposes of funding his big-budget production, *John Paul Jones* (dir. John Farrow, 1959). Film fans or otherwise, the members of the consortium all saw the logic of Bronston's proposal, which provided them with a way to potentially profit from their funds blocked in various European nations due to currency controls (restrictions on the export of hard currency). Bronston would use their frozen currency for production financing and repay the loan with the dollars that the film would earn in the U.S. market: a kind of currency swap agreement.[27] Pleased with both the investment strategy and the film it produced, Pierre du Pont became Bronston's limited partner, providing Bronston with loan guarantee notes worth a total of $35 million (equivalent to $220 million today) between 1959 and 1964.[28]

With access to this level of financing, Bronston could afford to produce on an epic scale and established his own studio, Las Matas, on the outskirts of Madrid, where production costs were even lower than in Italy, France, and the United Kingdom. Channeling much of his production budget into lavish salaries for international stars such as Sophia Loren and Charlton Heston, Bronston cut costs elsewhere by hiring blacklisted talent. Delighted with Ben Barzman's last-minute rewrite of *El Cid*, Bronston hired him to do *The Fall of the Roman Empire* (dir. Anthony Mann, 1964). Bernard Gordon wrote the scripts for two other Bronston productions, *55 Days at Peking* (dir. Nicholas Ray, 1963) and *Circus World* (dir. Henry Hathaway, 1964), and also contributed to *El Cid*. Likewise, Barzman received a writing credit for *55 Days at Peking*, reflecting Philip Yordan's fondness for circulating scripts among his writers. By the fall of 1963, Yordan and Bronston had five blacklisted writers—Arnaud d'Usseau, Guy Endore, and Julian Zimet, in addition to Barzman and Gordon—installed in Madrid, hard at work on various projects.[29]

Despite the seemingly limitless funds at his disposal, not to mention the comparatively modest salaries he paid some of his blacklisted personnel, Bronston still managed to spend with a rare profligacy. As Bernard Gordon recalls, "Expensive talent was hired and then dismissed and paid off on a whim. Personal expenses were unrestrained and had to come out of the budget."[30] This flair for excess and lack of supervision extended to Bronston's productions. The budget for *The Fall of the Roman Empire*, originally set at $10 million, quickly ballooned to more than twice that. In the spring of 1964, with *The Fall* still in production, du Pont—having lost millions in the course of his partnership with Bronston—withdrew his financial support. Although Yordan managed, through some creative financing with Paramount, to salvage the production, *The Fall of the Roman Empire* felled Bronston's empire, too.[31]

What sort of opportunity did Bronston's operations in Madrid provide for the blacklisted talent he employed? For star writers like Barzman and Gordon, the financial incentives and lifestyle perks were considerable. Norma Barzman recalls Ben receiving a $50,000 bonus from Bronston for his work on *El Cid* and suggests that Ben's deal for *The Fall of the Roman Empire* was even more lucrative.[32] Bernard Gordon's salary of $2,000 a week was very good by Hollywood standards and absolutely extravagant in light of the much lower cost of living in Europe.[33] In their accounts of the period, both Gordon and Norma Barzman describe a luxurious and highly social expatriate existence in Madrid, filled with late nights of drinking and dancing.

With regard to the blacklist and the issue of screen credit, however, "Hollywood in Madrid" did not present significant advantages over Hollywood, California. In a 1961 interview, Bronston attributed the screenplays for *El Cid* and the upcoming *Fall of the Roman Empire* to Philip Yordan.[34] When Bernard Gordon requested credit for his work on *55 Days at Peking*, Yordan countered that the film's American distributors would object.[35] Ultimately, Bronston's (and Yordan's) attitude toward the blacklist was inconsistent and presumably opportunistic; while Ben Barzman received screen credit for *The Fall of Roman Empire*, Yordan insisted on acting as Gordon's front for *Circus World*, released the same year (1964).

From Gordon's account, it seems clear that Yordan took advantage of the blacklist to accumulate screen credits for himself. Time and again, Yordan used the excuse that a film's distributors expected his name to be in the credits according to the terms of their arrangement.[36] Gordon speculates that he did not press Yordan on this issue out of a sense of gratitude, although he does not specify for what. The opportunity to work again, to earn a good salary, to live the high life in Europe? Did the money available in Fascist Spain act as an opiate, dulling the desire of those involved to continue to fight the blacklist, or even to maintain some semblance of artistic standards by rejecting such blatantly commercial projects? These questions were issues for some of the blacklisted exiles, for whom Bronston's Spanish colony presented both a lure and a challenge to their identity—and integrity—as a community. Sylvia Jarrico remembers that "some of the people who worked in Spain were looked down upon—they were regarded as hacks."[37] Similarly, Norma Barzman implied that Joseph Losey believed her husband Ben had betrayed himself (and by extension, Losey and their fellow blacklist victims) by going to work for Bronston. In a line that recalls the cocktail party communism of 1940s Hollywood with amusing literalness, she quotes Losey as accusing Ben of selling out "for a swimming pool."[38]

Cosmopolitan Cooperation

While the exiles' attitude toward Bronston's historical spectacles vacillated between opportunistic and dismissive, it is possible that their long-standing antipathy toward such blatantly commercial projects blinded them to the significance of Bronston's transnational mode of production. For Vanessa Schwartz, Bronston is a prime example of the new breed of cosmopolitan producers of the "cosmopolitan film" that emerged in the 1950s. Not only was Bronston himself a cosmopolitan by virtue of his upbringing (born in Moldova and educated in France), but his films were distinctly transnational in both their mode of production and thematic content. Because his financing model did not involve government subsidies, Bronston was not obliged to adhere to any national quotas in determining his cast and crew, nor did he need government approval of his scripts. With their casts of international stars and universal themes, his films were cosmopolitan in their refusal of any specific national identity. Instead, they "articulated a vision of transnationalism that matched a postwar international idealism with what mattered to filmmakers with big-budget pictures."[39] Another cosmopolitan producer of cosmopolitan films was the Polish-born and London-based Sam Spiegel, whose Horizon Pictures produced the big-budget epics *The Bridge on the River Kwai* and *Lawrence of Arabia,* both with screenplays by blacklisted authors (see chapter 3). Given the number of cosmopolitan films with similar pedigrees—in addition to Horizon's and Bronston's productions, Schwartz's list includes *Spartacus* (dir. Stanley Kubrick, scr. Dalton Trumbo, 1960), *Exodus* (dir. Otto Preminger, scr. Dalton Trumbo, 1960), and *Cleopatra* (dir. Joseph Mankiewicz, scr. Sidney Buchman et al., 1963)—Schwartz's observation that these films "had no vested interest in the American empire per se" takes on a more charged significance. As political exiles residing in Europe, the blacklisted had firsthand experience of the dark side of the "American Century" and would not have subscribed to any chauvinistic visions of American supremacy. At the same time, their political history suggests that spirit of "postwar internationalist idealism" common to these films may be less a reflection of Cold War politics than a remnant of the vision of international cooperation that infused the antifascist, progressive movement in Hollywood before the war.

The exiles understood the value of their transnational experience to an increasingly global film industry and gravitated toward projects that valorized their hybrid, expatriate perspective. Carl Foreman returned repeatedly to the subject of World War II in the films he produced for Columbia. *The Key* (dir. Carol Reed, 1958), *The Guns of Navarone* (dir. J. Lee Thompson, 1961), and *The Victors* (dir. Carl Foreman, 1963) all use World War II as the backdrop for stories of cross-cultural romance (between Sophia Loren and William Holden in *The Key*) and cooperation (between the British and the Greeks in *The Guns of*

Navarone and the American and European soldiers and civilians in *The Victors*). The casting of American stars, including Gregory Peck and Anthony Quinn as British soldiers in *The Guns of Navarone*, inserted America into the film's vision of Allied courage and solidarity. By returning repeatedly to a subject that dramatized transatlantic relations in terms of the fight against fascism, Foreman satisfied Columbia's expectations that he make films for the international market and simultaneously encouraged a level of cross-cultural identification that transcended the limits of national cinema.

Another popular formula for depicting postwar relations between America and Europe was the cross-cultural romance. Robert Shandley argues that the 1950s Hollywood "travelogue romance," in which an American (almost always a woman) finds love in Europe, constitutes a genre in the degree to which it adheres to a strict narrative scheme that reiterates a "stable set of ideological positions."[40] In films such as *Three Coins in the Fountain* (dir. Jean Negulesco, 1954), *Summertime* (dir. David Lean, 1955), and *Interlude* (dir. Douglas Sirk, 1957), the romance is filled with obstacles (usually the marital status of one or more partners) and typically culminates in the American's decision to return home. For Shandley, this narrative progression reflects America's fascination with European Old World sophistication but ultimate reluctance to forgo the advantages of the American way of life.

Carl Foreman gives instruction to George Peppard in *The Victors* (From the collections of the Margaret Herrick Library)

With their European settings and Euro-American love affairs, the Franco-American co-productions of the early 1950s discussed in chapter 2 anticipate aspects of Hollywood's "travelogue romance." However, in the Franco-American productions, the American heroines embrace their new lives in Europe, reflecting a position more in line with the experience of their blacklisted creators; *Pardon My French* (dir. Marcel Cravenne/Bernard Vorhaus, 1952) even offers a mild critique of American modernity. In a number of unproduced projects from the late 1950s, Michael Wilson likewise presented a vision of Franco-American relations that reflected a more nuanced appreciation of cultural difference than similar Hollywood fare. As Shandley notes, the Hollywood travelogue romances of the 1950s generally resorted to broad clichés in their depiction of Europeans; the English-speaking European lover is highly sexualized, while the non-English-speaking locals are a source of comic relief.[41] While bearing in mind the popularity of Hollywood productions such as *Roman Holiday* (dir. William Wyler, 1952) and *Love in the Afternoon* (dir. Billy Wilder, 1957) that combined European locations with cross-cultural romance, along with the need to adhere to the demands of the international coproduction, Wilson nonetheless sought to bring a more balanced, transatlantic perspective to his original projects.

Shortly after arriving in France, he began working on *The Grand Tour*, a comedy about a group of tourists on a five-day bus tour of the French countryside. The lead characters are an assortment of national stereotypes: the xenophobic French tour guide, the repressed British schoolmaster, the sexy and naïve young American woman (a part written with Marilyn Monroe in mind). In his preliminary notes for the project, Wilson lays out what he envisions as the film's "international" approach:

> Although this is primarily an American picture, it is not primarily an American's view of France. Nor is what we see limited to the frame of vision of any particular character in the story. The point of view is . . . one of objective and comic detachment in which all the national types come under the same scrutiny—a scrutiny, one hopes, that will be at once sharp and affirmative in the true comic terms—friendly, yet not sentimental; barbed but not bitter. In this sense we project a truly "international" film, in which there is no concession to the superiority of any national group, including the French hosts.[42]

Wilson initially brought the project to Spiegel, for whom he had recently completed work on *The Bridge on the River Kwai*, but he sold it to Dino de Laurentiis when Spiegel made it clear that he found the story "slight" and "somewhat disappointing."[43] Joseph Losey was enthusiastic about the film's prospects and asked Wilson about the possibility of showing the script to the producer Sydney Box "with (Alec) Guinness or (Dirk) Bogarde in mind."[44] But despite its relevance to the growth of mass tourism and America's fascination with France, the production never got off the ground.[45] After years of false starts, Wilson and his frequent writing partner, Paul Jarrico, bought back the rights from de Laurentiis in 1961.[46]

Wilson and Jarrico collaborated on two other Franco-American themed projects. In its basic plot, *April in Paris* foreshadows Jean-Luc Godard's *À bout de souffle* (1960) in recounting the adventures of an American girl in Paris eager to make her way as a journalist. In the former, however, Paris ultimately serves as little more than a backdrop for a marital comedy about a husband who feels threatened by his wife's successful career.[47] Another treatment, *Ambassador at Large,* used a Franco-American romance to probe Franco-American relations in a more meaningful fashion.[48] Abandoning the stereotypes of *The Grand Tour* and *April in Paris,* Wilson and Jarrico instead drew upon their intimate experience of radical politics to craft a narrative that dramatized the ideological journey of the Left in the postwar years. A wartime affair between Bill, an officer in the Office of Strategic Services (in which a number of the Hollywood Left, including Abraham Polonsky, had served), and Madeleine, a female Resistance leader, leads to Madeleine's pregnancy. An independent spirit, Madeleine rejects Bill's offer of marriage. Bill returns to America and marries Louise, the daughter of a wealthy industrialist. Fifteen years later, Bill and Louise arrive in Paris, where Bill has been appointed the U.S. ambassador. His former lover has become a prominent and influential journalist known for her strong anti-American views. She publishes an "I knew him when" article contrasting Bill's youthful idealism with his current incarnation as "a honey liberal, an opportunist." But Madeleine's daughter wants to meet her father and a rapprochement ensues.[49]

In his notes for the project, Wilson describes the film's themes in terms that make the connection with the lost world of radical Hollywood explicit: "Youth is a state of mind—a commitment to principles, a belief that the world can be changed. One can only remain young if one remains true to the radicalism of one's youth." That Bill regains his youthful idealism through his relationship with two French women, his former lover and his daughter, likewise can be seen as a commentary on the rejuvenating, and clarifying, effect life in France had on the careers of many of the blacklisted, not least Wilson.

Wilson had written the role of Madeleine for his close friend Simone Signoret, whose enthusiasm for the project helped spark the interest of producers on both sides of the Atlantic. For a brief period in the late fall of 1961, *Ambassador at Large* was poised to become a high-profile production, with Kirk Douglas, Gregory Peck, Paul Newman, and William Holden among the stars being considered for the role of the ambassador. The character of the ambassador's wife was modeled on Jackie Kennedy, a decision no doubt inspired by the First Lady's visit to Paris that spring. Yet despite its topicality and sensitive treatment of "a very important aspect of French and American relations" (according to the producer

Michel Bernheim), by the beginning of December *Ambassador at Large* had taken on "the chill of something tossed into the deep-freezer," as Wilson put it in a letter to Dalton Trumbo.[50] While containing all the elements associated with the "cosmopolitan" film (strong leading roles for international stars, Paris locations, and a thematic treatment of international diplomacy, both personal and political), it is possible that the project's political dimensions contributed to its ultimately unproduced status.[51]

Of all the exiles, it was Jules Dassin who took the notion of the cosmopolitan furthest, in both his filmmaking and his personal life. After being warmly adopted by the French as a result of *Rififi,* he turned his attention to Greece and Melina Mercouri, who would star in nearly all his subsequent films. Reflecting on his decision in a 1970 interview on French television, Dassin offered this explanation: "With *Rififi,* I was able to stay more or less in the tradition of American cinema, but I wasn't *chez moi,* I had neither a home nor a country. When I discovered Greece, it was a *coup de foudre*."[52] *Never on Sunday,* the second of five films he would make in Greece, satirizes the efforts of Homer, the sincere but naïve American played by Dassin, to reform Ilya, the free-spirited prostitute played by Melina Mercouri. The *New York Times,* in an appreciative discussion of the film, observed that despite the light, comic tone, it left "an itchy little question twitching around in the back of one's mind: may it not be presumptuous and futile to try to push other people into your way of life?"[53] That the American does not succeed in convincing the European to change her ways and instead goes home chastened at the end of this cross-cultural encounter suggests Dassin's awareness of the limitations of American exceptionalism.

Social Cinema and the Cold War

In testimony given in December 1961 before the Education and Labor Subcommittee on the Impact of Imports and Exports on American Employment, H. O'Neil Shanks of the Hollywood AFL Film Council painted a dramatic picture of the danger posed by American runaway production to national security: "If Hollywood is thus permitted to become 'obsolete as a production center' and the United States voluntarily surrenders its position of world leadership in the field of theatrical motion pictures, the chance to present a more favorable American image on the movie screens of non-Communist countries in reply to the Cold War attacks of our Soviet adversaries will be lost forever."[54] In other words, if Hollywood should lose its position of global dominance of the film industry, the cultural Cold War would be a lost cause.

While the Film Council found the Cold War discourse of anticommunism to be an expeditious vehicle for its labor concerns, as demonstrated in chapter 3, the question of what image of America emerged from the European films of the blacklisted is nonetheless a valuable one to consider in light of Cold War cultural politics. As Frances Stoner Saunders and others have documented, the CIA was involved in an extensive, secret program of cultural propaganda in Western Europe, funding publications such as the *Paris Review* and the British literary magazine *Encounter* in addition to art exhibitions, concerts, and international conferences through its Congress for Cultural Freedom.[55] As Saunders notes, the Congress's "mission was to nudge the intelligentsia of Western Europe away from its lingering fascination with Marxism and Communism towards a view more accommodating of 'the American way.'"[56] Yet as we saw in chapter 2 with regard to the French film industry in particular, a communist political orientation and popular anti-Americanism did not translate into a politically radical filmmaking practice, for a number of reasons. The popularity of Hollywood cinema was something French producers sought to emulate, not reject. Subsequently, the blacklisted exiles were of interest for their proficiency in American genre cinema, not on account of their aspirations to neorealism. Nor did indigenous filmmaking traditions such as the prestige *cinéma de qualité* or the popular *cinéma du samedi soir* attribute their success to radical politics. Likewise, in Britain, economic imperatives, particularly the desire to access the large U.S. market for English-language films, ensured that producers had reason to favor apolitical content.

Nonetheless, despite the obstacles to social cinema posed by both domestic considerations and America's presence in Europe's film industries during the postwar era, a number of the European films of the blacklisted did manage to present an oblique critique of aspects of America's Cold War culture—if not directly of America itself. Specifically, these films opposed the definition of "Americanism" that quickly came to dominate the political and cultural discourse of postwar America.[57] Whereas the liberal politics of the Roosevelt era encouraged an inclusive "Americanism" that was defined largely by its opposition to fascism, this progressive and pluralistic popular nationalism was swiftly replaced by an exclusionary, anticommunist version (with strong xenophobic and antisemitic undertones) in the early years of the Cold War. According to this new definition, the Hollywood radicals were now "un-American" in their support for antifascist and antiracist causes. Having been forced to choose between their careers and their country on account of their politics, the blacklisted exiles brought a complex perspective to their relationship with America. In her study of the community of left-wing American filmmakers, writers, and artists in Mexico during the same period, Rebecca Schreiber argues that the "distance of the U.S. exiles from the United States, and from sources of financial support allotted for the culture industries by the U.S. and Mexican governments, enabled these individuals to develop a critical transnationalist perspective in contrast to dominant Cold War culture."[58] Can the same be said of the blacklisted exiles in Europe?

Thom Andersen has suggested that the 1950s British noirs of Cy Endfield and Joseph Losey represent a continuation of *film gris,* a term he coined to refer to the small outpouring of socially conscious noirs by members of the Hollywood Left, including Berry, Dassin, Endfield, and Losey, during the political lull that prevailed between the 1947 and 1951 HUAC hearings. A distinct subgenre of noir, film gris, according to Andersen, emphasizes "social critique" over "psychological diagnosis," while themes relating to "work, class, money, and sometimes race" provide the "dramatic issues."[59]

Paul Buhle and Dave Wagner use related terms to express a similar insight, arguing that the integration of "American noir with Italian neo-realism" common to the early European films of the American exiles provides "a glimpse of the kinds of filmmaking that could have been part of U.S. cinema in the post-war era without a blacklist."[60] This concern with social issues and critique of unbridled capitalism, whether expressed through noir or neorealist aesthetics, is a distinctive characteristic of the blacklisted exiles' European films, from the very first exile production of *Christ in Concrete* to later works such as John Berry's *Tamango.*

As we saw in chapter 3, the production history of *Christ in Concrete* had close ties to Italian neorealism. Not only was the project spearheaded by Rod Geiger, the American producer of *Rome, Open City,* but it was originally envisioned as appropriate material for Roberto Rossellini's American debut. Peter Bondanella characterizes *Christ in Concrete* as "one of the first Hollywood representations of Italian Americans that reflects the influence of Italian cinema—specifically the post-war neo-realist film."[61] Yet although the Hollywood radicals were great admirers of Italian neorealism and were ideologically aligned with the movement's political and social concerns, *Christ in Concrete* shares few aesthetic continuities with Italian cinema of the immediate postwar years. Rather than using real locations, it was filmed entirely on sound stages. Its narrative does not focus on contemporary events (the story is set in the 1920s and early 1930s) and follows a clear causal structure that reflects screenwriter Ben Barzman's Hollywood training more than any influence of neorealism, with its more loosely constructed, episodic plots.

If Italian neorealism is a presence in the film, it reveals itself in *Christ in Concrete*'s thematic preoccupations and, specifically, its sympathetic and frank depiction of the lives of working-class immigrants. British critics were struck by the film's deglamorized depiction of American life, along with its "rather belated attack on *laissez-faire* capitalism."[62] In scene after scene, the film emphasizes the importance of solidarity among the workers, who refer to themselves as "five sticks in a bundle." When an unscrupulous, corner-cutting contractor offers a $100 bonus to the fastest bricklayer, the men decide—after some disagreement—to share the bonus if one of them should win it. The capitalist system is critiqued in scenes pitting the contractor's self-interested conception of the spirit of free enterprise against his workers' concerns for their safety. Nor does the America of *Christ in Concrete* have much to offer its new arrivals. Annunziata (Lea Padovani), the Italian wife of the bricklayer Geremio (Sam Wanamaker), must raise her family in the crowded tenements of New York's Lower East Side as the house Geremio promised her before their marriage continually eludes them. The film's dramatic climax, in which Geremio is buried alive in concrete as a result of a building accident, serves as a visual metaphor for the collapse of the American dream and the promise of a better life America held out to its immigrants.

While the American Legion ensured that *Christ in Concrete* did not make much of a splash in America, the film's triumph at the 1950 Karlovy Vary International Film Festival would seem in direct violation of the objectives of America's Cold War cultural policy and the promotion of the "American way of life." Founded in 1946 and located in the Czech spa town formerly known as Carlsbad, the festival's programming was guided by the principle that films should support the ideological struggle against the West. To the degree that films from the West were included, they had to be progressive in orientation and address issues of class and social justice.[63] *Christ in Concrete* certainly fit this bill, and the film was awarded the festival's grand prize, the Crystal Globe. However, in the press conference that followed the film's screening, the Eastern bloc journalists appeared baffled that "a Western nation [would] permit a film so implicitly critical of its own economy to be made at all," in the words of one reporter. Ben Barzman's retort that that such "direct censorship as you're suggesting doesn't exist in our country" seems either remarkably patriotic or naïve given the difficulties the production encountered on account of the blacklist.[64]

The influence of Italian neorealism is more prominent in the exiles' attempt at independent production in Italy under the auspices of Riviera Films. In *Stranger on the Prowl,* Losey made good use of the bombed-out ruins of the port city of Livorno, which had suffered extensive damage during World War II. The dilapidated settings were a vivid reminder of the recent war, which also provided the context for the film's narrative of poverty and desperation. The film's two central characters—the Man (Paul Muni) and Giacomo (Vittorio Manunta)—are bound together through the consequences of their attempts to fulfill their basic needs. The Man, about whom we know little besides his desire to book passage on a ship out of Livorno, inadvertently strangles a shop owner from whom he has stolen a piece of cheese. Giacomo, a young boy being raised by a single mother, has stolen a bottle of milk from the same store and is convinced that the police are after him. In its focus on the relationship between a man and a child, *Stranger on the Prowl* recalls other neorealist films such as *Paisan* (dir. Roberto Rossellini, 1946) and *Bicycle Thieves* (dir. Vittorio de Sica, 1948). Likewise, the film's unremitting emphasis on contemporary social issues—specifically the hardships that

Paul Muni as the Man and Vittorio Manunta as Giacomo, on the run in Livorno in *Stranger on the Prowl* (Cinémathèque française – Iconothèque)

characterized life for many in Italy in the aftermath of World War II—provides another connection with Italian neorealism, while its dramatic low-key lighting and "man-on-the-run" narrative bears the mark of Losey's background in American film noir.

The affinities between film noir and neorealism perhaps reach their apogee in the work of Jules Dassin, who never failed to acknowledge the influence of Italian neorealism on his work.[65] His late Hollywood noirs such as *The Naked City* (1947), *Thieves' Highway* (1949), and *Night and the City* (1950) all provided some measure of opportunity to channel his admiration for the aesthetic and social concerns of Italian neorealism, whether in the form of location shooting or social commentary. His first European film, *Du rififi chez les hommes* (1955), with its tightly constructed centerpiece heist sequence, veered on the side of film noir in its generic conventions. However, Dassin's skill with location shooting resulted in an intimate engagement with Paris that recalled neorealism's "environmental" approach to mise-en-scène and particularly André Bazin's notion of "density" in the way in which the actors and their actions are integrated into their milieu.[66]

The success of *Rififi* put Dassin in a position to fully indulge his appetite for social realism (and his fledging fascination with Greece) for the first time in his career. *The Greek Passion* (also known as *Christ Recrucified*) was a 1948 novel by the celebrated Greek author and fellow exile in France Nikos Kazantzakis, whose communist-inflected humanism was a good match for Dassin's political orientation. Set in a Greek village during the Ottoman occupation, the novel centers on the village's response to a group of refugees, who, having been forced to flee their homes by the Turks, seek refuge in the village. Fearful of the strain the presence of the refugees will place on the village's resources, the local priest tells his congregation that the refugees have cholera. At the same time as it is refusing shelter and water to the starving refugees, the village is preparing for its annual reenactment of Christ's Passion. The contradiction between Christ's words and the village's treatment of the refugees prompts Manolios (Pierre Vaneck), the shepherd who has been chosen for the role of Christ, to question the actions of the village elders. In the film's dramatic conclusion, Manolios, along with some other villagers, rises up in support of the refugees. He is subsequently accused of treason and dragged through the streets before dying in the arms of the village prostitute, Katerina (Melina Mercouri), the Passion play's Mary Magdalene.

For Dassin, *Celui qui doit mourir* (*He Who Must Die*), as the novel was retitled, provided the opportunity to make the "*film de sa vie.*"[67] What interested him about the film was the opportunity "to show a group of people suddenly becoming aware of their responsibility towards humanity."[68] The moral aspects of the story must have also had a clear appeal for Dassin in light of both his passion for social justice and personal experience of exile. With regard to aesthetics, *Celui qui doit mourir* provided Dassin with the long-awaited opportunity to shoot a film entirely according to his wishes. Toward the film's conclusion, he pays homage to Sergei Eisenstein, one of his heroes, in a scene that directly alludes to the celebrated Odessa Steps sequence in *Battleship Potemkin*. The film's three-month shoot in a small village in Crete also allowed Dassin to integrate the production into the lives of the locals, many of whom served as extras (Dassin later commented on his love for "those wonderful Cretan faces," a claim his lingering close-ups substantiate).[69]

Like Dassin, John Berry used his success in the film noir genre as a springboard from which to attempt more ambitious, socially conscious filmmaking. Even *Je suis un sentimental* (1955), his second popular *Série Noire* parody, contains elements of social critique. In a narrative reminiscent of the many "newspaper noirs" of the late 1940s and early 1950s, Eddie Constantine plays Barney Morgan, a star journalist who discovers his conscience in the course of investigating the murder of his boss's mistress. When his inquiries lead him to the LeContes, the wealthy owners of the newspaper where he works, Barney writes an exposé that lands him in jail. The power of social class and money is indicted in the film's depiction of the LeConte family, whose dissipation and corruption stand in opposition to Barney's quest for justice.

Berry's next film, a take on the legend of *Don Juan* (1956) starring the French comedian Fernandel, likewise contains a degree of class commentary. The film derives much of its comic effect from playing with class expectations when Don Juan (Erno Crisa) and his valet Sganarelle (Fernandel) swap identities. The film concludes with a popular revolt against the nobility and the elevation of Don Juan to people's hero, but its farcical tone distracts from any serious social message.

Tamango (1958), Berry's slave ship drama, was meant to be different. "[*Tamango*] was his dream, what he wanted to do," his daughter Jan recalled.[70] Working again with Lee and Tammy Gold, his collaborators on *Je suis un sentimental* as well as on numerous television scripts, Berry set about adapting Prosper Mérimée's novella. The changes that he and the Golds made were all calculated to emphasize the slaves' solidarity, dignity, and heroic martyrdom.[71] In

John Berry directing Dorothy Dandridge as Ayché in *Tamango* (Cinémathèque française – Iconothèque)

Mérimée's original, Tamango (Alex Cressan) is a slave-trading African chief and collaborator of the white traders, at least initially. Berry and the Golds' decision to make Tamango a captive himself and charismatic leader of his fellow slaves changed the racial dynamics of the film considerably, as did the love triangle they developed between Tamango and Ayché (Dorothy Dandridge), now the captain's mulatto mistress rather than Tamango's wife. The film dramatizes Ayché's mixed-race identity by forcing her to choose between the black slaves and her white captors; she ultimately commits herself to "her people" and dies with them when the captain puts an end to their uprising by directing his guns down in the ship's hold. The final massacre is another departure from Mérimée's original, in which the slaves successfully overthrow their captors but perish due to their inexperience and irresponsible behavior.

For Berry, *Tamango* was a vehicle to express his opposition to racial discrimination. His personal ties to the African American community dated back to his appearance in Orson Welles's 1941 stage adaptation of Richard Wright's *Native Son*. He remained close with Wright during their Paris exile, and he also appreciated France's "*anti-raciste*" tradition that allowed him to continue the affair he had begun in Hollywood with the singer Eartha Kitt more openly.[72] Years later, in his promotional interviews for *Claudine* (1974), the all-black family drama that marked his return to U.S. filmmaking, Berry was quick to refer to *Tamango* as evidence of his long-standing commitment to black representation and civil rights.[73]

With its narrative of black solidarity and revolt against Western colonial oppression, *Tamango* would seem to have been just the sort of blacklisted film that could "provide aid and comfort to the Communist conspiracy against the free world," as the AFL Film Council warned against.[74] In light of the State Department's purposeful use of black performers as Cold War cultural ambassadors to counter the perception of American racism, *Tamango*—and its blacklisted American director—would also seem likely to have attracted the attention of both the French and U.S. governments.[75] Nevertheless, while the film elicited controversy in France (discussed in the next chapter), its U.S. release went largely unremarked upon despite its resonance for the civil rights movement. In part this is due to the fact that, as Donald Bogle observes, "no major distributor would touch it": the film was ultimately released by the independent Hal Roach Distribution Company, which marketed it as an exploitation film.[76] Posters showing a scantily clad Dorothy Dandridge capitalized on the shock value of the interracial relationship between Dandridge's character and the ship's white captain. *Tamango* performed well in cities with large black populations such as Detroit and Washington, D.C., where it played for over a year. Yet while some reviews noted the film's relevance to the fight for racial equality, its polemical force was muted by its historical setting and presumed French origins.[77] Indeed, although John Berry is credited as director, no U.S. critics made the connection between Berry's blacklisted status and the film's politics.[78]

Like Dassin and Berry, Joseph Losey jumped at the first opportunity his European career afforded him to address a serious social issue. He had long been interested in adapting Emlyn Williams's 1953 thriller *Someone Waiting*, and by 1956 he had found backing from the independent Harlequin Productions for a film version, titled *Time Without Pity*. Both the film's budget and his fee were almost double those for his previous film, *The Intimate Stranger; Time Without Pity* also boasted a top-drawer English cast that included Michael Redgrave, Ann Todd, and Leo McKern.[79] Most significantly, the Hyams brothers, Americans whose Eros Films was providing financing and distribution, were willing to give credit to both Losey and Ben Barzman, who collaborated with Losey on the screenplay.[80]

In Williams's play, which Losey described as a "straight thriller . . . a suspense story in which you attempted to discover who the murderer was and why," Losey saw the chance to express his opposition to capital punishment, at the time still legal in the United Kingdom (and America, where the Rosenbergs had been electrocuted only three years earlier). Losey and Barzman retained the play's basic narrative—a young man, Alec Graham (Alec McCowan), is wrongly convicted of murder, prompting his estranged, alcoholic father, David (Michael Redgrave), to lead a last-minute hunt for the real killer—but they upped the stakes through an unrelenting emphasis on the young man's imminent execution. Images of clocks abound, visual reminders that Redgrave's character is fighting not only the criminal justice system but time itself. Losey later considered the effect "slightly artificial," and it was just one of the many baroque touches for which the film was attacked by British critics. Tellingly, the real murderer in the film, Robert Stanford (Leo McKern), is a wealthy industrialist who thinks that his money and influence will protect him from the consequences of his actions. Stanford's characterization also shows Losey's growing sensitivity to class and regional differences in British society. "One of the marks of the character was the fact that he had a strong Yorkshire accent and that he had all the inferiority complexes that go with being a north country man. And the stigma of commerce and all the rest of it."[81] More than the film's veiled capitalist critique, or direct indictment of capital punishment, it was Losey's fascination with Britain's strict class structures that would become a hallmark of his filmmaking.

As these examples of the European films of the blacklisted illustrate, the radical heritage of the 1930s left a lasting mark not only on the politics of the blacklisted exiles, but on their conception of cinema. In 1959, asked to comment on his predilection for socially conscious filmmaking, Dassin responded, "But that's all there is. Each film must have a message."[82] In 1969, John Berry chalked up his interest in social issues to his background: "I was formed during a period when we dreamed of a better world. . . . In my films, there will always be people who fight for freedom, justice, and truth."[83] Berry's comments hark back to the competing definitions of "Americanism" that emerged in the aftermath of World War II. The Hollywood radicals and Cold Warriors shared a vision of America as a bastion of democratic values, but their definitions of these values differed. For conservative Cold War ideologues, the atrocities of the Soviet Union and the threat of its imperial ambitions made any association with communism, and its claimed set of progressive ideals, suspect. Whereas the "Americanism" of the Roosevelt era was informed by the notion of America as a melting pot, a society of immigrants that offered equal opportunities to all, regardless of "race, color, or creed," postwar "Americanism," for the Cold Warriors, was about protecting the nation without, and policing it within, from the threat posed by the (communist) Other.[84]

Transatlantic Identities

With the exception of *Christ in Concrete*, none of the European films of the blacklisted discussed in this chapter was set in America. Nonetheless, it is possible to see in them the reflection of a pre–Cold War conception of what it meant to be American. The transnational (or supranational) orientation of the many "cosmopolitan" films written by the blacklisted can be seen as a rejection of the "American nationalist globalism"—a discourse that combined American national greatness, global responsibility, and containment of communism—that some historians consider fundamental to early Cold War ideology.[85] Likewise, in using their European films to promote themes of social justice and equity, including ethnic and racial tolerance, the blacklisted expressed a critical perspective on a country where this sort of social cinema could be considered "un-American." Nevertheless, perhaps even more than the films in which they were involved, their very presence in Europe attested to the political repression of the McCarthy era and challenged America's self-image as a haven of democratic freedom.

The cosmopolitan vision expressed in many of the films of the exiles from the late 1950s and early 1960s was also indicative of the distance they had traveled personally since first arriving in Europe ten years earlier. Arriving as political refugees, they had become important expatriate filmmakers whose transatlantic identities found appropriate expression through hybrid modes of filmmaking such as the international co-production. Carl Foreman, for example, leveraged his transnational experience to cast himself in the role of cross-cultural interpreter and critic, using his dual perspective to justify his critique of both Hollywood and the British film industry. In response to Hollywood's concern about runaway production, he repeatedly admonished the U.S. government for failing to follow Europe's example in providing aid or subsidies that would encourage

American producers to stay home and thus stem the overseas exodus.[86] He also accused Hollywood of no longer being capable of "establishing a cultural link or empathy with foreign audiences."[87] Likewise, he attacked the British film industry for a variety of ills: high production costs, restrictive unions, and an "archaic and monopolistic . . . distribution system."[88] In his opinion, both the United States and the United Kingdom were not doing enough to nurture young talent, which should be developed and cultivated through government-sponsored film schools and industry support for local film festivals.[89] That Foreman would feel secure enough to express his opinions so freely speaks not only to Hollywood's confusion and the cachet of the cosmopolitan, but to the personal distance he had traveled in the years since his flight to England.

Cinema's "European moment" also gave the blacklisted further incentive to sever themselves from their Hollywood roots. Having solicited Hugo Butler's help on the screenplay for *Eve* (1962), Losey found himself unable to see eye-to-eye with his old friend, a difference he chalked up to their disparate experiences over the previous ten years: "Hugo was being very *Hollywood* in his writing, very cold in his approach to it. It was a difference taking place during those years, because the kind of film I made with him on *The Prowler*, we were in complete accord about. The kind of film I was aiming at with *Eve* he wasn't in accord with at all because he was still back in that other place. I'm not saying one is better or worse but our European experiences had affected us differently."[90] In Butler's stead, Losey hired the English playwright Evan Jones, whom he had also brought in to replace Ben Barzman on *The Damned* (1961), and who would become one of his principal collaborators during the 1960s.[91] Jules Dassin likewise began working almost exclusively with European screenwriters after 1960, a decision he saw as a natural extension of the direction his life was taking. His collaborations with other blacklisted writers, such as Ben Barzman, had been "a matter of all of us being in the same boat, in the same place, sharing the work. Then I went off on my own, made a new life in Greece."[92] Indeed, his final attempt to work with a fellow exile imploded as a result of Michael Wilson's insistence on giving *Topkapi* (1964) an action-filled robbery sequence that had more in common with Hollywood than with Dassin's increasingly "European" sensibilities and self-image.[93]

6 • BLACKLISTED DIRECTORS, ART CINEMA, AND THE CAPRICES OF FILM CRITICISM

EMERGING IN TANDEM WITH the international co-production and "cosmopolitan" film was another filmmaking trend that played a significant role in shifting attention away from Hollywood. The rise of the European art film—both as a mode of film practice and an institution, to combine David Bordwell's and Steve Neale's well-known definitions—presented a distinct challenge to Hollywood filmmaking, as well as to the careers of some of the blacklisted in Europe.[1] While also intended for an international audience, the European art film employed rather different formal and economic strategies from the Anglo-American or Euro-American co-productions, or the Hollywood "runaway" productions previously discussed. Whether through aesthetic qualities such as fractured narratives or emphasis on personal expression or through its dependence on funding systems designed to support the production specifically of "quality" films, the European art film functioned as an oppositional cinema to commercial production—whether Hollywood or European—and as a bulwark for Europe's national cinemas.

A number of concurrent developments in Europe and America contributed to this new emphasis on cinema as art. In France, the ciné-club movement, which dated from the 1920s, experienced a dramatic revival in the postwar period, with numbers increasing from one in 1944 to more than 250 by 1960.[2] In 1955, the creation of the Association of French Art Cinemas (Association française des cinémas d'arts et d'essai), which granted formal recognition to designated theaters along with government support in the form of a tax break, reflected the interest in non-mainstream cinema that the ciné-club movement had helped foster. The critical discourse and debates promoted in new journals such as *L'Age du cinéma* (1951–1952,) *Cahiers du cinéma* (1951-present), *Ciné-Club* (1947–1954) and its replacement, *Cinéma 55* (1954–present), *Positif* (1952–present), and *Raccords* (1950–1952) similarly played a significant role in shifting the public perception of cinema away from that of an entertaining diversion to a fundamental part of cultural life.[3] In the United Kingdom, the postwar period also saw the arrival of a number of influential new film journals—*Sequence* (1947–1952), *Motion* (1961–1963), and *Movie* (1962–2000)—that emphasized aesthetics and attempted to reinvent film criticism by "finding ways of writing about cinema that escapes the limits of the reviewer's craft," in the words of V. F. Perkins, one of *Movie*'s co-founders.[4]

The career paths of the blacklisted exiles were profoundly affected by these changes taking place within European film criticism. In both Britain and France, the committed humanism of an earlier generation of critics made way for a new apolitical emphasis on the director as *auteur*. For many of the exiles, whose intellectual and artistic orientation remained profoundly influenced by their progressive politics, these developments put them firmly at the margins of the zeitgeist. Unlike the critics associated with communist publications such as *L'Écran français* and *L'Humanité* who admired the Hollywood exiles as fellow "hommes de gauche" and evaluated their films through the lens of their political experiences, the *Cahiers* group had little patience for the mystique of the blacklist.[5] Likewise, in Britain, the young critics of *Movie* magazine were less interested in Joseph Losey's radical background than in the passion for stylization that prompted them to laud him as the only "British" director who could be recognized as an auteur. The fact that he was actually American only fueled their conviction that British cinema was just as "dead" as it had been before the so-called "New Wave" began in the late 1950s.[6] At a time when British cinema was experiencing a dramatic renaissance thanks largely to the influx of American financing, the success of exiles like Losey further complicated the charged debates surrounding national cinema and identity.

The new cachet of European art cinema in the United States also had a significant effect on the careers of the blacklisted exiles. A number of historical and demographic factors contributed to the American movie-going public's growing interest in looking beyond Hollywood. The experience of World War II had created a demand for films that portrayed individual and social problems with greater realism. Likewise, the G.I. Bill led to a population of college-educated veterans whose experience living abroad contributed to an interest in more cosmopolitan, sophisticated films. As the 1950s progressed and the children of the postwar baby boom became young adults, changing social mores and frustration with the Production Code also spurred interest in foreign films in which adult themes were articulated and explored with greater freedom. By the early 1960s, U.S. "art houses" accounted for over 500 screens nationwide.[7] The growing number of theaters devoted to the exhibition of "films from other countries, reissues of old-time Hollywood 'classics,' documentaries, and independently made films on offbeat themes," as defined by a contemporary observer, created an expanded exhibition space for the European films of the blacklisted exiles.[8] In turn, the critical and, in some instances, commercial success of their films in America not only improved the work opportunities available to them, but provided empirical evidence of the increasing irrelevance of the blacklist. Likewise, their U.S. reception illuminates the significance attributed to European art cinema in U.S. film culture and the degree to which this association between European filmmaking and a certain type of cinema established an interpretive distance between the blacklisted exiles and their Hollywood roots.

The major international film festivals also played an important role in promulgating the conception of cinema as art. The London Film Festival was founded in 1957; the New York Film Festival followed six years later in 1963 and soon established itself as the premier showcase for foreign films seeking access to the U.S. market. By providing an institutional framework that elided "foreign film" with "art film," the New York Film Festival further contributed to the perception of art cinema—European or otherwise—as distinct and superior to commercial Hollywood production. In his review of the 1964 festival, critic Robert Gessner wrote that it "reminded New Yorkers once again what most urban Americans realize, namely the most imaginative and intelligent film is likely to come from abroad."[9] Among the highlights of the first New York Film Festival in 1963 was Joseph Losey's *The Servant,* which brought his reputation as one of *Britain*'s leading directors to America's attention.

This chapter focuses on the career trajectories of the émigré directors—particularly Jules Dassin, John Berry, and Joseph Losey—in relation to a number of key developments in European cinema in the 1950s and early 1960s: the European co-production, the emergence of the Free Cinema movement in Britain and the New Wave in France, and the ascendance of the concept of the *auteur.* By virtue of the visibility of their profession, blacklisted directors—unlike their screenwriter friends—could not work surreptitiously on international co-productions backed by U.S. studios and were more likely to be restricted to opportunities available in European film production. One result of this situation was that their films were evaluated in relation to the national cinemas of their host countries; they are thus revealing of both European ambivalence toward Hollywood and the revolutions occurring in Europe's own film cultures.

By the beginning of the 1960s, Dassin and Losey found themselves on opposite ends of critical favor largely because of these changes. Although it was one of the loudest champions of *Rififi,* the *Cahiers du cinéma* was ultimately critical of Dassin's departure from genre filmmaking and condemned his attempts to address "European" subjects in *Celui qui doit mourir* (1957) and *La Loi* (1959).

These films were both Franco-Italian co-productions, which accounted for roughly half of French film production during these years and provide helpful context for understanding Dassin's fall from critical grace.[10] Losey, in contrast, took advantage of his position as an exile to cast an appraising eye over the British class system, a focus that no doubt contributed to his popularity among the French critics (and for different reasons, British critics as well). By 1960, the *Cahiers* was ready to declare that Dassin's stay in Europe had proved "fatal" to him even as it devoted an entire issue to Losey, an honor that elevated Losey to the rank of *auteur*.[11]

European Co-productions

In his revisionist history of European art cinema, Mark Betz presents a compelling argument regarding the relationship between the European art film, Hollywood, and notions of national cinema. Noting that most histories of the period depict the relationship between European and American cinema in terms of David and Goliath, with Europe trying valiantly to protect itself from and compete with its more powerful rival across the Atlantic, Betz adjusts his critical framework to acknowledge the role of other factors, most significantly the formation of the European Economic Community in 1957. Situating European art cinema within this broader context provides another, typically overlooked rationale for the conventional reading of the European art cinema in terms of national cinema, he contends. Betz argues that the various "New Waves" that emerged in Europe during the 1950s and 1960s should be considered "nation-building responses at the cultural level to transnational cooperation and European unification at the economic and industrial level. . . . The casts, the production, and the distribution of the canonical postwar French and Italian cinema are prominently transnational, and as such may be read in terms of discourses concerning national authenticity during the first years of the EEC." Returning to the theme of American cultural imperialism, Betz also suggests that "European art cinema, with its elevation of the film director to artist status . . . can certainly be seen as a similar effort on the part of the nations of Europe to quell the tide of the massive influx of American mass culture and commodities."[12] The blacklisted exiles were situated at the nexus of these competing discourses, their involvement complicating the status of the European co-productions on which they worked as both national cinema and European art cinema. Specifically, a focus on the French reception of the "European" films of Jules Dassin and John Berry from the late 1950s reveals the degree to which the elision of art cinema with European national cinema encouraged the perception that, in moving away from genre cinema, these directors were trespassing on cinematic territory not their own.

While the numerous high-profile Euro-American co-productions of the 1950s and 1960s reflect an important development in international cinema during this period, they do not represent the majority of European production. As Betz notes, European co-productions produced during these years were usually intra-European and, most often, Franco-Italian in their composition. Since the signing of the Franco-Italian co-production agreement in October 1949, the number of such productions had grown steadily, peaking in the early-to-mid 1960s. According to Betz's investigations, in 1959, 30 of France's 39 co-productions were with Italy; in 1963, 43 of 47; and in 1968, 21 of 30. Because of the strict regulations concerning the amount of national participation necessary for these productions to qualify for state subsidies, Franco-Italian co-productions tended to have significantly higher budgets than normal national production.[13]

The success of *Rififi* allowed Jules Dassin to make the leap into the more lavishly funded realm of the Franco-Italian co-production. For his next two films, *Celui qui doit mourir* (1957) and *La Loi* (1959), his *Rififi* producer Henri Bérard partnered with a consortium of French and Italian production companies in order to raise budgets almost three times the size of *Rififi*'s.[14] In both instances, Dassin's cast was multinational, including the Austrian Carl Möhner and the Greek Melina Mercouri, in addition to the French and Italian actors required by the terms of the co-production. In its funding, genre, and religious and ethical themes (discussed in chapter 5), *Celui qui doit mourir* represented a startling departure from the crime films for which Dassin was best known and, as a result, instigated heated debates amidst the French critical establishment even before its premiere at the 1957 Cannes Film Festival. Opinions of the film were so divergent as to effectively divide Cannes into two camps, according to Jean de Baroncelli, the film critic for *Le Monde.*

In Baroncelli's view, the violence of the controversy provoked by the film was a measure of the director's ambition: "Dassin has made an impassioned film; you reap what you sow." While acknowledging the film's imperfections (a schematic Manichaeism, the absence of the novel's solemn mysticism), he praises Dassin for having the courage to break out in a new direction. "We know that he could have remade *Rififi* ten times and we would have been ready to cover him with accolades. But he chose a more difficult path, one strewn with pitfalls."[15] Continuing this line of thought, Jacques Doniol-Valcroze—writing in the *Cahiers du cinéma*—attacked the reluctance of French critics (and, by extension, the French public) to allow artists to depart from the molds in which they had been cast by their previous successes. "Here [at *Cahiers*], as elsewhere, the same critics who praised Dassin to the stars are now ready to publicly vilify him, as happened recently to [Jacques] Becker, and as will happen to all those who stray from their assigned seats or suddenly deliver a message somehow incompatible, in its form or its substance, with our too limited conception of their artistic destiny."[16]

Skepticism toward the sort of "*grand film*" with ample funding and trans-European casts that the European co-production agreements encouraged also contributed to the debates surrounding the film. Like *Rififi*, *Celui qui doit mourir* represented France in competition at Cannes, causing some critics to query what was "French" about a European co-production filmed in Crete with an international cast and American director.[17]

Both of these critical tendencies are evident in *Celui qui doit mourir*'s most scathing review, authored by François Truffaut. In a dramatic *volte-face* considering the ardor with which he had previously lauded Dassin's talents, Truffaut attacked what he felt to be the film's misguided sincerity. For Truffaut, Dassin's failure was all the more distressing considering the facility he had shown for "saving" the "*petits films policiers*" he had been assigned in Hollywood; now, given the chance to express himself freely, "all we get are noble sentiments, and more noble sentiments." Truffaut fell back on knee-jerk anti-Americanism to explain his disappointment:

> The bottom line is that Dassin is American and that many Americans are children at heart. Just like children, they have more spirit, imagination, and intuition than adults, which is why Hollywood cinema is so much more vibrant than ours. But when children try to imitate adults, while you can get Mozart, you can also get Minou Drouet! When Americans (with the exception of Faulkner) try to 'rethink' the world, they lean naturally toward the left, and left-wing Americans are the most childish of all.[18]

Despite the controversy swirling about the film, most reviews were positive, regardless of the political leanings of the publication. The widely read Communist Party daily *L'Humanité* provided Dassin—"a courageous man chased from Hollywood for his refusal to bow before the witch hunts"—with unwavering support, attacking the "*mauvaise foi*" (bad faith) of those journalists whose determination to demolish the film led them to attribute false statements and intentions to its director.[19] The violent polemics carried into the Cannes Festival's closing ceremony, during which catcalls and boos alternated with cries of "Dassin! Dassin!" from the film's supporters when the results of the Palme d'Or were announced.[20] *Celui qui doit mourir* lost to *Friendly Persuasion* (dir. William Wyler, 1956), a result that by some accounts came about through the American delegation's determination to deny the award to a blacklisted filmmaker.[21]

Four years later, discussing the reaction to *Celui qui doit mourir* in a televised interview, Dassin exclaimed, in no uncertain terms, "*C'était une catastrophe!*" He purported to remain baffled by the French critics' antipathy for the film, which was well received elsewhere in Europe and even in America.[22] Nonetheless, the critical and commercial failure of *Celui qui doit mourir* put a temporary halt to his blossoming European career. Melina Mercouri remembers a period of financial difficulties following the film's release, during which the only offers of work Dassin received were projects along the lines of *Rififi*.[23] By February 1958, however, his career—and finances—were back on track. For his next project, an adaptation of Roger Vailland's award-winning novel *La Loi*, he would receive a salary of 21.5 million francs (about $51,200), plus 25 percent of the net profits.[24]

Another Franco-Italian co-production, *La Loi* was filmed largely on location in southern Italy with a budget of 273 million francs (about $650,000) and an all-star cast that included Marcello Mastroianni, Yves Montand, Gina Lollobrigida, and Melina Mercouri.[25] Its preproduction history illustrates some of the pitfalls of European co-production and the intermingling of financial concerns with issues of national and cultural identity that this form of production necessitated. The film's original budget required the Italian co-producers, Titanus and Monica Films, to contribute 60 percent of the costs, making the film a majority Italian production. However, the publication of the Italian translation of Vailland's novel in May 1958 prompted such outrage in the Italian press about what was considered the book's defamatory and insulting depiction of Italian provincial life that the head of Italy's film council withdrew his support for the production on the grounds that it violated the Franco-Italian co-production agreements, which stated that the films produced under the agreement were not to harm the prestige of either nation. To salvage the production just forty-eight hours before filming was due to begin, the film's French producer Jacques Bar assumed the 60 percent share of the budget and agreed to film the interiors in Paris with a French crew, thereby making *La Loi* a majority French production and averting catastrophe.[26]

Set in Puglia, Vailland's novel draws its title from the French translation of *la legge*, a card game common in southern Italy. Also known as *la passatella*, the game permits the winner to use his position as *patron* to insult and humiliate a victim selected from among the other players. For Vailland, a former member of the Communist Party and *écrivain engagé*, the game offered a lens through which to explore class structure and social hierarchy in a remote and impoverished region of Italy. While certainly appreciative of Vailland's politics, Dassin bowed to practical considerations that required changes to the script, shifting the film's emphasis away from social critique and toward melodrama. The casting of Gina Lollobrigida as Marietta, the local beauty, required that the role be expanded; Lollobrigida's request for a new love interest led Dassin to develop the part of Enrico (Mastroianni), a government agronomist charged with draining the region's swamps and who represents the intrusion of modernity into the community's closed way of life. Showing his characteristic attention to location, Dassin uses the picturesque Mediterranean setting to contrast with the internecine tensions that fuel the plot, which abounds in love affairs and betrayals.

Dassin checks the light on location in Puglia for *La Loi* (Cinémathèque française – Iconothèque)

Despite significant advance publicity touting the film as "one of the most important commercial productions of the year," French reviewers fixated on the film's shortcomings.[27] Much of the criticism focused on aspects stemming from the film's status as a European co-production. *Le Monde* noted that it was bizarre to hear the inhabitants of a small Italian village speaking French, and that certain actors had a screen presence and style inconsistent with their roles as Italian villagers.[28] *Le Figaro* likewise called attention to the film's disconcerting linguistic mélange (*La Loi* was filmed in both French and Italian, with some of the actors speaking both languages and some being dubbed) and the strange effect of hearing "'Ciao Francesco,' 'Ciao Marietta!'" pronounced with a working-class Parisian accent.[29] In arguments that foreshadowed the "Euro pudding" charge leveled at contemporary policy-driven European co-productions, numerous reviewers described the film as an unsuccessful hodgepodge of elements that did a disservice to the national cinemas of both France and Italy. Writing in *Les Nouvelles littéraires*, Georges Charensol explained that his "uncertainty about this film stems from the fact that this intrinsically Italian story is being told to us by an American working from a novel by a Frenchman. I must confess, I am not at all convinced by the arguments of Georges Sadoul [film critic for *Lettres françaises*, rival publication to *Nouvelles littéraires*] who is convinced that cinema transcends the frame of the national."[30] Dassin's American nationality only complicated matters further and prompted some critics to attribute the film's *cinema du samédi soir* sensibility to the director's Hollywood training.[31]

This strict conception of national cinema defined by territory and language informs another common theme in reviews of *La Loi*: the notion that Dassin had lost his way in Europe. *Le Figaro* wrote, "It's no longer clear what's to become of Jules Dassin, who, having brought neo-realism to Hollywood with *The Naked City*, now makes a film in Italy filled with artificial effects."[32] And *Le Figaro littéraire*, after reviewing Dassin's trajectory from Hollywood to Europe, concluded that "alas, with *La Loi*, one fears that this talented man has taken a wrong turn."[33] Jean-Luc Godard offered the most biting articulation of this sense of disappointment in Dassin:

> We loved the Dassin who filmed on the sly among the fruit vendors of San Francisco, in New York's old wooden subway, on London's dreamlike docks. But alas, our Jules started taking himself seriously when he came to France wearing his martyr's badge. A few years ago, we were taken in by *Rififi* but now, we see that it doesn't come up to the ankles of [*Touchez pas au*] *Grisbi*, which it copied, much less those of *Bob* [*le flambeur*], which copied it. What happened next is all too familiar. If Billy Graham made films, no doubt he'd be called Jules Dassin. Permitting our aspiring philosopher to preach from European sound stages is like allowing an unschooled athlete to believe he is capable of explaining Aristotle.[34]

Finding inspiration in Godard's critique, that's just what Dassin (tongue firmly in cheek) would do in his next film, *Never on Sunday*.

John Berry's forays into the realm of European co-production would be no more successful than Dassin's. In 1956, with two hits to his name, Berry was in a position to write his own ticket. He signed a two-picture deal with Les Films du Cyclope, one of the larger Parisian production companies presided over by the wealthy Madame Carbuccia. Ironically, Madame Carbuccia's husband was a fascist and had been living in exile in Spain since the end of World War II. For this reason, Berry's contract stipulated that his first film be a Franco-Italian-Spanish co-production of *Don Juan*, starring the French comic Fernandel and filmed in Spain. At the time, this condition did not seem unduly onerous to Berry, who otherwise found the terms of the contract highly attractive: "They were going to pay me a fair amount of money just to sit and pick my second picture from those things that they were going to suggest, and I could turn any one of them down, etc., over a period of three years. It was a marvelous setup on the surface, and I signed for it."[35] As a European co-production, however, *Don Juan* was subject to a host of restrictions Berry did not reckon with, particularly concerning casting. For the leading female role, Berry was forced to accept the Spanish actress

Carmen Sevilla, an important star in Spain but not his actress of choice. He was also unhappy with the screenplay by Maurice Clavel and Juan Antonio Bardem, whose treatment of the legend was more political than the farce Berry had in mind.[36] Berry had his heart set on Vittorio De Sica for the role of Don Juan, who in Berry's version has grown tired of women and decides to trade places with his valet Sganarelle, played by Fernandel. But unable to get De Sica, he had to settle for Erno Crisa, a "fortyish, nice fellow, charming, half-assed star from Italy."[37]

When *Don Juan* opened in Paris in May 1956, these compromises were evident to many reviewers, who praised the concept but criticized its execution.[38] The *Cahiers du cinéma* caught Bardem's allusions to Franco's regime, noting the dictatorial nature of the chief of police, Don Inigo, and the popular revolution suggested by the film's final scenes, in which the people rise up against the "police state of 17th century Toledo." [39] Berry emerged mostly unscathed from the reviews, with many critics charitably blaming the film's inconsistencies of tone on other factors, such as the commercial demands of creating a vehicle for Fernandel. Berry's daughter Jan remembers the profound sense of optimism that buoyed their family's spirits at the time: "After *Ça va barder* and up until *Tamango*, there was a feeling that things were getting better, that we were on an upward trajectory."[40] This trajectory took a terrible turn, however, with Berry's second project for Les Films du Cyclope, the disastrous *Tamango*.

Costing over 300 million francs, filmed in color in both French and English and with international stars in the leading roles, *Tamango* was a European "superproduction."[41] That Berry was entrusted with such a big-budget film underscores his reputation at the time as one of France's most successful commercial filmmakers.[42] Through a contact at Twentieth Century–Fox's Paris office, Berry had learned that Dorothy Dandridge was in Europe, where she hoped to find a greater range of roles than the stereotypical parts offered by Hollywood. Berry's friend and assistant director Jacques Nahum suggested that Prosper Mérimée's novella *Tamango* could provide the source material for a Dandridge vehicle. Berry asked Lee and Tammy Gold to help him with the screenplay. According to Berry's son, Denis, the film's problems began with this choice of collaborators. "[*Tamango*] showed my father's fundamental lack of understanding of European culture. He wrote it with the Golds and what did they know?"[43] Nor did the attitude of Madame Carbuccia, whose Films du Cyclope had channeled its profits from *Don Juan* into the production, help.[44] "She didn't pay attention to details," Nahum recalls. "She assigned the costumes to one of the leading Paris fashion designers of the day as a means of paying off her account. The costumes were awful; they looked like what Mardi Gras dancers wear. Dorothy Dandridge took one look at them and refused to do the film."

A more basic cause of consternation for Dandridge was Berry's script; the story of a shipboard slave rebellion that she agreed to do had been transformed into a melodrama anchored by a love triangle among her character, Ayché, the ship's white captain (Curd Jürgens), and Tamango (Alex Cressan), the leader of the slave revolt. Although Berry agreed to script changes, their relationship did not improve after this rocky start.[45] Other production problems provide a window into the state of race relations in France on the cusp of decolonization. "We had trouble finding actors who were black, not *café au lait*, to play the slaves," recalled Nahum, whose imperfect solution was to hire the soldiers from France's African colonies stationed at a nearby army base. According to Nahum, the soldiers had great difficulty accepting their roles: "They objected to having oil applied to give luster to their skin, to wearing leg irons, even to eating peanuts. 'We're not monkeys!' they would cry."[46]

Tamango opened in Paris on 24 January 1958, its star-studded première attended by Simone Signoret and Yves Montand, Jean Marais, and Jacques Becker, among others.[47] The left-wing press was divided in its response. *L'Humanité* praised Berry for having taken liberties with Mérimée's text, particularly with regard to the character of Tamango, the leader of the slave rebellion whom Berry portrays in more heroic terms than the original novella. Calling attention to *Tamango*'s contemporary relevance for a country embroiled in a war of independence with Algeria, the reviewer lauds the film's moral courage along with its value as entertainment.[48] *Combat* was less forgiving, suggesting that the film's good intentions would have been better served by a screenplay that hewed more closely to the original text and by a directing style that showed greater concern for realism (the reviewer notes that the slave ship never seems to move).[49] The *Cahiers du cinéma* and *France Observateur* both express nostalgia for Berry's earlier work. Writing in the latter publication, Jacques Doniol-Valcroze suggests that none of Berry's French films approximate the energy and audacity of his Hollywood productions.[50] As he had for *Celui qui doit mourir*, François Truffaut provided the most sensational and nationalist review, exclaiming in his headline, "They betrayed Mérimée!" and proceeding to excoriate the film's acting, cinematography, and direction.[51] On 31 January, *Tamango* was struck another blow when the French government announced its decision to ban the film's exhibition in its overseas territories, having evidently deemed the tale of rebellion too politically sensitive for its volatile colonies.[52]

Berry tried to counterattack, defending the film on the popular radio program *Le Masque et la plume*.[53] However, his characteristic chutzpah masked his serious disappointment. "I don't know if he ever recovered from *Tamango*," observed his son, Denis, who attributed the film's shortcomings to his father's Hollywood training. "He wrote a film about a slave rebellion that spent all its time on the bridge, not down in the hold. It was a Hollywood film."[54] Yet many of *Tamango*'s commercial aspects owe as much to 1950s French cinema as to Hollywood. The film's release coincided with the publication of *Cinéma 58*, in which Pierre Billard put forth his annual assessment of the French film industry. Among the factors to which Billard attributed French cinema's lack of vitality was the "tendency in French production to develop 'big international films' co-produced with other countries, featuring foreign stars, in color, with high budgets, and which are thus offered to established directors who have already proven themselves, at least commercially, with other projects."[55] As a period film adapted (however loosely) from a literary classic, *Tamango* derived from the *tradition of qualité* in French cinema that the New Wave would challenge.

Dassin and Berry's experiences with *Celui qui doit mourir, La Loi,* and *Tamango* indicate some of the minefields the American exiles had to cross in the course of their European careers. On the one hand, their blacklisted status gave them an undeniable *caché,* especially with the coterie of communist critics both more tolerant of political art and more constant in their admiration for their American comrades' political courage. On the other hand, as Americans from Hollywood, the blacklisted were saddled with a certain set of expectations regarding the sort of films they should make. Dassin's post-MGM Hollywood films were highly regarded in France, while Berry was admired for his work with John Garfield in *He Ran All the Way.* Their facility with the noir genre gained them entry into the French industry, where the relative freedom of the French mode of production allowed them to explore other subjects and genres.

Their excursions into unknown territory were unsuccessful for a variety of reasons. The critical backlash that their efforts precipitated reveals the degree to which the Americans exiles occupied a very specific—and restricted—place within French culture. As refugees from "le MacCarthyisme," they reinforced France's self-image as a bastion for political tolerance, but as "Hollywood" filmmakers who tried to leave Hollywood behind, they made ready targets for the nationalist and anti-American (if not anti-Hollywood) strains of the emerging French critical discourse exemplified by the *Cahiers du cinéma.* At the same time, both Dassin and Berry were tackling cultural material that was profoundly foreign to them and indeed to the blacklisted Hollywood screenwriters they chose to work with. *Celui qui doit mourir* was the most successful of these films. Dassin's understanding of Greece was undoubtedly helped by his relationship with Melina Mercouri, while the film's status as a parable allowed its moral significance to transcend its immediate cultural context. Berry, on the other hand, was dealing with source material freighted with cultural and historical meaning, not to mention explosive contemporary import. Mérimée was revered in France and his short story was part of the French canon, in addition to being part of France's history of colonization. That the middle of the Algerian war may not have been an opportune moment to call attention to France's role as a colonial oppressor seems not to have occurred to Berry, who would tackle the subject of race more successfully years later in *Claudine* (1974), set in his native New York.

The production histories and critical receptions of *Celui qui doit mourir, La Loi,* and *Tamango* also reflect changes taking place in the French cinemascape that had nothing to do with Dassin's and Berry's distinctive backgrounds as blacklisted Americans. By virtue of their age, Dassin (b. 1911) and Berry (b. 1917) both belonged to the older generation of filmmakers that the New Wave would supplant.[56] Not only did they dare to stray from their film noir roots in these films, but in doing so they situated themselves within certain established trends in commercial French cinema of the 1950s—most notably the big-budget European co-production—to which the new generation of French filmmakers (many of whom were still developing their vision of cinema through their work as film critics) opposed themselves.

Joseph Losey and "La Politique des Auteurs"

Joseph Losey's transformation from a *cinéaste maudit* to one of Europe's foremost directors, whose name was frequently cited alongside those of Michelangelo Antonioni, Ingmar Bergman, Federico Fellini, and Alain Resnais in the cinematic discourse of the period, provides a revealing contrast with Dassin's and Berry's European experience.[57] As Losey frequently acknowledged, his professional resurrection owed much to the French, and to a number of devoted advocates such as Pierre Rissient and Bertrand Tavernier in particular. In June 1960, Rissient and other young cinephiles affiliated with the Cinéma MacMahon organized the Paris release of *Time Without Pity.*[58] Rissient had seen the film three years earlier when Losey had come to Paris to screen the print for Ben Barzman, who was unable to travel to London for the premiere due to ongoing passport problems.[59] In 1957, however, the critical climate in France was not ready for Losey, in Rissient's opinion. "It took a few years for *Time Without Pity* to come out in France because at the time, there were more people against Losey than for him."[60] Rissient is referring to the evolution that occurred in French critical discourse toward the close of the 1950s, as politically committed social criticism continued its fall from favor.[61] "La nouvelle critique" that replaced it put new emphasis on questions of form and mise-en-scène, as well as on the importance of the director as the source of the vision reflected in the film. This *politique des auteurs,* associated principally with the *Cahiers du cinéma* but also promulgated in the pages of rival journals such as *Positif* (albeit with different favored *auteurs*) and newspapers, was rapidly becoming the new standard of interpretation for French film criticism.[62]

By June 1960, the Parisian critical establishment was ready to welcome the arrival of a new *auteur,* though not with universally open arms. Jean Douchet, a critic of the *Cahiers* school, set the stakes high with a hyperbole-studded review of *Time Without Pity* in which he called Losey "*un metteur en scène cosmique*" and one of the cinema's greatest masters. Reflecting his adherence to the new criticism, Douchet attributes the film's success entirely to its exemplary use of mise-en-scène, which "approaches truth by maintaining a lucid gaze on reality."[63] *Le Monde* and *Libération* both referred to the nascent cult of Losey in their reviews, which—while favorable—maintain a more measured tone.[64] Georges Sadoul, demonstrating his allegiance to the older, sociopolitical approach to film criticism, barely discussed the film at all, choosing instead to present Losey as an example of the "lost generation" of American postwar filmmakers whose careers were cut short by the Hollywood blacklist, much to the detriment of American cinema.[65] With its relentless pacing and no-holds-barred performances from Leo McKern and Michael Redgrave, *Time Without Pity* maintains a hysterical edge that can be exhausting, but for those French critics with sterner nerves, the film's suspense and visual flair more than compensated for its more melodramatic aspects.

Pierre Rissient and Michel Fabre followed up *Time Without Pity*'s release by persuading Eric Rohmer, then editor of the *Cahiers du cinéma*, to devote the entire September 1960 issue to Losey, an honor that placed Losey in the company of Hitchcock and Renoir, previous recipients of the *Cahiers*' undivided attention. Including a lengthy interview with Losey and a complete "biofilmography," in addition to analyses of Losey's inimitable mastery of style, the issue provided a thorough, if tendentious, introduction to Losey's oeuvre.

Losey's *étoile* continued to rise during the first half of 1961 with the release of *L'Enquête de l'Inspecteur Morgan* (*Blind Date*) in late January and his prison-break thriller *Les Criminels* (*The Criminal*) two months later. While Losey's talent was unquestioned, critical opinion remained divided as to the issue of degree: Was Losey simply a superlative *metteur-en-scène* or a true *auteur* capable of imprinting a film with his own distinctive style and vision of the world? An overview of the critical response elicited by Losey reveals the degree to which the *politique des auteurs* put forward in the pages of the *Cahiers, Positif,* and other specialty film journals had influenced mainstream critical discourse by the early 1960s. Just a few years earlier, communist publications such as *L'Humanité* and *Combat* privileged a very different set of criteria in their reviews, emphasizing realist aesthetics and the political commitment of the filmmaker. Yet in its review of *Les Criminels, L'Humanité* lauded "the perfection of the mise-en-scène, which demonstrates not only the technical mastery of the director, but also his temperament and intelligence." Not to be outdone, *Combat* declared that in *Les Criminels,* "cinema achieves its highest potential: that of revelation through style. The work is purely visual; words don't count." Only *Les Nouvelles littéraires*' George Charensol, while conceding that Losey demonstrated a perfect knowledge of his craft, still wondered whether the cult of Losey was either an instance of "fraud or a collective aberration."[66]

Losey remembered this period as a "turning point": "Basically, it gave me confidence that I could do something again that was all right, and original, and strong—because I had begun to wonder, you know. . . . I was relieved to have some enthusiastic people call me again because the last picture to have received any kind of acclaim was *The Prowler* seven years before. It's a long time when you're in your forties."[67] With the support of the French, Losey began to judge his own work, and that of others, in distinctly auteurist terms. In a 1961 interview with *Sight and Sound,* he spoke of the need for a filmmaker to have "a 'signature,' an immediately recognizable style."[68] Of the new wave of European directors, Losey felt particular admiration for Antonioni. In a letter to the French critic Louis Marcorelles in February 1961, he praised *L'Avventura* as "one of the most complete and satisfying films of its kind I have ever seen."[69] Later that year, Losey would pay a more direct homage to Antonioni's style by employing the same director of photography (Gianni Di Venanzo) and leading lady (Jeanne Moreau) that Antonioni had used in *La Notte* (1961) on his next project, *Eve* (1962).[70]

Losey was also keenly aware of the need to capitalize professionally on his explosive popularity in France. In a letter to *The Criminal*'s U.K. distributors, Anglo-Amalgamated, he urged them to use the film's success in France to promote its sale to a U.S. distributor: "I understand that THE CRIMINAL is doing top business in France, and I understand this can be a highly lucrative market, in fact much better than the English one. In the light of this, what further efforts are being made toward New York and American distribution? I should think the first step would be to make Gordon aware of the French response and business, and of my standing there."[71] He also asked Moura Budberg, a Russian émigré and friend of many of the blacklisted exiles in Paris, to help him find a "suitable subject . . . to do as an English/French co-production." "I'll show you the notices on THE CRIMINAL from Paris," he continued; "they are so good and the coverage so extensive that I am in demand in France but have no subject."[72] That was soon to change, however, as sometime in May, while on location with his next film, *The Damned,* Losey received a phone call from the French producers, Robert and Raymond Hakim, regarding *Eve,* an adaptation of a pulp novel by James Hadley Chase for which they had already signed Jeanne Moreau and Stanley Baker. Losey saw a connection between the critical cult he inspired in France and the opportunity to work with the producers of Antonioni's two most recent films. "It's possible that owing to the new and fairly intense interest in my work in France the Hakims, being nothing if they aren't alert to changes and fashions, thought that I was a good idea."[73]

Losey's standing in the United Kingdom, however, was a different story. British reviews of *The Criminal* had been mixed and Anglo-Amalgamated had not devoted many resources toward promoting it.[74] Discussing *The Damned,* his next project, Losey explained that it was "probably the only film that I had any chance to do at that moment, because the backers of *The Criminal* didn't like the film very much and *Blind Date* had been blacklisted." Unenthusiastic about *The Damned*'s science fiction genre, Losey focused his energies on what could interest him in the project, namely the opportunity to say something about the "danger of playing around with other people's lives in connection with atomic fission," while commenting upon the British public school system and "certainly the control of education." He was also drawn to the film's visual possibilities, selecting the location of Portland Bill, a bleak promontory on England's south coast, for the contrast "its savagery and military installations" (Portland Bill was home to a naval base where experiments on biological warfare were conducted) provided with the "seedy victoriana of Weymouth," a nearby seaside resort.[75]

The film opens with a number of startling juxtapositions. An aerial tour of the coastline reveals several large pieces of sculpture incongruously perched on the cliff's edge. In the long takes that follow, Losey establishes a vivid contrast between the Old England evoked by Weymouth's Victorian boardwalk and the new generation represented by the gang of Teddy boys hanging disrespectfully from a statue of a unicorn, one of the boardwalk's attractions.[76] The contrast is brought home when the gang brutally attacks and robs an American tourist, while the sound track chants, "Black leather, black leather, smash, smash, smash." This opening sequence foreshadows the themes of loss and destruction the film explores through the story of a group of children who, on account of their mothers having been "accidentally" exposed to radiation while pregnant, are themselves radioactive and thus impervious to the effects of radiation. The children are being raised in complete isolation by scientists for whom they represent the future of the human race in the inevitable event of a nuclear holocaust. For Losey, the children's fate presented a way to expose the "indirect, secret, hidden, hypocritical violence of the men who assumed the right, through some kind of old school educational system, to corrupt, pervert, and brainwash the minds of the young."[77] Cynical and bleak, the film offers little consolation to the viewer; in the closing shots of the coastline, the children's cries of "Help us, please help us" are slowly overwhelmed by the sound of gulls.

The Damned would prove to be another turning point for Losey, boosting his critical reputation in the United Kingdom much as *Blind Date* and *The Criminal* had done in France. Philip French in the *Observer* hailed the film as "one of the most significant recent British movies, a disturbing work of real importance," while the *Times* began its positive review by proclaiming Losey's status as "one of the most intelligent, ambitious, and constantly exciting film-makers now working in this country, if not indeed the world."[78] Referring to the two-year delay in the film's release (Columbia had tried to shelve it on account of its political content), Philip Oakes of the *Sunday Telegraph* called Losey "a director whose talent is exceeded only by his incredible bad luck."[79]

By 1963, however, Losey's luck was dramatically improving thanks in part to the generational change occurring in British film criticism. Between 1960 and 1964, more than half of Britain's most prominent film critics either died or retired.[80] In their stead rose a new generation of critics much less opposed to auteur-driven perspectives than their predecessors. Whereas the *engagé* critics of *Sight and Sound*, with their dedication to a politically committed humanism, could not stomach the *Cahiers du cinéma*'s adulation of commercial Hollywood directors such as Howard Hawks, Otto Preminger, and Alfred Hitchcock, the young critics of the new journals *Motion, Movie,* and the *Oxford Opinion* held no such prejudices against the popular. Indeed, *Movie* made clear its allegiance to a *Cahiers*-inspired *politique des auteurs* by including a "pantheon" of directors in its inaugural issue. Third on the list, after Hawks and Hitchcock, was Joseph Losey.[81] By the end of the year, with the triumphant November release of *The Servant,* Losey had finally "arrived" in Britain.[82]

National Cinemas, New Waves

To a degree that distinguished him from other prominent directors in 1960s Britain, Losey was able "to command the support of disparate critical schools," a facility that Robert Murphy attributes to his "impeccable credentials as an auteur": "He had done interesting work in the theater as a disciple of Brecht, he had made a couple of good Hollywood films, he had fought against anti-Communist hysteria and B-movie producers to maintain his personal and artistic integrity, and above all he was not British."[83] Losey's Brechtian views on realism appealed to the new guard of French critics and their British acolytes. In an interview published in the *Oxford Opinion,* Losey explained: "I hate naturalism—as much as Brecht did . . . the only way to approach reality is to break down the thing, clean it out . . . then select the reality symbols that you want and place them back in the scene . . . in a heightened way."[84] His Hollywood films were admired by devotees of auteurism, with their insistence on the possibility for individual statements even within the limitations of the studio system, while his political status endeared him to the older generation of left-wing critics such as Georges Sadoul. Losey also believed in a filmmaker's responsibility to concern himself with what he called "social content," a perspective that aligned him with the critics and filmmakers affiliated with *Sight and Sound* and the Free Cinema movement.[85] However, securing his appeal in Britain, above and beyond these other elements, was the fact that he was *not* British.

By virtue of his American nationality, Losey provided welcome ammunition for the tradition of opposition to the cinema establishment that united the divergent strands of British film criticism. As much as Lindsay Anderson and his Free Cinema co-founders, Karel Reisz and Tony Richardson, had advocated a cinema that combined personal expression with social awareness, a cinema that was "free" from the industry's conventions of style and technique, the younger critics of *Motion*, *Movie*, and the *Oxford Opinion* opposed what they saw as the narrow social realism of the "New British Cinema" that the Free Cinema movement had helped spawn. In 1962, *Movie* launched its inaugural issue with an all-out attack on the so-called British New Wave:

> Five years ago the ineptitude of British films was generally acknowledged. The stiff upper lip movie was a standard target for critical scorn. But now the British cinema has come to grips with Reality. We have had a break-through, a renaissance, a New Wave. . . . All we can see is a change of attitude, which disguises the fact that the British cinema is as dead as before. Perhaps it was never alive. Our films have improved, if at all, only in their intentions. We are still unable to find evidence of artistic sensibilities in working order.[86]

Raymond Durgnat of *Motion* shared *Movie*'s disdain for British social realism, although for reasons as much political as aesthetic. His opposition was to the notion that art should serve a "high moral purpose," that social commitment was the ultimate criterion by which a film's value should be judged. He considered the New British Cinema's emphasis on the working class to be hypocritical, arguing that "what masquerades as vaguely leftish goodness is really middle-class fear of the brutal and licentious proletariat."[87]

Just as *Movie* judged Losey to be the one "British" director who could undoubtedly be classed as an auteur, *Motion* declared that "it should—but apparently doesn't—go without saying that Losey's recent works are incomparably the greatest 'British' films so far made."[88] The quotation marks drive home the intended insult to British cinema. The reverse chauvinism practiced by the new generation of British film critics stood in stark contrast to the anti-Hollywood bias of the British mainstream press, for whom "American" served as an insult of sorts. For instance, with regard to *The Criminal*, the *Times* accused it of "self-consciously setting out to prove that it can be as tough as anything produced in America," while the *Guardian* again charged Losey with giving "his own special treatment—which is 'American plus'—to a British subject. There lies the trouble."[89] As they had with *Time Without Pity*, certain British reviewers seemed to be objecting to something overwrought in Losey's style, an excess of violence or emotion that could be most easily dismissed as "American."

As the language of these reviews suggests, popular conceptions of national cinema were coded in terms of genre. Hollywood had the market cornered on violent crime films, on efficient and exciting thrillers such as *The Criminal*, whereas Britain excelled at . . . ? The reviews tended to leave this question unanswered, instead giving a definition by default (British cinema was bloodless, insipid, dishonest, etc.). Through its film criticism and programming, the Free Cinema movement had begun to make strides toward a more positive definition of British cinema. Its intellectual preoccupations (with the traditional working class and youth culture), however, remained outside the cinematic mainstream.[90] *Room at the Top* (dir. Jack Clayton, 1959), with its bracing endorsement of the material and sexual ambitions of its working-class protagonist, had a greater impact on the industry due to its commercial success. By August 1959, eight months after *Room at the Top*'s release, reviews of *Blind Date* included references to "the new British effort to face up to sex without blinking" and the "new look" of films, or to "sociological studies," such as *Room at the Top* and *Look Back in Anger* (1958) (Tony Richardson's film adaptation of John Osborne's generation-defining play).[91] The early 1960s saw an explosion of these "sociological studies" or "kitchen sink" films. With their working-class themes, unabashed treatment of sexuality, location shooting, and lack of established stars, these films were a clear departure from the cautious conformity that had characterized much British cinema of the 1950s.[92]

The blacklisted exiles in London were largely bystanders to these developments. Although Losey admired writers such as Alan Sillitoe (*Saturday Night and Sunday Morning, The Loneliness of the Long Distance Runner*), David Storey (*This Sporting Life*), and Willis Hall (*Billy Liar*) and certain directors (Lindsay Anderson, with qualifications), he was generally skeptical of the British "new wave." In a letter to the London-based American producer Charles Schneer from February 1960, he expressed his lack of confidence in the abilities of the "Royal Court boys"—a reference to the Chelsea theater focused on modern British drama, where *Look Back in Anger* had premiered in 1956—none of whom he deemed "very safe on a screenplay project."[93] Nonetheless, he did pursue a number of projects that became important examples of British social realism—*The Loneliness of the Long Distance Runner* (dir. Tony Richardson, 1962), *Billy Liar* (dir. John Schlesinger, 1963), and *This Sporting Life* (dir. Lindsay Anderson, 1963)—but was unable to find financing for them within his network of independent producers.[94]

Carl Foreman approved of Lindsay Anderson's call to British filmmakers to address the country's contemporary issues and praised films like *Room at the Top, The Entertainer,* and *Saturday Night and Sunday Morning* for their willingness to address "challenging subjects."[95] His own artistic choices, however, were circumscribed by his understanding of his status as an exile and his professional orientation. As an American and a self-perceived "outsider" to British society, Foreman felt it was not his place to comment upon the problems of a nation not his own. "I feel that I should accept the hospitality that's been given me and do my best to make what I consider worthwhile films if I can. . . . Maybe after ten years I can say, 'Yes, I am a part of the community,' and have a right to comment after making some contribution."[96] More than any self-imposed ethical dictates (whether genuinely held or not), Foreman's arrangements with Columbia determined the type of films he would write and produce. The terms of Foreman's deal meant that he needed to make films for the international market, with the result that *The Key* (dir. Carol Reed, 1958), *The Guns of Navarone* (dir. J. Lee Thompson, 1961), and *The Victors* (dir. Carl Foreman, 1963) all adhered to Hollywood's formula for international co-productions: star-studded international casts, exotic locations, and universal themes.

While Losey and Foreman may have wanted, in some capacity, to avail themselves of the talent and tenor of the British New Wave, they were limited by both their own career choices and by the strict associations between genre and national cinema. The strong affinity between Hollywood (and subsequently, the Hollywood exiles) and genre—especially that of the crime film—also persisted in France, as the experiences of John Berry and Jules Dassin discussed earlier illustrate. Joseph Losey's French agent, Jean Rossignol, pitched him projects in this vein such as *Classe tous risques*, which Losey rejected as "very ordinary" (the film, now considered a classic *film policier*, was made by Claude Sautet in 1960 with Lino Ventura and Jean-Paul Belmondo).[97] But whereas the British New Wave was indigenous in its derivation and topical orientation, the French New Wave self-consciously engaged with Hollywood's genre production in its quest to rid French cinema of its hidebound *tradition de qualité.*

François Truffaut launched the offensive against the *tradition de qualité* in 1954 when the *Cahiers du cinéma* published—after a year of revisions and deliberations on the part of the journal's editors, André Bazin and Jacques Doniol-Valcroze—his polemic, "Une certaine tendance du cinéma français." In this essay, Truffaut argued that French cinema was dying under the weight of its *quality*: the literary adaptations and costume dramas that, with their high production values, consistently won prizes despite their lack of aesthetic innovation. For Truffaut, the strength of the *tradition* was stifling to creativity: "We say *la qualité française,* and don't think about it any further."[98] He was particularly scornful of the emphasis placed on screenwriters (with their lack of understanding of cinematic language) as opposed to directors. Instead, Truffaut lay the groundwork for *la politique des auteurs* by championing directors such as Jacques Becker, Robert Bresson, Jean Cocteau, Abel Gance, Roger Leenhardt, Max Ophuls, Jean Renoir, and Jacques Tati, who often wrote their own dialogue and whose films were consequently a closer reflection of their personal vision. Indeed, Truffaut asserted that he did not believe in the "peaceful co-existence of the *tradition of qualité* and *cinema of auteurs*" on the grounds that in the former, the director manipulated his characters like puppets, while in the latter, the director treated his characters with respect.[99]

In mounting his attack against the *tradition of qualité,* Truffaut and the other "young Turks" associated with the *Cahiers* such as Jean-Luc Godard, Jacques

Rivette, and Eric Rohmer were objecting to a mode of production that was becoming increasingly common in 1950s French cinema. Between 1955 and 1959, the average budget of a French film rose by almost $100,000. Twenty percent of France's production output was shot by the same nine directors between 1945 and 1957. Michel Marie offers this summary of the state of the French film industry on the cusp of the New Wave's arrival in 1959: "By 1958, the French cinema had clearly become increasingly industrial, even if film production remained, at least in strictly economic terms, somewhat artisanal. It churned out picture shows principally to entertain and turn a healthy profit."[100] In their desire to redirect French cinema toward personal, artistic expression, the critic-directors of the New Wave saw a model in American B-movies. The vitality and originality of these films, usually independent, low-budget productions lacking stars, affirmed the New Wave's adherence to marginal production made outside the dominant, commercial system as a means of maintaining artistic integrity. The depth of admiration these directors had for American B-pictures and the pulp fiction sources they often drew upon was indicated by Godard's and Truffaut's early choices, with Godard dedicating *À bout de souffle* (1960) to Monogram Pictures (producer of B-movies such as Joseph Lewis's *Gun Crazy*) and Truffaut adapting *Shoot the Piano Player* (1960) from *Down There* (by the American noir fiction author David Goodis).

In light of its devotion to low-budget American genre cinema, the New Wave critics' rejection of Jules Dassin and John Berry was predictable. Not only did Dassin and Berry belong to the same "generation of aging leftists" as the seasoned French filmmakers (such as Claude Autant-Lara) that the young cinephiles blamed for French cinema's stagnation, but they had the temerity, as Americans, to reject U.S. low-budget genre production in favor of a more typically "French" cinema; *Celui qui doit mourir, Tamango,* and *La Loi* were all examples of the sort of "*cinéma littéraire*" scorned by the *Cahiers* crew.[101] That Dassin and Berry were depicted as having committed an act of transgression by daring to make more "European" films betrays the degree to which the New Wave filmmakers, for all their desire to create a more modern French cinema, still adhered to a restrictive notion of national cinema. Ironically, the New Wave's success would inspire filmmakers and film movements around the world and, in doing so, would contribute to cinema's increasingly transnational character.

Truffaut's and Godard's antipathy toward Dassin's European turn seems to have blinded them to the ways in which Dassin actually used his increased autonomy as a filmmaker to make films that were in many ways consistent with aspects of the New Wave. Beginning with *La Loi,* Dassin wrote or co-wrote the screenplays to all his films with the exception of *Topkapi* (1964) and *Circle of Two* (1981). He also privileged shooting in natural locations and had a long-standing interest in the documentary form (which he explored in *Survival 1967,* his documentary on Israel's Six Day War). *Never on Sunday* (1960), released the same year as *À bout de souffle* and *Tirez sur le pianiste*, differs starkly from Godard's and Truffaut's works in tone, but could be considered a *film d'auteur* in view of the degree of Dassin's involvement in its production. Not only did Dassin write, direct, produce, and star in the film, but he used its tale of an American abroad to address the critique often leveled at him by French critics that he had lost his bearings in Europe. In the film, Dassin plays Homer, an American scholar who travels to Greece in pursuit of Truth. Instead, he finds Ilya (Melina Mercouri), a happy-go-lucky prostitute whom he takes for a symbol of the fall of Greece and sets about trying to reform. For Dassin, the film was a lighthearted comment on American cultural imperialism, on "this awful tendency that Americans have to try to remake the world in their image, in their thinking. Often half-baked, often without any real understanding of what different countries are about."[102] Having arrived in Europe during a periodic upswing in anti-American sentiment, Dassin would have been well versed in the discourse of American domination. Considering his blacklisted political status, his choice to cast himself as a one-man Marshall Plan, come to save the prostitutes of the Piraeus from themselves, is as ironic as his depiction of the informer in *Rififi*. Godard, however, among others, failed to get the joke.

Perhaps not surprisingly, Dassin was no fan of *la nouvelle vague*, although he did acknowledge the "tremendous importance" of what it demonstrated about the possibility of making dynamic, meaningful films for very little money, "with complete liberty."[103] Losey likewise admired the independence of New Wave filmmaking, complaining wistfully that "Jean-Luc Godard can work with a crew of seven. I have to work with 60." Nevertheless, according to Andrew Sarris, who queried Losey on the subject in 1968, Losey "takes much of the Nouvelle Vague with more than a grain of salt" and was particularly dismissive of Godard.[104] Ben Barzman, while praising Godard's talent and Truffaut's humanity, expressed concerned over the dark vision of a film like *À bout de souffle* and others by the New Wave filmmakers, which he saw as "more dangerous than the most rushed Hollywood Z-movie."[105] Despite their professed ambivalence about the new generation of French filmmakers who were suddenly at the industry's vanguard, Dassin, Losey, and their fellow exiles were inevitably influenced by the changes the New Wave ushered in. Regardless of whether they would succeed as *auteurs*, they embraced the freedom and recognition accorded to filmmakers in the new climate of European cinema.

"European" Auteurs in America

By the early 1960s, an idealized opposition between the role of the director in Europe as compared with Hollywood had gained popular recognition and was often cited in the American press as one of the principal reasons behind the exodus of Hollywood filmmakers to Europe. A 1962 article in the *Los Angeles Times* posed the question: "Why have so many of our movie-makers flocked to England and the Continent?" In Rome, Paris, Madrid, and London, filmmakers expressed similar views regarding the creative advantages of working in Europe. "I am here because of the humiliation I have suffered at the hands of editorial supervision," noted one respondent. "The filmmaker in Europe has autonomy. The filmmaker makes it and it comes out as his film—not a product of executive memos," observed another.[106]

Both Jules Dassin and Carl Foreman attributed the vitality of contemporary European cinema to the degree of respect and importance granted the director. "In Italy, for example, a director might say 'I'm going to do a picture about horses,' and if he's a good director, that's all he need say to secure financing and the proper cast," Dassin observed. "Here [in America] the director is often the last man to be hired."[107] Carl Foreman credited Ingmar Bergman's films with reminding him of his long-standing desire to direct. "I said to myself: My God, how I envy that man! He made a movie. It's him. But before it was possible for me to direct my first film, *The Victors,* I had to spend twenty years in the kind of apprenticeship our system demands. Most of all, I had to come up with important money-making successes. In Europe artistic success is the main criterion in determining whether someone can handle the total job of filmmaking."[108]

This perception of the superiority of the European mode of production was itself an offshoot of Hollywood's European turn and of the American public's increased cinephilia. A brief survey of the U.S. reception of the European films of the blacklisted reflects European cinema's growing prestige (and Hollywood's growing anxieties) along with changing attitudes toward the blacklist. As Dalton Trumbo argued, the best weapon against the blacklist was talent, and the European triumphs of the exiles played a significant role in transforming the industry's attitude toward the blacklist.

As the most prominent of the exiled directors, Jules Dassin and Joseph Losey once again provide revealing case studies. Prior to *Rififi*'s American release in June 1956, none of the European films of the blacklisted was exhibited in the United States with the names of their blacklisted writers or directors in the credits.[109] While this practice began to change in the wake of *Rififi*'s strong box-office performance, most reviews either made no mention of the writer or director or, if they did, omitted their American nationality. As Dassin noted, "Most reviewers of *Rififi* wrote about me as though I was a foreigner."[110]

In the case of *Rififi,* the film's independent distributor adopted a marketing and exhibition strategy that served to further distance *Rififi* from any political taint carried by Dassin. One display ad mentioned neither the film's national origin nor the name of its director, placing the emphasis squarely on its genre instead. Other ads, while including Dassin's name in the credits, chose to highlight the film's strong notices; the *New York Times* called it "the keenest crime film that ever came from France," while the *New York Daily Mirror* considered it "the best foreign film of the year." In New York, *Rififi* played at the Art Theatre in Greenwich Village and at the Fine Arts on Fifty-eighth Street alongside titles such as René Clair's *The Grand Maneuver* and Alexander Korda's *Fire Over England,* its exhibition context thus affirming its status as a foreign art film.

Buoyed by the success of *Rififi's* New York release, the distributors dubbed the film into English and released it nationwide in April 1957. Without exception, the reviews evaluated *Rififi* in terms of its origins and contribution to the crime film, a genre that "has heretofore been the exclusive province of British and American filmmakers," in the opinion of the *Hollywood Reporter.* The *Los Angeles Times* described the film as a French version of John Huston's *Asphalt Jungle,* while *Variety* noted that it took an American director to give the French gangster film the proper treatment. This tone of Franco-American rivalry—and anxiety—even colored the film's marketing materials; a full-page spread in the *New York Times* declared that "Frenchmen have muscled in on what was once exclusive Yankee territory—the gangster movie."[111]

Rififi rehabilitated Jules Dassin's career in America. Every film he made over the next ten years would be released in the United States, where he was developing a reputation as one of "the most interesting directors to emerge in France," as the *Saturday Review* observed with a certain irony.[112] While *Rififi* was marketed as a French gangster film, Dassin's next film—*He Who Must Die* (*Celui qui doit mourir* directly translated)—was promoted the next year as a serious European art film, albeit one directed by an American. In stark contrast to the reviews of *Rififi,* reviews of *He Who Must Die* noted Dassin's American nationality with remarkable consistency, and a number made more explicit reference to his political past. The *Los Angeles Times* mentioned that Dassin "left this country under a political cloud," while *Time* magazine called attention to the irony of a man who had been blacklisted as a communist directing a film that it considered to be "one of the most powerful religious statements the screen has made in many a year."[113]

By 1960, however, new trends in the film industry were to prove more interesting to reviewers than rehashing the story of the blacklist. *La Loi,* renamed *Where the Hot Wind Blows,* provided the centerpiece for a *Los Angeles Times* feature about the "new kind of movie flooding the American market": the international co-production that combined aspects of the European art film with more commercial production.[114] A number of other reviews made a similar point about the film's hybridity, but very few mentioned either Dassin's nationality or political background, suggesting that his reputation was by now sufficiently well established as not to merit further explanation. Only one review of *Never on Sunday,* released to great acclaim almost concurrently with *Where the Hot Wind Blows,* referred to Dassin's past troubles—and did so in a sympathetic fashion.[115]

Dassin and Melina Mercouri celebrating the success of *Never on Sunday* (Cinémathèque française – Iconothèque)

Joseph Losey had to wait longer for his career in America to take off again. While Dassin's critical reception in the United States and France often diverged, with American critics showing more tolerance for Dassin's commercial streak than their French colleagues, Losey's reputation in America was influenced more directly by his growing fame in Europe. Beginning with *Time Without Pity*, all his British films were exhibited in the United States. However, until the release of *Blind Date* (U.K.)/*Chance Meeting* (U.S.) in February 1960, Losey's background was not mentioned in reviews, which subsumed his nationality into that of his films. The American Legion ensured this would not be the case with *Chance Meeting*, launching a campaign to halt the release of a film made by known "subversives." After waiting several months for the controversy to die down, Paramount did release the film, to positive reviews with Losey's name intact. Few critics lingered over Losey's past, preferring instead to focus on the relationship between the film's genre and nationality. The *New York Times* judged the film an exemplary thriller of "the vintage British brand," while the *Motion Picture Herald* declared that "nobody makes a thriller like the British" and praised "the American director" Joseph Losey for "setting a swift pace in the British style."[116] The reviews also sounded two more contemporary notes indicative of the changes rapidly transforming the film industry. The *Hollywood Reporter* compared the film favorably to Jack Clayton's *Room at the Top*, while *Variety* situated the film's German, French, and English leads in relation to "the current vogue of mixed international casts."[117]

Two years later, *The Criminal* (retitled *The Concrete Jungle*) had a limited U.S. release, with reviewers again categorizing the film as a "British crime movie," albeit a rather "strange," "odd and uneven" one.[118] Despite his misgivings about the film, one critic suggested:

> U.S. audiences seem bound to hear a lot more about Losey during the next few years. First portent: "The Concrete Jungle," released abroad as "The Criminal," received the Nouvelle Critique prize, awarded each year by young French critics, as the best foreign movie of 1961. With their recherché tastes, this group is often completely off base, but just as often they hit home. Second portent: Jeanne Moreau, no mean prognosticator herself, has just finished starring in Losey's first major-league production, "Eva." The appearance of Miss Moreau in a movie nowadays seems an almost certain sign that a director has arrived.[119]

While Losey had most certainly "arrived" in Europe by this point, it would take *The Servant*'s attention-grabbing premiere at the 1963 New York Film Festival for his talent to be fully recognized in the America. Numerous reviews and interviews note the lag between Losey's eminence abroad and lack of renown at home. The *New York Times*' Eugene Archer observed: "International as the motion picture industry has become, there are still sharp divergences between European and American film tastes. Nowhere is the contrast illustrated more strikingly than in the embattled career of Joseph Losey. Mr. Losey, as few Americans are yet aware, is a Wisconsin-born filmmaker who, at the moment, is just about the leading director in the British film industry." *Newsweek* called attention to Losey's week-long retrospective at the Paris Cinémathèque in 1962 and the distinction accorded him by *Movie* of being the only brilliant *British* director.[120]

A number of factors contributed to America's belated embrace of Europe's critical darling. Most immediate was the festival context in which *The Servant* debuted. As Britain's entry to the first-ever New York Film Festival, whose establishment testifies to the new internationalism of American film culture, *The Servant* came to the American public's attention in the company of films by Luis Buñuel, Jean-Luc Godard, Alain Resnais, and Roberto Rossellini. The presence of these European heavyweights would certainly have lent *gravitas* to *The Servant*, as did Harold Pinter's script given the recent Broadway success of his play *The Caretaker*. And much as the ascent of a new generation of film critics in France and Britain had facilitated Losey's rise to prominence, changes in the American critical establishment likewise worked in his favor. In 1962, the alternative journal *Film Culture*, founded by Jonas and Adolfus Mekas in 1954 to provide a forum for exploring avant-garde and independent cinema, published Andrew Sarris's seminal essay "Notes on the Auteur Theory." In 1960, Eugene Archer, one of Sarris's colleagues at *Film Culture*, joined the staff of the *New York Times*. And while *The Servant* left Archer's senior colleague Bosley Crowther, the *Times* long-established chief film critic, baffled, Crowther had nonetheless played an important role in shifting the public's attention toward the vitality of European cinema in opposition to the often stilted and stultifying spectacles coming out of Hollywood in the 1950s.[121] By the time of *The Servant*'s U.S. release in the spring of 1964, American cinemagoers had already had the chance to familiarize themselves with the work of other practitioners of modern European art cinema such as Antonioni, Bergman, Fellini, and Resnais. Reflecting the degree to which movies mattered in the new American film culture of the 1960s, by 1965 even a mainstream news magazine like *Newsweek* could assume that its readers would be familiar with these European auteurs, to whom it compared Losey in its review of *Eve*.[122]

Why was *Celui qui doit mourir* considered a European art film in the United States but an overreaching Euro-mélange in France? Why was *Chance Meeting* received as an above-average British crime film in America but an auteurist triumph in France? As this chapter has demonstrated, changes in film criticism, in conjunction with the economic and industrial considerations animating the surge in European co-productions during the late 1950s, all contributed to these transatlantic differences in reception. Were the French less inclined to see a film like *Celui qui doit mourir* as the work of an auteur because it was—with its multinational cast and exotic setting—an (obvious) European co-production and thus antithetical to the national cinema paradigm of auteurist art cinema? American critics and audiences, less sensitive to the nationalist concerns of Europe's smaller film industries in the face of Hollywood interference and the move toward European unification, were more flexible in their definition of European art cinema, which was above all an oppositional cinema to commercial (Hollywood) film culture.

Yet, as Mark Betz cautions, the bias of film criticism (and subsequently film history) in favor of national cinema has obscured the origin of many prototypical French and Italian art films of this era as actual European co-productions.[123] For instance, Losey's *Eve*—filmed on location in Italy with a European cast and Franco-Italian funding—transcended national boundaries in its mode of production as much as *Celui qui doit mourir*. Yet while Dassin's American nationality and, by extension, sensibility, problematized his attempts to tackle European subjects, at least in the perception of European critics, Losey's American roots were readily absorbed into his new identity as a European auteur. What this difference indicates, apart from a certain critical caprice, is that form and content, as opposed to mode of production, were determining features of modern European art cinema. While Losey's highly stylized explorations of alienation and anomie in films such as *Eve* were entirely in keeping with the aesthetic and thematic concerns of other European filmmakers such as Antonioni and Resnais, Dassin maintained his commitment to a particular vision of social cinema. His expression of this vision through the visual and industrial tropes of the European co-production was more in keeping with the *tradition de qualité* and European cinema's own attempts to compete with Hollywood on terms that the new critics considered aesthetically moribund.

7 • THE LEGACY OF THE BLACKLIST

Predicting the end of the blacklist was, not surprisingly, a favorite pastime of the blacklisted. On a trip to Europe during the summer of 1958, Adrian Scott advised his exiled friends that by his estimation, the blacklist would be dead within a year.[1] Six months later, Paul Jarrico echoed Scott's sentiments in a letter to the Czech director Jirí Weiss. Noting recent signs of improvement in Hollywood, Jarrico concluded that "the blacklist, in fact, seems to be on its last legs, at long last."[2] Changes within the industry and at the governmental level contributed to the sense of optimism. The growing weakness of the U.S. domestic market meant that American independent producers could increasingly afford to ignore industry prohibitions like the Production Code or the blacklist and instead concentrate on recouping their investment in other world markets such as Europe, where television had yet to decimate cinema attendance to the degree that it had in the United States.[3] Another sign of the changing status of the blacklist came from an unlikely source: Richard Nixon. Early in June 1958, the actor and independent producer Kirk Douglas had arranged a meeting with the vice president. Douglas's production company, Bryna Productions, employed a number of blacklisted writers, and Douglas hoped to persuade Nixon to issue a statement condemning the blacklist. While not acceding to Douglas's request, Nixon emphasized that the blacklist was an industry, not a government, issue—a startling declaration of neutrality from such a high-profile former member of HUAC.[4]

The industry's increasing disregard for the blacklist did not go unnoticed in the national press. In May 1958, *The Reporter*, an important biweekly political magazine, published a feature-length survey of recent events in Hollywood that concluded with the assessment that "slowly, the blacklist is being abandoned."[5] That Hollywood's poor economic performance was forcing the studios to relax their standards prompted *The Reporter* to observe satirically that "if they thought they could turn a buck doing it they might even hire Paul Robeson to sing in a musical written by Dalton Trumbo and produced by Adrian Scott." The article also referred to a number of "catastrophes" involving the 1957 Academy Awards: not only did the Academy amend its bylaws to avert the embarrassment of having a blacklisted writer (Michael Wilson) receive an Oscar nomination (for *Friendly Persuasion*), but it awarded the Oscar for Best Original Screenplay to the mysterious Robert Rich, whose real identity remained the subject of much speculation.[6]

The Reporter reserved star billing, however, for Carl Foreman. The article described the shock waves generated by Foreman's recent deal with HUAC and Columbia: "It wasn't but a few days before the word got out that Foreman's testimony had *not* included what had previously been a No. 1 essential—the names. Phones rang in offices and next to barbecue pits all over Hollywood." And despite pressure from anticommunist organizations such as the Veterans of Foreign Wars (VFW), neither Columbia nor HUAC chairman Francis E. Walter backed down from their positions. In a public statement, Walter presented the following justification of his treatment of Foreman: "I wasn't interested in getting names from Foreman of people who had already been identified as Communists. I wanted someone who could get up and tell what a sucker he'd been. I thought Foreman was the kind of important man we needed for this, and I think he did a service to the country in his testimony."[7]

What *The Reporter* article (which received coverage in *Variety*) made abundantly clear was the extent to which the blacklist had become a public relations conundrum for the industry by 1958.[8] On the one hand, conservative pressure groups like the American Legion and the VFW were still capable of stirring up bad press for perceived violations of the blacklist. On the other hand, the blacklist had become a source of embarrassment to the industry, as the Academy of Motion Pictures kept handing out Oscars to films written by blacklisted screenwriters (just as the 1957 Academy Awards were marked by the Robert Rich and *Friendly Persuasion* fiascos, the 1958 awards were notable for the scandal surrounding *The Bridge on the River Kwai*, whose purported screenwriter, the novelist Pierre Boulle, could not speak English).

In a letter to Richard Nixon that he entrusted to Kirk Douglas (in advance of the actor's meeting with the vice president), Dalton Trumbo outlined the detrimental effect of these events: "Academy night is probably the most widely publicized cultural event in the world. It is also uniquely American. A situation that brings it into disrepute year after year is greatly damaging to American prestige. The blacklist, which other nations use as an excuse for anti-American propaganda, is not good for the Academy, nor for the troubled American motion picture industry, nor for our government, which detractors of America invariably blame for it."[9] After broadly emphasizing to Nixon the harm the blacklist had done to the U.S. film industry and America's reputation overseas, Trumbo used the examples of the blacklisted in Europe as his chief body of evidence. Citing the successes of Carl Foreman and Donald Ogden Stewart, he commented that "wherever an American motion picture personality goes in London he is subject to politely satirical remarks about his blacklisting homeland." He noted that in France Jules Dassin had become "an ornament to the world of French cinema" and that his case was "regularly cited in French intellectual circles as a criticism of American democracy." And in Italy, Trumbo continued, the "most important film producers . . . are now availing themselves of blacklisted American writing talent. This is perfectly open, and occasions a good deal of cynical comment." Referring to the U.S. industry's current state of economic crisis, he concluded: "Under such circumstances it is unfortunate that many of the most successful foreign films presently competing with it for [the world] market are now being written or directed by blacklisted persons whose talents may not be used by the American industry that first discovered and developed them."[10]

Although Trumbo put a positive gloss on the experiences of the blacklisted in Europe, failing to mention that many of them were still forced to work under assumed names, he nonetheless articulated the vital role that the exiles played in making a pragmatic counterargument to the blacklist. Clearly, according to this rationale, the authority of the blacklist suffered when Jules Dassin's name shone down from the credits of *Rififi* during the film's successful 1957 U.S. release, just as it did from the open speculation that the Oscar for *The Bridge on the River Kwai* should have gone to Carl Foreman and Michael Wilson. As David Lean commented in a letter to Michael Wilson from early 1958: "The farce is also accentuated by our friend Jules Dassin. Everyone here keeps saying what a success he's made of rubbing his nose at the situation here by having his films exhibited in spite of the blacklist. The situation has become more and more ridiculous and I think it must soon become untenable."[11]

What Trumbo's and Lean's argument points to is the significant role played by the blacklisted exiles in Europe in breaking the blacklist. Conventional accounts of the end of the blacklist center upon the year 1960 and the success of *Spartacus* (dir. Stanley Kubrick) and *Exodus* (dir. Otto Preminger), two big-budget epics written by Dalton Trumbo and the first to be released with his name in the credits since his blacklisting in 1947 as one of the Hollywood Ten. This domestic focus overlooks the transnational dimensions of the blacklist revealed by the experiences of the European exiles and serves more as a *terminus post quem* rather than a *terminus ante quem*. This chapter challenges the narrative surrounding the end of the blacklist by exploring the inconsistencies in its enforcement as reflected in the careers and choices of the blacklisted exiles. The director Cy Endfield's late-season HUAC testimony in 1960 provides a revealing case study, as does Twentieth Century–Fox's half-hearted attempt to profit from Jules Dassin's new

European prestige. In conclusion, the chapter considers what the blacklist continued to mean for the exile community in Europe even in its aftermath.

The End of the Blacklist

Within Hollywood, the momentum against the blacklist continued to build as the 1950s reached their close. Suspecting that *The Defiant Ones* (dir. Stanley Kramer, 1958), written by the blacklisted Nedrick Young under the pseudonym Nathan E. Douglas, would earn an Oscar nomination, and anxious to avoid a repeat of the disastrous 1957 and 1958 award ceremonies, on 15 January 1959 the Academy repealed its bylaw excluding communist or suspected communists from Oscar eligibility.[12] Two days later, Dalton Trumbo revealed that he was the real Robert Rich. Jeff Smith offers a cogent analysis of the impact of these events: "The Academy decision and Trumbo's 'Rich' announcement confirmed what had been implied by the publicity surrounding the black market: the blacklist simply had not worked. After each public relations embarrassment, the general public was forced to ask itself the question . . . : what was so subversive about these writers if they were winning major awards?"[13] In a letter to Michael Wilson in Paris the following month, Trumbo outlined his strategy for bringing the blacklist to its knees. Since the blacklist had never been officially acknowledged by the industry, the industry could not officially rescind it. "There *was*, however, the Academy rule. Revocation of the Academy rule was the nearest thing to an official recision [*sic*] of the blacklist that could or will occur."[14] The next step, in Trumbo's opinion, was for writers of the caliber of himself, Wilson, and Albert Maltz to band together and use their talent as a "weapon" against the blacklist. With the industry in such an advanced state of fragmentation that there was "no longer a centralized control . . . tight enough to enforce the blacklist," Trumbo perceived an opening. "Each of us [Trumbo, Wilson, and Albert Maltz] must very soon use the excellence of our work to compel the use of our names."[15]

Less than a year later, on 20 January 1960, Otto Preminger announced that Dalton Trumbo was the screenwriter of *Exodus* and that he "naturally will get the credit on screen that he amply deserves."[16] Bryna Productions followed suit that August, stating that Trumbo would receive screenplay credit for *Spartacus.* Both *Spartacus* and *Exodus* performed very strongly at the box office following their respective releases in October and December 1960, and vied for the top two spots throughout the early months of 1961.[17]

Preminger's announcement prompted a stream of reports in the press that contributed to the impression of the blacklist's imminent demise. In early February 1960, Stanley Kramer went public with his opposition to the blacklist, declaring his determination to hire any writer of his choice, regardless of "past affiliations or suspected affiliations."[18] A week later, *New York Times* critic Bosley

Crowther discussed Preminger's and Kramer's actions in an opinion piece in which he made clear his disdain for the blacklist: "Now is a good time for the industry to re-examine its stand on the validity of its 'Waldorf manifesto' in the light of all that has occurred. To permit this precautionary policy . . . to collapse through violation without acknowledging its obsolescence and demise is only to continue a hypocrisy that has already too much prevailed."[19] The following month, Frank Sinatra announced that he had hired Albert Maltz to write the film adaptation of *The Execution of Private Slovik* and that he would be granting Maltz screen credit.[20]

The more permissive atmosphere surrounding the blacklist is reflected in the fact that even the normally reticent exhibition sector weighed in with its opinion. Harry Brandt, president of the Independent Theatre Owners Association and head of the Brandt theater chain, called for "an end to the era of the blacklist, a shameful chapter in the industry's history." Brandt singled out for criticism the power of the "private pressure groups which have taken unto themselves a special guardianship of the screen," noting that if the industry was going to free itself of their influence, then "the Kramer-Preminger position is entitled to support from other motion picture producers, distributors, and exhibitors."[21]

Independent producers and the studios alike took up Brandt's challenge to such a degree that, by September 1960, the *New York Times* was prompted to declare that the "American Legion is clearly being ignored."[22] Earlier that year, Martin McKneally, the national commander of the Legion, had condemned the growing industry practice of "clearance," whereby producers sought to protect themselves from criticism by demanding statements from blacklist victims declaring they were no longer communists as a precondition for employment. Despite the Legion's censure, the trend continued, fueled by the industry's opportunistic determination to find a solution to its slump. As Murray Schumach noted: "Though most of the producers seeking letters are obviously unhappy about the existence of a blacklist, they are motivated by more than ethical consideration. These are days when producers and studios are trying for the smash hit, the movie that will make millions of dollars. The stars, as well as producers, have become increasingly fastidious about scripts. They want the best. If some of the best writers are on a blacklist, then they will try to pry them loose. The letter is the lever."[23] Their success in doing so was such that by the year's close, the *New York Times* felt confident reporting that it seemed that "the industry might be ready to end its hypocritical approach to the blacklist" once and for all.[24]

Albert Maltz and Nedrick Young, among others, might have begged to differ. Frank Sinatra rescinded his offer to Maltz less than a month after making it, stating that he felt compelled to accede to the wishes of the American public, who had made clear their objection to the hiring of Maltz on moral grounds.[25] And when *Inherit the Wind* was released in November 1960, it bore the name of

Nedrick Young's pseudonym, Nathan E. Douglas. Unlike Trumbo, neither Maltz nor Young was working with a showboating personality like Otto Preminger, for whom any publicity was good publicity. And as Jeff Smith notes, Trumbo himself had manipulated his public image so effectively that, by 1960, his "name had become a rather unusual form of product differentiation."[26]

Although Trumbo's strategy proved effective in his own case, his personal triumphs did not have the broader effect he had envisioned. Despite the "evidence" of progress presented by the successful exhibition of *Spartacus* and *Exodus,* twelve blacklisted film professionals including Herbert Biberman, John Howard Lawson, and Albert Maltz filed suit against all the major Hollywood studios (with the exception of United Artists) at the end of December 1960, convinced that the studios were in fact returning to a policy of stricter enforcement of the blacklist.[27] A few months later, Adrian Scott wrote to Paul Jarrico of the false expectations Trumbo's achievements had generated among the blacklisted: "Many thought that after Trumbo's break through that there would be many more. Not so. . . . Trumbo is secure now, mining a narrow vein but of pure gold."[28] Indeed, circumstances were still so difficult by the end of 1961 that Scott—who had been eking out a living as a television writer for detective shows including *Meet McGraw, 77 Sunset Strip,* and *Surfside Six,* using his wife as his front—finally decided to give up on Hollywood.[29] "It was only when things got really hopeless that he considered the offer from a former college mate who was then an executive at MGM to go [to London]," his wife Joan recalled.[30] Nor did Trumbo's theory about talent winning out prove to be the case for Michael Wilson. As noted in chapter 3, Sam Spiegel refused to credit Wilson for his work on *Lawrence of Arabia* on account of Wilson's adamant refusal to provide him with a noncommunist statement. Wilson would not receive a screen credit until *The Sandpiper* (dir. Vincente Minnelli), released in 1965 and co-scripted with Trumbo.

The Case of Cy Endfield

The preceding overview of the blacklist's decline reveals the unpredictable vicissitudes of its enforcement. Some independent producers, like Sam Spiegel, required noncommunist statements, while others, such as Otto Preminger and Kirk Douglas, did not. Some studios, like Columbia and United Artists, were willing to disregard the American Legion, while others, such as Paramount, were shaken by its threats of picket lines and public censure. And while the blacklisted community in Europe played a significant role in breaking the blacklist (their employment and accolades overseas being frequently evoked by the American press to show the damage to U.S. prestige from the blacklist), their professional experiences, particularly for those based in England or working on

Anglo-American productions, were subject to many of the same restrictions and humiliations as those of their colleagues in the United States.

The confusion surrounding the status of the blacklist was manifest in Cy Endfield's efforts to clear himself before the committee without naming names. On 18 August 1958, Endfield sent an impassioned, handwritten letter to HUAC chairman Francis E. Walter. In the letter, he made clear his abhorrence for "a party and program that has long since . . . become repugnant to me, standing opposed to all I since believed," but maintained his opposition to naming names:

> The difficulty has been that I was not, nor still am not, prepared for what has seemed often to be the final or confirming criterion of anti-Communism in a former Communist sympathizer—that is, the naming of individuals who were associated with one's political past. But I have probed my conscience unendingly, and know with total certainty that this divulgence would be valueless, except for its possible opportunistic benefits to myself—and after these many years of professional deprivation for this factor alone, I still cannot find the resources within myself to overcome the emotional repugnance I feel against informing against others, solely for self-gain.[31]

In the letter, Endfield initially referred only indirectly to his goal, which was to arrange for a deal similar to that of Carl Foreman's. He continued: "I hope that the naming of past associates as an absolute pre-condition for establishing one's rejection of a communist past might be now mitigated or abandoned by those who have maintained it." He is similarly oblique with regard to his motivation in appealing to the committee at this time, although his closing request makes clear that it is for reasons of professional advancement: "Can your committee take cognizance of my anti-communist position *so that reference can be made to it by any concerned entity in the USA which wishes to make enquiries relevant to the earlier allegations?* If so, what are the further procedures I need undergo, if any?"[32]

Endfield's decision to contact the committee at this time, and in this way, was curious for a number of reasons. Having spent his first years in England making low-budget films for small, independent producers, Endfield had entered a new phase of his career the previous year with the release of *Hell Drivers*, produced and distributed by Rank. As his widow Maureen recalled, "*Hell Drivers* was a big step up for him, to be making a film for Rank. After he started working for Rank, life became much more normal. Before, each film was such a struggle."[33] Indeed, Endfield composed his letter to the committee only ten days prior to the premiere of his next film, *Sea Fury*, which was also released by Rank and marked his debut as a producer/director. It was also odd that, unlike his good friend Carl Foreman, Endfield did not approach the committee through the offices of a skilled lawyer like Sidney Cohn. What does seem clear is that some "concerned entity in the USA" had expressed an interest in hiring Endfield—most likely for a sum far beyond those offered by British producers—but only on condition that Endfield first clear himself.

Endfield received a prompt reply from Congressman Walter. Walter reaffirmed the committee's policy of affording "any person who feels that he has been adversely affected by any testimony the opportunity to appear and testify," but he refused to meet either of Endfield's requests. Although he assured Endfield that the committee would retain his letter in its files, "since it is not a matter of a formal hearing, it cannot be incorporated into our public references." Nor did Walter suggest that Endfield would be able to get away without naming names: "Should you at any time avail yourself of the privilege to appear before this Committee, I think I should advise you that the Committee will not be precluded from interrogation of you respecting any persons whom you may have known as a Communist or any incidents involving Communist activity."[34] Evidently, this was a line Endfield was still unwilling to cross, for another year and a half would elapse before he contacted the committee again.

When Endfield renewed his relations with Walter, he was fueled by a strong sense of urgency. On 5 February 1960, he sent Walter a telegram in which he stated his willingness to "furnish testimony openly without reservation or qualification" at the chairman's "earliest convenience," noting that "time is of the essence."[35] Walter responded two weeks later by letter, in which he granted Endfield's request to testify on the condition that he agree to answer questions relating not only to his own activities, but also to those of any of his former Communist Party associates.

On 31 March 1960, Endfield gave executive session testimony before Richard Arens, HUAC staff director, and Donald T. Appell, a staff investigator. In a memo prepared in advance of Endfield's appearance, Appell noted that Endfield's previous affidavits (filed with the U.S. Consul in London when Endfield requested a renewal of his passport) gave the impression of much more limited Communist Party involvement than reported in the testimony of friendly witnesses such as Martin Berkeley, David Lang, and Pauline Townsend. Accordingly, Appell recommended that "Endfield be given an opportunity to tell his story in his own way and, after he has finished, refer back to the testimony of Berkeley, Lang, and Townsend for his explanation of their testimony."[36] Following Arens's prompts, Endfield provided an extremely thorough account of his personal history, beginning with his time at Yale and his professional training in the New York social theater of the 1930s and continuing through his years in Hollywood. In addition to describing the extent of his membership in the Communist Party, he named over thirty names, including those of his friends and fellow exiles Carl Foreman, Paul Jarrico, and Bernard Vorhaus.

Asked why he had waited so long to approach the committee, Endfield first framed his answer in terms of his changing views on the responsibility of the individual toward the community, but his high-minded rationalizations soon gave way to the more mundane motivations of ambition and jealousy:

> There was a series of incidents that led me to reverse my position . . . about the using of names of other past associates. . . . I was offered a job . . . by an American producer who subsequently discovered I was on the banned list as far as working in Hollywood was concerned, and the job offer was withdrawn. Rather recently, I was made another offer like this, an attractive job, and my answer was the same. I said I was terribly sorry, I would love to do it and provide any testamentary material necessary to show that I was not and have not been a Communist for many, many, many years, but I still had these reservations about naming of other individuals, partly as a principle reservation, and part of it had to do with direct feelings for some of these people. I would not like to come under their disapproval, purely as individuals.
>
> That afternoon I encountered some people I knew who told me of a writer who was blacklisted, Mike Wilson . . . who was working under the table, by arrangement with the producers. . . . And suddenly it occurred to me that as a director, in a public function, I was carrying the burden of a moral position far in excess of that carried by individuals who had, by my understanding, much deeper principle feelings about the whole matter. . . . And I realized, why should I turn down the job . . . to do something for and on behalf of individuals who to me were taking an unprincipled position?[37]

In an indirect and rather incoherent fashion, Endfield seems to have been querying why a committed Marxist like Michael Wilson should have been able to have a lucrative black-market career by virtue of the "invisibility" of his profession while Endfield, who felt no allegiance to communism, continued to suffer professionally.

Endfield's sour grapes would be easier to explain if his career had been more visibly in dire straits. But since *Hell Drivers*, he seemed to be on a roll; his most recent films—*Sea Fury* and *Jet Storm*—had both been well received, the caliber of the cast of the latter (which included Richard Attenborough and Mai Zetterling, in addition to Stanley Baker) attesting to Endfield's rising status within the British film industry. A clue to Endfield's actions may lie in the fact that, at the time, he was having difficulty raising money for the project that would become *Zulu* (1964). With Stanley Baker as his co-producer, Endfield approached as many as thirty production companies and distributors without success. "It took about two years of literally carrying that script under one's arm and being thrown out of every distribution office from here to California," he later recalled.[38] As for the identity of the project he referred to in his testimony, it could be *Mysterious Island*, Endfield's next film. On 27 January 1960—just ten days before Endfield sent his telegram to Walter—*Variety* announced that the London-based American independent producer Charles Schneer was preparing *Mysterious Island* for a Columbia release.[39] However, if this is the case, it raises the question of why Columbia would accept a noncommunist statement from Joseph Losey (signed in September 1960 as a condition for *The Horizontal Man*, which Carl Foreman was to produce as part of his deal with Columbia), but not from Endfield.

Although the precise circumstances surrounding Endfield's decision to testify remain obscure, his testimony and treatment by HUAC reveal the complex negotiations that occurred between the government, studios, conservative pressure groups, and the blacklisted themselves during the blacklist's slow demise. When Endfield first approached the committee in 1958, the backlash that Carl Foreman's testimony had elicited was still fresh in the minds of committee members like Richard Arens, for whom Walter's decision to allow Foreman not to name names had come as a surprise during Foreman's testimony.[40] Foreman's appearance had remained a source of public embarrassment for the committee, thanks to the efforts of anticommunist groups like the American Legion, the VFW, and AWARE.[41] In 1958, Lee R. Pennington, assistant director of the American Legion, expressed his dismay regarding Columbia's treatment of *The Key*, Carl Foreman's first credited work since he was blacklisted and the first film produced as part of his deal with the studio. "Apparently Columbia Pictures has adopted the attitude of 'The Public Be Damned,'" he wrote, adding that he had written to "Jim O'Neil [of the American Legion] to see whether we can really start something but I will discuss it with you before taking any action. I don't want any boomerangs."[42] Clearly, the American Legion was aware that it no longer had Hollywood's full support in its opposition to the blacklist. Nonetheless, at its annual convention in 1959, it requested that the committee call Foreman to testify again, as his status as a cooperative witness remained in doubt.[43] The negative publicity that the so-called "Foreman affair" continued to generate was such that it effectively precluded the possibility that the committee would again risk its reputation by cutting a similar deal with others on the blacklist.

In his decision to approach the committee again in 1960, did Endfield simply misread the signs that the blacklist's efficacy was weakening? Could his experience have been more satisfactory had he not committed the tactical error of forgoing legal counsel? Was his mistake one of perspective, in that he took an emotional, moralizing view of the blacklist rather than the pragmatic one advocated by Dalton Trumbo? In 1958, Trumbo predicted that "before this thing is over, a number of persons who were not outstandingly successful before the blacklist are going to have to face some bitter truths.... Only the best blacklisted writers will profit from the end of the blacklist, while the rest will be confronted with a terrible competitive struggle for their existence."[44] Trumbo's persistent emphasis on the issue of talent brings us to another possible explanation for

Endfield's actions. Did Columbia fail to offer him "clearance" as it did Losey because it did not consider him as talented? Was Endfield not getting the work he felt he merited because of the blacklist, or was the blacklist instead simply an excuse for the studios to reject him? That Endfield's insecurity and jealousy could lead him to such extreme actions as naming names offers some insight into the pervasive and corrosive psychological effects of the blacklist.

Clearing the Way to *Never on Sunday*

In the spring of 1959, Dassin signed a contract with United Artists to direct four films in Europe. The terms were similar to those of Losey's ill-fated Paramount deal: United Artists promised Dassin complete artistic freedom and in return demanded . . . nothing, at least according to Melina Mercouri. While Mercouri was adamant that UA imposed no conditions, Carl Foreman believed that Dassin furnished UA with a noncommunist statement, suggesting in a letter to Paul Lazarus of Columbia that Losey planned to use Dassin's statement as a model for his own.[45] Lew Kerner, an independent producer who initiated the UA deal, tried to check Dassin's status with the committee prior to finalizing the arrangements in January 1959, but was told he would need to make his request through his local congressman.[46] Whether Kerner made further inquiries is unclear, but Dassin provided his attorney Leon Kaplan with a letter stating that he left the Communist Party in 1949, at which time he ceased all political activities.[47] The deal went forward, with *Daily Variety* announcing Dassin's partnership with Kerner on 3 March 1959.[48] Kerner had joined forces with Ilya Lopert, a producer and foreign film distributor who had sold his company to UA but maintained a large degree of autonomy in its continued operations. Although UA executives were involved in the negotiations, Dassin's deal was with Lopert Films, a strategy that offered UA a degree of protection from charges of defying the blacklist.[49]

Shortly after Dassin signed his deal with United Artists, he was approached by Spyros Skouras, president of Twentieth Century–Fox. Skouras, who had emigrated to the United States from Greece at the age of thirteen, spoke with Dassin about making a film for him in Greece with Melina Mercouri; it is possible that Dassin pitched him *Never on Sunday*, which he was working on at the time. The negotiations between Dassin and Twentieth Century–Fox dragged on for a year and provide yet another example of the Hollywood studios' continued squeamishness with regard to the blacklist. Following his initial meeting with Dassin in June 1959, Skouras set about trying to clear him with HUAC, contacting staff director Richard Arens directly about the matter. Informed by Arens that Dassin would need to come to Washington to testify, Skouras expressed his fear that any film made with Dassin would be boycotted by groups like the American Legion. Darryl Zanuck—who had left Fox in 1956 in order to concentrate on independent production—responded with skepticism, pointing out that Dassin's "last two films are playing all over America and his name is on the marquee of Warners' Beverly Hills and there has been no criticism, picketing, or boycotting of any sort."[50] In March of the following year, Dassin sent a "clearance" letter to Zanuck, assuring his old friend that "there is no reason—moral, ethical, professional, or political—why we can't work together."[51] Zanuck promptly hired Dassin to write and direct one of his forthcoming films; the timing suggests it was *The Big Gamble* (dir. Richard Fleischer, 1961). However, the deal soon fell apart as a result of comments Zanuck made at a press conference in Paris that offended the American Legion (although the details are obscure, the statement made reference to Dassin, Nikita Khrushchev, and the Waldorf Astoria meeting).[52] Skouras's subsequent attempts to appease the American Legion were unsuccessful, and no film was ever made with Dassin.

These communications between Skouras and Zanuck about Dassin's situation indicate how the industry's view of the blacklist evolved during the 1950s. Zanuck, whose independent DFZ Productions was based in Paris, repeatedly called attention to the hypocrisy surrounding the blacklist's enforcement.[53] "It just seems incredible to me," he wrote, "that acknowledged and known Communists are employed 'under cover' and men who left the Party twenty years ago are still suspect."[54] Skouras, whose conservative politics made him more inclined to defer to the Legion, was nonetheless concerned with not disabusing Dassin of the notion that he was "one of the fantastic crusaders against innocent people."[55] That Skouras would imply that the blacklisted were innocent and that those who supported them were heroes indicates the sea change occurring in attitudes toward the blacklist. Even the FBI, which had begun a file on Dassin in 1944, felt that it was no longer in the government's best interests to call Dassin in for questioning when he visited the United States. In a report submitted to J. Edgar Hoover on 26 September 1960—just weeks before the U.S. premiere of *Never on Sunday*—the special agent in charge articulated how Dassin had strengthened his position through his "voluntary self-exile" and professional success:

> The fact that Dassin has chosen to maintain permanent residence outside the U.S. affords him with at least a psychological advantage should he prefer to decline cooperation with this government on matters pertaining to his personal past activities that would not accrue to a person who had not pursued such a course. It is the belief of this office that Dassin, who has acquired considerable prestige in the movie industry abroad in recent years, could seize upon any attempted discussion of his former CP affiliations conducted during a visit here as an opportunity to criticize the government for hounding him about matters that occurred many years ago and that he could publicize any unfavorable reaction to such an interview in a manner that could be a source of embarrassment to the Bureau.[56]

That the FBI feared embarrassment at the hands of a famous expatriate blacklisted filmmaker suggests that, as in Trumbo's case, success was the best revenge against the blacklist.

A Separate Peace

The ultimately successful European careers of many of the exiles, while never removing them entirely from the shadow of the blacklist, did make the blacklist increasingly irrelevant to their new lives as cosmopolitan filmmakers. In March 1964, Herbert Biberman wrote to Paul Jarrico to solicit his help raising funds among the exile community for their suit against the Motion Picture Association of America regarding its efforts to thwart the release of *Salt of the Earth* (dir. Herbert Biberman, 1954) ten years earlier.[57] He described meeting Joseph Losey at *The Servant*'s New York opening.

> [Losey] knew nothing of our efforts really. Only some general information. I found him still alive, concerned and desirous of talking to whomever he could properly address on the subject of the case's need for money. We spoke of Jules Dassin. I stated my utter inability to understand how this man could fail to interest himself to the extent of a decent sum of money for this case. Remembering your great closeness to him, I wonder if you still see him. I am unable to believe that Carl Forman [*sic*] would not wish to associate himself to the extent of a decent cash boost for our needs. I cannot believe that Ben Barzman would not wish to do something in this direction. . . . I find that the case is so remote to people that it takes time for them to warm to it. The lackadaisical attitude of most of our friends . . . is shocking. There seems to be some kind of relationship between the former aliveness and present imperviousness to sensation. So be it. The world will stop for no one's self-declared disinterest.[58]

Jarrico's response is indicative of the tensions within the exile community that were contributing to Biberman's fund-raising difficulties. Rather than concur with Biberman's observations or suggest ways to revive concern about the blacklist among the émigrés, Jarrico focused on his personal grievances:

> Looking back over your earlier letter and trying to analyze what it was that angered me so, I think it was the following sentence that made my hackles rise: 'I undertook to write to you, knowing from what I hear that you are not in any position or condition to do anything about this yourself, because I saw Joe Losey yesterday.' Aside from running into him briefly in [producer Max] Youngstein's hotel suite a year or so ago, I haven't seen Losey in years. I've accumulated, nevertheless, considerable resentment of the man, for reasons too complicated to recount at the moment,

> and the thought that he was retailing to my friends in New York the latest estimates of my position or condition made me boil. The more so since the estimates are so clearly damaging. I don't mind your knowing, or other close friends' knowing that on the chart of economic ups and downs that have marked my life I'm currently down. But if people like Losey are saying it (people who can't possibly know except on the basis of industry 'talk'), I'm in worse trouble than I thought.[59]

Jarrico's manifest insecurities are indicative of the extent to which professional rivalries had come to supplant the sense of loyalty that the experience of the blacklist had initially fostered among the exiles.[60] The competitive professional environment of European cinema in the 1960s accentuated the differences between those in positions of power or influence and their less successful friends. In 1962, at a moment when the imbalance in their professional fortunes was acute, Carl Foreman withdrew his support for *The Horizontal Man*, a project Joseph Losey had long hoped to direct. Losey ended his friendship with Foreman as a result.[61] And when Adrian Scott refused to use his position at MGM Britain to pull in a favor for a down-on-his-luck Paul Jarrico, mutual friends among the blacklisted took sides.[62]

Despite these patent tensions, those who resisted the blacklist remained bound through—if nothing else—their moral conduct and undiminished sense of outrage. Jules Dassin explained the enduring nature of the exiles' ties: "Many of them changed their political ideas, many became disillusioned, many were angry about the way things turned out—particularly about the Soviet Union, which they had set great store by, had such hopes for, hopes that were frustrated, defeated, and betrayed. But what held and holds them together is that they behaved well. And they respect each other for it, whatever differences there may be among them."[63] Implicit in Dassin's comments is his opinion of those who *didn't* behave well. Unlike the radicals who remained in Hollywood, the exiles were for the most part spared the pain of regular contact with former friends turned informers, and thus the feelings of "disconnectedness, alienation, depression, and further loss of a sense of community" that often accompanied the loss of friendship.[64] When encounters with informers did occur, the exiles were not shy about making their feelings known. In his unpublished autobiography, Lewis Milestone remembers walking through Paris with Robert Rossen, who had testified before the committee in 1953, and bumping into Jules Dassin. When Rossen offered his hand, Dassin exploded: "You must be kidding. I wouldn't shake hands with you if my life depended on it." Discussing the incident later, Dassin defended his actions to Milestone, naming one of his fellow exiles as a counterexample. "'So many people we know fought for their principles . . .' he said. 'Who, for instance?' [Milestone] asked. 'Well,' he said, 'men like Carl Foreman. I know he would never do that.'"[65]

Nor did these feelings diminish with the passage of time. Joan LaCour Scott recalls that, while living in London in the early 1960s, she and her husband Adrian attended a party where an informer figured among the guests. Rather than risk an encounter, they departed immediately. And when Joseph Losey learned that Elia Kazan—who named names in his testimony before HUAC in 1952—was in the audience for *The Servant*'s Paris premiere, he abandoned the screening for a meal at Fouquet's that he ate still "shaking with rage," according to Dirk Bogarde, whom he had brought along for company.[66] Michael Wilson stated his position bluntly: "I'm not one who says, Let bygones be bygones. I don't defend my attitude in terms of principle. It's just a visceral reaction, that's all. I just don't like the fuckers. Socially, I don't acknowledge their existence. I wouldn't say hello. I have good friends who don't do that—and that's their right. It's simply not my attitude."[67] Perhaps because he was also a member of their expatriate community, Cy Endfield was one of the few informers for whom the exiles made an exception; as Endfield's friend Paul Jarrico explained, "We pretend it (the informing) never happened."[68]

Nonetheless, most of the exiles ultimately made their personal peace with the blacklist and the unexpected direction it gave to their lives. As Michael Wilson eventually observed: "Many of us grew during that period rather than withered. It tested our mettle; we came out the better for it. We attained a more abiding and profound humanism, a greater compassion, and a philosophical perspective on our own lots, which could certainly have been much worse. Compared to political refugees in other lands we had it relatively easy."[69] The exiles' sense of indignation at the injustice of the blacklist as a historical fact nevertheless remained undiminished and continued to unite them. Paul Jarrico devoted his later years to the mission of restoring screen credits to blacklisted writers. Thanks to his efforts, by July 2000, the Writer's Guild of America had designated almost 100 films from the blacklist period for credit changes.[70] And in 1999, Norma Barzman, Bernard Gordon, and other members of the blacklisted in Los Angeles rallied together to protest the Academy's decision to award Kazan an honorary Oscar. In their refusal to let the blacklist be forgotten, the survivors honored the memory of those who suffered on its account.[71]

CONCLUSION

> Back in this ghost town called Paris where there doesn't seem to be anyone left whom I know. But there are reminders of you, little mementoes which recall that once you were here too, in this very apartment.
>
> —Lee Gold

LEE GOLD'S ELEGIAC TONE in this letter to Paul Jarrico from September 1964 gives a sense of the losses their formerly "tight little Paris colony" had suffered in the preceding years.[1] The Wilsons had decamped to Ojai, California, that summer; the Barzmans were living full-time in Provence; John Berry had spent much of the year in New York directing for stage and television; and Jules Dassin was on the road promoting his latest film, *Topkapi.* Two years earlier, Jarrico had left the Paris group, convinced that the booming British film industry would offer better professional opportunities for an Anglophone screenwriter. Betsy Blair had also crossed the Channel, moving to London in 1963 when she married the English Czech director Karel Reisz.[2]

Nor was the London community intact. Hannah Weinstein's Sapphire Productions had ceased operations abruptly in the winter of 1961 as a result of financial mismanagement on the part of Weinstein's husband, Jonathan Fisher. Joseph Losey offered this description of her situation in a letter to their mutual friend, Vladimir Pozner:

> Her empire has collapsed totally, apparently through the mistakes (not to give them an uglier name) of Jonathan. He had apparently disappeared from the house and was finally discovered in Edinburgh; though I don't know the details, I gather that he has still not regained consciousness. Meantime, the studio has been taken over by receivers, as was also her house, her cars, and apparently everything. They are keeping it as quiet as possible, and she is in Edinburgh so I have not yet spoken to her. The children are being wonderful, and are being taken care of, so I think there is really nothing anyone can do at this moment excepting to hope that something will be rescued for her.[3]

Shortly thereafter, Weinstein returned to New York, where she eventually reestablished herself as a film producer; her first credit was for *Claudine* (1974), directed by her old friend John Berry and nominated for an Academy Award.

Those who remained in London were separated by the ever-widening gulf left by their diverging professional and personal paths. For some, the lingering influence of the blacklist along with a thriving (and thus competitive) British film industry posed frequent roadblocks to success. "Everything seemed to fall through," remembers Adrian Scott's widow, Joan LaCour Scott. "A film that was supposed to star Warren Beatty and have Joseph Losey as a director didn't happen. Adrian wasn't credited for films he did writing on, *Night Must Fall* (dir. Karel Reisz, 1964) among others."[4] During his five years in England, the screenwriter Lester Cole saw only one commercial project come to fruition: *Born Free* (dir. James Hill, 1966), produced by Columbia through the auspices of Carl Foreman, who intervened when the studio balked at Cole's blacklisted status.[5] Other exiles, however, were rapidly becoming film industry fixtures. In 1965, Carl Foreman was appointed to the British Film Institute's Board of Governors. Five years later, he was made a CBE to honor his contributions to the British film industry. Joseph Losey was likewise a VIP in England as a result of the success of *The Servant* (1963), which he followed with a string of films, most notably *King and Country* (1964), *Accident* (1967), and *The Go-Between* (1970), in which his sensitive dissection of the British class system and its mores secured his reputation as being "more English than the Brits."[6]

With its members either dispersed to the winds or immersed in their European careers, by the mid-1960s the blacklisted exile community had ceased to function as such. However, the experience of the blacklist and exile created lasting bonds among the émigrés. Denis Berry recalls the importance his father placed on attending the Los Angeles premiere of Jules Dassin's *A Dream of Passion* in 1978.[7] When Paul Jarrico died in 1997, Berry wrote his eulogy, which Norma Barzman read at the funeral in California. Joseph Losey maintained a close correspondence with the Barzmans in his later years and visited them in Los Angeles a number of times in the early 1980s. Whereas HUAC succeeded in fracturing the radical community in Hollywood, exile gave the blacklisted the opportunity to extend the sense of being part of a meaningful shared experience, political or otherwise.

In concluding, I wish to explore the effect of exile on the artistic identity and creative output of the émigrés. Did they see their European sojourn as conducive or detrimental to their development as filmmakers? To what degree did they define themselves through the experience of blacklist and exile? Many of the exiles harbored the strong desire to return to Hollywood, at least in a professional if not permanent capacity, and to be recognized as "American" filmmakers.

To their immense frustration, exile had stripped them of their nationality. Jules Dassin squarely rejected the "cosmopolitan" label so often attached to him, countering that his experience making *Up Tight!* (1968), his first American film since *Thieves' Highway* (1949), confirmed to him that "I am just . . . deeply American."[8] And in an interview given four years before his death in 1984, Joseph Losey articulated the confusion his expatriate career had created. "I am an American. . . . But I didn't say I was an American director. . . . The French now think I'm English. A lot of the English think I'm English. The Italians think I'm French."[9] The distinction Losey made between his nationality and identity as a filmmaker suggests how the blacklisted exiles continued to define themselves in terms of national cinema even as their European careers spoke to cinema's increasingly transnational future.

The Inheritance of Exile

For the blacklisted, exile evoked the experiences of the European émigré filmmakers they had known in Hollywood during the 1930s and early 1940s. How was it possible that they found themselves uprooted from a country that had so recently provided others with a political haven? Their sense of disbelief created a reluctance to embrace an exilic identity. Paul Jarrico said they did not use the word "exile" to describe themselves, and Norma Barzman recalled her astonishment when Pablo Picasso pronounced her and her husband Ben to be "exiles who don't yet know they're exiles."[10] For John Berry, the notion of "exile" emphasized victimhood as opposed to volition. "I made a choice," he explained. "A victim doesn't have one. I wasn't exiled, I chose exile."[11]

Of the exiles, John Berry was perhaps ultimately the most comfortable embracing a hybrid American European identity, both personally and as a filmmaker. Whereas Joseph Losey spoke of "being an alien everywhere" and Jules Dassin made Greece his permanent home, both repeatedly asserted their identities as Americans.[12] Berry, on the other hand, called himself a "European American." In a radio interview given two years before his death in 1999, he articulated his feelings about his bi-cultural identity:

> I came to France and I stayed here for many years because I couldn't work in my profession in the U.S. I can't say I'm proud of having chosen not to stay, but I couldn't. In any case, what effect does this have? It creates two cultures, two sets of roots, because now I have fairly deep roots in France. My wife Myriam Boyer, my young son with her. So you see, I'm always between the two countries, so to have a big success in the U.S. really made me feel great. I'm always between the two cultures, between America which is the culture of my roots, of my youth, and French culture, which has stolen my heart as well.[13]

Berry believed that his approach to filmmaking reflects his dual perspective. "With *Claudine*," he added, "I set up certain scenes the way I did because of the work I had done in France, because of that influence."[14]

Most of Berry's blacklisted cohort found the experience of exile profoundly disruptive on a creative level. Speaking to an American reporter in 1971, Jules Dassin offered a dispiriting assessment of his career and the difficulties of working in a cultural context not his own. "I had to pretend, and I still am pretending, that I identify with European culture. I've done films in Greece, in France, in Italy and so on, about subjects of those countries. They're not mine, and I'm being ersatz about it, and I know it. . . . I should be making films about Harlem, about things and places I know. My problem is that of an artist separated from his sources. I'd have been a better film director had I been able to continue my work in the United States."[15] Ben Barzman likewise found the challenges of working in a foreign cultural context emotionally stressful. "The feelings of exclusion, alienation, and uprootedness never really left me," he told Larry Ceplair shortly after his return to Hollywood in the late 1970s. "As a writer, I felt circumscribed, a writer needs to be steeped in the mainstream of the culture he is writing about. I did not feel I was part of the French community."[16] Carl Foreman considered that his work "suffered tremendously" as a result of the blacklist and exile.[17] "I know nobody who wasn't bumped hard, who didn't develop such a trauma, who wasn't affected," he explained. "All the writers wrote very badly, without exception."[18] Losey described the debilitating effect of exile, which caused him to lose his creative stride between 1949 and 1959. "We were working under terrible conditions. Working anonymously, with no salary, exploited, under constant pressure about passports, pressure about everything, you were cut off from your family, you were under suspicion even from some of your friends. . . . A lot of people were destroyed."[19]

Dassin, Barzman, Foreman, and Losey were among the lucky ones, as they readily acknowledged. Unlike some of their blacklisted friends, they were able to continue their careers. Bernard Vorhaus, for instance, never stopped regretting being forced to abandon his filmmaking career just as he was learning his strengths and limitations as a director.[20]

But what of the creative benefits of exile? The flipside of being separated from one's roots is the not inconsiderable gift of fresh vision and heightened powers of observation. Responding to comments that his *Voyage à Paimpol* (1985) succeeded as a film *à la française*, Berry suggested that, as a foreigner, his eye for *la vie française* was more acute. "If you are a Parisian and have lived your life in Paris, you appreciate its beauty less than a stranger does."[21] Joseph Losey, whose exilic perspective was fundamental to his European successes, saw the advantages enjoyed by a Hollywood-trained filmmaker in Europe as twofold: "An American making English-language films in Europe not only possesses the energy and

Bernard Vorhaus and John Berry, c. 1989, at the Cinémathèque française (Cinémathèque française – Iconothèque)

technical expertise conferred by his Hollywood heritage, but also a fresh eye with which to evaluate the benefits and disadvantages of the English or Continental approach to both life and filmmaking respectively."[22]

Losey's comments indicate another major challenge that the blacklisted in Europe faced; in addition to working in a foreign cultural context, they had to adapt to a European mode of film production that differed in significant ways from their Hollywood experience. John Berry recalled these differences in a 1988 interview: "The French approach to developing and directing a film was completely different. In France, the director was considered an auteur, which wasn't the case in the U.S. I found myself completely involved in all aspects of the production, from coming up with the story to selecting the posters. As we well know, in the U.S., the director is usually treated like a technician. Once the shoot is over, he has only a limited impact on the editing, the music, and all other aspects of post-production."[23] While the exiles relished the more relaxed European mode of production, the relative autonomy it offered was not always creatively productive.[24] Berry's son, Denis, a film and television director who has worked in both France and America, believes that the culture of production his father encountered in France was detrimental to his career: "[In France] you were expected to select your own creative team, to have a clear vision for all aspects of the film. In Hollywood, this was all done for you. The team was there, they were well trained and expected to give the director more input. This is why people like my father and Dassin were lost in Europe. They weren't able to adapt and their work suffered for it."[25]

Transatlantic Waves

Did the European exile of the blacklisted really deprive Hollywood of a social cinema tradition, as Paul Buhle and David Wagner have proposed?[26] At a press conference for the New York premiere of *Accident* in 1967, Joseph Losey suggested that the blacklist must have had a negative impact on Hollywood because of what it indicated about the state of America. "I hope and flatter myself and my colleagues and associates that it was a loss to the American film industry and to the whole culture," he stated. "Because you can't have anything of this sort without a stultification of the whole nation."[27] And in a letter to Paul Jarrico written from the vantage point of April 1970, Michael Wilson used the recent successes of a number of formerly blacklisted screenwriters to refute the notion that the blacklisted were generally untalented and their absence therefore no loss to Hollywood. "Remember the days when our enemies, grumbling about public concern over the blacklist, asserted it was much ado about nothing?" he asked, while noting that "it's been a good period for some of our friends." "Ring's (Lardner) M*A*S*H* is a S*M*A*S*H*. Waldo (Salt) won both the Writers Guild and Academy Awards for MIDNIGHT COWBOY. Trumbo won the Guild LAUREL Award. . . . He is about to produce and direct JOHNNY GOT HIS GUN on a six-hundred thousand dollar budget raised from sources outside the industry. . . . Abe's (Polonsky) picture [*Tell Them Willie Boy is Here*] got great notices."[28] But although the blacklist certainly deprived Hollywood of the talents of many gifted individuals, it did not drive the production of socially conscious films to a complete halt. As Denise Mann observes, "The late 1940s and 1950s managed to generate a remarkable collection of creative and progressive Hollywood films, often with the full cooperation of the studios"—a paradox she explains in terms of the rise of the "package" system and the new power wielded by independent producers and agents in postwar Hollywood.[29]

Perhaps the more salient question concerns the effect of the blacklist on the development of European cinema during the postwar years. Buhle and Wagner make the grandest claim in this regard, suggesting that in their integration of American and European generic and stylistic traditions, a number of the exiles' films from the 1950s provided the "political and aesthetic rock" on which "the short-lived church of the French New Wave was built."[30] Yet as we have seen, the critic-filmmakers whose films would launch the New Wave at the decade's close had a complex relationship with the American exiles, their admiration for

Losey equaled by their disdain for the "Europeanized" Dassin. Also, although the influence of the "Young Turks" over the development of French critical discourse proved profound, in the early 1950s theirs was just one voice among many. *Cahiers du cinéma* had a circulation of only 4,000 in 1954, the year Truffaut published his *tradition de qualité* manifesto.[31] During the course of the decade, France continued to produce the period films and literary adaptations that Truffaut railed against as well as another traditional (if hybrid) genre of French cinema: the French film noir.

Appropriately, in view of the complex relationship between French and American cinema manifested in film noir, it was here that the Paris-based blacklisted directors made their mark on postwar French cinema.[32] As discussed in chapter 4, the early 1950s saw a spate of French films that caricatured the American noirs that had flooded French screens in the aftermath of World War II. While John Berry's *Ça va barder* and *Je suis un sentimental* were clearly in this vein, they were seen as superior examples and influenced the development of French noir by establishing the parody as a profitable sub-genre.[33] Jules Dassin's contribution to French film noir was of a different nature. Rather than use his Hollywood know-how to make superlative spoofs of American films, Dassin expressed his admiration for Italian neorealism and documentary aesthetics through his lyrical depiction of Paris's grandeur and grit. Along with Jacques Becker's *Touchez pas au grisbi* (1954) and Jean-Pierre Melville's *Bob le Flambeur* (1956), *Rififi* represents a continuation of the prewar tradition established in films such as *La Nuit du Carrefour* (dir. Jean Renoir, 1932), *Pépé le Moko* (dir. Julien Duvivier, 1937), and *Le Dernier Tournant* (dir. Pierre Chenal, 1939). Compared with their American counterparts, these films placed greater emphasis on the milieu of the French underworld than on the nature of crime itself.[34] In its sympathetic depiction of a band of domesticated gangsters, *Rififi* helped to (re)establish the French film noir as an *étude de moeurs.* And while its success spawned numerous lesser imitations,[35] *Rififi* also proved an inspiration to French filmmakers of the caliber of Jean-Pierre Melville, who paid homage to the film's celebrated silent robbery sequence in *Le Cercle Rouge* (1970).[36]

In Britain, Joseph Losey played a key role (along with two other foreign directors, Michelangelo Antonioni and Roman Polanski) in transforming British cinema through the incorporation of art cinema practices. Dirk Bogarde called attention to the significance of Losey's achievements in a 1970 interview: "I've never said this before, because it sounds so pompous. But I will say it now. When Joe Losey and I made those terribly important films which no British companies wanted to touch, we were doing it for Britain. We honestly wanted to make British cinema important, to lift it out of the domestic rut. And I think we did."[37] In terms of its effect on the next generation of filmmakers, Losey's work was perhaps even more influential in France, where he first achieved his cult status.

Bertrand Tavernier's admiration for *Time Without Pity* was such that he felt compelled to write about it and submitted his first two film reviews to *Cinéma* and *Positif*. The film would later provide the inspiration for his directorial début, *L'Horloger de Saint-Paul* (1974), which also explored the relationship between a father and son who had been accused of murder.[38]

Much as Losey raised the artistic profile of British cinema through his highly individual vision, Carl Foreman contributed to its reputation for high-quality commercial entertainment. His long-standing relationship with Columbia, which provided his company with production financing and distribution, ensured that Foreman's work as a writer and producer would target the growing international market. With their international casts and exotic foreign locations, films such as *The Guns of Navarone* (1961) and *The Victors* (1963) epitomized the blockbuster formula. At the same time, the British bent of other projects such as *The Key* (1958), a romance set in World War II England, and *Young Winston* (1972), about the early life of Winston Churchill, reflected Foreman's engagement with his adopted home. Foreman credited the presence of the Americans (blacklisted or otherwise) in London with the dramatic expansion of the number of "topflight" British directors during the 1950s. He contended that, by 1958, Ken Annakin, Phil Leacock, Alexander Mackendrick, and J. Lee Thompson had joined the ranks of David Lean and Carol Reed as British directors with "international" reputations. In his opinion, the experience many of these directors had gained working with the American exiles had been "a dynamic factor" in achieving their new, international stature.[39]

Foreman's comments touch upon what was perhaps the exiles' most significant contribution to postwar European cinema. As Hollywood-trained, European-based professionals, they critically and materially facilitated the transatlantic economic and artistic exchange that had become a fundamental component of American and European film culture by the mid-1960s. During their years in Europe, they worked on low-budget, black-market projects for American producers, on big-budget, high-profile films for a coterie of cosmopolitan producers (de Laurentiis, Spiegel et al.), as well as on European co-productions and smaller, domestically financed films—a range of projects that covered the gamut of postwar European film production. While the blockbusters of de Laurentiis and Spiegel aimed to compete with Hollywood for the international mass audience, this audience was increasingly inclined to see European cinema—and especially the European art film—as an attraction in and of itself.

Initially, the allure the blacklisted held for European producers was premised on the notion that some of their Hollywood magic would rub off and thereby improve a film's chances of attracting the notoriously insular and provincial American audience. But with Hollywood's economic decline and the surge in runaway production, Americans became accustomed to seeing European locations onscreen and to watching narratives that dramatized these foreign locales. In this sense, by implementing the blacklist, Hollywood created the space filled by the international blockbuster, which combined the familiar (the action genre, Hollywood stars) with the unfamiliar (exotic locations, foreign stars). The rise of the European art film—aided in no small part by the increased prominence of the film festival circuit—further contributed to the decentering of production away from Hollywood and the erosion of the traditional boundaries of national cinema. By 1967, Robert Favre Le Bret, president of the Cannes Film Festival, would note that "it has become harder and harder to determine the nationality of films."[40] On a trip to Hollywood that same year, Carl Foreman told the *Los Angeles Times:* "Now I'm returning as something of a conquering hero, bringing work to the Hollywood movie industry which has lost so many jobs to overseas productions."[41]

This concatenation of industry and cultural changes fundamentally altered the dynamic between Hollywood and Europe's national cinemas. The blacklisted exiles were uniquely positioned, if not forced by circumstance, to take advantage of the opportunities created by these developments for European film production. And as American expatriates whose transnational perspective can be attributed to a combination of political orientation and personal experience, the blacklisted in Europe contributed not to the Americanization, but to the globalization, of postwar film culture. As such, they functioned as gadflies in the cultural politics of the Cold War: while their filmmaking, bound as it was by industrial practicalities, may not have constituted a fully oppositional film culture per se, their presence in Europe, box office success, and social consciousness reflected in some of their films challenged America's image as a haven for freedom of expression. Likewise, the influence of their European careers on the blacklist's demise reflects the shifting balance of power between Hollywood and European cinema at the beginning of the 1960s.

Asked to evaluate the "radical changes taking place in the field of cinema" for a special issue of *Positif* published in 1964, Losey responded unequivocally: "The future belongs to international filmmakers . . . who use their freedom to work all over the world—in Italy, England, France, Russia—who communicate with a global audience, not easily, but intensely, and to a much greater degree than was ever before possible." Losey, at least in this instance, viewed his exile positively, in that it allowed him to be part of cinema's future. "I don't belong to any country and I feel at home everywhere," he explained, adding: "One of the cinema's essential functions should be to demolish national boundaries and cross-pollinate the world."[42] The transnational cultural production of the blacklisted exiles in Europe made significant strides in accomplishing this goal.

NOTES

INTRODUCTION

1. Brian Neve addresses the experiences of the blacklisted in Europe, both in his book *Film and Politics in America: A Social Tradition* (New York: Routledge, 1992) and his recent article "Cases in European Film Culture and the Hollywood Blacklist Diaspora," in *The Lost Decade? The 1950s in European History, Politics, Society, and Culture*, ed. Heiko Feldner, Claire Gorrara, and Kevin Passmore (Newcastle: Cambridge Scholars Publishing, 2011). Neither publication, however, is intended as a comprehensive analysis of the blacklisted diaspora's history and accomplishments. The most extensive study of the Hollywood blacklist, Larry Ceplair and Steven Englund's magisterial *The Inquisition in Hollywood: Politics in the Film Community 1930–1960* (Urbana: University of Illinois Press, 2003), addresses the émigrés briefly. Similarly, the experiences of the exiles crop up only occasionally in *Naming Names*, 3rd ed. (New York: Hill and Wang, 2003), Victor Navasky's psychologically oriented investigation of the period. One of the only secondary sources on the activities of the émigrés is Paul Buhle and Dave Wagner's *Hide in Plain Sight: The Hollywood Blacklistees in Film and Television, 1950–2002* (New York: Palgrave Macmillan, 2003), but its comprehensive focus on the creative work of the blacklisted means that its discussion of the European exiles is limited.

More recent publications relating to the Hollywood blacklist include Brian Neve, *The Many Lives of Cy Endfield* (Madison: University of Wisconsin Press, 2013); Steven J. Ross, *Hollywood Left and Right: How Movie Stars Shaped American Politics* (New York: Oxford University Press, 2011); Reynold Humphries's *Hollywood's Blacklists: A Political and Cultural History* (Edinburgh: Edinburgh University Press, 2010); Joseph Litvak's *The Un-Americans: Jews, the Blacklist, and Stoolpigeon Culture* (Durham, N.C.: Duke University Press, 2009); Jennifer Langdon's *Caught in the Crossfire: Adrian Scott and the Politics of Americanism* (New York: Columbia University Press, 2008); Larry Ceplair's *The Marxist and the Movies: A Biography of Paul Jarrico* (Lexington: University Press of Kentucky, 2007); Gerald Horne's *The Final Victim of the Blacklist: John Howard Lawson, Dean of the Hollywood Ten* (Berkeley: University of California Press, 2006); Ronald Radosh and Allis Radosh's *Red Star Over Hollywood: The Film Colony's Long Romance with the Left* (San Francisco: Encounter Books, 2005); and Mona Z. Smith's *Becoming Something: The Story of Canada Lee* (New York: Faber and Faber, 2004).

2. One notable exception to the dearth of scholarly literature on the international ramifications of the Hollywood blacklist is Rebecca Schreiber's *Cold War Exiles in Mexico: U.S. Dissidents and the Culture of Critical Resistance* (Minneapolis: University of Minnesota Press, 2008), which includes a thorough and insightful analysis of the community of blacklisted writers, artists, and filmmakers who gathered in Mexico during the 1950s and their transnational cultural production.

3. Two recent dissertations address the shortage of historical studies of runaway production: Daniel Steinhart's "Hollywood Overseas: The Internationalization of Production and Location Shooting in the Postwar Era" (Ph.D. diss., University of California, Los Angeles) and Camille K. Yale's "Runaway Production: A Critical History of Hollywood's Outsourcing

Discourse" (Ph.D. diss., University of Illinois, 2011). *Contracting Out Hollywood: Runaway Productions and Foreign Location Shootings*, ed. Greg Elmer and Mike Gasher (Lanham, Md.: Rowman and Littlefield, 2005), examines contemporary runaway production. Robert Shandley's *Runaway Romances: Hollywood's Postwar Tour of Europe* (Philadelphia: Temple University Press, 2009) explores Hollywood's European productions of the 1950s and 1960s, but focuses more on the content of the films produced than the industrial circumstances of their production.

With regard to Cold War film studies, Tony Shaw has published a number of books examining Cold War film propaganda. See (with Denise J. Youngblood) *Cinematic Cold War: The American and Soviet Struggle for Hearts and Minds* (Lawrence: University Press of Kansas, 2010); *Hollywood's Cold War* (Edinburgh: Edinburgh University Press, 2007); and *British Cinema and the Cold War: The State, Propaganda, and Consensus* (London: I. B. Tauris, 2006). Nora Sayre's *Running Time: Films of the Cold War* (New York: Doubleday, 1982) and J. Hoberman's *An Army of Phantoms: American Movies and the Making of the Cold War* (New York: The New Press 2012) both offer numerous examples of anticommunism in Hollywood films of the 1950s. Vanessa R. Schwartz makes the important point that studies of Cold War culture need to move beyond the emphasis on the "centrality of propaganda about the 'American way of life' to establishing its even more complex achievement: the globalization of capitalist culture, the century's greatest weapon against Communism." See *It's So French!: Hollywood, Paris, and the Making of Cosmopolitan Film Culture* (Chicago: University of Chicago Press, 2007), 10.

4. The records of the House Un-American Activities Committee, housed at the National Archives in Washington, were declassified in 2001. The papers of Paul Jarrico became available at the Academy of Motion Picture Arts and Sciences in June 2007.

5. See Stephanie Barron, ed., *Exiles and Emigrés: The Flight of European Artists from Hitler* (New York: Harry Abrams, 1997); John Baxter, *The Hollywood Exiles* (New York: Taplinger Publishing Co., 1976); Thomas Elsaesser, "Ethnicity, Authenticity, and Exile: A Counterfeit Trade? German Filmmakers and Hollywood," in *Home, Exile, Homeland: Film, Media, and the Politics of Place*, ed. Hamid Naficy (New York: Routledge, 1999); Anthony Heilbut, *Exiled in Paradise: German Refugee Artists and Intellectuals in America from the 1930s to the Present* (Berkeley: University of California Press, 1997); Jan-Christopher Horak, "German Exile Cinema, 1933–1950," *Film History* 8 (1996): 373–389; Gene D. Phillips, *Exiles in Hollywood: Major European Film Directors in America* (Bethlehem, Pa.: Lehigh University Press, 1998); and John Russell Taylor, *Strangers in Paradise: The Hollywood Emigrés 1933–1950* (London: Faber and Faber, 1983).

6. For a thorough accounting of the CIA's manipulation of the cultural sphere to promote its political agenda in Europe during the Cold War, see Frances Stoner Saunders, *The Cultural Cold War: The CIA and the World of Arts and Letters* (New York: New Press, 1999).

7. Richard Maltby, "Made for Each Other: The Melodrama of Hollywood and the House Committee on Un-American Activities, 1947," in *Cinema, Politics, and Society in America*, ed. Philip Davies and Brian Neve (Manchester: Manchester University Press, 1981), 76.

8. Two recent publications successfully challenge this perception of postwar European-American cultural relations. In *It's So French!*, Vanessa Schwartz suggests that the changes occurring in postwar Franco-American film culture are better characterized by notions of cultural hybridity than cultural hegemony. In *Beyond the Subtitle: Remapping European Art Cinema* (Minneapolis: University of Minnesota Press, 2009), Mark Betz argues that European art films (many of which were European co-productions) need to be understood not just as a reaction to Hollywood, but as a distinctly European phenomenon in keeping with the cross-cultural initiatives of the nascent European Economic Community (EEC).

9. Catherine Gallagher and Steven Greenblatt, *Practicing New Historicism* (Chicago: University of Chicago Press, 2000), 67.
10. In "Red Hollywood," his influential 1985 essay on the historiography of the Hollywood blacklist, Thom Andersen reviews the major scholarly histories of the blacklist and how they have subsequently influenced our understanding of this historical phenomenon. The essay appears, along with an afterword, also by Andersen, in *"Un-American" Hollywood: Politics and Film in the Blacklist Era*, ed. Frank Krutnik, Steve Neale, Brian Neve, and Peter Stanfield (New Brunswick, N.J.: Rutgers University Press, 2007).
11. Norma Barzman, *The Red and the Blacklist: The Intimate Memoir of a Hollywood Expatriate* (New York: Thunder's Mouth Press/Nation Books, 2003); Betsy Blair, *The Memory of All That: Love and Politics in New York, Hollywood, and Paris* (New York: Knopf, 2003); Lester Cole, *Hollywood Red: The Autobiography of Lester Cole* (Palo Alto, Calif.: Ramparts Press, 1981); Bernard Gordon, *Hollywood Exile: Or How I Learned to Love the Blacklist* (Austin: University of Texas Press, 1999); Mickey Knox, *The Good, the Bad, and the Dolce Vita: The Adventures of an Actor in Hollywood, Paris, and Rome* (New York: Nation Books, 2004); Howard Koch, *As Time Goes By: Memoirs of a Writer* (New York: Harcourt Brace Jovanovich, 1979); Jean Rouverol, *Refugees from Hollywood: A Journal of the Blacklist Years* (Albuquerque: University of New Mexico Press, 2000); Donald Ogden Stewart, *By a Stroke of Luck! An Autobiography* (New York: Paddington Press, 1975); and Bernard Vorhaus, *Saved from Oblivion: An Autobiography* (Lanham, Md.: Scarecrow Press, 2000). Patrick McGilligan and Paul Buhle's *Tender Comrades: A Backstory of the Hollywood Blacklist* (New York: St. Martin's, 1997) includes interviews with Norma and Ben Barzman, Leonardo Bercovici, John Berry, Jules Dassin, Bernard Gordon, Julian Halevy Zimet, Paul Jarrico, Mickey Knox, Joan LaCour Scott and Adrian Scott, as well as with the actress Betsy Blair, the screenwriter Frank Tarloff, and the director Bernard Vorhaus; Bertrand Tavernier's *Amis Américains: entretiens avec les grands auteurs d'Hollywood* (Lyons: Institut Lumière: Actes Sud, 1993) includes John Berry, Sidney Buchman, Carl Foreman, Julian Halevy Zimet, and Joseph Losey.
12. Schreiber, *Cold War Exiles*, xii.
13. In addition to Schwartz, *It's So French!*, and Betz, *Beyond the Subtitle*, see Dudley Andrew and Hervé Joubert-Laurencin, eds., *Opening Bazin: Postwar Film Theory and Its Afterlife* (Oxford: Oxford University Press, 2011); Janet Bergstrom, "Genealogy of *The Golden Coach*," *Film History: An International Journal* 21, no. 3 (2009); and Saverio Giovacchini and Robert Sklar, eds., *Global Neorealism: The Transnational History of a Film Style* (Jackson: University Press of Mississippi, 2012).
14. Koch was not technically "blacklisted" but "graylisted." However, he experienced the same work restrictions as his blacklisted friends and was an important figure in the blacklisted community in London from 1952 to 1956.
15. The epics produced by Bronston include *King of Kings* (dir. Nicholas Ray, 1961), *El Cid* (dir. Anthony Mann, 1961), and *The Fall of the Roman Empire* (dir. Anthony Mann, 1964).
16. Andersen, "Red Hollywood," 257.
17. Ceplair and Englund note that this period is frequently (and erroneously) referred to as the McCarthy Era, after the notorious red-baiting senator from Wisconsin. McCarthy, however, focused his communist investigations on the U.S. government, not Hollywood. In the authors' opinion, "'McCarthyism' should refer only to a political style composed of bullying, intimidation, thuggery, and undocumented accusations. It should not designate a historical era." See Ceplair and Englund, *The Inquisition in Hollywood*, xv.
18. Edward Said offers these distinctions between exiles, refugees, expatriates, and émigrés:

> Exile originated in the age-old practice of banishment. Once banished, the exile lives an anomalous and miserable life, with the stigma of being an outsider. Refugees, on

> the other hand, are a creation of the twentieth-century state. The word 'refugee' has become a political one, suggesting large herds of innocent and bewildered people requiring urgent international assistance, whereas 'exile' carries with it, I think, a touch of solitude and spirituality.
>
> Expatriates voluntarily live in an alien country, usually for personal or social reasons. Hemingway and Fitzgerald were not forced to live in France. Expatriates may share in the solitude and estrangement of exile, but they do not suffer under its rigid proscriptions. Emigré enjoys an ambiguous status. Technically, an émigré is anyone who emigrates to a new country.

See Edward Said, *Reflections on Exile and Other Essays* (Cambridge, Mass.: Harvard University Press, 2000), 181.

19. See Barzman, *The Red and the Blacklist;* and Blair, *The Memory of All That.*

20. Vanessa Schwartz notes that the term "Atlantic world" is often used to refer to Euro-American relations, especially as pertaining to commerce and culture, in the early modern period, but that a number of recent studies have demonstrated how twentieth-century postwar history also benefits from a more "Atlanticist framework" highlighting the complex interactions between culture, economics, and politics that shaped relations between America and Europe during the Cold War. See Schwartz, *It's So French!*, 7–8.

21. See Jon Lewis, "We Do Not Ask You to Condone This: How the Blacklist Saved Hollywood," *Cinema Journal* 39, no. 2 (Winter 2000).

CHAPTER 1: THE RADICAL COMMUNITY IN HOLLYWOOD

1. The California Department of Employment estimates that 33,400 individuals were employed as wage and salary workers in motion picture production and distribution in California in 1946. This figure includes administrative, supervisory, sales, technical, and office personnel, as well as production and related workers, but does not take into account freelance or temporary employment. See Irving Bernstein, *Hollywood at the Crossroads: An Economic Study of the Motion Picture Industry* (Hollywood: Hollywood A.F. of L. Film Council, 1957), 35. Larry Ceplair and Steven Englund estimate that the total population of the film community, including extras, fluctuated between 50,000 and 60,000 people during the 1930s, which suggests that the figure quoted by the California Department of Employment is conservative on account of not including freelance workers. See Larry Ceplair and Steven Englund, *The Inquisition in Hollywood: Politics in the Film Community 1930–1960* (Urbana: University of Illinois Press, 2003), 125.

2. Because the Communist Party was underground in Hollywood, branch meetings had to masquerade as cocktail parties, so that members would be found with a glass in hand in case a nonmember walked in. See Nancy Lynn Schwartz, *The Hollywood Writers' Wars* (New York: Alfred A. Knopf, 1982), 89.

3. *The Boy with Green Hair* would have been produced by Adrian Scott had not the 1947 hearings intervened. Other writer-director collaborations include Hugo Butler on *Miss Susie Slagle's* (dir. John Berry, 1946, adaptation: Adrian Scott), *From This Day Forward* (dir. John Berry, 1946), and *The Big Night* (dir. Joseph Losey, 1951, co-author: Ring Lardner Jr.); Ben Barzman on *Back to Bataan* (dir. Edward Dmytryk, 1945); Albert Maltz on *The Naked City* (dir. Jules Dassin, 1948); Lee Gold on *The Affairs of Martha* (dir. Dassin, 1942); and Ian McLellan Hunter on *Young Ideas* (dir. Jules Dassin, 1943) and *The Amazing Mr. X* (dir. Bernard Vorhaus, 1948). Adrian Scott produced *Murder, My Sweet* (1944), *Cornered* (1945), *So Well Remembered* (1947), and *Crossfire* (1947), all of which were directed by Dmytryk.

4. Paul Buhle, "John Weber," in Paul Buhle and Patrick McGilligan, *Tender Comrades: A Backstory of the Hollywood Blacklist* (New York: St. Martin's Press, 1997), 693; Michael Butler, "Shock Waves," *Cinema Journal* 44, no. 4 (Summer 2005): 81.
5. Victor S. Navasky, *Naming Names*, 3rd ed. (New York: Hill and Wang, 2003), 347.
6. Eric Sherman, *An Oral History with Howard Koch*, April 1974, American Film Institute, 101–102.
7. Eric Sherman, *An Oral History with Abraham Polonsky*, 1974, American Film Institute, 128–129.
8. In his testimony before the committee in 1947, RKO producer Dore Schary expressed this sentiment: "I would feel I was an incompetent producer if I could allow political opinions I disagreed with to infiltrate a film." Quoted by Joseph Losey in Michel Ciment, *Conversations with Losey* (London: Methuen, 1985), 70.
9. Brooks Atkinson, "'The Revolt of the Beavers,' or Mother Goose Marx, Under WPA Auspices," *New York Times*, 21 May 1937, 19. The play was shut down by the New York police commissioner after three weeks. See Brian Neve, *Film and Politics in America: A Social Tradition* (London: Routledge, 2000), 7.
10. Ciment, *Conversations*, 43, 45.
11. The committee also objected to other Federal Theatre productions, including the plays of the known communist Christopher Marlowe, whom Federal Theatre director Hallie Flanagan had to identify as a Shakespearean-era English dramatist during her testimony in front of the committee. See R. C. Reynolds, *Stage Left: The Development of the American Social Drama in the Thirties* (Troy, N.Y.: Whitston Publishing Company, 1986), 80.
12. Patrick McGilligan, "Jules Dassin," in Buhle and McGilligan, *Tender Comrades*, 202.
13. Ibid. See also Christian Viviani, "Jules Dassin: Décidé à être un héros," *Positif*, no. 466 (December 1999): 93.
14. MGM's initial reaction to *The Tell-Tale Heart* was so negative that the studio decided not to take Dassin under contract. However, when a local movie theater misplaced a newsreel and asked Paramount to send them some additional programming content, a studio hand sent them *The Tell-Tale Heart* by mistake. The film was a hit, and Dassin was signed to a seven-year contract with MGM. See Cynthia Grenier, "Jules Dassin," *Sight and Sound* 22, no. 3 (Winter 1957–58): 41. See also McGilligan, "Jules Dassin," 207; Viviani, "Jules Dassin," 94.
15. David Caute, *Joseph Losey: A Revenge on Life* (New York: Oxford University Press, 1994), 83; Ciment, *Conversations*, 66.
16. Ciment, *Conversations*, 65.
17. Brian Neve, "An Interview with Cy Endfield," *Film Studies: An International Review* 7 (Winter 2005): 119.
18. Ring Lardner Jr., *I'd Hate Myself in the Morning: A Memoir* (New York: Thunder's Mouth Press/Nation Books, 2000), 98.
19. Ceplair and Englund estimate that about 300 film people joined the Hollywood branch of the CPUSA between 1937 and 1947. See Ceplair and Englund, *The Inquisition in Hollywood*, 58, 65.
20. Patrick McGilligan, "Maurice Rapf," in Buhle and McGilligan, *Tender Comrades*, 520.
21. Albert Maltz quoted in David Talbot and Barbara Zheutlin, *Creative Differences: Profiles of Hollywood Dissidents* (Boston: South End Press, 1978), 35.
22. *The Reminiscences of Carl Foreman*, April 1959, 14, Oral History Collection of Columbia University.
23. Schwartz, *Hollywood Writers' Wars*, 45.
24. Neve, *Film and Politics*, 8

25. Donald Ogden Stewart, *By a Stroke of Luck! An Autobiography* (New York: Paddington Press, 1975), 213, 216–217.
26. Schulberg quoted in Schwartz, *Hollywood Writers' Wars*, 92.
27. Losey's involvement with the Communist Party dates back to the mid-1930s, when he worked as a courier for the communist underground. Caute speculates that Losey was more useful (i.e., inconspicuous) outside the Party. Caute, *Joseph Losey*, 48–49 and 99–100.
28. Patrick McGilligan, "Paul Jarrico," in Buhle and McGilligan, *Tender Comrades*, 331.
29. Larry Ceplair, "Norma Barzman," in Buhle and McGilligan, *Tender Comrades*, 6.
30. Talbot and Zheutlin, *Creative Differences*, 4; Paul Buhle and Dave Wagner, "Abraham Polonsky," in Buhle and McGilligan, *Tender Comrades*, 493.
31. Ceplair, "Norma Barzman," 6.
32. As Nancy Lynn Schwartz observes, while the "variety of movements that proliferated during those years . . . undoubtedly would have existed without the CP . . . what the Party did do was to lend a structure and a context to political efforts in Hollywood." Schwartz, *Hollywood Writers' Wars*, 85.
33. Ceplair and Englund, *The Inquisition in Hollywood*, 104–112; see also Paul Buhle and Dave Wagner, *Radical Hollywood: The Untold Story behind America's Favorite Movies* (New York: New Press, 2002), 78–79.
34. Ceplair and Englund, *The Inquisition in Hollywood*, 125.
35. Stewart, *By a Stroke of Luck*, 257.
36. Schwartz, *Hollywood Writers' Wars*, 185. Ceplair and Englund offer a similar assessment: "In sum, Axis aggression, by creating a new international alliance and restoring an old domestic alliance, allowed the CPUSA to reverse itself and proclaim a patriotism and an anti-fascism acceptable to a broad current of Americans. Once again, and to an even greater extent than in the thirties, being a Communist did not automatically insulate one from the center ring of American political activity." See Ceplair and Englund, *The Inquisition in Hollywood*, 186.
37. This surge in Party membership was also a result of developments within the Communist Party USA, which was formally dissolved in 1944 by its head, Earl Browder. Browder saw the war as an opportunity to soften the party line and promote a more inclusive, mainstream vision of communism. With its emphasis on education and coalition building with liberal groups, the new Communist Political Association (CPA) alienated the communist hard line, but also attracted much broader membership to the Party. See Schwartz, *The Hollywood Writers' Wars*, 204; see also Ceplair and Englund, *The Inquisition in Hollywood*, 183.
38. Ceplair and Englund estimate that the Hollywood branches included approximately 150 screenwriters, roughly 50 percent of the 300 industry people who joined the Party between 1936 and 1946. See Ceplair and Englund, *The Inquisition in Hollywood*, 65 and 68.
39. Ceplair, "Norma Barzman," 3; Schwartz, *The Hollywood Writers' War*, 163–164, 194.
40. In 1935, the "call" put forth for the first American Writers' Congress, which led in turn to the formation of the League of American Writers, describes the situation of writers faced with the challenge of "presenting in our work the fresh understanding of the American scene that has come from our enrollment in the revolutionary cause. A new Renaissance is upon the world; for each writer there is the opportunity to proclaim both the new way of life and the revolutionary way to attain it. Indeed, in the historical perspective, it will be seen that only these two things matter. The revolutionary spirit is penetrating the ranks of the creative writers." See Joseph North, ed., *New Masses: An Anthology of the Rebel Thirties* (New York: International Publishers, 1969), 313–314.
41. Paul Buhle and Dave Wagner, "Robert Lees," in Buhle and McGilligan, *Tender Comrades*, 431.

42. Barzman's friend Edward Dmytryk also taught at the school. See Neve, *Film and Politics*, 95. Carl Foreman likewise taught courses in screenwriting in 1947. Carl Foreman File, Box 3, Records of the House Un-American Activities Committee, National Archives, Washington, D.C.
43. Dan Georgakas and Petros Anastasopoulos, "A Dream of Passion: An Interview with Jules Dassin," *Cinéaste* 9, no. 1 (Fall 1978): 23.
44. Ciment, *Conversations*, 70.
45. Carl Foreman Oral History, 14.
46. Paul Jarrico Oral History, 38.
47. Maltz in Talbot and Zheutlin, *Creative Differences*, 15–16.
48. Abraham Polonsky, "How the Blacklist Worked in Hollywood," *Film Culture*, no. 50–51 (Fall/Winter 1970): 44.
49. President Roosevelt requested that Jack Warner personally supervise the production of *Mission to Moscow*. Ceplair and Englund, *The Inquisition in Hollywood*, 312. The script for *Song of Russia* was vetted and approved by the Office of War Information, which encouraged the film's pro-Soviet stance. Ronald Radosh and Allis Radosh, *Red Star over Hollywood: The Film Colony's Long Romance with the Left* (New York: Encounter Books, 2006).
50. Ceplair and Englund, *The Inquisition in Hollywood*, 311–312.
51. Lary May argues that the postwar labor disputes spurred studio heads to strengthen their ties to corporate interests. Rejecting the liberal, New Deal culture of the 1930s, Hollywood chose to instead align itself with "the new 'American' ideology of corporate consensus, class harmony, and abundance," drawing on "anticommunism and HUAC to discredit opposition to monopoly capital." See Lary May, "Movie Star Politics: The Screen Actors' Guild, Cultural Conversion, and the Hollywood Red Scare," in *Recasting America: Culture and Politics in the Age of Cold War*, ed. Lary May (Chicago: University of Chicago Press, 1989), 127. See also Steven J. Ross, *Hollywood Left and Right: How Movie Stars Shaped American Politics* (Oxford: Oxford University Press, 2011), 108.
52. In the prepared statement he was prevented from reading at his hearing before HUAC, the producer Adrian Scott listed the cinematic contributions made by the Hollywood Nineteen toward the fight against antisemitism and racism: "Robert Rossen wrote the anti-lynch picture *They Won't Forget*. His latest picture is *Body and Soul*, which treats Negro and Jew with dignity and justice as free men. Howard Koch wrote *Casablanca* and *In This Our Life*. The Negro is treated honestly as a free man. Albert Maltz wrote *Pride of the Marines* and *The House I Live In*. . . . Both pictures exposed anti-Semitism and religious and racial intolerance. Waldo Salt wrote *The Comington Story* for the OWI, an attack on anti-Semitism. Ring Lardner, Jr. wrote *The Brotherhood of Man*, calling for more understanding among races and religions. Herbert Biberman produced *New Orleans*, hailed by the Negro press as an intelligent treatment of Negroes. Lewis Milestone directed *Of Mice and Men*, in which the Negro was handled with dignity. And lest we forget, Nazi storm troopers stopped the showing of his anti-war film *All Quiet on the Western Front* in 1939, in Germany. Lester Cole wrote *None Shall Escape*, which exposed Nazi brutality to the Jews. Richard Collins wrote *Don't Be a Sucker* for the armed services. It exposed anti-Semitism and kindred hatreds. Irving Pichel directed *A Medal for Benny*, which treated a Mexican minority with dignity. Will the American people allow this bigoted committee to sit in judgment of these men and their records?" Quoted in Schwartz, *The Hollywood Writers' Wars*, 273–274.
53. Gold, quoted in Ceplair and Englund, *The Inquisition in Hollywood*, 234.
54. Polonsky, "How the Blacklist Worked in Hollywood," 44.
55. Bertrand Tavernier, *Amis Américains: Entretiens avec les grands auteurs d'Hollywood* (Lyons: Institut Lumière/Actes Sud, 1993), 512.

56. *Rome, Open City* was not released in America until 1946.
57. Dassin, interview with author, 23 March 2006.
58. Ciment, *Conversations*, 131.
59. Malvin Wald, a member of the First Motion Picture Unit of the Army Armed Forces, recalls seeing the films of Robert Flaherty and Joris Ivens for the first time as part of the lunchtime documentary screening series organized by the radical screenwriter and fellow conscript Ben Maddow. He attributes his interest in the documentary form, which he would go on to explore in his screenplay for *The Naked City*, to this screening series. See Malvin Wald, "Afterword," in *The Naked City: A Screenplay by Malvin Wald and Albert Maltz*, ed. Matthew J. Bruccoli (Carbondale: Southern Illinois University Press, 1979), 137.
60. Philip K. Scheuer, "Movie Realism at Peak in 1948. But Signs Begin to Hint That Crust of Postwar Hardness Is Cracking," *Los Angeles Times*, 26 December 1948.
61. Neve, "An Interview with Cy Endfield," 121.
62. Caute, *Joseph Losey*, 84.
63. Inter-Office Memo from Jerry Wald to Mike Curtis, 4 September 1948 (*Flamingo Road* Special Box, file 1905 "Story—Memos and Correspondence file 2 of 3," Warner Bros. Archives, School of Cinematic Arts, University of Southern California). With special thanks to Haden Guest.
64. In an early script conference for *The House on 92nd Street* (dir. Henry Hathaway, 1945), the first of the semi-documentary cycle, Zanuck doesn't mask his disdain for the documentary. He warns: "We have to do what we do dramatically or it will fall into the category of documentary features and there is just no market for them. . . . We have to make up our minds to make an entertaining picture or we should just turn the material over to *The March of Time* and forget about making a picture out of it." Quoted in Haden R. Guest, "The Police Procedural Film: Law and Order in the American Cinema, 1930–1960" (Ph.D. diss., University of California, Los Angeles, 2005), 125.
65. By 1947, there were fifteen independent production companies for every one that had existed in 1940. Dramatically declining revenues (from $121 million in 1946 to $48 million in 1948) led to massive layoffs, including significant reductions in the number of writers, directors, and actors under contract. With fewer contract players, the studios increasingly relied on independent production units to fulfill their production needs. Bernstein, *Hollywood at the Crossroads*, 17 and 23.
66. Jules Dassin, interview with author, 23 March 2006. See also McGilligan, "Jules Dassin," 207.
67. *Brute Force* features a number of Dassin's friends from the Actors' Lab, including Hume Cronyn, Jeff Corey, and Roman Bohnen. In an interview with *Daily News* drama editor Virginia Wright, Dassin gives a diplomatic response regarding the number of Lab members among the cast of *Brute Force*, claiming he cast them "not because the Lab people are particular friends of mine, but because I think the best actors around are with the Lab." See Virginia Wright, *Daily News*, 9 April 1947. See also Robert E. Kopp to Mark Hellinger, 8 April 1947, Box 1, Mark Hellinger Collection, University of Southern California Library.
68. Quoted in Tom Milne, *Losey on Losey* (New York: Doubleday, 1968), 79.
69. Berry was hired to direct *Caught* (1949) after Max Ophuls fell ill. However, having fallen behind schedule and with Ophuls on the mend, Berry was fired after only two weeks. For a detailed discussion of *Caught*'s production history, see Lutz Bacher, *Max Ophuls in the Hollywood Studios* (New Brunswick, N.J.: Rutgers University Press, 1996), 204–263. See also "John Berry" in Tavernier, *Amis Américains*, 600.
70. Robert Aldrich quoted in Bacher, *Max Ophuls*, 204.

71. After Enterprise's demise in 1949, Aldrich worked on other independent productions, serving as Joseph Losey's assistant director on *M* (1951) (starring the future blacklist victims Karen Morley and Howard DaSilva) and again on *The Prowler* (1951). Jules Dassin suggested that Albert Maltz, a friend from New York, be hired to polish Malvin Wald's script for *The Naked City*. Bernard Vorhaus provided Ring Lardner and Ian McLellan Hunter with some of their first jobs in Hollywood, hiring them to write his independent B-movies *Meet Dr. Christian* (1939) and *The Courageous Doctor Christian* (1940), both of which were produced by Stephens-Lang Productions; Vorhaus would again work with McLellan Hunter on *The Amazing Mr. X* (1948), produced by Ben Stoloff Productions. Vorhaus's last Hollywood production would be a collaboration with Hugo Butler's wife, Jean Rouverol, who wrote the script for *So Young, So Bad* (1950), a film about a reform school for girls, also an independent production (Danziger/Individual Pictures). Joseph Losey signed a contract to direct three films for the Kramer Company, the independent production unit founded by Stanley Kramer along with an old friend from the army, Carl Foreman, at Columbia; among the films Losey recalls being slated to direct are *High Noon* and *The Wild One* (Kramer canceled Losey's contract in September 1951 after Losey was called to appear before HUAC). See "John Berry," in Tavernier, *Amis Américains*, 600. See also Caute, *Joseph Losey*, 104–107.

72. See Ciment, *Conversations*, 116. There is speculation that Losey and Frances Lardner were in fact having an affair at the time and that Losey's offer of work to Ring, who had recently returned to Hollywood after serving his time in prison, was motivated by guilt. See Caute, *Joseph Losey*, 109–110.

73. Milne, *Losey on Losey*, 83.

74. Cited in Neve, *Film and Politics*, 84–85.

75. See Thom Andersen's astute accounts of the historiography of the Hollywood blacklist, "Red Hollywood" and "Afterword," in *"Un-American" Hollywood: Politics and Film in the Blacklist Era*, ed. Frank Krutnik, Steve Neale, Brian Neve, and Peter Stanfield (New Brunswick, N.J.: Rutgers University Press, 2007), 225–243 and 269–275.

76. Norma Barzman, *The Red and the Blacklist: An Intimate Memoir of a Hollywood Expatriate* (New York: Thunder's Mouth Press/Nation Books, 2003), 93. The Nineteen sent Losey a thank-you note, which read as follows: "We cannot leave our home town without expressing to you our gratefulness for the unselfish and effective work you have contributed to the common defense of our Constitution and our industry. You have launched a counterattack from which our people will profit. This is small thanks, but you don't need any anyway." See Caute, *Joseph Losey*, 101–102.

77. Ceplair and Englund, *The Inquisition in Hollywood*, 275.

78. Ibid., 285.

79. Lawson's statement denounces the hearings as "illegal and indecent" and charged the committee with trying to "subvert orderly government and establish an autocratic dictatorship." In his conclusion, Lawson exposes the fascist ideology he sees at work in the hearings: "I am plastered with mud because I happen to be an American who expresses opinions that the House Un-American Activities Committee does not like. . . . The Committee's logic is obviously: Lawson's opinions are properly subject to censorship; he writes for the motion picture industry, so the industry makes pictures for the American people, so the minds of the people must be censored and controlled. . . . The struggle between thought-control and freedom of expression is the struggle between the people and a greedy unpatriotic minority which hates and fears the people." See Robert Vaughn, *Only Victims: A Study of Show Business Blacklisting* (New York: G. P. Putnam's Sons, 1972), 330.

80. The text of the statement reads: "We are frank to recognize that such a policy involves dangers and risks. There is the danger of hurting innocent people. There is the risk of creating

an atmosphere of fear. Creative work at its best cannot be carried on in an atmosphere of fear. We will guard against this danger, this risk, this fear. To this end we will invite the Hollywood talent guilds to work with us to eliminate any subversives, to protect the innocent, and to safeguard free speech and a free screen wherever threatened." "The Waldorf Statement," reprinted in Ceplair and Englund, *The Inquisition in Hollywood,* Appendix 6, 455.

81. Ceplair and Englund, *The Inquisition in Hollywood,* 291, 345.

82. Ibid., 344.

83. Barzman, *The Red and the Blacklist,* 103.

84. Schwartz, *The Hollywood Writers' Wars,* 259.

85. Paul Jarrico Oral History, 86.

86. Barzman, *The Red and the Blacklist,* 91.

87. Ibid., 105–115.

88. Betsy Blair, *The Memory of All That: Love and Politics in New York, Hollywood, and Paris* (New York: Knopf, 2003), 179; Jean Rouverol, *Refugees from Hollywood: A Journal of the Blacklist Years* (Albuquerque: University of New Mexico Press, 2000), 5.

89. Blair, *The Memory of All That,* 179; Navasky, *Only Victims,* 335.

90. Quoted in Milne, *Losey on Losey,* 92.

91. Dassin, interview by Virginia Wright, *Daily News,* 9 April 1947.

CHAPTER 2: LIFE ON THE BLACKLIST: PRODUCTION AND POLITICS IN POSTWAR EUROPE

1. Joseph Losey to Ring Lardner Jr., 11 December 1954, Folder 162, Ring Lardner Jr. Collection, AMPAS.

2. Patrick McGilligan, "Jules Dassin," in Patrick McGilligan and Paul Buhle, *Tender Comrades: A Backstory of the Hollywood Blacklist* (New York: St. Martin's Press, 1997), 218.

3. Norma Barzman, *The Red and the Blacklist: An Intimate Memoir of a Hollywood Expatriate* (New York: Thunder's Mouth Press/Nation Books, 2003), 252.

4. Betsy Blair, *The Memory of All That: Love and Politics in New York, Hollywood, and Paris* (New York: Knopf, 2003), 147. See also Betsy Blair, "FBI's Merry Dance with Mrs. Gene Kelly," *Sunday Times* (London), 14 June 1998.

5. "John Berry," *A Voix Nue,* FranceCulture2, 20 May 1999.

6. Carl Foreman, Autobiography, Item 1, Carl Foreman Collection, British Film Institute.

7. Donald Ogden Stewart Jr., letter to author, 8 February 2007.

8. Berry would later earn as much as 500 francs a day dubbing French stars, including Michel Simon and Jean Gabin. "John Berry," *A Voix Nue,* FranceCulture2, 20 May 1999.

9. Michel Ciment, *Conversations with Losey* (London: Methuen, 1985), 135; Barzman, *The Red and the Blacklist,* 169.

10. Adrian Scott quoted in Bruce Cook, *Dalton Trumbo* (New York: Scribner's Sons, 1977), 282.

11. McGilligan, "Jules Dassin," 212. Dassin was finally called to Washington to testify in November 1952, only to have the hearings canceled in the wake of the election of Dwight D. Eisenhower to the presidency. See Christian Viviani, "Jules Dassin: Décidé à être un héros," *Positif,* no. 466 (December 1999): 96.

12. Losey waited to see the results of the presidential election; as soon as Eisenhower's victory became clear, he was on the plane back to London. See Ciment, *Conversations,* 133–134.

13. Tina Daniell, "Marguerite Roberts (and John Sanford)," in McGilligan and Buhle, *Tender Comrades,* 580.

14. Paul Buhle and Dave Wagner, *A Very Dangerous Citizen: Abraham Polonsky and the Hollywood Left* (Berkeley: University of California Press, 2001), 144.
15. Jean-Pierre Jeancolas, "From the Blum-Byrnes Agreement to the GATT Affair," in *Hollywood and Europe: Economics, Culture, National Identity, 1945–1965*, ed. Geoffrey Nowell-Smith and Steven Ricci (London: British Film Institute, 1998), 48.
16. The slogan was such a prevalent symbol of the virulent anti-Americanism of the early 1950s that the director André Hunnebelle used it as a leitmotiv in *L'Impossible Monsieur Pipelet* (1955), albeit to comic effect. Patricia Hubert-Lacombe, *Le cinéma français dans la guerre froide, 1946–1956* (Paris: Editions L'Harmatton, 1996), 128.
17. Ridgeway was labeled a war criminal in the communist press on account of his alleged use of biological weapons in Korea. Kuisel, *Seducing the French*, 48, 51–52.
18. Signed on 28 May 1946, the Blum-Byrnes agreement concerned U.S. imports into France, of which cinema was of key interest. Irwin Wall notes that State Department files for the cinema portion of the agreement are equal in size to the files concerning all other aspects of the agreement. See Irwin M. Wall, *The United States and the Making of Postwar France, 1945–1954* (Cambridge: Cambridge University Press, 1991), 56.
19. See Colin Crisp, *The Classic French Cinema, 1930–1960* (Bloomington: Indiana University Press, 1997), 74; Hubert-Lacombe, *Le cinema français*, 92.
20. Pierre Billard calls attention to the eighteen-month lag between the committee's establishment and the anti-Blum-Byrnes demonstration. He suggests that the catalyst for the demonstration was less the precipitous decline in French production, for which the Blum-Byrnes made a handy scapegoat, than certain geopolitical and ideological developments that had occurred between 1946 and the beginning of 1948. During this period, the United States (along with France, as its ally) had entered the Cold War, and French politics had split into two antagonistic camps: pro-American and pro-Soviet. "In this context, the Blum-Byrnes agreement became a perfect target for attacks on both the 'American imperialists' who threatened the future of French cinema just as they threatened world peace and on [the French president] Léon Blum, a 'traitor' who sold French cinema to Washington for a plate of beans. . . . The debate surrounding the place of American film in France was no longer about economics or industry concerns but had entered the realm of the political and ideological." See Pierre Billard, *L'Age classique du cinema française: Du cinéma parlant à la nouvelle vague* (Paris: Flammarion, 1995), 516–518.
21. The Parti Communiste Français (PCF) won 26 percent of the vote in France's 1945 elections, the most in its history. Although the PCF did not participate in any Fourth Republic administration (the premier Paul Ramadier having barred PCF members from cabinet positions in May 1947, when they voted against the government's policy in Vietnam), the PCF won an average of 22 percent of the vote in the six general elections between 1951 and 1968 and held a large number of seats in the Assemblée Nationale. Philippe Roger, *Rêves et cauchemars américains: Les Etats-Unis au miroir de l'opinion publique française, 1945–1953* (Paris: Presses Universitaires de Septentrion, 1996), 235.
22. Daquin represented the Fédération in its negotiations with the British cinema's trade union leader, George Elvin, regarding the co-production regulations for *Pardon My French*. *Dans la vie tout s'arrange*, Dossier d'Archives, Fonds: Credit National, cote CN 421 B292, Bibliothèque du Film, Paris.
23. Larry Ceplair, "Norma Barzman," in McGilligan and Buhle, *Tender Comrades*, 15.
24. For further discussion of the role played by the French Communist Party in the film industry in France during the late 1940s and early 1950s, see Hubert-Lacombe, *Le cinema français*, 106–126.
25. McGilligan, "John Berry," in McGilligan and Buhle, *Tender Comrades*, 77.

26. Most of the French papers, including the conservative *Le Figaro* and the neutralist (on account of its refusal to favor either Washington or Moscow) *Le Monde*, published reports on the hearings of the Hollywood Ten in October 1947. It was not until the ascent of Senator Joseph McCarthy, however, that the anticommunist witch hunts began to attract more widespread attention. In November 1953, *Le Monde* published a series of three articles that were highly critical of President Eisenhower's failure to rein in McCarthy's excesses. Marcelle Henry, "Qu'est-ce que c'est le MacCarthyisme?," *Le Monde*, 13–15 November 1953. As the title of the series indicates, European anxiety about the American anticommunist movement focused on the very visible—and unpopular—figure of McCarthy. A CIA survey of European radio broadcasts between March and September 1953 found that out of 173 mentions of McCarthy, only 3 were favorable; of the remaining 170, 67 were mildly unfavorable and 100 were strongly unfavorable. See John P. Rossi, "The British Reaction to McCarthyism, 1950–54," *Mid-America: An Historical Review* 70, no. 1 (1988): 14. See also Roger, *Rêves et cauchemars*, 123, 315–317.

27. *L'Ecran français* began life in December 1943 as the underground publication of the film committee of the French Resistance. Founded by the actor and militant communist René Blech, the weekly journal was not favorably inclined toward Hollywood, with some contributors systematically favoring Soviet film in the 1950s. *L'Ecran français* ceased publication in 1953, having become increasingly isolated from its readership due to its unwavering support of the communist party line. For a history of the journal, see Olivier Barrot, *L'Ecran Français, 1943–1953: Histoire d'un journal et d'une époque* (Paris: Les Editeurs français réunis, 1979); see also Crisp, *Classic French*, 249. Articles pertaining to the Hollywood blacklist include: Henri Robillot, "La Commission des Activités 'non américaines' . . . une sinistre comédie!," *L'Ecran français*, no. 168 (Noël 1947); "Quand l'épicerie voit rouge . . . ," *L'Ecran français*, no. 207 (15–21 June 1949); "Pour avoir réalisé 'Crossfire,' le chômeur Ed. Dmytryk est retenu prisonnier à Hollywood," *L'Ecran français*, no. 239 (1–7 February 1950); Vladimir Pozner, "Neuf cineastes et un producteur américains sont en prison," *L'Ecran français*, no. 251 (26 April–2 May 1950); "L'Affaire des Dix, jugée par Frederic March, Gregory Peck, Evelyn Keyes, Paul Henreid, Robert Ryan, and William Wyler," *L'Ecran français*, no. 252 (3–9 May 1950); "Une declaration de Joris Ivens à propos de 'l'Affaire des Dix,'" *L'Ecran français*, no. 253 (3–9 May 1950); "Letter from Hollywood: Un film est en préparation sur les Dix, pour les Dix, et par les Dix," *L'Ecran français*, no. 255 (22 May 1950); "Charlie Chaplin et cinq cents cinéastes américains luttent pour les 10 otages de la liberté," *L'Ecran français*, no. 258 (14–20 June 1950).

28. Michel Favier-LeDoux, "L'autre visage d'Hollywood: Trois cinéastes américains à Paris," *L'Ecran français*, no. 56 (29 May 1946); Harold J. Salemson, "Hollywood: Les rivalités politiques s'accentuent . . . Katharine Hepburn (gauche) contre Ginger Rogers (droite)," *L'Ecran français*, no. 115 (9 September 1947).

29. Norma Barzman recalls being invited to the home of Georges and Ruta Sadoul as a result of the success of *Christ in Concrete*. See Barzman, *The Red and the Blacklist*, 201. For more on the role of Sadoul within the French film milieu, see Antoine de Baecque, *La cinéphilie: Invention d'un regard, histoire d'une culture, 1944–1968* (Paris: Fayard, 2003), 74–75.

30. Jean-Charles Tacchella, "Hollywood est en décadence," *L'Ecran français*, no. 307 (23–27 May 1951).

31. McGilligan, "John Berry," 77–78.

32. Crisp, *The Classic French Cinema*, 86, 196–202. Under the French system, production companies neither owned production facilities nor kept personnel under contract, in addition to lacking any reliable funding base. Jacques Nahum, interview with author, 2 February 2007.

33. The Centre national de la cinématographie was established by law on 25 October 1946. Despite these regulations, the American influence on set often dominated, at least according to an article published in *L'Ecran français* on the making of *Traqué / Gunman in the Streets* (dir. Frank Tuttle, 1950). "The studio at Joinville seems to have been transformed into Hollywood, since although 50% of the cast and crew are French, everyone is speaking English since the Americans speak French so poorly!" Claude Daire, "Simone Signoret part avec un homme 'tracqué' mais espère bientôt changer la peau . . . de ses personnages," *L'Ecran français,* no. 240 (6 February 1950).

34. These productions included *Alice aux pays des merveilles / Alice in Wonderland* (dir. Lou Bonin, 1948), *L'Homme de la Tour Eiffel / The Man on the Eiffel Tower* (dir. Burgess Meredith, 1948), *La Taverne de New Orleans / Adventures of Captain Fabian* (dir. Robert Florey/ William Marshall, 1950), *Traqué / Gunman in the Streets* (dir. Boris Lewin/Frank Tuttle, 1950), *Le Gantelet vert / The Green Glove* (dir. Rudolph Maté, 1950), *Nous Irons à Monte Carlo / Monte Carlo Baby* (dir. Jean Boyer/Lester Fuller, 1950), *Dans la vie, tout s'arrange / Pardon My French* (dir. Marcel Cravenne/Bernard Vorhous, 1951), *C'est arrivé à Paris / It Happened in Paris* (dir. Henri Lavorel/ John Berry, 1952), and *Un Acte d'amour* (dir. Anatole Litvak, 1953). See Hubert-Lacombe, *Le cinema français,* 55–58.

35. Vorhaus is not listed on any of the film's accounting documents. The only reference to his participation is in a letter from the Centre Nationale de la Cinématographie stating that it will renew the work permits for foreigners employed on the film, including "Bernard Vorhaus who is directing the English-language version." *Dans la vie tout s'arrange,* Dossier d'Archives, Fonds: Credit National, cote CN 421 B292, Bibliothèque du Film, Paris.

36. A future friendly witness, Ronald Kibbee would give eighteen names in his HUAC testimony. See John Baxter, "Bernard Vorhaus," in McGilligan and Buhle, *Tender Comrades,* 678. The production records make no mention of either Adrian Scott or Madeleine Dmytryk, giving story credit to a Madeleine Robinson, who is described as an American writer. *Dans la vie tout s'arrange,* Dossier d'Archives, Fonds: Credit National, cote CN 421 B292, Bibliothèque du Film, Paris.

37. George Thomas Jr., "Under Three Flags," *New York Times,* 12 March 1950.

38. Kristin Ross calls attention to the cult of cleanliness that emerged in France in the 1950s. She connects its hold on the French subconscious with the desire to purge *la patrie* of the taint of German occupation, but also with the intense embrace of consumer goods that followed years of wartime deprivation. See Kristin Ross, *Fast Cars, Clean Bodies: Decolonization and the Reordering of French Culture* (Cambridge, Mass.: MIT Press, 1995), 71–104.

39. Roland Barthes, *Mythologies* (Paris: Editions du Seuil, 1957).

40. In 1954, 76 percent of French households had no hot running water; only 10 percent of the population had a washing machine and only 9 percent owned refrigerators. Betsy Blair remembers her American refrigerator being an object of wonder when she imported one for her Paris apartment in 1957. See Victoria de Grazia, *Irresistible Empire: America's Advance through Twentieth-Century Europe* (Cambridge, Mass.: Harvard University Press, 2005), 361; Blair, *The Memory of All That,* 288.

41. As Catherine Gaston-Mathé notes in her study of French postwar cinema, films inspired by "le mythe américain" tended to fall into two categories. The first depicts the adventures of Americans in France, whether in the form of an attractive American heiress or the gauche and vulgar "Amerloque," a common figure in films of the period such as *Les Femmes sont folles* (dir. Gilles Grangier, 1950) and *L'Air de Paris* (dir. Marcel Carné, 1954). The second spoke to France's fascination with the "American way of life." In *Jour de Fête* (1949), Jacques Tati satirized the perception of America as the land of modern efficiency, while *Le Voyage en Amérique* (dir. Henri Lavorel, 1951) sent a young couple to America to experience its prosperity firsthand. See Catherine Gaston-Mathé, *La Société française au miroir de son cinéma: De la débâcle à la décolonisation* (Paris: Collections panoramiques/

Arléa-Corlet, 1996), 165. See also Hubert-Lacombe, *Le cinema français,* 126–133, and Roger, *Rêves et cauchemars,* 59.

42. *Rencontre à Paris / Meeting in Paris* (dir. Georges Lampin, 1956), a French production starring Betsy Blair as Nancy Blanding, the heir to a Chicago meatpacking fortune, takes a similar approach when Nancy abandons the Ritz for a small hotel in the Latin Quarter. The trope of the American heiress in France also appears earlier in *Mademoiselle s'amuse / Mademoiselle Has Fun* (dir. Jean Boyer, 1948). See Gaston-Mathé, *La Société française,* 165.

43. Lavorel's production company, Le Monde en images, had produced one previous film, *Le Voyage en Amérique,* about the experiences of a young French couple who travel to America.

44. McGilligan, "John Berry," 78. See also Barzman, *The Red and the Blacklist,* 262.

45. Louis Chauvet, "C'est Arrivé à Paris," *Le Figaro,* 16 February 1953; Jean de Baroncelli, "C'est Arrivé à Paris," *Le Monde,* 21 February 1953.

46. Michel Fourré-Cormeray, *Combat,* 11 April 1950, cited in Hubert-Lacombe, *Le cinéma français,* 60.

47. Jean Rosenthal, "Pour ou contre les coproductions cinématographiques," *Combat,* 11 April 1950. The underground paper of the Resistance founded in 1944, *Combat* was led by the militant Marxist Victor Fay from 1948 until 1960.

48. Pierre Bloch-Delahaie, quoted in Hubert-Lacombe, *Le cinéma français,* 74.

49. André Sarrut, "Une question de vie ou de mort pour le cinéma français," *Combat,* 19 April 1950.

50. "L'Affaire Dassin Irks Paris Press; See U.S. Dictation," *Variety,* 27 May 1953. The story was also picked up in Britain. Anthony Asquith, president of the Association of Cine Technicians (ACT), the communist-dominated industry union, cabled Dassin the following message of support: "Associate ourselves with protest of French film makers at intolerable interference in your personal beliefs and the consequent attack on freedom of opinion and freedom to work." See *Cine Technician* 19, no. 103 (July 1953); see also Sydney Smith, "Zsa Zsa has a beeg poleetical affair," *Daily Express,* 30 April 1953.

51. Among these projects was a play about "a Hollywood writer who faces a choice of trading his principles for money," the blacklist having given him the time to finally write up an idea he had first mentioned in an interview in 1947. Dan Georgakas and Petros Anastasopoulos, "A Dream of Passion: An Interview with Jules Dassin," *Cinéaste* 9, no. 1 (Fall 1978): 23; Sam Zolotow, "*Little Hut* Listed for a Fall Opening; Robert Morley Sought to Fill Leading Role in London Hit Headed for the Coronet," *New York Times,* 21 July 1952.

52. See Christian Viviani, "Jules Dassin: Décidé à être un héros," *Positif,* no. 466 (December 1999): 96.

53. Bar had originally planned to limit Dassin's role to that of supervisor and technical director, but "in light of [Dassin's] views on the screenplay, professional skills, rapport with Fernandel, and *French origins,*" decided to assign him the film's direction. Jacques Bar, Cité Films, letter to Crédit National, 2 March 1953, Cote CN620, Fonds Crédit National, Bibliothèque du Film. Emphasis added.

54. Alastair Phillips, *Rififi* (London: I. B. Tauris, 2009), 10; "Cinema: Hollywood Boss," *Time,* 27 April 1953; Jacques Bar, Cité Films, letter to Crédit National, 20 April 1953, Cote CN620, Fonds Crédit National, Bibliothèque du Film.

55. "Une lettre ouverte signée de huit cinéastes français," *Combat,* 30 April 1953.

56. This support extended into reviews of the film, which was released the following April. For the *Cahiers du cinéma,* "the only interesting question one can ask about the film is what would Dassin have done with it had he remained the director?" "Notes sur d'autres films: *L'Ennemi public no. 1,*" *Cahiers du cinéma* 6, no. 34 (April 1954): 63.

57. McGilligan, "Jules Dassin," 216–217.

58. Lee Gold had written the screenplay for *The Big Break* (1953), the film adaptation of *All You Need Is One Good Break*, the Arnold Manoff play that John Berry had directed to much acclaim at the Actors' Lab. McGilligan, "John Berry," 76–77; Jan Berry, interview with author, 5 February 2007; *Cinéfilms du 31 mai: John Berry*, France Inter, 31 May 1997.

59. The film historian Pierre Billard, who was active in the ciné-club movement during the 1950s, describes Ciné Action as "animated by Communism, its vision of filmmaking being very closely linked to political action." He also recalls that Ciné Action screened a print of *Christ in Concrete*, which was perhaps the occasion of the Barzmans' attendance. Pierre Billard, interview with author, 6 July 2006.

60. Ceplair, "Norma Barzman," 15.

61. Agnes Schneider, the consul in charge of passports, was infamous within the American community in Paris. As Stanley Karnow, a journalist at *Time* magazine's Paris office, explains, "[Schneider] had been dubbed 'Schneider the Spider' for the subterfuges she devised to confiscate the passports of allegedly disloyal Americans. Among her ruses, she would ask to verify some technicality, then slam the passport into her drawer, thus depriving the owner of a vital document." See Stanley Karnow, *Paris in the Fifties* (New York: Random House, 1997), 63. See also Barzman, *The Red and the Blacklist*, 247–248; Jan Berry, interview with author, 5 February 2007; Ellie Boris, interview with author, 11 November 2006.

62. A memo dated 9 March 1959 includes the following assessment of Paul Jarrico: "The present activities of PAUL JARRICO are unknown. He claims to be a writer and reportedly receives frequent visits from non-French persons. These visitors, who are occasionally extremely noisy, are reported to leave very late at night. The neighbors have protested because of the noise." Paul Jarrico, FBI Files, FOIPA No. 1055532.

63. In Paris, members of the African American community, such as Richard Wright and Chester Himes, also suspected other black Americans in Paris of spying on them for the CIA. See Tyler Stovall, *Paris Noir: African-Americans in the City of Light* (Boston: Houghton Mifflin, 1996), 208, 219. See also James Campbell, *Exiled in Paris: Richard Wright, James Baldwin, Samuel Beckett, and Others on the Left Bank* (Berkeley: University of California Press, 2003), 196–197.

64. Ciment, *Conversations*, 118.

65. Ellie Boris, interview with author, 11 November 2006.

66. McGilligan, "Jules Dassin," 218.

67. Jan Berry, interview with author, 5 February 2007.

68. Recently declassified MI5 files reveal that the BBC permitted MI5 officers to review the records of all editorial applicants throughout the Cold War. David Smith, "BBC Banned Communists in Purge," *Observer*, 5 March 2006. See Tony Shaw, *British Cinema and the Cold War: The State, Propaganda, and Consensus* (London: I. B. Tauris, 2006), 35–62, for a discussion of British films made between 1945 and 1965 that address the theme of Cold War domestic insecurity.

69. Carl Foreman, Autobiography, Item 1, Carl Foreman Collection, British Film Institute.

70. David Caute's investigations suggest that Losey may have been exaggerating the precariousness of his situation. Losey's correspondence with his American lawyers during this period in the early 1950s "offers not a glimmer of evidence that he was facing deportation." Upon his arrival in London in January 1953, Losey was granted a four-month residency permit. However, the stamps in his Alien Registration Certificate show that until April 1959, he was obliged to renew his residency every few months and sometimes with greater frequency. See David Caute, *Joseph Losey: A Revenge on Life* (New York: Oxford University Press, 1994), 114–117.

71. Donald Ogden Stewart Jr., letter to author, 8 February 2007. Taking this approach, Joseph Losey was able to successfully renew his passport at the U.S. Consulate in Glasgow in August 1954. Caute, *Joseph Losey*, 116.
72. "Carl Foreman," *Take One* 3, no. 9 (May 1973): 24; "Carl Foreman," Autobiography, Item 1, Carl Foreman Collection, British Film Institute.
73. Caute, *Joseph Losey*, 116–117.
74. Donald Ogden Stewart Jr., letter to author, 8 February 2007; Sam Wanamaker mentions a subpoena being delivered to his apartment in London shortly after he had finished work on *Christ in Concrete*. Sam Wanamaker, *Remembering the Blacklist Era: A Personal Account*, Clippings File, British Film Institute.
75. Cahal Milmo, "How MI5 Opened a Surveillance File on Star Who Fled US Persecution," *Independent*, 1 September 2009. With thanks to Kevin Brownlow for bringing this article to my attention.
76. Howard Koch, *As Time Goes By: Memoirs of a Writer* (New York: Harcourt Brace Jovanovich, 1979), 208–209.
77. Carl Foreman, Autobiography, Item 1, Carl Foreman Collection, British Film Institute; Caute (1994), 114.
78. Losey suggests that British reserve also accounted for the less aggressive attitudes he encountered toward the blacklist: "Very few people were deterred by the fact that there was a witch hunt and that it was a 'Red' scare and that of course, if you were blacklisted, you were presumed to be a dangerous 'Red.' There wasn't much inquiry about ideas and in the United States there was none. In England there wasn't any either, but for quite a different reason—it was out of politeness. Sometimes it got around to it but never as a challenge and never as an inquisition." Joseph Losey Collection, Item 75 (transcript of *Moviemen* interview, 24 March 1970), British Film Institute.
79. Erik Tarloff, interview with author, 9 January 2007.
80. Donald Ogden Stewart Jr., letter to author, 8 February 2007; Koch, *As Time Goes By*, 207. See also Nora Sayre, *On the Wing: A Young American Abroad* (Washington, D.C.: Counterpoint, 2001), 123–126, 130–140, 156–170.
81. The British public favored American films throughout the 1950s. See Paul Swann, *The Hollywood Feature Film in Postwar Britain* (London: Croom and Helm, 1987), 31–47. In comparison, French films were becoming increasingly popular with French audiences during the same period, while attendance figures for American films steadily declined. See Richard Kuisel, "The Fernandel Factor: The Rivalry between French and American Cinema in the 1950s," *Yale French Studies* 98 (2000): 121; and Crisp, *The Classic French Cinema*, 82.
82. Robert Murphy, "Under the Shadow of Hollywood," in *All Our Yesterdays: 90 Years of British Cinema*, ed. Charles Barr (London: British Film Institute, 1986), 62.
83. Sayre, *On the Wing*, 136–137; Carl Foreman, "The Road to the Victors," *Films and Filming* 9, no. 12 (September 1963).
84. Ciment, *Conversations*, 134.
85. *The Limping Man* (1953), *The Master Plan* (1955), and *Hell Drivers* (1957). Charles de la Tour was an English friend willing to lend Endfield his name; Hugh Raker and C. Raker Endfield were pseudonyms. Maureen Endfield, interview with author, 2 May 2007. After an article appeared in the *Hollywood Reporter* suggesting the real identity of Joseph Walton, RKO decided to take no chances with the film's U.S. release, changing the title to *Finger of Guilt* and removing the name Joseph Walton from the credits. See Caute, *Joseph Losey*, 134.
86. Donald Ogden Stewart Jr., letter to author, 8 February 2007.
87. Arden Winch, "The Persecution of Jules Dassin," *Picture Post*, 3 December 1955. Winch, an advertising executive with J. Walter Thompson and a future television writer, would later

approach Joseph Losey with a number of projects. Joseph Losey Collection, Item 105, Special Collections, British Film Institute.

88. Foreman says that he came up with the idea for *The Sleeping Tiger* specifically as a favor to Losey, who needed to be employed in order to get his residence permit renewed. "It was a vicious circle," he recalls. "No one wanted to give him any work because he didn't have a permit, and no one would extend his permit because he didn't have any work." Bertrand Tavernier, *Amis américains: Entretiens avec les grands auteurs d'Hollywood* (Lyons: Institut Lumière/Actes Sud, 1993), 516–517. David Caute notes that Losey's residence permit was extended on 12 January 1954—toward the end of *The Sleeping Tiger*'s shoot—and marked, "Allowed by Secretary of State to finish Sleeping Tiger." Caute, *Joseph Losey*, 115.

89. Ciment, *Conversations*, 135.

90. Foreman lists David Lean's *Hobson's Choice* in addition to *The Man Who Loved Redheads* among the films on which he worked for no credit. See Tavernier, *Amis américains*, 512.

91. Carl Foreman clipping file, British Film Institute; Item 1, Carl Foreman Collection, British Film Institute; Kevin Brownlow, *David Lean* (London: Richard Cohen, 1996), 346.

92. The ACT's monthly publication, the *Cine Technician*, kept abreast of the blacklist, publishing Paul Jarrico and Herbert Biberman's account of the making of *Salt of the Earth* and Adrian Scott's analysis of the effect of the blacklist on Hollywood and campaigning to bring Paul Robeson to London. *Cine Technician* 19, no. 108 (December 1953): 164–165; 21, no. 132 (November 1955): 165; 23, no. 151 (August 1957): 100.

93. Michael Seifert, interview with author, 25 April 2007.

94. Caute, *Joseph Losey*, 113.

95. Richard Roud, "The Reluctant Exile," *Sight and Sound* 48, no. 3 (Summer 1979): 145. Although the decision of whether or not to issue a work permit lay with the Ministry of Labour, the ACT closely monitored work permit applications by foreign technicians and informed the ministry of their approval or disapproval on a case-by-case basis. Throughout the 1950s, the ACT was very concerned with the number of foreign—particularly American—technicians employed on British productions, publishing an editorial on the subject entitled "A Thorn in Our Flesh." *Cine Technician* 23, no. 150 (June/July 1957): 83.

96. Caute, *Joseph Losey*, 115; Roud, "The Reluctant Exile," 145.

97. Cy Endfield Clipping File, British Film Institute; Jonathan Rosenbaum, "Pages from the Endfield File," *Film Comment* 29, no. 6 (November 1993): 48–55.

98. Caute, *Joseph Losey*, 123–124

99. A 1955 report on the state of French cinema states that three sound stages at Epinay, two sound stages at Billancourt, and all the stages at Neuilly had been booked by American television companies. See Marcel L'Herbier, "Vers les Etats Généraux du Cinématographie," *Cinéma* 55, no. 2 (1955): 3.

100. Barzman, *The Red and the Blacklist*, 260. Prior to coming to Europe, Reynolds had worked as a writer on *Danger*, a television series that employed the blacklisted writers Walter Bernstein, Arnold Manoff, and Abraham Polonsky, all of whom could have easily put him in touch with the Paris group. See Steve Neale, "Swashbucklers and Sitcoms, Cowboys and Crime, Nurses, Just Men, and Defenders: Blacklisted Writers and TV in the 1950s and 1960s," *Film Studies* 7 (Winter 2005): 83–103.

101. The French film industry was highly unionized and required that for every non-union member employed on a film, a union member must also be hired, thereby effectively doubling the size of the crew. Jacques Nahum, interview with author, 2 February, 2007. For more on the history of French unionization, see Crisp, *The Classic French Cinema*, 196–202.

102. Cy Endfield directed the three pilot episodes for the series in 1952, after which time production ceased until 1954, when Hannah Weinstein produced another twenty-two episodes

for Fountain Films. Another of the American exiles, Phil Brown, acted in and directed a number of these later episodes. Tise Vahimagi, *Hannah Weinstein*, British Film Institute Screen Online. Maureen Endfield, interview with author, 2 May 2007.

103. Sidney Cole, BECTU interview, British Film Institute, 20. Cole was politically on the Left and was responsible for the inclusion of television technicians in the film industry's trade unionthe Association of Cinematograph Technicians (ACT)which became the Association of Cinematograph Television and Allied Technicians (ACTT) in 1955.

104. Ian McLellan Hunter Collection, Box 4, Folder 7, AMPAS. Howard Koch's wife, Anne, was another early contributor to the series. See Koch, *As Time Goes By*, 202; see also Neale, "Swashbucklers and Sitcoms," 92.

105. The first episode of *The Adventures of Robin Hood* was broadcast on Britain's ITV network on 26 September 1955. See Neale, "Swashbucklers and Sitcoms," 89, and Vahimagi, *Hannah Weinstein*.

106. Lindsay Anderson, "Notes from Sherwood," *Sight and Sound* 26, no. 3 (Winter 1956–1957): 159–160.

107. In addition to Hunter and Lardner, the blacklisted writers Weinstein employed on these series include Mischa Altman, Norma Barzman, Arnaud D'Usseau, Gordon Kahn, Millard Lampell, Robert Lees, Arnold Manoff, Maurice Rapf, Fred Rinaldo, Waldo Salt, Adrian Scott, and Michael Wilson. For a description and listing of the episodes for these series, see Steve Neale, "Swashbuckling, Sapphire, and Salt: Un-American Contributions to TV Costume Adventure Series in the 1950s," in *"Un-American" Hollywood: Politics and Film in the Blacklist Era*, ed. Frank Krutnik, Steve Neale, Brian Neve, and Peter Stanfield (New Brunswick, N.J.: Rutgers University Press, 2007), 198–209.

108. Losey consulted Weinstein prior to signing his noncommunist affidavit in 1956. David Caute suggests that Losey and Weinstein were romantically involved during this period. See Caute, *Joseph Losey*, 115.

109. Pierre Rissient, "Connaissance de Joseph Losey," *Cahiers du Cinéma* 19, no. 111, (September 1960): 25. See also Ciment, *Conversations*,134.

110. Sayre, *On the Wing*, 125.

111. Koch, *As Time Goes By*, 203; Caute, *Joseph Losey*, 116.

112. Carl Foreman, Autobiography, Item 1, Carl Foreman Collection, British Film Institute.

113. "John Berry," *Etoiles et Toiles*, TF1, 11 November 1985.

114. Carl Foreman, Autobiography, Item 1, Carl Foreman Collection, British Film Institute.

115. Cy Endfield's first three British films—*The Limping Man* (1953), *Impulse* (1954), and *The Secret* (1955)were independent productions that he directed using various pseudonyms; Losey's *The Sleeping Tiger* was also independently produced.

116. Ben Barzman suggests this attitude in his description of the British response to the American exiles: "The English knew who we were, but were never sure what official stance to take with regard to our situation. In fact, they really didn't understand anything about the blacklist. So they gave us residency permits and work permits so that we could continue to make films. They would say 'America has stolen so many of our talents and now it's sending them back to us thanks to MacCarthy' [*sic*]!" See Ben Barzman, "Profession scénariste," *Cinématographe* 90 (June 1983): 74; see also Jean-Charles Tacchella, "Hollywood perd ses vedettes: Depuis quelques années, de nombreuses 'stars' préfèrent l'Europe à l'Amérique . . . ," *L'Ecran français*, no. 271 (20–26 September 1950).

117. John Nasht, the English producer of the *Orient-Express* television series, was particularly notorious among the blacklisted community for his underhanded dealings. Howard Koch, whom Nasht had led on a wild goose chase around Europe in 1952, explained the producer's technique in a letter to Losey written in 1959: "One of Nasht's favorite tricks is to profess

sympathy for progressives in that situation, hire them at bargain-counter prices, then default on payments, using the black-list as an excuse." After receiving Koch's letter, Losey wrote to John Berry to see if he had any advice about Nasht, who seems to have reneged on payments owed to Berry and Lee and Tammy Gold for their work on *Orient-Express.* Howard Koch to Joseph Losey, 7 May 1959, Item 88, Joseph Losey Collection, British Film Institute. Joseph Losey to John Berry, 14 May 1959, Item 88, Joseph Losey Collection, British Film Institute.

CHAPTER 3: THE BLACKLIST AND "RUNAWAY" PRODUCTION

1. Although subpoenaed in 1947 as one of the Hollywood Nineteen, Koch was never called to testify, nor was he ever named by an informer, the two hard-and-fast criteria for blacklisting.
2. Larry Ceplair and Steven Englund, *The Inquisition in Hollywood: Politics in the Film Community 1930–1960* (Urbana: University of Illinois Press, 2003), 386; Lewis Milestone Collection, Autobiography, Folder 170, p. 273, AMPAS. Milestone lived mainly in Europe from 1950 to 1955, during which time he directed a number of films in England and Italy, including *Melba* (1953), *They Who Dare* (1954), and *The Widow* (1954).
3. Kelly spent the period of 1952–1953 in Paris and London, where he made *The Devil Makes Three* (dir. Andrew Marton, 1952), *Seagulls Over Sorrento* (dir. John Boulting, Roy Boulting, 1954), and *Invitation to the Dance* (dir. Gene Kelly, 1956). See Betsy Blair, *The Memory of All That: Love and Politics in New York, Hollywood, and Paris* (New York: Knopf, 2003), 164–167.
4. Daniel Steinhart, "Hollywood Overseas: The Internationalization of Production and Location Shooting in the Postwar Era" (Ph.D. diss., University of California, Los Angeles, in progress), 10.
5. This trend would reach its peak in 1968, when American sources provided 90 percent of all capital for British productions. See Robert Murphy, "Under the Shadow of Hollywood," in *All Our Yesterdays: 90 Years of British Cinema*, ed. Charles Barr (London: British Film Institute, 1986), 64. See also Irving Bernstein, *Hollywood at the Crossroads: An Economic Study of the Motion Picture Industry*, prepared for the Hollywood AFL Film Council December 1957, 48, cited in Vanessa R. Schwartz, *It's So French!: Hollywood, Paris, and the Making of Cosmopolitan Film Culture* (Chicago: University of Chicago Press, 2007), 187. Schwartz observes that Bernstein based his report on incomplete data, but that his conclusions reflect a contemporary perspective on the issue of runaway production. It is important to note that the report was prepared for the Hollywood AFL Film Council, a group adamantly opposed to runaway production on account of the challenge it posed to Hollywood labor interests.
6. Steinhart, "Hollywood Overseas," 4. Robert R. Shandley, *Runaway Romances: Hollywood's Postwar Tour of Europe* (Philadelphia: Temple University Press, 2009), 11.
7. The American Legion counted nearly three million members in the early 1950s and sponsored over 17,000 posts nationwide. That its membership in 2008 is comparable when the population of the United States has almost doubled since 1950 gives a sense of its social influence at the time. See http://www.legion.org and http://www.census.gov. The power of the Legion's censure was such that in the spring of 1952, Eric Johnston, head of the Motion Picture Association of America, arranged a meeting with Donald Wilson, the Legion's national commander, to discuss how best to address Hollywood's problem with "subversives." At Johnston's request, the Legion provided a list of 300 suspected communists and communist sympathizers. Although only two names belonged to recipients of HUAC subpoenas, the studios nonetheless gave credence to the list and began checking the loyalties of those named. See Ceplair and Englund, *The Inquisition in Hollywood*, 392–393.

8. Thomas Guback, *The International Film Industry: Western Europe and America since 1945* (Bloomington: Indiana University Press, 1969), 165.

9. Although his Hollywood negotiations reached the option stage, Rossellini ultimately decided to remain in Italy out of a sense of patriotism and loyalty; "In Italy there is hardly enough work already and I was afraid of betraying my friends and the people who usually worked with me," he explained. Erica Sheen notes the irony of Rossellini's decision in light of the very different choices the film's director, Edward Dmytryk, would make concerning friendship and betrayal in his HUAC testimony. See Erica Sheen, "Un-American: Dmytryk, Rossellini, and *Christ in Concrete*," *Film Studies* 7 (Winter 2005): 32–42. See also A. H. Weiler, "Random Notes on the Film Scene," *New York Times*, 28 April 1946, and Thomas F. Brady, "Geiger Doing Film at Rank's Studios," *New York Times*, 13 January 1949.

10. Tom Ryall, *Britain and the American Cinema* (London: Sage Publications, 2001), 65–67; Sue Harper and Vincent Porter, *British Cinema of the 1950s: The Decline of Deference* (Oxford: Oxford University Press, 2003), 15.

11. Philippe Carcassonne and Jacques Fieschi, "Ben Barzman," *Cinématographe* 66 (March-April 1981): 42. See also Vincent Ostria, "Qui êtes-vous, Mr. B.B.?," *Le Journal des Cahiers du Cinéma* 31 (February 1983): 3.

12. By the beginning of the postwar period, Rank was the largest and most powerful company in the British film industry. Having acquired the Gaumont British and Odeon firms with their large exhibition circuits, Rank was vertically integrated and possessed assets on a par with those of the major American studios. Ryall, *Britain and the American Cinema*, 59, 61–62, 92–93. See also Geoffrey Macnab, *J. Arthur Rank and the British Film Industry* (London: Routledge, 1993), 176–177, 182–183.

13. Norma Barzman, *The Red and the Blacklist: An Intimate Memoir of a Hollywood Expatriate* (New York: Thunder's Mouth Press/Nation Books, 2003), 149–153; Edward Dmytryk, *Odd Man Out: A Memoir of the Hollywood Ten* (Carbondale: Southern Illinois University Press, 1996), 108.

14. After an initial flurry of censorious articles in the fall of 1947, coverage in the *Times* fell off precipitously. The left-wing *Manchester Guardian* was the most assiduous in its reporting of HUAC's activities, with their correspondent Alistair Cooke submitting a series of articles regarding the anticommunist witch hunts between 1948 and 1953. Cooke's book on the Alger Hiss case, *A Generation on Trial*, was published in 1950.

15. "Free Comment," *Sequence* (Autumn 1948): 3. Discussing the imprisonment of the Hollywood Ten, Lindsay Anderson castigates the British press for their silence in another editorial in 1950: "To Britons, the silence which our Press has preserved over the whole affair is particularly disquieting, for its implications spread far beyond Hollywood or the United States; in recording our sympathetic indignation for these victims of intolerance and hysteria, it is all well that we should remember that witch-hunting is not altogether obsolete here either." *Sequence* 11 (Summer 1950): 1. As *Sequence*'s circulation never exceeded 5,000 copies, Anderson's ability to call attention to the plight of the Hollywood Ten was limited. For more on the history of *Sequence* and its influence, see Erik Hedling, "Lindsay Anderson: *Sequence* and the Rise of Auteurism in 1950s Britain," in *British Cinema of the 1950s: A Celebration*, ed. Ian MacKillop and Neil Sinyard (Manchester: Manchester University Press, 2003), 23–31; see also Hedling, "Lindsay Anderson and the Development of British Art Cinema," in *The British Cinema Book*, ed. Robert Murphy (London: British Film Institute, 2001), 241–247.

16. British censorship laws prohibited the use of the word "Christ" in a title. The film was released as *Give Us This Day* in Europe and as *Salt to the Devil* in the United States. Barzman, *The Red and the Blacklist*, 155.

17. Joan Lester, "Give Us This Day," *Reynolds News*, 30 October 1949; Richard Winnington, "Give Us This Day," *Sight and Sound* 18, no. 72 (1 January 1950): 19–20.
18. Bosley Crowther, "'Give Us This Day,' Film Based on Pietro di Donato Novel, Unveiled at the Rialto," *New York Times*, 21 December 1950; Earl H. Donovan, "'Salt to the Devil' Powerful Film," *Los Angeles Examiner*, 17 June 1950; John McCarten, "Give Us This Day," *New Yorker*, 24 December 1950; Lowell E. Redelings, "Brickbats and Bouquets," *Hollywood Citizen-News*, 20 June 1950; Philip K. Scheuer, "Absorbing Picture Made from Novel of Little Italy," *Los Angeles Times*, 17 June 1950; "Christ in Concrete," *Variety*, 19 June 1950; "Direction, Acting Register in Drama," *Hollywood Reporter*, 19 June 1950; "Give Us This Day," *Motion Picture Herald*, 17 December 1950.
19. Dmytryk, *Odd Man Out*, 110; Barzman, *The Red and the Blacklist*, 121–123.
20. Steinhart, "Hollywood Overseas," 4, 12.
21. C. A. Lejeune, "American Influence Changing British Films," *New York Times*, 19 June 1949.
22. "New York Is the Star of 'Naked City': Hellinger's Last Film Is Manhattan Melodrama," *Cue*, 14 February 1947.
23. Stephen Watts, "Cameras On 'Night and the City' in London," *New York Times*, 2 October 1949.
24. "Night after night, crowds of Londoners, visitors from the provinces and tourists from abroad, drawn by the glare of the arc lamps and the lined up caravans of the inevitable impediments of movie-making, have stood in patient fascination for hours, watching the seemingly snail-like activities by which perhaps two-minutes of motion picture are created." Ibid.
25. Robert Murphy suggests that Dassin "brings more of London to the screen than any film before the 'Swinging London' films of the sixties." See Murphy, *Realism and Tinsel: Cinema and Society in Britain 1939–1948* (London: Routledge, 1989), 164. Twentieth Century–Fox's publicity campaign for *Night and the City* emphasized the "54 different London locations" used in the film, including a list of these locations in its publicity materials. "Night and the City," British Film Institute clipping file. Dassin was not unique in his interest in shooting on location, but rather part of a postwar wave embracing cinematic realism. Taking a tack similar to Fox, Universal's public relations department had seized upon Dassin's extensive use of location shooting in *The Naked City* (1948), boasting of the "107" authentic New York City locations shown in the film. See Rebecca Prime, "Cloaked in Compromise: Jules Dassin's 'Naked' City," in *"Un-American" Hollywood: Politics and Film in the Blacklist Era*, ed. Frank Krutnik, Brian Neve, Steve Neale, and Peter Stanfield (New Brunswick, N.J.: Rutgers University Press, 2007), 142–151.
26. Dassin recalls that Douglas Fairbanks Jr. was particularly helpful in casting the smaller roles. See Philippe Garnier, "Les Forbans de Hollywood," *Cinéma* 8 (Autumn 2004): 43; Christian Viviani, "Jules Dassin: Décidé à être un héros," *Positif*, no. 466 (December 1999): 96.
27. Dassin remembers receiving a call from Zanuck, who asked him to write in a role for Gene Tierney as a favor; Tierney had had an unhappy love affair and Zanuck thought that the change of scene and distractions of work in London would be good for her. Viviani, "Jules Dassin," 96. See also Patrick McGilligan, "Jules Dassin," in Patrick McGilligan and Paul Buhle, *Tender Comrades: A Backstory of the Hollywood Blacklist* (New York: St. Martin's, 1997), 208; John Francis Lane, "I See Dassin Make 'The Law,' *Films and Filming* 4, no. 12 (4 September 1958): 28.
28. In a number of interviews from both the 1950s and more recent years, Dassin was very positive about the film, crediting it as some of his best work and with teaching him his craft. However, he has also referred to *Night and the City* as a film he has "chosen to forget," and in 2004 described the production as an awful, painful experience in a letter to Philippe Garnier.

See Garnier, "Les Forbans," 42; Gordon Gow, "Style and Instinct," *Films and Filming* 16, no. 4 (February 1970): 26; Cynthia Grenier, "Jules Dassin," *Sight and Sound* 22, no. 3 (Winter 1957–58): 142; Lane, "I See Dassin," 28; Viviani, "Jules Dassin," 96.

29. "I still can't believe that I remained ignorant of these changes for 53 years after having made the film. What hurts me the most is that Zanuck—towards whom I really was in debt, for his honorable behavior on another occasion—could have done this behind my back and never mentioned it to me when he lived in Paris in the late 1950s and we used to see each other frequently." Dassin quoted in Garnier, "Les Forbans," 42.

30. Composers in Britain retain the rights to their work, a practice that may have encouraged Fox to commission a separate American version for which the studio could own the rights. Garnier, "Les Forbans," 40. For more on the quota system, see Margaret Dickenson and Sarah Street, *Cinema and State: The Film Industry and the Government 1927–84* (London: British Film Institute, 1985), 195–198.

31. For a detailed discussion of *Night and the City* in relation to American and British traditions of film noir, see chapter 4.

32. "Night and the City," *Times*, 19 June 1950; Dilys Powell, "Night and the City," *Sunday Times*, 18 June 1950.

33. Roy Nash, "This Film Insults London," *Star*, 13 June 1950; "Night and the City," *Evening Standard*, 15 June 1950.

34. François Truffaut and Claude Chabrol, "Entretien avec Jules Dassin II," *Cahiers du cinema* 8, no. 47 (May 1955): 9; "Protest U.S. Actors in British Film Roles," *New York Times*, 29 June 1950, 36. Tensions between the British and American film industries had peaked the previous year, when Hollywood imposed a total boycott of the British market in retaliation for the 75 percent import tax on foreign films that went into effect in August 1947. The boycott lasted through the following March, when the British government, considering the interests of exhibitors most affected by the shortage of product, repealed the tax.

35. In a letter to Philippe Garnier, Dassin says that before he left London, Douglas Fairbanks Jr., acting as Darryl Zanuck's messenger, indicated that he wouldn't be welcome at Fox when he returned to Los Angeles. See Garnier, "Les Forbans," 26–43. See also Jules Dassin, Twentieth Century–Fox Legal Files, Box 690, Performing Arts Special Collections, University of California, Los Angeles.

36. Losey's biographer suggests that Vorhaus was originally to have directed *A Bottle of Milk* as well, but he ceded the job to Losey after being named by Edward Dmytryk in April 1951. See David Caute, *Joseph Losey: A Revenge on Life* (New York: Oxford University Press, 1994), 96.

37. Forzano's father had served as a minister of culture of sorts under Mussolini. Salvatore was by all accounts an unsavory character, known as "the lemon-squeezer of Livorno" because of his work as a private tax collector for Mussolini, according to John Weber. Losey goes even further, stating that Salvatore had been condemned to death as a war criminal. See Paul Buhle, "John Weber," in McGilligan and Buhle, *Tender Comrades*, 696; Michel Ciment, *Conversations with Losey* (London: Methuen, 1985), 128; Barzman, *The Red and the Blacklist*, 242.

38. Bernard Vorhaus was named by Edward Dmytryk in his testimony on 26 April 1951; Ben and Norma Barzman, Joseph Losey, and John Weber were named by the screenwriter Leo Townsend in September 1951. See Victor S. Navasky, *Naming Names*, 3rd ed. (New York: Hill and Wang, 2003), 283.

39. Buhle, "John Weber," 696.

40. See Larry Ceplair, "Norma Barzman," in McGilligan and Buhle, *Tender Comrades*, 14; Barzman, *The Red and the Blacklist*, 252; Ciment, *Conversations*, 130.

41. Buhle, "John Weber," 696–697; Caute, *Joseph Losey*, 96–97; Ciment, *Conversations*, 128–131.

42. "U.S. Actors Seek Ban on Red Films," *New York Times*, 26 August 1952.

43. Philip K. Scheuer, "Muni Returns," *Los Angeles Times*, 3 December 1953.

44. Shandley, *Runaway Romances*, 20, 26.

45. Bernard Vorhaus, *Saved from Oblivion: An Autobiography* (Lanham, Md.: Scarecrow Press, 2000), 122.

46. Paul Buhle, "John Weber," in McGilligan and Buhle, *Tender Comrades*, 697.

47. Bertrand Tavernier, *Amis américains: Entretiens avec les grands auteurs d'Hollywood* (Lyons: Institut Lumière/Actes Sud, 1993), 515.

48. "Writer Files Suit for U.S. Passport," *New York Times*, 2 May 1956. Two months earlier—and three years into his fight to regain his passport—Stewart had finally submitted a signed affidavit regarding his past Party membership to the American Embassy in London, but he was still denied a passport. In November 1957, when the Federal Court of Appeals in Washington ruled that Stewart's affidavit made him eligible to receive a passport, Stewart held a "wake" for his alias Gilbert Holland at the embassy's bar. "Donald Ogden Stewart, Playwright, Wins 5-Year Battle for Passport to Continent," *New York Times*, 8 November 1957; "A Witch Hunt Film Man Holds a Wake," *News Chronicle*, 7 November 1957.

49. "Carl Foreman Gets New U.S. Passport," *Hollywood Reporter*, 16 January 1956; "Film Writer Wins Return of Passport," *Los Angeles Times*, 14 January 1956. See also Navasky, *Naming Names*, 161.

50. Sidney Cohn, Interview, Carl Foreman Collection, Item 1, Special Collections, British Film Institute.

51. By 1961, four years after the film's release, this profit participation has already earned Foreman $250,000. See Kevin Brownlow, *David Lean: A Biography* (London: St. Martin's Press, 1996), 387–388.

52. David Lean was not aware that Spiegel had hired Wilson until the producer arrived in Sri Lanka on 8 September 1956 with Wilson in tow. Brownlow, *David Lean*, 352–358; Natasha Fraser-Cavassoni, *Sam Spiegel: The Incredible Life and Times of Hollywood's Most Iconoclastic Producer* (New York: Simon & Schuster, 2003), 177–185.

53. House Un-American Activities Committee, Box 37, Carl Foreman Executive Session Transcript, Records of the House of Representatives, National Archives, Washington, D.C.

54. Cohn notes that Foreman could have signed a deal with Fox worth $1 million, but stayed with Columbia in gratitude for their help with *The Bridge on the River Kwai*. Sidney Cohn, Interview, Carl Foreman Collection, Item 1, Special Collections, British Film Institute. To celebrate the deal, Columbia threw Foreman a star-studded party at Claridge's, with guests ranging from Carol Reed to Alec Guinness to "Britain's Marilyn Monroe," Diana Dors. David Lewin, *Daily Express*, 22 March 1957; "Carl Foreman, Clearing Self with Red Probers, to Produce 4 Col Pix," *Daily Variety*, 1 March 1957.

55. "Ask for Full Testimony in Carl Foreman Case," *Hollywood Reporter*, 18 April 1957; "Veterans of Foreign Wars Blasting Carl Foreman; Columbia Deal Stands," *Variety*, 24 April 1957.

56. Sidney Cohn, interview, Carl Foreman Collection, Item 1, Special Collections, British Film Institute. The final transcript shows that the committee strategically deleted large portions of Foreman's original testimony, specifically those in which Foreman expresses his opposition to naming names. House Un-American Activities Committee, Box 37, Carl Foreman Executive Session Transcript, Records of the House of Representatives, National Archives, Washington, D.C.

57. Paul Jarrico to Michael Wilson, 21 March 1957, Michael Wilson Papers, Box 48, Folder 4, Performing Arts Special Collections, University of California, Los Angeles.

58. Marguerite Roberts and John Sanford to Joseph Losey, 17 December 1958, Joseph Losey Collection, Item 104, Special Collections, British Film Institute.
59. Donald Ogden Stewart Jr., letter to author, 7 February 2007.
60. Navasky, *Naming Names*, 163.
61. Michael Seifert, interview with author, 25 April 2007; Robin Dalton, interview with author, 1 May 2007; Maureen Endfield, interview with author, 2 May 2007; Joseph Losey Collection, British Film Institute Special Collections. Losey, who read Foreman's testimony, confirms that Foreman did not name names. Nonetheless, "he made statements that would have stuck in my throat. I never understood how he could do that. I'm reasonably sure he didn't believe what he said, and I charged him with this privately. But he said, 'Well, you don't appear before people like that if you aren't prepared to give them something. What did you want me to do?'" See Navasky, *Naming Names*, 164. Michael Wilson also asserts that Foreman never named names, explaining to Alvah Bessie in 1974 that "the best evidence is that he took a diminished fifth position." Michael Wilson to Alvah Bessie, 14 May 1974, Michael Wilson Papers, Box 48, Folder 2, Performing Arts Special Collections, University of California, Los Angeles.
62. Jan Berry, interview with author, 8 February 2007; Denis Berry, interview with author, 17 March 2007.
63. Richard Kuisel offers this summary of the effect of the events of 1956 on the French Left: "The Red Army's invasion of Hungary shook confidence in the USSR and communism as forced for human liberation. Khrushchev's denunciation of Stalin's crimes seemed to confirm the worst anti-Communist charges about the Soviet Union. Sartre and others broke with the PCF [Parti Communist Français]." Richard Kuisel, *Seducing the French: The Dilemma of Americanization* (Berkeley: University of California Press, 1996), 127.
64. "*Sel de la terre*," *Cahiers du cinema* 7, no. 40 (November 1954): 29–30; *Cine Technician* 27, no. 138 (June 1956).
65. Although Wyler publicly acknowledged Wilson's participation in the film at the festival and was known for his liberal politics, he had bowed to industry pressure to exclude Wilson from the credits, an omission all the more notable for the fact that the film was independently produced and released by Allied Artists. Samuel Lachize, "Un Bon Film Américain: *La Loi du Seigneur*," *L'Humanité*, 14 May 1957; R. M. Arlaud, "Au Festival de Cannes: Un cadavre vient d'animer la fête," *Combat*, 14 May 1957; R. M. Arlaud, "Au Festival de Cannes: La farandole des favoris," *Combat*, 15 May 1957; François Roche, "La 'B.B. Party' soulève une tempête sur le festival," *France-Soir*, 15 May 1957; *Lettres et Arts*, 16 May 1957.
66. "A Cannes, Michael Wilson s'élève contre *La Loi du seigneur*," *Le Monde*, 15 May 1957.
67. Ben Barzman describes meeting Marcel Pagnol, the president of the French jury, on a train back to Paris after the festival. "[He] told me openly that pressure had been brought on him and the other French members of the jury by elements of the American delegation, to avoid giving our film a major prize. . . . He also indicated that even Jean Cocteau, who had also been on the jury, had submitted to the pressure." Navasky, *Naming Names*, 343.
68. The Academy reinstated Wilson's nomination in December 2002.
69. David Lean to Michael Wilson, 30 January 1958, Michael Wilson Papers, Box 48, Folder 4, Performing Arts Special Collections, University of California, Los Angeles.
70. Ibid.
71. Michael Wilson to Paul Jarrico, 21 November 1957, Michael Wilson Papers, Box 48, Folder 1, Performing Arts Special Collections, University of California, Los Angeles; Dino de Laurentiis to Michael Wilson, 27 November 1957, Box 48, Folder 10, Performing Arts Special Collections, University of California, Los Angeles; Michael Wilson to Sam Spiegel, 30 November

1957, Michael Wilson Papers, Box 46, Folder 13, Performing Arts Special Collections, University of California, Los Angeles.

72. During the 1950s and early 1960s, the King brothers hired members of the blacklisted exile community for various projects, including the West German production *Carnival Story* (1954, scr. Michael Wilson and Dalton Trumbo) and, most famously, *The Brave One* (1956), for which Dalton Trumbo (as Robert Rich) was awarded the Oscar for Best Screenplay. Dalton Trumbo to Michael Wilson, 9 January 1958, Michael Wilson Papers, Box 48, Folder 1, Performing Arts Special Collections, University of California, Los Angeles; Michael Wilson to Dalton Trumbo, 28 April 1958, Michael Wilson Papers, Box 48, Folder 1, Performing Arts Special Collections, University of California, Los Angeles.

73. David Lean to Michael Wilson, 3 February 1960, Michael Wilson Papers, Box 18, Folder 8, Performing Arts Special Collections, University of California, Los Angeles.

74. Fraser-Cavassoni, *Sam Spiegel*, 221.

75. Michael Wilson to Robert Bolt, 29 November 1962, Michael Wilson Papers, Box 18, Folder 8, Performing Arts Special Collection, University of California, Los Angeles.

76. Ibid.

77. Michael Wilson to Robert Bolt, 29 November 1962, Michael Wilson Papers, Box 18, Folder 8, Performing Arts Special Collection, University of California, Los Angeles. The "American producer" to which Wilson refers is probably Samuel Goldwyn Jr., who had agreed to give Wilson credit for his adaptation of Howard Fast's novel *April Morning*. The film was never made.

78. Joseph Losey to Michael Wilson, 1 October 1957, Michael Wilson Papers, Box 48, Folder 3, Performing Arts Special Collections, University of California, Los Angeles.

79. Ciment, *Conversations*, 151–153.

80. Edith de Rham, *Joseph Losey* (London: Deutsch, 1991), 107.

81. Ciment, *Conversations*, 154.

82. Rank did produce the project, although not with Barzman's script (*SOS Pacific*, dir. Guy Green, 1959).

83. Joseph Losey to John Collier, 20 August 1958, Joseph Losey Collection, Item 88, British Film Institute.

84. Caute, *Joseph Losey*, 131.

85. Joseph Losey Collection, Item 104, British Film Institute.

86. David Robinson, "Blind Date," *Financial Times*, 24 August 1959; "Blind Date," *Guardian*, 22 August 1959; Isobel Quigley, "Blind Date," *Spectator*, 28 August 1959; "Blind Date," British Film Institute Clipping File.

87. Caute, *Joseph Losey*, 132.

88. Murray Schumach, "Studio Buys Film By 'Subversives': Paramount Will Distribute Movie Made by 3 Suspected of Left-Wing Leanings," *New York Times*, 9 February 1960.

89. Ciment, *Conversations*, 171.

90. Caute, *Joseph Losey*, 135. The film opened in Brooklyn as the second feature in a double bill. Joan Barthel, "'I'm an American, for God's Sake!,'" *New York Times*, 26 March 1967.

91. Hollis Alpert, "Chance Meeting," *Saturday Review*, 27 February 1960; Eugene Archer, "Chance Meeting," *New York Times*, 27 October 1960.

92. Joseph Losey to Evan Jones, 4 April 1960, Joseph Losey Collection, Item 88, British Film Institute.

93. Joseph Losey to Dirk Bogarde, 5 May 1961, Joseph Losey Collection, Item 87, British Film Institute. The project collapsed when Foreman withdrew his support at the last minute, prompting an irrevocable rift in his friendship with Losey. See Ciment, *Conversations*, 284, 397.

94. The text of the statement, dated 26 September 1960, reads as follows:

To whom it may concern.

I make this statement voluntarily and under oath hoping thereby to put an end to any possible question about my loyalty to the United States and to remove once and for all any doubt as to my position and my opinion on communism.

I am unreservedly opposed to anything that communism represents and espouses. I join with those who fight totalitarianism and I will support and defend the United States against its enemies.

I am not a communist and I disavow any previous association which may have involved me in any way with the communist party or any front organization.

Joseph Losey

See Caute, *Joseph Losey*, 135.

95. Association of Motion Picture and Television Producers (AMPTP) Records, 1931–1990, Item no: 17-f.171, AMPAS.

CHAPTER 4: THE BLACKLIST, EXILE, AND THE TRANSATLANTIC NOIR

1. David Caute, *Joseph Losey: A Revenge on Life* (New York: Oxford University Press, 1994), 104.
2. Quoted in Tom Milne, *Losey on Losey* (New York: Doubleday, 1968), 93.
3. Patrick McGilligan, "John Berry," in Patrick McGilligan and Paul Buhle, *Tender Comrades: A Backstory of the Hollywood Blacklist* (New York: St. Martin's Press, 1997), 74.
4. "He came to my house in the middle of the night—and coming to my house was like visiting the tenements, because I lived on the wrong side of town. He said, 'Get out. Get out fast. Here's a book. You're going to London. Get a screenplay as fast as you can and start shooting the most expensive scenes. Then they might let you finish it.' That was *Night and the City.*" See Patrick McGilligan, "Jules Dassin," in McGilligan and Buhle, *Tender Comrades*, 208.
5. Caute, *Joseph Losey*, 106.
6. Bertrand Tavernier, *Amis américains: Entretiens avec les grands auteurs d'Hollywood* (Lyons: Institut Lumière/Actes Sud, 1993), 611–612.
7. Both Blair and Barzman give accounts of Berry fleeing through a bathroom window while government agents waited at the front door. Betsy Blair, interview with author, 9 July 2005, and Norma Barzman, interview with author, 10 July 2006.
8. Jules Dassin, Twentieth Century–Fox Legal Files, Box 690, Performing Arts Special Collections, University of California, Los Angeles.
9. Vincent Brook, *Driven to Darkness: Jewish Emigré Directors and the Rise of Film Noir* (New Brunswick, N.J.: Rutgers University Press, 2009).
10. Jonathan Auerbach, *Dark Borders: Film Noir and American Citizenship* (Durham, N.C.: Duke University Press, 2011), 1.
11. Ibid., 2.
12. "The hard facts of economic life are transmuted, in these movies, into corresponding moods and feelings. Thus the feelings of loss and alienation expressed by the characters in film noir can be seen as the product both of post-war depression and of the reorganization of the American economy." Sylvia Harvey cited in David Reid and Jayne L. Walker, "Strange Pursuit: Cornell Woolrich and the Abandoned City of the Forties" in *Shades of Noir*, ed. Joan Copjec (New York: Verso, 1993), 58–59.
13. For a clear and thorough discussion of film noir's diverse cultural influences, see Andrew Spicer, *Film Noir* (London: Pearson Education Limited, 2002), 5–19; Sheri Chinen Biesen

provides a detailed analysis of film noir's wartime genesis in *Blackout: World War II and the Origins of Film Noir* (Baltimore: Johns Hopkins University Press, 2005).

14. For example, James Naremore, *More Than Night: Film Noir in Its Contexts* (Berkeley: University of California Press, 1998); see also Marc Vernet, "Film Noir on the Edge of Doom," in Copjec, *Shades of Noir*, 1–31.

15. Vernet, "Film Noir," 4–5.

16. Paul Schrader, "Notes on Film Noir," in *Film Noir Reader*, ed. Alain Silver and James Ursini (New York: Limelight Editions, 1996), 63.

17. J. P. Telotte, "Noir Narration," in *Post-War Cinema and Modernity: A Film Reader*, ed. John Orr and Olga Taxidou (Edinburgh: Edinburgh University Press, 2000), 33.

18. Steve Neale, "Film Noir," in *Genre and Hollywood* (London: Routledge, 2000), 152–153, 169; Biesen, *Blackout*, 2.

19. Jules Dassin, interview, *Night and the City* DVD (Criterion Collection, 2005).

20. Richard Maltby articulates the pitfalls of a "Zeitgeist theory of film as cultural history, which is based more on critical ingenuity in textual interpretation than on any precise location of movies within the historical circumstances of their production and consumption. . . . As history . . . it is notoriously difficult to substantiate, since it is inevitably dependent on the selective presentation of its evidence." For example, film noir represented only a small percentage of Hollywood's production during the 1940s and 1950s, which raises the question of how other, more prominent genres of production reflected the postwar zeitgeist. See Richard Maltby, "The Politics of the Maladjusted Text," in *The Movie Book of Film Noir*, ed. Ian Cameron (London: Studio Vista, 1992), 41.

21. Vivian Sobchack, "Lounge Time: Postwar Crises and the Chronotope of Film Noir," in *Refiguring American Film Genres: History and Theory*, ed. Nick Browne (Berkeley: University of California Press, 1998), 130–136. The French anthropologist Marc Augé uses the phrase "non-place" to refer to places of transience that do not hold enough significance to be regarded as "places." Examples include airports, highways, hotel rooms, and supermarkets. See Marc Augé, *Non-Places: Introduction to an Anthropology of Supermodernity*, trans. John Howe (London: Verso, 1995).

22. Andrew Dickos, *Street with No Name: A History of the Classic American Film Noir* (Lexington: University Press of Kentucky, 2002), 76; Glenn Erickson, "Expressionist Doom in *Night and the City*," in Silver and Ursini, *Film Noir Reader*, 203; Foster Hirsch, *The Dark Side of the Screen: Film Noir* (Cambridge, Mass.: Da Capo Press, 2001), 128.

23. Raymond Borde and Etienne Chaumeton, *A Panorama of American Film Noir, 1941–1953*, trans. Paul Hammond (San Francisco: City Lights Books, 2002), 137; Andrew C. Mayer, "Films from Abroad: Crime Wave," *Quarterly of Film, Radio, and Television* 11, no. 2 (Winter 1956): 168.

24. Virginia Graham, "Night and the City," *Spectator*, 16 June 1950.

25. Robert Murphy, *Realism and Tinsel: Cinema and Society in Britain 1939–1948* (London: Routledge, 1989), 149–159.

26. Peter Wollen, *Paris Hollywood: Writings on Film* (London: Verso, 2002), 189.

27. William K. Everson, "British Film Noir," *Films in Review* 38, no. 5 (May 1987): 287. While Andrew Spicer also acknowledges the influence of Poetic Realism on the British noir, he sees *It Always Rains on Sunday* as more representative of noir semi-documentary films such as *Pool of London* (promoted as Britain's *Naked City*) that combined a "documentary-style exploration of a topical issue with an evocative use of a noir visual register." See Spicer, "Film Noir," 190.

28. Graham, "Night and the City," 1950.

29. Murphy, *Realism and Tinsel*, 152.

30. Ibid., 163; Spicer, *Film Noir*, 177; Stephen Watts, "Cameras on *Night and the City* in London," *New York Times*, 2 October 1949.
31. Ginette Vincendeau suggests the rapport between characters and their environment to be greatly emphasized in both French Poetic Realist cinema (an antecedent of French *noir*) and American film noir, the difference being that "in French films, action is steeped in social milieu, and violence tends to be motivated, not gratuitous." See Ginette Vincendeau, "Noir Is Also a French Word: The French Antecedents of Film Noir," in *The Book of Film Noir*, ed. Ian Cameron (New York: Continuum, 1993), 49. See also Ginette Vincendeau, *Jean-Pierre Melville: An American in Paris* (London: British Film Institute, 2003), 100.
32. Alastair Phillips, *Rififi* (London: I. B. Tauris, 2009), 30n48.
33. Borde and Chaumeton, *Panorama*, 135.
34. Vincendeau, *Jean-Pierre Melville*, 101.
35. Peter Wollen notes that the spiv cycle coincides with the years of Clement Attlee's reforming Labour government, "which brought the working class—or its representatives—to power for the first time in British history." See Wollen, "Paris Hollywood," 189.
36. "Many books and films feature a protagonist who, after a period in jail, experiences failure and disappointment; nostalgia for the prewar is rife. Chronotopes of confinement and stasis can also be related to the war and German occupation, as can the pessimism and violence of the genre, the death-drive of its characters." Vincendeau, *Jean-Pierre Melville*, 102.
37. Through the intervention of a French producer and a government official, friends from the Resistance, Dassin was able to obtain a *titre de voyage* that allowed him to travel within Europe. Patrick McGilligan, "Jules Dassin Interviewed," *Film Comment* 32, no. 6 (November/December 1996): 45.
38. Burt Bernstein, interview with author, 14 March 2007.
39. McGilligan, "Jules Dassin," 217. A version of *Maestro Don Gesauldo*, directed by Giacomo Vaccari, was made for Italian television in 1964.
40. John Francis Lane, "I See Dassin Make 'The Law,'" *Films and Filming* 4, no. 12 (4 September 1958): 29.
41. Claude Chabrol and François Truffaut, "Interview with Jules Dassin," *Cahiers du cinéma* 8, no. 47 (May 1955): 12.
42. As Dassin remembers the experience: "The producer said I was the only person who could make the book into a film. I asked why. He said, 'The problem is that all the bad guys in this story are North African, and at this moment relations between France and Algeria are explosive. But *you* can make the bad guys American.' I said, 'Has it occurred to you to make them French?' He was stunned at first and then accepted." McGilligan, "Jules Dassin," 218–219.
43. *La Croix* named *Thieves' Highway* one of the year's top films, while *Le Figaro littéraire* called Dassin one of the most brilliant new American directors in its review of the film. "Les Bas Fonds de Frisco," *La Croix*, n.d., CNC clipping file for *Thieves' Highway;* Claude Mauriac, "Le Bas Fonds de Frisco," *Le Figaro littéraire*, 8 July 1950. François Truffaut considered *Night and the City* to be the pinnacle of Dassin's pre-*Rififi* oeuvre. François Truffaut, "Jules Dassin et le *Rififi*," *Arts*, 15 December 1954.
44. *Rififi* was budgeted at 90 million francs, slightly below the 100 million franc average at the time but hardly as minuscule as Dassin claims it to have been. The film ended up costing almost 140 million francs. *Du rififi chez les hommes*, cote 658B450, Fonds Crédit National, dossiers d'archives, Bibliothèque du Film. Colin Crisp, *The Classic French Cinema, 1930–1960* (Bloomington: Indiana University Press, 1997), 86–87.
45. Melville was paid two million francs (about $5,700) for his participation in *Rififi*. *Du rififi chez les hommes*, Fonds Crédit National, cote 658B450, Bibliothèque du Film. According to Melville, he had persuaded Bérard to buy the rights to the book, who in turn promised him

the job of director. When Melville finally heard from Bérard again six months later, the producer had replaced him with Dassin. However, Dassin "had the extreme courtesy to say that he would do it only if I wrote to tell him that I was happy about the arrangement. Which I did." See Rui Nogueira, ed., *Melville on Melville* (London: Secker and Warburg/British Film Institute, 1971), 154.

46. Dassin's share of the profits went up to 25 percent once the producers had made back over 50 million francs. *Du rififi chez les hommes*, cote 658B450, Fonds Crédit National, dossiers d'archives, Bibliothèque du Film. Although Dassin's salary was small compared to what he had been making in Hollywood (over $4,300 a week with fifteen weeks employment guaranteed according to the terms of his last contract with Fox), it was more than double the average cost of living for a white-collar French family of four, which was estimated at 1.9 million francs in 1956. *Annuaire Statistique de la France*, Institut Nationale de la Statistique et des Études Économiques, Imprimerie Nationale et Presses Universitaires de France, 1960. George Wasson to Donald Henderson, 6 February 1950. Jules Dassin, Twentieth Century–Fox Legal Files, Box 690, UCLA Arts Library Special Collections.

47. "Jules Dassin," *Étoiles et Toiles*, TF1, 3 June 1985.

48. Auguste Le Breton, "Le *Rififi* trente ans après," *Le Matin*, 17 July 1984.

49. The shoot ran from 20 September to 25 December 1954. *Du rififi chez les hommes*, Fonds Crédit National, Cote 658 B450 and Cote CN 1440 B643, Bibliothèque du Film.

50. "From the worst pulp novel I've ever read, Dassin has created the best film noir I've ever seen." François Truffaut, "*Du rififi chez les hommes*," *Arts*, April 1955.

51. Louis Chauvet, "Du rififi chez les hommes," *Le Figaro*, 14 April 1955.

52. Vance Bourjaily, "Movies Uptown: Rififi," *Village Voice*, 4 July 1956; Henry Hart, "Rififi," *Films in Review* 7, no. 6 (June-July 1956): 290.

53. Jean-Paul Marquet,"Le Vrai Dassin," *Positif*, no. 14–15 (November 1955): 73.

54. Borde and Chaumeton, *Panorama*, 135; Marquet, "Le Vrai Dassin," 73.

55. Naremore, *More Than Night*, 22; Vernet, "Film Noir," 5–6.

56. John Berry, a close friend of Altman's, was outraged by Dassin's sly reference. Jacques Nahum, interview with author, 14 March 2007.

57. "Jules Dassin," *Étoiles et Toiles*, TF1, 10 June 1985. Ironically, Dassin ended up playing the role of César himself, after the Italian actor hired for the part dropped out at the last minute.

58. "Tournage du film de Jules Dassin, *Du rififi chez les hommes*," 26 October 1954, Inathèque.

59. *Nulle Part Ailleurs*, Canal+, 21 June 1999; *20H: Le Journal Cinéma*, France 2, 12 August 1999.

60. Borde and Chaumeton, *Panorama*, 136–137.

61. Marquet observes that *Rififi* does contain one allusion to the "loi du milieu" when Tony le Stéphanois executes César le Milanais. Marquet, "Le Vrai Dassin," 72.

62. Catherine Gaston-Mathé, *La Société Française au Miroir de son Cinéma: De la débâcle à la décolonization* (Paris: Arléa-Corlet, 1996), 160.

63. Philippe Carcassonne, "Trois hommes du Milieu," *Cinématographe* 63 (December 1980): 38.

64. Vincendeau, *Jean-Pierre Melville*, 112–113.

65. *The Naked City* (1947) and *Thieves' Highway* (1949) likewise include scenes of domestic life with young children.

66. Vincendeau, "Noir Is Also a French Word," 58.

67. Chabrol and Truffaut, "Interview with Jules Dassin," 14.

68. Truffaut, "Du rififi chez les hommes," 2–26.

69. Watts, "Cameras on *Night and the City*."

70. George Bluestone, "Interview with Jules Dassin," *Film Culture*, no. 17 (February 1958): 4.

71. Borde and Chaumeton, *Panorama*, 136–137.

72. For a discussion of changes in French film culture during the 1950s, see Claude Forest, "De Vichy au Quartier latin: l'âge d'or du cinéma populaire," in *CinémAction: Le Cinéma du Sam'di Soir*, ed. Gérard Dessère and Nicholas Schmidt (Editions Corlet/Telerama: Condé-sur-Noireau 2000), no. 95, 50–60.

73. These developments are examined more extensively in chapter 6.

74. Examples include André Hunnebelle's *Mission à Tanger* (1949), *Méfiez-vous des blondes* (1950), and *Massacre en dentelles* (1951) and Bernard Borderie's *Les Loups chassent la nuit* (1952), *La Môme vert-de-gris* (1953), and *Les femmes s'en balancent* (1954).

75. Borde and Chaumeton, *Panorama*, 128–129.

76. Pierre Billard, *L'Age Classique du Cinéma Française: du cinéma parlant à la Nouvelle Vague* (Paris: Flammarion, 1995), 550. Constantine would play Lemmy Caution for the last time in 1991, in Jean-Luc Godard's *Allemagne année 90 neuf zero;* previously, he starred as Caution in Godard's science fiction–inspired *Alphaville* (1965).

77. Berry described screening two of Constantine's earlier films: "I realized right away he didn't know what he was doing, but man, he really did come off the screen. I think it was his terror." Patrick McGilligan, "John Berry," in *Tender Comrades*, 80.

78. Berry had previously worked with Dekobra as a dialogue coach on the writer's directorial debut, *La Rafle est pour ce soir* (1954). Berry's role may have extended to that of director; "They kept asking me where to put the camera," he recalls. "Hommage à John Berry," *Projection Privée*, France Culture, 31 May 1997. See also Christian Viviani, "J'ai eu une vie magnifique: Entretien avec John Berry," *Positif*, no. 436 (June 1997): 64.

79. McGilligan, "John Berry," 79.

80. Ibid.

81. With the founding of the Centre national de la cinématographie in 1946, the process of obtaining work permits became highly regulated. For instance, to be eligible for a director's permit, it was necessary to have worked on at least three films in the capacity of assistant director. The French film trade union (Syndicat national des techniciens et réalisateurs) exercised a virtual monopoly on the distribution of these permits, which presented a serious obstacle to the introduction of new talent into the industry. See Billard, *L'Age Classique*, 508–509.

82. Viviani, "Une vie magnifique," 64.

83. While many reviewers dismissed the film as a rehash of earlier Constantine adventures, exceptions were *L'Humanité*, which called the film "a minor comic masterpiece," and *France-Observateur*, whose critic—André Bazin—praised Berry for fulfilling the comic promise hinted at in an earlier Constantine film, Bernard Borderie's *Les femmes s'en balancent* (1954). "Je suis un sentimental," *L'Humanité Dimanche*, 16 October 1955; André Bazin, "Je suis un sentimental," *France-Observateur*, 3 November 1955.

84. Tavernier, *Amis américains*, 613.

85. The production histories of his period films *Don Juan* (1956) and *Tamango* (1958) are discussed in chapter 6.

86. Brian Neve, "Cases in European Film Culture and the Hollywood Blacklist Diaspora," in *The Lost Decade? The 1950s in European History, Politics, Society, and Culture*, ed. Heiko Feldner, Claire Gorrara, and Kevin Passmore (Newcastle: Cambridge Scholars Publishing, 2011), 238; see also Brian Neve, "An Interview with Cy Endfield," *Film Studies: An International Review* 7 (Winter 2005): 124.

87. Neve, "Cases in European Film Culture," 238.

88. Jonathan Rosenbaum, "Pages from the Endfield File," *Film Comment* 29, no. 6 (November 1993): 53.

89. Spicer, *Film Noir*, 194.

90. Neve, "Interview with Cy Endfield," 125.

91. "Hell Drivers," *Spectator*, 2 August 1957.
92. "Duel with Lorries," *Daily Times*, 27 July 1957.
93. Milne, *Losey on Losey*, 161.
94. Ginger Rogers was probably in England to make *Twist of Fate* (dir. David Miller, 1954). See Caute, *Joseph Losey*, 121–122.
95. Colin Gardner, *Joseph Losey*, (Manchester: Manchester University Press, 2004), 36–37.
96. Milne, *Losey on Losey*, 45–46.
97. Maureen Endfield describes Baker as a "very close friend" of her husband's; in addition to starring five of Endfield's films (*Hell Drivers, Sea Fury, Jet Storm, Zulu*, and *Sands of the Kalahari*), he became his producing partner in 1960. Maureen Endfield, interview with author, 2 May 2007; Sheldon Hall, *Zulu: With Some Guts Behind It—The Making of the Epic Movie* (Sheffield: Tomahawk Press, 2005), 118–119. Losey also describes having "a very good relationship" with Baker, whom he worked with in *The Criminal* and *Accident* in addition to *Blind Date* and *Eve*. Michel Ciment, *Conversations with Losey* (London: Methuen 1985), 175.
98. Ciment, *Conversations*, 178.
99. In a closing voiceover laden with despair, Jones offers the following self-assessment: "Part-time writer, part-time guide, full-time exile in my Babylon."
100. Ciment, *Conversations*, 210, 178.
101. Norma Barzman, interview with author, 10 July 2006.
102. Phillips, *Rififi*, 1, 76.
103. Naficy defines "accented cinema" in opposition to Hollywood and proposes three key differences, of which the first two appear relevant to blacklisted production in Europe: (1) accented cinema places greater emphasis on the personal or autobiographical; (2) accented cinema is produced, distributed, and exhibited outside of a studio system; and (3) ethnic collectives and media arts organizations play important roles as funders and producers. See Hamid Naficy, *An Accented Cinema: Exilic and Diasporic Filmmaking* (Princeton, N.J.: Princeton University Press, 2001).

CHAPTER 5: COSMOPOLITAN VISIONS, COLD WAR FEARS

1. Bosley Crowther, "The Swing Abroad: Film Production Moving to European Studios," *New York Times*, 19 June 1960.
2. Stephen Watts, "British Report—Heavy Foreign Agenda for Columbia," *New York Times*, 9 July 1961.
3. Murray Schumach, "Fox Studio Defies Movie Blacklist," *New York Times*, 12 May 1960.
4. "Lopert Does What UA Cannot," *Weekly Variety*, 15 April 1959.
5. Murray Schumach, "Fox Studio Defies Movie Blacklist," *New York Times*, 12 May 1960.
6. Murray Schumach, "Movie Industry Seeks U.S. Help: Report on Runaway Films Cites Unfair Practices," *New York Times*, 25 January 1963. Carl Foreman frequently expressed similar sentiments, using his self-appointed position as a cultural emissary between the British film industry and Hollywood to urge the U.S. government to follow Europe's example by providing both financial and promotional support for its films. See "Foreman Urges Gov't Film Aid to Solve 'Runaway' Problem," *Hollywood Reporter*, 3 July 1961.
7. This final point evokes the charge levied by the Hollywood AFL Film Council in 1959 that films made by American "runaway" producers in Europe "give aid and comfort to the Communist conspiracy against the free world." This claim, of course, reiterates HUAC's central accusation that Hollywood's radicals were slipping communist propaganda into their films and also resonates with Hollywood's heightened involvement in foreign policy during the

postwar years. Association of Motion Picture and Television Producers (AMPTP) Records, 1931–1990, Item no: 17-f.171, AMPAS.

8. In 1948, the producer Walter Wanger noted that the "motion picture industry has been the nearest thing to Senator Benton's conception of a Marshall Plan for ideas." Walter Wanger, "Donald Duck and Diplomacy," *Public Opinion Quarterly* (Fall 1950): 443–452, cited in Vanessa R. Schwartz, *It's So French!: Hollywood, Paris, and the Making of Cosmopolitan Film Culture* (Chicago: University of Chicago Press, 2007), 12.

9. The Eady Levy was introduced on a voluntary basis in 1950 and was made mandatory in 1957. Although modeled after similar incentives in place in France and Italy, the Eady Levy did not limit the availability of its funds to "quality" films deemed to represent the character of the nation and thus did not have the effect of encouraging a distinctive national cinema. On the contrary, by the mid-1960s it was evident to commentators such as Alexander Walker that "what the levy did was make the rich man richer still," and that the rich man in question was very often an American running a British subsidiary. See Alexander Walker, *Hollywood England: The British Film Industry in the 1960s* (London: Michael Joseph, 1974), 460–461. In contrast, the French system specified its preference for "films of a nature to serve the cause of French cinema and to open new perspectives in filmic art or to promote the great themes and problems of the French Union." Colin Crisp's industrial analysis of the period leads him to credit the system with encouraging the New Wave of young filmmakers and with boosting production despite declining cinema admissions. See Colin Crisp, *The Classic French Cinema, 1930–1960* (Bloomington: Indiana University Press, 1997), 78.

10. Having worked exclusively in television in Hollywood, Anton Leader directed *Children of the Damned* (1963) for MGM Britain. Tarloff's hopes for a film career were also fulfilled. While in London, he wrote the Oscar-winning script for *Father Goose* (dir. Ralph Nelson, 1964). Erik Tarloff, interview with author, 9 January 2007.

11. Bernard Gordon, *Hollywood Exile, or How I Learned to Love the Blacklist* (Austin: University of Texas Press, 1999), 133. The epic spectacles produced by Bronston include *King of Kings* (dir. Nicholas Ray, 1961), *El Cid* (dir. Anthony Mann, 1961), and *The Fall of the Roman Empire* (dir. Anthony Mann, 1964).

12. Dalton Trumbo Papers, Box 114, Folder 14, Department of Special Collections, University of California, Los Angeles. Ring Lardner Jr. also spent time in Rome while working on *A Breath of Scandal* (dir. Michael Curtiz, 1960). Jean Rouverol Butler, interview with author, 3 August 2005.

13. Ellie Boris, interview with author, 1 November 2006.

14. On 16 June 1958, the Supreme Court struck down the State Department's interdiction against issuing passports to anyone whose activities abroad might be considered "prejudicial to the orderly conduct of foreign relations or otherwise be prejudicial to the interests of the United States." According to the ruling, the State Department could still withhold passports from those found to be "participating in illegal conduct," a loophole used to delay the issuance of passports to some of the blacklisted. *Kent v. Dulles*, 357 U.S. 116 (1958).

15. Larry Ceplair, *Paul Jarrico Oral History*, UCLA Special Collections, 165.

16. Sue Harper and Vincent Porter, *British Cinema of the 1950s: The Decline of Deference* (Oxford: Oxford University Press, 2003), 175

17. Michael Wilson to Burt Lancaster, 12 April 1963, Michael Wilson Papers, Box 48, Folder 2, Performing Arts Special Collections, University of California, Los Angeles; Ilse Lahn to Zelma and Michael Wilson, 14 January 1961, Michael Wilson Papers, Box 48, Folder 1, Performing Arts Special Collections, University of California, Los Angeles.

18. Joseph Losey to Jean Rossignol, 2 May 1961, Joseph Losey Collection, Item 105, British Film Institute.

19. Many of these marriages did break up. John Berry, Jules Dassin, Carl Foreman, and Paul Jarrico all divorced their American wives in order to marry European women (Cy Endfield and Joseph Losey also remarried in England, but were already divorced when they arrived). Sylvia Jarrico saw a direct connection between the disruptive, dislocating experience of exile and the dissolution of so many marriages: "I think the frustration that [the men] felt contributed to their adventures, their love affairs." Carl Foreman's American wife, Estelle, similarly blamed the blacklist for the break-up of her marriage: "Carl went to England, and when I joined him he was a different man. He suffered terribly and I think he felt at that time that nothing was any use anymore, including loyalty to one's spouse." Sylvia Jarrico, interview with author, 23 August 2006; Victor S. Navasky, *Naming Names*, 3rd ed. (New York: Hill and Wang, 2003), 357; Carl Foreman Collection, Item I, Special Collections, British Film Institute.

20. Hannah Weinstein gave the young critics Lindsay Anderson and Karel Reisz the chance to direct, hiring them for *The Adventures of Robin Hood*. Mordecai Richler made an uncredited contribution to the screenplay for *Room at the Top* (dir. Jack Clayton, 1959), and Harry Saltzman produced the film version of John Osborne's hit play *Look Back in Anger* (dir. Tony Richardson, 1958) and *Saturday Night and Sunday Morning* (dir. Karel Reisz, 1960).

21. A true cosmopolitan, Litvak, originally from Kiev, had made films in Russia, Germany, England, and France before leaving Europe for Hollywood in 1937. For more on James Jones, see Frank MacShane, *Into Eternity: The Life of James Jones, American Writer* (Boston: Houghton Mifflin, 1985).

22. Berry had a starring role in Orson Welles's Broadway dramatization of Richard Wright's *Native Son* and is likely to have encountered Wright in Paris through their mutual acquaintance, Jean-Paul Sartre. Jan Berry, interview with author, 5 February 2007. Pierre Rissient, interview with author, 6 July 2005. William Marshall appeared in *Rencontre à Paris* (dir. Georges Lampin, 1956), starring Betsy Blair. William Marshall to Michael Wilson, n.d., Michael Wilson Papers, Box 18, Folder 8, Performing Arts Special Collections, University of California, Los Angeles; Betsy Blair, *The Memory of All That: Love and Politics in New York, Hollywood, and Paris* (New York: Knopf, 2003), 282; Betsy Blair, interview with author, 9 July 2005; Norma Barzman, interview with author, 10 July 2006. For more on the African American expatriate community in Paris in the 1950s, see Tyler Stovall, "The Fire This Time: Black American Expatriates and the Algerian War," *Yale French Studies* 98 (2000): 182–200; and James Campbell, *Exiled in Paris: Richard Wright, James Baldwin, Samuel Beckett, and Others on the Left Bank* (Berkeley: University of California Press, 2003), 196–197.

23. Maureen Endfield, interview with author, 2 May 2007. Endfield also provided Chester with uncredited assistance on the script for *Crashout* (dir. Lewis Foster, 1955).

24. Paul Buhle, "Frank Tarloff," in Patrick McGilligan and Paul Buhle, *Tender Comrades: A Backstory of the Hollywood Blacklist* (New York: St. Martin's Press, 1997), 650–651.

25. For a thorough overview of Bronston's career, see Neal Moses Rosendorf, "The Life and Times of Samuel Bronston, Builder of Hollywood in Madrid: A Study in the International Scope and Influence of American Popular Culture" (Ph.D. diss., Harvard University, 2000).

26. Philip K. Scheuer, "Bronston Plan Seen as Film Revolution. Madrid Operation Is Based on Pre-Selling Productions," *Los Angeles Times*, 31 July 1962. See also Gordon, *Hollywood Exile*, 100.

27. Bernard Gordon describes a more complicated barter system involving three or four different countries. Bronston, acting as an international broker, would trade Spanish goods for whatever products Spain needed. The pesetas generated by the retail value of these goods would then be put toward his below-the-line costs. See Gordon, *Hollywood Exile*, 99.

28. Neal Moses Rosendorf, "'Hollywood in Madrid': American Film Producers and the Franco Regime, 1950–1970," *Historical Journal of Film, Radio, and Television* 27, no. 1 (March 2007): 89–90.
29. Gordon, *Hollywood Exile*, 122, 182. Other staff included the blacklisted producer-director Irving Lerner and Lou Brandt, a progressive who had been active in the theater in New York and Hollywood.
30. Gordon notes that while he negotiated for a proper salary, some of the other blacklisted writers in Bronston's employ received only "expense money" and the promise of profit participation. This "expense money" was nonetheless generous given the low cost of living in Franco's Spain. According to Bronston Productions senior vice president Paul Lazarus, all company employees received a weekly envelope stuffed with hundreds of dollars in pesetas at a time when a luxury, ten-room apartment in Madrid had a monthly rent of $250. See Gordon, *Hollywood Exile*, 134, 152; and Rosendorf, *Life and Times*, 287–288.
31. Samuel Bronston Productions declared bankruptcy in June 1964. "Bronston Film Productions Files Bankruptcy Petition," *New York Times*, 6 June 1964.
32. Norma Barzman, *The Red and the Blacklist: The Intimate Memoir of a Hollywood Expatriate* (New York: Nation Books, 2003), 334, 348.
33. Gordon, *Hollywood Exile*, 171.
34. A. H. Weiler, "View from a Local Vantage Point," *New York Times*, 9 July 1961.
35. Gordon won this argument, using the example of Trumbo to persuade Paul Lazarus to risk putting his name on the screen (Lazarus agreed on the condition that Gordon sign a loyalty statement, which he did). Gordon, *Hollywood Exile*, 160–161.
36. Yordan used this explanation to deny Gordon credit for *The Day of the Triffids* (dir. Steve Sekely, 1962) and *Battle of the Bulge* (dir. Ken Annakin, 1965). Gordon, *Hollywood Exile*, 144, 194.
37. Sylvia Jarrico, interview with author, 23 August 2006.
38. Barzman, *The Red and the Blacklist*, 337.
39. Schwartz, *It's So French!*, 188, 196.
40. Robert Shandley, *Runaway Romances: Hollywood's Postwar Tour of Europe* (Philadelphia: Temple University Press, 2009), xx.
41. Shandley, *Runaway Romances*, xxi–xxii.
42. Michael Wilson Papers, Box 11, Folder 13, Performing Arts Special Collections, University of California, Los Angeles.
43. Michael Wilson to Sam Spiegel, 30 November 1957, Michael Wilson Papers, Box 46, Folder 13, Performing Arts Special Collections, University of California, Los Angeles.
44. Joseph Losey to Michael Wilson, 28 November 1957, Michael Wilson Papers, Box 48, Folder 3, Performing Arts Special Collections, University of California, Los Angeles.
45. For more on the growth of American tourism in postwar France, see Christopher Endy, *Cold War Holidays: American Tourism in France* (Chapel Hill: University of North Carolina Press, 2004).
46. Michael Wilson to Dino de Laurentiis, 1 June 1961, Michael Wilson Papers, Box 11, Folder 15, Performing Arts Special Collections, University of California, Los Angeles.
47. Michael Wilson Papers, Box 2, Folder 3, Performing Arts Special Collections, University of California, Los Angeles.
48. Michael Wilson Papers, Box 1, Folder 6, Performing Arts Special Collections, University of California, Los Angeles.
49. Ibid.
50. Michel Bernheim had worked in Hollywood during the war; his brother, Alain, became a successful Hollywood talent agent. Both were close with many of the future exiles. Alain

Bernheim, interview with author, 8 December 2005; Michel Bernheim to Michael Wilson, 3 November 1961, Michael Wilson Papers, Box 1, Folder 6, Performing Arts Special Collections, University of California, Los Angeles; Michael Wilson to Dalton Trumbo, Michael Wilson Papers, Box 1, Folder 6, Performing Arts Special Collections, University of California, Los Angeles.

51. In the 1990s, Paul Jarrico was still trying to sell the script, this time packaged as a miniseries. Paul Jarrico Papers, Special Collections, AMPAS.

52. "Jules Dassin," *L'Invité de dimanche,* France 2, 21 May 1970.

53. Bosley Crowther, "Ingenious Paradox: 'Never on Sunday' Puts a Wry Idea on Screen," *New York Times,* 23 October 1960.

54. Statement of H. O'Neil Shanks, Executive Secretary, Screen Actors Guild & Chairman, Foreign Film Committee, AFL Film Committee, cited in Pamela Conley Ulich and Lance Simmens, "Motion Picture Production: To Run or Stay Made in the U.S.A.," *Loyola L.A. Entertainment Law Review* 21 (2001): 357.

55. See Frances Stoner Saunders, *The Cultural Cold War: The CIA and the World of Arts and Letters* (New York: New Press, 1999); David Caute, *The Dancer Defects: The Struggle for Cultural Supremacy during the Cold War* (Oxford: Oxford University Press, 2003); and Penny M. Von Eschen, *Satchmo Blows Up the World: Jazz Ambassadors Play the Cold War* (Cambridge, Mass.: Harvard University Press, 2004).

56. Saunders, *The Cultural Cold War,* 1.

57. Jennifer E. Langdon offers an extensive discussion of the shifting discourse of twentieth-century Americanism in *Caught in the Crossfire: Adrian Scott and the Politics of Americanism in 1940s Hollywood* (New York: Columbia University Press, 2008).

58. Rebecca M. Schreiber, *Cold War Exiles in Mexico: U.S. Dissidents and the Culture of Critical Resistance* (Minneapolis: University of Minnesota Press, 2008), xiii.

59. Andersen considers the following films as examples of *film gris: Body and Soul* (dir. Robert Rossen, 1947), *Force of Evil* (dir. Abraham Polonsky, 1948), *Road House* (dir. Jean Negulesco, 1948), *Not Wanted* (dir. Ida Lupino, 1949), *Thieves' Highway* (dir. Jules Dassin, 1949), *They Live By Night* (dir. Nicholas Ray, 1949), *Knock on Any Door* (dir. Nicholas Ray, 1949), *We Were Strangers* (dir. John Huston, 1949), *Quicksand* (dir. Irving Pichel, 1950), *Shakedown* (dir. Joseph Pevney, 1950), *The Asphalt Jungle* (dir. John Huston, 1950), *Night and the City* (dir. Jules Dassin, 1950), *The Breaking Point* (dir. Michael Curtiz, 1950), *The Lawless* (dir. Joseph Losey, 1950), *The Prowler* (dir. Joseph Losey, 1951), *Try and Get Me* (dir. Cy Endfield, 1951), and *He Ran All the Way* (dir. John Berry, 1951). See Thom Andersen, "Red Hollywood" and "Afterword," both in *"Un-American" Hollywood: Politics and Film in the Blacklist Era,* ed. Frank Krutnik, Steve Neale, Brian Neve, and Peter Stanfield (New Brunswick, N.J.: Rutgers University Press, 2007), 257, 265.

60. Paul Buhle and Dave Wagner, *Hide in Plain Sight: The Hollywood Blacklist in Film and Television, 1950–2002* (New York: Palgrave Macmillan, 2003), 109–110.

61. Peter Bondanella, *Hollywood Italians: Dagos, Palookas, Romeos, Wise Guys, and Sopranos* (New York: Continuum, 2005), 29–35.

62. "Give Us This Day," *Times,* 31 October 1949; Milton Shulman, "Give Us This Day," *Evening Standard,* 27 October 1949; Dilys Powell, "Death in Concrete," *Sunday Times,* 30 October 1949.

63. At the 1948 festival, William Wyler was awarded the prize for best director for *The Best Years of Our Lives* (1946). Karlovy Vary International Film Festival, http://www.kvif.com/en/about-festival/fesitval-history.

64. Barzman, *The Red and the Blacklist,* 230.

65. See Christian Viviani, "Jules Dassin: Décidé à être un héros," *Positif,* no. 466 (December 1999): 95. See also Tom Charity, "Red Nightmare," *Time Out London,* 7–12 August 2002, 78.

66. Andre Bazin, "An Aesthetic of Reality: Neorealism," in *What Is Cinema?* vol. 2, trans. Hugh Gray (Berkeley: University of California Press, 1971), 38.
67. "For the first time in my life, I've made a film that I like." Dassin quoted in *L'Humanité*, 4 May 1957; most articles by the French press emphasized this theme.
68. Jacques Doniol-Valcroze, "Passion interdite," *Cahiers du cinéma* 12, no. 72 (June 1957): 45.
69. "Dassin Calls 'Runaway Production' a Natural Development of Films," *Box Office*, 22 October 1962.
70. Jan Berry, interview with author, 5 February 2007.
71. For an in-depth critical analysis of *Tamango* and its production history, see Christopher L. Miller, *The French Atlantic Triangle: Literature and Culture of the Slave Trade* (Durham, N.C.: Duke University Press, 2007), 222–241.
72. John Berry, "A Voix Nue," FranceCulture2, 20 May 1999.
73. Berry had directed the South African playwright Athol Fugard's anti-apartheid drama *Blood Knot* on stage in London and New York in the early 1960s. His final film would be a screen adaptation of another Fugard play, *Boesman and Lena* (2000), starring Angela Bassett and Danny Glover.
74. Association of Motion Picture and Television Producers (AMPTP) Records, 1931–1990, Item no: 17-f.171, AMPAS.
75. For an account of the State Department's use of black jazz luminaries as a propaganda tool during the Cold War era, see Von Eschen, *Satchmo Blows Up the World.*
76. Donald Bogle, *Dorothy Dandridge* (New York: Amistad, 1997), 454.
77. Richard Nason, "*Tamango* from France," *New York Times*, 17 September 1959; Geoffrey Warren, "*Tamango* Low Grade New Race Melodrama," *Los Angeles Times*, 23 October 1959; "Movie of the Week: *Tamango*," *Jet*, 27 August 1959.
78. As Christopher Miller notes, *Tamango* is not the only film by blacklisted filmmakers in which slavery and the slave trade stand in for the contemporary forms of oppression practiced during the McCarthy era, *Spartacus* being another prominent example. Nor is it unique in its emphasis on race; it can be considered one of a "group of 'progressive' protoblaxploitation films by black-listed directors," according to J. Hoberman. See Miller, *The French Atlantic Triangle*, 226, and J. Hoberman, "Tamango," *Village Voice*, 1 July 1997. Other examples of "black" films by blacklisted filmmakers include *Up Tight* (dir. Jules Dassin, 1968), *Slaves* (dir. Herbert Biberman, 1969), and *Claudine* (dir. John Berry, 1974). For a discussion of these films, see Rebecca Prime, "From Black Lists to Black Films: The Hollywood Radicals Return Home," in *Cinematic Homecomings: Exile and Return in Transnational Cinema*, ed. Rebecca Prime (New York: Continuum Books, forthcoming).
79. From a budget of £100,412, Losey was paid £4,500, about £45,000 in today's value. Caute, *Joseph Losey*, 126.
80. The brothers' motivation in giving credit to Losey and Barzman remains obscure. While Eros had proved itself eager to work with the blacklisted Americans, releasing four of Cy Endfield's early British films in addition to *Born for Trouble* (1955), a compilation of Carl Foreman's *Aggie* television series, and *Escapade* (1955), for which Donald Ogden Stewart contributed the screenplay, in all these instances they insisted on the use of pseudonyms.
81. Michel Ciment, *Conversations with Losey* (London: Methuen, 1985), 144–148.
82. "Jules Dassin," *La Masque et la Plume*, Paris 4, 1 January 1959.
83. Bertrand Tavernier, *Amis américains: Entretiens avec les grands auteurs d'Hollywood* (Lyons: Institut Lumière/Actes Sud, 1993), 613.
84. The science fiction B-movies of the 1950s provide allegorical readings of the paranoia and anxiety provoked by the un-American Other during the Cold War. See, for example, David

Seed, *American Science Fiction and the Cold War: Literature and Film* (Edinburgh: Edinburgh University Press, 1999).

85. See John Fousek, *To Lead the Free World: American Nationalism and the Cultural Roots of the Cold War* (Chapel Hill: University of North Carolina Press, 2000).

86. Hy Hollinger, "Foreman Sees Foreign Government Concessions to Picture Producers a Message Uncle Sam Must Heed," *Variety*, 22 June 1960; "Foreman Urges Gov't Film Aid to Solve 'Runaway' Problem," *Hollywood Reporter*, 3 July 1961. Philip K. Scheuer, "Producer Analyzes Lost Film Market: Has Hollywood Lost Cultural Empathy? Foreman Says Yes," *Los Angeles Times*, 5 December 1961.

87. Philip K. Scheuer, "Producer Analyzes Lost Film Market," *Los Angeles Times*, 5 December 1961.

88. Carl Foreman, "The Cost of Independence: An Enquiry," *Sight and Sound* 30, no. 3 (Summer 1961): 112.

89. "Disgrace, Says Top U.S. Film Writer," *Daily Worker*, 2 September 1958; "Industry's Festival Support 'a Disgrace'—Carl Foreman's attack," *Evening Dispatch*, 2 September 1958; "Foreman's Crusade: School for Talent," *Variety*, 16 October 1963. In 1998, the British Academy of Film and Television Arts (BAFTA) honored Foreman's efforts to improve opportunities for young filmmakers in Britain by creating the Carl Foreman Award for Special Achievement by a British Director, Writer, or Producer in their First Feature Film.

90. Ciment, *Conversations*, 211–212. Emphasis added. Hugo Butler spent the 1950s as part of the blacklisted community in Mexico, only arriving in Europe in 1960. Jean Rouverol Butler, interview with author, 3 August 2005.

91. Jones wrote the screenplays to *King and Country* (1964) and *Modesty Blaise* (1966).

92. Patrick McGilligan, "Jules Dassin," in McGilligan and Buhle, *Tender Comrades*, 220.

93. Jules Dassin to Michael Wilson, 31 May 1963, Michael Wilson Papers, Box 48, Folder 2, Performing Arts Special Collections, University of California, Los Angeles.

CHAPTER 6: BLACKLISTED DIRECTORS, ART CINEMA, AND THE CAPRICES OF FILM CRITICISM

1. For a detailed exploration of the history and definition of the art film, see David Bordwell, "The Art Cinema as a Mode of Film Practice," in *Film Theory and Criticism: Introductory Readings*, ed. Leo Braudy and Marshall Cohen, 5th ed. (New York: Oxford University Press, 1999), and Steve Neale, "Art Cinema as Institution," *Screen* 22, no. 1 (1981). As Mark Betz notes in his historiography of European art cinema, however, the influence of these works has resulted in two main threads of art cinema scholarship, one privileging formal analysis of individual films and auteurs and one that analyzes art cinema as national production exemplified by specific film movements. See Mark Betz, *Beyond the Subtitle: Remapping European Art Cinema* (Minneapolis: University of Minnesota Press, 2009), 13–14.

2. Colin Crisp, *The Classic French Cinema, 1930–1960* (Bloomington: Indiana University Press, 1997), 229.

3. The house publication of the *Fédération français de ciné-clubs* and edited by the film historian Pierre Billard, *Cinéma 55* renamed itself according to the year of publication, becoming *Cinéma 56, Cinéma 57*, etc. to reflect its dedication to a new, cutting-edge French cinema.

4. V. F. Perkins, "Ian Cameron: A Tribute," *Movie: A Journal of Film Criticism* 1 (2010): 2. When *Sequence* folded in 1952, its critics joined the staff of *Sight and Sound*, the prestigious journal published since 1934 by the British Film Institute, and thus brought their ideological concerns to a wider audience. See Erik Hedling, "*Sequence* and the Rise of Auteurism," in

British Cinema of the 1950s: A Celebration, ed. Ian MacKillop and Neil Sinyard (Manchester: Manchester University Press, 2003), 24.

5. As Antoine de Baecque observes, for the new generation represented by Truffaut and Godard, the obstinate refusal of the communist critics even to consider the merits of Hollywood cinema simply extended the zero-sum, East-versus-West logic of the Cold War into intellectual and artistic domains. Antoine de Baecque, *La cinéphilie: invention d'un regard, histoire d'une culture, 1944–1968* (Paris: Fayard, 2003), 74–75.

6. "The British Cinema," *Movie,* no. 1 (June 1962): 3–9. *Movie* was founded in 1962 by Ian Cameron, V. F. Perkins, and Mark Shivas; Robin Wood and Paul Mayersberg were also regular contributors to the journal, which was distinguished from its rivals by its focus on close visual analysis.

7. Thomas Schatz, *Old Hollywood/New Hollywood: Ritual, Art, and Industry* (Ann Arbor: University of Michigan Research Press, 1983), 175.

8. John E. Twomey, "Some Considerations on the Rise of Art Film Theater," *Quarterly of Film, Radio, and Television* 10 (Spring 1956): 240, cited in Barbara Wilensky, *Sure Seaters: The Emergence of Art House Cinema* (Minneapolis: University of Minnesota Press, 2001), 13.

9. Cited in Paul Monaco, *The Sixties: 1960–1969,* History of American Cinema, vol. 8 (Berkeley: University of California Press, 2001), 55.

10. See Mark Betz, "The Name above the (Sub)title: Internationalism, Coproduction, and Polyglot European Cinema," *Camera Obscura 46* 16, no. 1 (2001): 22.

11. Jean-Luc Godard, "Jamais le dimanche," *Cahiers du cinema* 18, no. 108 (June 1960): 37–38.

12. Betz, *Beyond the Subtitle,* 33–35.

13. Ibid., 75–78.

14. *Rififi,* Fonds Crédit National, Cote CN 658 B450, Bibliothèque du Film; *La Loi,* Fonds Crédit National, Cote CN 740 B497, Bibliothèque du Film.

15. Jean de Baroncelli, "La France a présenté à Cannes *Celui qui doit mourir* de Jules Dassin," *Le Monde,* 7 May 1957.

16. Jacques Doniol-Valcroze, "Passion Interdite," *Cahiers du cinéma,* no. 72 (June 1957): 46–47.

17. Marcel Ranchal, "Celui qui doit mourir," *Positif* 3, no. 25–26 (Autumn 1957): 58; O'Picratt, *Le Canard Enchainé,* 10 May 1957.

18. François Truffaut, "Celui qui doit mourir," *Arts,* 10 May 1957. Minou Drouet was a much-fêted child poet and musician of questionable talent.

19. "Celui qui doit mourir," *L'Humanité,* 13 May 1957.

20. Doniol-Valcroze, "Passion Interdite."

21. See chapter 3 for a discussion of *l'affaire Wilson.*

22. "Jules Dassin," *Cinépanorama,* 2 December 1961.

23. Melina Mercouri, *Je suis née grèque* (Paris: Editions Stock, 1972), 159; *Cinépanorama* (1961).

24. *La Loi,* Fonds Crédit National, Cote CN 740 B497, Bibliothèque du Film.

25. Ibid.

26. "Lollobrigida fait la Loi," *L'Express,* 17 July 1958; *La Loi,* Fonds Crédit National, Cote CN 740 B497, Bibliothèque du Film.

27. Yves Boissey, "Otello Martelli, Jules Dassin, Gina Lollobrigida, Yves Montand, gagneront-ils au jeu de 'la loi'?," *Cinéma* 31/40, n.d.; Robert F. Hawkins, "Secluded, Rustic Area Used as Site for 'La Loi," *New York Times,* 12 October 1958; John Francis Lane, "I See Dassin Make 'The Law,'" *Films and Filming* 4, no. 12 (4 September 1958).

28. Jacques de Baroncelli, "La Loi," *Le Monde,* 28 January 1959.

29. Louis Chauvet, "La Loi," *Le Figaro,* 24 January 1959.

30. Georges Charensol, "La Loi," *Les Nouvelles littéraires*, 29 January 1959.
31. *"La Loi," L'Express*, 29 January 1959.
32. Chauvet, "La Loi," 24 January 1959.
33. Claude Mauriac, "Quand la camera fait 'La Loi,'" *Le Figaro littéraire*, 31 January 1959.
34. Jean-Luc Godard, "Dura Lex," *Cahiers du cinéma* 15, no. 93 (March 1959): 61.
35. Patrick McGilligan, "John Berry," in Patrick McGilligan and Paul Buhle, *Tender Comrades: A Backstory of the Hollywood Blacklist* (New York: St. Martin's, 1997), 81.
36. An outspoken critic of the Franco regime, Bardem was temporarily jailed later that year on political grounds.
37. McGilligan, "John Berry," in *Tender Comrades*, 81.
38. Jean de Baroncelli, "Don Juan," *Le Monde*, 23 May 1956; Henry Magnan, "Don Juan . . . Fernandélisé," *Lettres Françaises*, 17 May 1956; Louis Chauvet, "Don Juan," *Le Figaro*, 15 May 1956; R. M. Arlaud, "Don Juan," *Combat*, 24 May 1956; André Lang, "Don Juan," *France Soir*, 12 May 1956.
39. Jacques Siclier, "Le mythe fait le moine (Don Juan)," *Cahiers du cinema* 10, no. 60 (June 1956): 48–49.
40. Jan Berry, interview with author, 5 February 2007.
41. Although a Franco-Italian co-production, *Tamango* does not seem to have been subject to the same restrictions in terms of casting and location as *Don Juan* and *La Loi. Tamango* does not feature any Italian actors and was shot entirely in the south of France.
42. Jacques Doniol-Valcroze, "Tamango," *France Observateur*, 30 January 1958; Jacques Nahum, interview with author, 2 February 2007.
43. Denis Berry, interview with author, 17 March 2007.
44. *Don Juan/Tamango*, Fonds Crédit National, Cote 1089 B549, Bibliothèque du Film.
45. Donald Bogle, *Dorothy Dandridge: A Biography* (New York: Amistad Press, 1997), 379–380.
46. Jacques Nahum, interview with author, 2 February 2007.
47. François Roche, "Le noir perd . . . et gagne," *France-Soir*, 26 January 1958.
48. Jacques Deltour, "*Tamango:* la révolte des exclaves," *L'Humanité*, 29 January 1958.
49. R. M. Arlaud, "*Tamango:* de l'idée révolutionaire au spectacle complaisante," *Combat*, 29 January 1958.
50. Etienne Loinod, "Aiche menu," *Cahiers du cinéma* 14, no. 80 (February 1958): 61; Jacques Doniol-Valcroze, "Tamango," *France Observateur*, 30 January 1958.
51. François Truffaut, "On a trahi Mérimée! Navet somptueux *Tamango* est devenu monument d'ennui," *Arts*, 31 January 1958.
52. "Après l'interdiction du film *Tamango*, une declaration de M. Senghor au *Monde*," *Le Monde*, 1 February 1958.
53. John Berry, *Cinéma: Le Masque et la plume*, France Inter, 15 February 1958.
54. Denis Berry, interview with author, 17 March 2007.
55. Pierre Billard quoted in Michel Marie, *The French New Wave: An Artistic School*, trans. Richard Neupert (Oxford: Blackwell Publishing, 2003), 18.
56. Billard's aforementioned issue of *Cinéma 58* also included a report, entitled "40 under 40: The Young Academy of French Cinema," that distinguished between "*les anciens*" (directors born prior to 1914) and "new" directors born after 1918. Cited in Marie, *The French New Wave*, 8.
57. British, French, and American critics make regular reference to Antonioni in particular in their reviews of *Eva* and *The Servant*. Losey greatly admired these filmmakers and maintained a correspondence with Fellini and Resnais. David Caute, *Joseph Losey: A Revenge on Life* (New York: Oxford University Press, 1994), 314–318.

58. The "Cercle du Mac-Mahon," the influential ciné-club that met on Sunday mornings at the Cinéma Mac-Mahon, privileged the work of certain directors, most notably the "four aces": Fritz Lang, Otto Preminger, Raoul Walsh, and Joseph Losey. See Alain and Odette Virmaux, *Dictionnaire du Cinéma Mondial* (Paris: Editions du Rocher, 1994), 487–488.

59. Rissient first learned of Losey via Jules Dassin, who mentioned the presence of Losey and other American blacklist victims in Europe in an interview with *Cahiers du cinéma* published in conjunction with the release of *Rififi* in April 1955. Undeterred by his own youth and inexperience, Rissient befriended the blacklisted community and made it his mission that their films be shown in Paris. According to his description, the Parisian blacklistees and their friends came out en masse for Losey's 1957 screening of *Time Without Pity*, with John Berry, Betsy Blair, Jules Dassin, Michael Wilson, Yves Montand, Roger Pigaut, and Simone Signoret among those in attendance. Pierre Rissient, "L'Univers de Joseph Losey," *CinémAction*, no. 96 (3me trimestre, 2000): 186. See also Norma Barzman, *The Red and the Blacklist: An Intimate Memoir of a Hollywood Expatriate* (New York: Thunder's Mouth Press/Nation Books, 2003), 284–285.

60. Rissient, "L'Univers de Joseph Losey," 186.

61. Colin Crisp notes that it was only once *Positif* relinquished its commitment to interpreting film as a sociopolitical text that the magazine became financially viable. See Crisp, *The Classic French Cinema*, 249.

62. *Positif* favored Orson Welles to Alfred Hitchcock and Jean Rouch to Jean-Luc Godard; its preferred New Wave directors included none of the critics-cum-directors associated with the *Cahiers*. See Richard Neupert, *A History of the French New Wave Cinema* (Madison: University of Wisconsin Press, 2007), 32–34. See also Crisp, *The Classic French Cinema*, 238–239, 249.

63. Jean Douchet, "Un des plus grands maîtres," *Arts*, 7 June 1960.

64. Jean de Baroncelli, "Temps sans pitié," *Le Monde*, 11 June 1960; Jeander, "Temps sans pitié," *Libération*, 15 June 1960.

65. Sadoul attributed Hollywood's declining fortunes to the blacklist, which "decapitated American cinema." Georges Sadoul, "Une génération perdue," *Les Lettres françaises*, 9 June 1960.

66. Samuel Lachize, "Les Criminels," *L'Humanité*, 25 March 1961; Pierre Marcabru, "Les Criminels," *Combat*, 27 March 1961; Georges Charensol, "Les Criminels," *Les Nouvelles littéraires*, 7 April 1961.

67. Michel Ciment, *Conversations with Losey* (New York: Methuen & Co., 1985), 145–146.

68. Penelope Houston and John Gillett, "Conversations with Nicholas Ray & Joseph Losey," *Sight and Sound* 30, no. 4 (autumn 1961).

69. Caute, *Joseph Losey*, 316.

70. Losey cited Antonioni's *L'Avventura* as an influence on *The Servant* on account of the film's social meaning. See Raymond Bellour, "Joseph Losey: 'The Servant' est un film sur le mensonge et l'hypocrisie," *Lettres Françaises*, 9 April 1964.

71. Joseph Losey to David Deutsch, 10 July 1961, Joseph Losey Collection, Item 105, Special Collections, British Film Institute. *The Criminal*, retitled *The Concrete Jungle* and cut from ninety-seven to eighty-six minutes, was not released in the United States until May 1962. It was not booked into any major New York theaters and did not reach the West Coast until 1965. Caute, *Joseph Losey*, 141.

72. Joseph Losey to Moura Budberg, 5 April 1961, Joseph Losey Collection, Item 105, Special Collections, British Film Institute.

73. Ciment, *Conversations*, 207.

74. The *Guardian* dismissed the film as a "hot, intense thriller" and a "phoney" American take on a British subject. "The Criminal," *Guardian*, 29 October 1960. The *New Statesman*

praised the film's originality but also found its intensity, particularly in its depiction of prison life, hard to swallow. "The prison is meant to be 'real,' yet it heaves with that hysteria which the needs of the plot will bring out." "The Criminal," *New Statesman*, 5 November 1960.

75. Ciment, *Conversations*, 196, 198; Joseph Losey, "Mirror to Life," *Films and Filming* 5, no. 9 (June 1959): 54.

76. Teddy boys affected the dress of Edwardian ("Teddy") dandies and became an identifiable subculture in Britain in the 1950s. Despite the violence associated with some Teddy boy gangs, Losey felt a kind of naïve admiration for the working-class youths attempting to "recapture some kind of power out of past elegance by wearing Edwardian clothes." Ciment, *Conversations*, 200.

77. Ibid., 201.

78. Philip French, "The Damned," *Observer*, 19 May 1963; "An Exciting Director: Joseph Losey's Latest Film," *Times*, 20 May 1963.

79. Philip Oakes, "The Damned," *Sunday Telegraph*, 26 May 1963.

80. Robert Murphy, *Sixties British Cinema* (London: British Film Institute, 1992), 58.

81. Lindsay Anderson, "Book Reviews: French Critical Writing," *Sight and Sound* 24, no. 2 (October–December 1954): 105; "The British Cinema," *Movie*, 9.

82. An unqualified critical and commercial success, *The Servant* (released 14 November 1963) was included on many critics' lists of the year's top ten films. Alexander Walker of the *Evening Standard* named it the film of the year, as did the London Film Critics Guild. See Caute, *Joseph Losey*, 22.

83. Murphy, *Sixties British Cinema*, 88.

84. Quoted in Caute, *Joseph Losey*, 141.

85. Losey offered this definition of "social content": "Well, it certainly need not be propaganda in the stigmatized sense of proselytizing. To me it means a social point of view, a moral one if you like. Telling a story to a purpose. Not knowingly perpetuating false ideas, or prejudices, or fostering dangerous concepts. It means having an attitude toward life and accepting fully the social responsibility which goes with any media of communication, and particularly a mass media." See Joseph Losey, "Mirror to Life," 54.

86. For added emphasis, *Movie* compared several of the most acclaimed films of the British "kitchen sink" school to low-brow British comedies: "There is as much genuine personality in *Room at the Top*, method in *A Kind of Loving* and style in *A Taste of Honey* as there is wit in *An Alligator Named Daisy*, intelligence in *Above Us the Waves* and ambition in *Ramsbotttom Rides Again*." "The British Cinema," *Movie*, 9.

87. Quoted in Murphy, *Sixties British Cinema*, 68–69.

88. *Movie* places Losey on the "British" side of the ledger in its pantheon of great directors. "The British Cinema," *Movie*, 9. Robin Wood, "The Criminal," *Motion*, no. 4 (February 1963).

89. "Cinematic Study of Crime and Prison Life," *Times*, 31 October 1960; "The Criminal," *Guardian*, 29 October 1960.

90. Between 1956 and 1959, the Free Cinema group organized six programs at London's National Film Theatre, three of which showcased "New Wave" films from Poland, France, and America while three featured recent British documentaries, including a number of their own (Lindsay Anderson: *Wakefield Express* [1952], *O Dreamland* [1953], and *Every Day Except Christmas* [1957]; Karel Reisz: *Momma Don't Allow* [1955], co-directed with Tony Richardson, and *We Are the Lambeth Boys* [1958]).

91. Isobel Quigley, "Blind Date," *Spectator*, 28 August 1959; "Blind Date," *Guardian*, 22 August 1959. *Look Back in Anger*, with its disaffected antihero, Jimmy Porter, and equally disaffected creator, John Osborne, prompted critics to pronounce the arrival of a new social type—the Angry Young Man—upon the play's debut at London's Royal Court Theatre in 1956.

92. Prominent example of British "new wave" films include *Saturday Night and Sunday Morning* (dir. Karel Reisz, 1960), *A Taste of Honey* (dir. John Schlesinger, 1961), *The Loneliness of the Long Distance Runner* (dir. Tony Richardson, 1962), *A Kind of Loving* (dir. John Schlesinger, 1962), *Billy Liar* (dir. John Schlesinger, 1963), and *This Sporting Life* (dir. Lindsay Anderson, 1963).
93. Quoted in Caute, *Joseph Losey*, 280. Home to the English Stage Company, whose members included Tony Richardson, London's Royal Court Theatre developed a reputation as a launching pad for serious contemporary drama following the explosive debut of John Osborne's *Look Back in Anger* in 1956.
94. In September 1960, Losey sent a copy of the script for *This Sporting Life* to the producer Daniel Angel, who rejected it on the grounds that films about sports did not make for good box office. Three years later, the film was produced by Julian Wintle, whom Losey had mentioned in relation to the project in a letter to Stanley Baker back in March of 1960, but with Lindsay Anderson as the director. Joseph Losey Collection, Item 104, Special Collections, British Film Institute.
95. Carl Foreman, "One Man's Credo. Scenarist Takes Firm Stand in Favor of Important, Current Themes," *New York Times*, 29 June 1958; Carl Foreman, "The Cost of Independence: An Enquiry," *Sight and Sound* 30, no. 3 (Summer 1961): 112.
96. Penelope Houston and Kenneth Cavander, "Interview with Carl Foreman," *Sight and Sound* 27, no. 5 (Summer 1958).
97. Joseph Losey to Jean Rossignol, 12 August 1958, Joseph Losey Collection, Item 104, Special Collections, British Film Institute.
98. Cited in Pierre Billard, *L'Age Classique du Cinema Française: Du cinéma parlant à la Nouvelle Vague* (Paris: Flammarion, 1995), 569, my translation.
99. Marie, *La Nouvelle Vague*, 31–35, 37–38.
100. Ibid., 18, 24, 49.
101. Neupert, *French New Wave Cinema*, xvii.
102. Gordon Gow, "Style and Instinct," *Films and Filming* 16, no. 6 (March 1970): 68.
103. "Dassin Understands, Doesn't Practice Producer Presold Property Fixation," *Weekly Variety*, 7 November 1962.
104. Andrew Sarris, ". . . and the Man Who Made It," *New York Times*, 17 November 1968.
105. Ben Barzman, "Comment j'ai travaillé avec Joseph Losey," *Les Lettres françaises*, 17 January 1962.
106. Philip Scheuer, "The Tea Break Notwithstanding, London Studios Humming," *Los Angeles Times*, 12 August 1962.
107. "Dassin Understands, Doesn't Practice Producer Presold Property Fixation," *Weekly Variety*, 7 November 1962.
108. Hollis Alpert, "Something Worth Fighting For," *Saturday Review*, 28 December 1963.
109. *Time Without Pity* (1957) was the first of Joseph Losey's European films to be shown in the United States with his name in the credits; Cy Endfield had to wait until 1961 and the U.S. release of *Mysterious Island*.
110. Murray Schumach, "Hollywood Turns: Changing Intellectual Climate Notes by Blacklisted Director Dassin," *New York Times*, 16 October 1960.
111. James Powers, "'Rififi' Very Well Done Suspense Crime Picture," *Hollywood Reporter*, 4 April 1957; "Les Gangsters," *New York Times*, 20 May 1956.
112. Hollis Alpert, "A Greek Passion," *Saturday Review*, 20 December 1958.
113. Philip K. Scheuer, "'He Who Must Die' Is Modern Christ Parable," *Los Angeles Times*, 19 February 1959; "He Who Must Die," *Time*, 29 December 1958.
114. Philip K. Scheuer, "Hybrid 'Hot Wind': Art or Box Office?" *Los Angeles Times*, 9 October 1960.

115. *Time*, 31 October 1960.
116. Eugene Archer, "Chance Meeting," *New York Times*, 27 October 1960; Richard Gertner, "Chance Meeting," *Motion Picture Herald*, 30 January 1960.
117. Jack Moffitt, "Chance Meeting," *Hollywood Reporter*, 29 January 1960; "Chance Meeting," *Variety*, 29 January 1960.
118. "Kingdom of Crime," *Time*, 13 July 1962.
119. "The Concrete Jungle," *Show*, September 1962.
120. Eugene Archer, "Expatriate Retraces His Steps," *New York Times*, 15 March 1964; "Who Is the Master?" *Newsweek*, 23 March 1964.
121. Crowther frequently used his opinion pieces as a bully pulpit for foreign films. See, for example, "Which Way Salvation? A 'Trapeze' Won't Save the Screen But Films Like 'Rififi' Can," *New York Times*, 10 June 1956, and "Touting Foreign Films: Their Possibilities Are Commended to the Theatre Owners of America," *New York Times*, 16 September 1956.
122. "Lobster Woman," *Newsweek*, 14 June 1965.
123. For example, *Zazie dans le métro* (dir. Louis Malle, 1960); *L'Année dernière à Marienbad* (dir. Alain Resnais, 1961); *Jules et Jim* (dir. François Truffaut, 1961); along with most of the 1960s films of Antonioni, Fellini, Godard, and Visconti. See Betz, *Beyond the Subtitle*, 78.

CHAPTER 7: THE LEGACY OF THE BLACKLIST

1. Joseph Losey to John Collier, 20 August 1958, Joseph Losey Collection, Item 88, British Film Institute.
2. Paul Jarrico Collection, Correspondence T–Z, Special Collections, Academy of Motion Picture Arts and Sciences.
3. By the early 1960s, this was less true of Britain than it was of France and Italy, where television ownership rates were lower. "European Movies; Surging Exports Keep Producers Prosperous Despite Spread of TV," *Wall Street Journal*, 22 August 1961.
4. Jeff Smith, "A Good Business Proposition: Dalton Trumbo, Spartacus, and the End of the Blacklist," in *Controlling Hollywood: Censorship and Regulation in the Studio Era*, ed. Matthew Bernstein (New Brunswick, N.J.: Rutgers University Press, 1999), 220.
5. Paul Jacobs, "Good Guys, Bad Guys, and Congressman Walter," *Reporter*, 15 May 1958.
6. Trumbo revealed his identity as Robert Rich in January 1959, but he only received his Academy Award in 1975 and his screen credit in 1992.
7. Jacobs, "Good Guys," 31.
8. "Nat'l Mag Cites Foreman-Col Deal as Example of Blacklist Fadeout," *Daily Variety*, 12 May 1958.
9. Dalton Trumbo to Edward Lewis, 31 May 1958, in *Additional Dialogue: Letters of Dalton Trumbo, 1942–1962*, ed. Helen Manfull (New York: M. Evans and Company, 1970), 428–429.
10. Manfull, *Additional Dialogue*, 429.
11. David Lean to Michael Wilson, 30 January 1958, Michael Wilson Papers, Box 48, Folder 4, Performing Arts Special Collections, University of California, Los Angeles.
12. Thomas M. Pryor, "Academy Repeals Ruling on 'Oscars,'" *New York Times*, 14 January 1959.
13. Smith, "A Good Business Proposition," 222–223.
14. Dalton Trumbo to Michael Wilson, 24 February 1959, Michael Wilson Collection, Box 49, Folder 10, Performing Arts Special Collections, University of California, Los Angeles.
15. Dalton Trumbo to Michael Wilson, 24 February 1959, Michael Wilson Collection, Box 49, Folder 10, Performing Arts Special Collections, University of California, Los Angeles.

16. A. H. Weiler, "Movie Maker Hires Blacklisted Writer," *New York Times*, 20 January 1960.
17. Smith, "A Good Business Proposition," 228–229.
18. Murray Schumach, "Kramer Defies American Legion Over Hiring of Movie Writers," *New York Times*, 8 February 1960.
19. Bosley Crowther, "Hitting the Blacklist. Policy of Banning 'Labeled' Writers Frankly Defied by Film Producers," *New York Times*, 14 February 1960.
20. Murray Schumach, "Sinatra Defying Writer Blacklist. Hires Albert Maltz for His Filming of 'The Execution of Private Slovik,'" *New York Times*, 20 March 1960.
21. "Exhibitor Calls for End of Blacklists; Scores American Legion 'Persecution,'" *Weekly Variety*, 2 March 1960.
22. Murray Schumach, "Hollywood Test. Hiring of Banned Writers Indicates Challenge to Industry Blacklist," *New York Times*, 11 September 1960.
23. Ibid.
24. Murray Schumach, "Hollywood Reviewed. Profits, TV Sales, Realistic Views Marked Confident Industry's Year," *New York Times*, 25 December 1960.
25. Sinatra was also closely associated with John F. Kennedy, whose presidential campaign had come under attack for Sinatra's actions. Murray Schumach, "Sinatra Dismisses Blacklisted Writer," *New York Times*, 9 April 1960.
26. Smith, "A Good Business Proposition," 225.
27. The $7.5 million suit, charging that in conspiring to enforce a blacklist, the studios acted as a monopoly and violated U.S. antitrust laws, was settled out of court for $80,000 in 1965. Murray Schumach, "Hollywood Trial. Suit by Blacklisted Writers, Actors, Puts Controversy into Spotlight," *New York Times*, 8 January 1961; "Blacklisting Suit Ended by Payment," *New York Times*, 2 June 1965.
28. Adrian Scott to Paul Jarrico, 9 February 1961, Paul Jarrico Collection, Correspondence: S, Special Collections, AMPAS.
29. Paul Buhle, "Joan LaCour Scott (and Adrian Scott)," in Patrick McGilligan and Paul Buhle, *Tender Comrades: A Backstory of the Hollywood Blacklist* (New York: St. Martin's Press, 1997), 596.
30. Joan LaCour Scott, interview with author, 21 August 2006; Adrian Scott, FBI File, Foia No. 100287200.
31. Cy Endfield to Francis E. Walter, 18 August 1958, House Un-American Activities Committee, Cy Endfield File, Box 138, Records of the House of Representatives, National Archives, Washington, D.C.
32. Ibid. Emphasis added.
33. Maureen Endfield, interview with author, 2 May 2007.
34. Francis E. Walter to Cy Endfield, 27 August 1958. House Un-American Activities Committee, Cy Endfield File, Box 138, Records of the House of Representatives, National Archives, Washington, D.C.
35. Cy Endfield to Francis E. Walter, 5 February 1960, House Un-American Activities Committee, Cy Endfield File, Box 138, Records of the House of Representatives, National Archives, Washington, D.C.
36. Memo from D. T. Appell to Richard Arens, 28 March 1960, House Un-American Activities Committee, Cy Endfield File, Box 138, Records of the House of Representatives, National Archives, Washington, D.C.
37. Records of the House of Representatives, House Un-American Activities Committee, Cy Endfield, Executive Session Testimony, Box 49.
38. Sheldon Hall, *'Zulu': With Some Guts Behind It—The Making of the Epic Movie* (Sheffield: Tomahawk Press, 2005), 128.

39. "Schneer to Film J. Verne Sequel," *Weekly Variety*, 27 January 1960.
40. In the unedited version of Foreman's executive session testimony, Arens asked Foreman whether he would name names, to which Foreman replied that he would not. This exchange was deleted from the final transcript of the testimony. See Records of the House of Representatives, House Un-American Activities Committee, Carl Foreman Executive Session Transcripts, Box 37.
41. Calling itself "An Organization to Combat the Communist Conspiracy in Entertainment-Communications and the Fine Arts," AWARE sent an open letter to the committee regarding the Foreman case in April 1957 urging the committee to make public the full transcripts of Foreman's testimony.
42. Lee R. Pennington to Richard Arens, 7 July 1958, House Un-American Activities Committee, Carl Foreman file, Box 92 (683–76), Records of the House of Representatives, National Archives, Washington, D.C.
43. "Legion-Hollywood Balance Sheet," *Variety*, 2 September 1959.
44. Dalton Trumbo to Michael Wilson, 24 February 1959, Michael Wilson Collection, Box 49, Folder 10, Performing Arts Special Collections, University of California, Los Angeles.
45. Melina Mercouri, *Je suis née grèque* (Paris: Editions Stock, 1972), 165; David Caute, *Joseph Losey: A Revenge on Life* (New York: Oxford University Press, 1994), 135.
46. Telegram from Lewis Kerner to Chairman of HUAC (no name given), 30 January 1959: "I am about to close a deal with Jules Dassin under which he will (write) and direct one or more motion pictures in association with me for world wide distribution including the United States. He has assured me he is not a communist. To be doubly certain I am checking with you to see if there is any reason why I should not make the deal with Mr. Dassin. Because time is of great importance please advise me immediately by return wire collect." House Un-American Activities Committee, Box 134, Jules Dassin File, Records of the House of Representatives, National Archives, Washington, D.C.
47. Darryl Zanuck to Spyros Skouras, 20 June 1959, Department of Special Collections, Stanford University.
48. "Kerner, Jules Dassin Join to Produce Films," *Daily Variety*, 3 March 1959.
49. Alain Bernheim, letter to author, 7 June 2007. "Lopert Does What UA Cannot," *Weekly Variety*, 15 April 1959. Over the course of the next year, United Artists repeatedly denied the rumors that it had entered into any sort of arrangements with Dassin. Murray Schumach, "Fox Studio Defies Movie Blacklist," *New York Times*, 12 May 1960.
50. Darryl Zanuck to Spyros Skouras, 24 June 1959. Spyros Skouras Papers, Box 34, Folder 11, Department of Special Collections, Stanford University. With thanks to Peter Lev for bringing these materials to my attention.
51. Dassin continues: "I used to be a communist. I stopped being a communist about 19 or 20 years ago. Never in my life have I had an un-American thought or committed an un-American act. That's as simply and as briefly as I can put it." Jules Dassin to Darryl Zanuck, 1 March 1960, Spyros Skouras Papers, Box 34, Folder 11, Department of Special Collections, Stanford University.
52. Darryl Zanuck to Spyros Skouras, 30 March 1960, Spyros Skouras Papers, Box 34, Folder 11, Department of Special Collections, Stanford University; Spyros Skouras to Darryl Zanuck, 18 April 1960, Spyros Skouras Papers, Box 34, Folder 11, Department of Special Collections, Stanford University.
53. Although personal factors also played a role in Zanuck's decision to relocate to France in 1956, he was also motivated to leave Hollywood on account of the changes that had occurred in the industry in the postwar years. The role of the producer was no longer that of the creative supervisor it had been when he started out in the business in the 1930s; instead, according

to Zanuck, he found himself acting as "a negotiator, an executive, a peacemaker" in a Hollywood where "everyone was becoming a corporation, with their own managers, their own agents, their own lawyers. . . . You can't deal with individuals any longer." Quoted in George F. Custen, *Twentieth Century's Fox: Darryl F. Zanuck and the Culture of Hollywood* (New York: Basic Books, 1997), 354.

54. Darryl Zanuck to Spyros Skouras, 30 March 1960, Spyros Skouras Papers, Box 34, Folder 11, Department of Special Collections, Stanford University.

55. Spyros Skouras to Darryl Zanuck, 18 April 1960, Spyros Skouras Papers, Box 34, Folder 11, Department of Special Collections, Stanford University.

56. Jules Dassin, FBI File, FOIPA No. 1126133–000.

57. The suit seeking $6 million in damages was dismissed by a federal court in November 1964. "Film Blacklist Suit Dismissed by Jury," *New York Times*, 14 November 1964.

58. Herbert Biberman to Paul Jarrico, 18 March 1964, Paul Jarrico Papers, Special Collections, AMPAS.

59. Paul Jarrico to Herbert Biberman, 11 April 1964, Paul Jarrico Papers, Special Collections, AMPAS.

60. It is possible that Jarrico's grudge against Losey stemmed from their exchanges concerning *All Night Long* (dir. Basil Dearden, 1962), a jazz version of *Othello* and pet project of Jarrico's. In November 1960, Losey expressed his interest in directing the film from Jarrico's script; Jarrico replied bluntly that he thought "the possibility of your directing ALL NIGHT LONG . . . very small. There are just too many people lined up ahead of you, including me." Losey's otherwise measured response ended with some advice that could hardly have failed to rile Jarrico. Expressing his personal preference for a clear division of labor between writer and director, he wrote: "I strongly advise you against directing the film yourself; I can't think of one first-rate writer who has made a first-rate director, and I'm as much against writers falsely aspiring to be directors as I am against directors presuming to be writers." Joseph Losey to Paul Jarrico, 27 November 1960, Paul Jarrico Papers, Special Collections, AMPAS.

61. Foreman was coasting on the success of *The Guns of Navarone* (dir. J. Lee Thompson, 1961) and preparing to make his directorial debut with another World War II drama, *The Victors* (1963). Losey, on the other hand, was struggling to save his latest—and most personal—film, *Eve* (1962), from his scissor-wielding producers. Michel Ciment, *Conversations with Losey* (New York: Methuen & Co., 1985), 397. Foreman attributed the project's failure to Losey's refusal to take suggestions from anyone other than his friend George Tabori, who wrote the film's screenplay. See Bertrand Tavernier, "Carl Foreman, 1969," *Amis Américains* (Lyons: Institut Lumière/Actes Sud, 1993), 517.

62. Lester Cole's wife, Kay, writes in a letter to Paul Jarrico dated 1 May 1964: "Lee Gold, Sam and Charlotte Wanamaker & the Sullivans (Lou and Wilma) and Lester had a big going over of the Jarrico and Scott feud. We're all Jarricos." Paul Jarrico Papers, Special Collections, AMPAS.

63. Patrick McGilligan, "Jules Dassin," in McGilligan and Buhle, *Tender Comrades*, 223.

64. Victor S. Navasky, *Naming Names*, 3rd ed. (New York: Hill and Wang, 2003), 348.

65. Lewis Milestone Papers, Folder 170, Special Collections, AMPAS. Dassin's example is ironic considering the rumors that would later surround Foreman's status as an unfriendly witness.

66. Caute, *Joseph Losey*, 313.

67. Navasky, *Naming Names*, 379.

68. Paul Jarrico to Matti Salo, 26 April 1991, Paul Jarrico Papers, Special Collections, AMPAS.

69. Larry Ceplair and Steven Englund, *The Inquisition in Hollywood: Politics in the Film Community, 1930–1960* (Urbana: University of Illinois Press, 2003), 421.

70. Larry Ceplair, *The Marxist and the Movies: A Biography of Paul Jarrico* (Lexington: University Press of Kentucky, 2007), 239.
71. "Maybe if I hadn't lived with a man whose guts were torn out by [the blacklist], I'd feel differently," Joan LaCour Scott explained to Victor Navasky. "But I feel personally responsible not to let anyone think he is forgiven." Navasky, *Naming Names*, 378.

CONCLUSION

1. Lee Gold to Paul Jarrico, 23 September 1964, Correspondence F–H, Paul Jarrico Papers, Special Collections, AMPAS.
2. Betsy Blair, *The Memory of All That: Love and Politics in New York, Hollywood, and Paris* (New York: Knopf, 2003).
3. Joseph Losey to Vladimir Pozner, 18 January 1961, Item 87, Joseph Losey Collection, British Film Institute.
4. Paul Buhle, "Joan LaCour Scott (and Adrian Scott)," in Patrick McGillian and Paul Buhle, *Tender Comrades: A Backstory of the Hollywood Blacklist* (New York: St. Martins, 1997), 604. The Warren Beatty project was an adaptation of a best seller by Gavin Lyall called *The Most Dangerous Game*. For more on Adrian Scott's years in London, see Jennifer E. Langdon, *Caught in the Crossfire: Adrian Scott and the Politics of Americanism in 1940s Hollywood* (New York: Columbia University Press, 2008), 354–390.
5. Lester Cole, *Hollywood Red: The Autobiography of Lester Cole* (Palo Alto, Calif.: Ramparts Press, 1981), 381–382. See also Bertrand Tavernier, "Carl Foreman, 1969," *Amis Américains* (Lyons: Institut Lumière/Actes Sud, 1993), 518.
6. Michel Ciment, *Conversations with Losey* (London: Methuen, 1985), 144.
7. He also recalls his father's dismayed reaction to the film: "All we do is shit." Denis Berry, interview with author, 17 March 2007.
8. Gordon Gow, "Jules Dassin: Style and Instinct II," *Films and Filming* 16, no. 6 (March 1970): 70.
9. "Dialogue on Film: Joseph Losey," *American Film* 6, no. 2 (November 1980): 59–60.
10. Larry Ceplair, Paul Jarrico Oral History, UCLA Special Collections (1991), 165; Norma Barzman, *The Red and the Blacklist: An Intimate Memoir of a Hollywood Expatriate* (New York: Thunder's Mouth Press/Nation Books, 2003), 169.
11. "John Berry," *A Voix Nue*, FranceCulture2, 20 May 1999.
12. Joan Barthel, "I'm an American, for God's Sake!," *New York Times*, 26 March 1967; "Jules Dassin," *L'Invité de Dimanche*, France 2, 21 May 1970.
13. "John Berry," *A Voix Nue*, FranceCulture2, 21 May 1999.
14. Ibid.
15. Arthur Friendly, "Jules Dassin: Victim of the 'Great American Red Hunt,'" *Washington Post*, 4 April 1971. Here Dassin took a very different stance with regard to his exile than that expressed a year earlier on French television, suggesting that he may have been tailoring his undoubtedly mixed feelings to his American audience.
16. Larry Ceplair and Steven Englund, *The Inquisition in Hollywood: Politics in the Film Community 1930–1960* (Urbana: University of Illinois Press, 2003), 402.
17. Alfred Friendly, "'The World Had Rocked,'" *Washington Post*, 9 April 1971.
18. "Carl Foreman," *Take One* 3, no. 9 (May 1973): 21.
19. Alfred Friendly, "Joseph Losey Is Back: He Isn't Scared Any More," *Washington Post*, 6 April 1971.
20. John Baxter, "Bernard Vorhaus," HUAC Collection, Item 31, British Film Institute.
21. "John Berry," *A Voix Nue*, FranceCulture2, 21 May 1999.

22. Joseph Losey, "Un Américain à l'étranger," *Positif*, no. 293/294 (July-August 1985): 36.
23. "Sept questions aux cinéastes étrangers ayant tourné en France," *Positif*, no. 325 (March 1988).
24. Losey felt that only the crème de la crème of European directors (Bergman, Fellini, Resnais, and Godard) had any real freedom of choice, and that this freedom stemmed largely from their own creative choices. "Godard does exactly what he wants to do insofar as he knows what he wants to do, but he does it by cutting a lot of corners and working very cheaply." Barthel, "I'm an American, for God's Sake!," *New York Times*, 26 March 1967.
25. Denis Berry, interview with author, 17 March 2007.
26. Paul Buhle and Dave Wagner, *Hide in Plain Sight: The Hollywood Blacklist in Film and Television, 1950–2002* (New York: Palgrave Macmillan, 2003), 109.
27. Joseph Losey, "Losey on McCarthyism," *Film Culture*, no. 50–51 (Fall and Winter 1970): 62.
28. Michael Wilson to Paul Jarrico, 8 April 1970, Paul Jarrico Papers, Special Collections, AMPAS.
29. Under the "package" system, an independent producer—often the film's star, director, or writer—assembled a film's creative team in order to use the "package" as leverage in exchange for studio financing and/or distribution. See Denise Mann, *Hollywood Independents: The Postwar Talent Takeover* (Minneapolis: University of Minnesota Press, 2008), 20, 243.
30. Buhle and Wagner, *Hide in Plain Sight*, 110.
31. Pierre Billard, *L'Age Classique du Cinema Française: du cinéma parlant à la Nouvelle Vague* (Paris: Flammarion, 1995), 568.
32. Pierre Billard views the French film noir as the reflection of the love-hate relationship between French cinema and Hollywood: "At their best, French film noirs are fake Hollywood films made with all the tenderness and scorn French filmmakers feel toward American cinema." Billard, *L'Age Classique*, 550.
33. Subsequent "comic" noirs include *La Bande à Papa* (dir. Lefranc, 1956) and *Le Caïd* (dir. Borderie, 1960). François Guérif, *Le Cinéma policier français* (Paris: Editions Henri Veyrier, 1981), 100.
34. Ginette Vincendeau, *Jean-Pierre Melville: An American in Paris* (London: British Film Institute, 2003), 100.
35. *Rififi in Amsterdam* (dir. Giovanni Korporaal, 1962), *Du Rififi à Tokyo* (dir. Jacques Deray, 1963), *Rififi en la ciudad* (dir. Jesus Franco, 1963), and *Du Rififi à Paname* (dir. Denys de la Patellière, 1966).
36. Melville, who had initially been assigned to direct *Rififi*, indicated his approbation by incorporating a reference to the film in an early draft of the script for *Bob le Flambeur*. Confronted with a safe to crack, a character suggests, "Why don't we do as in *Rififi?*" Vincendeau, *Jean-Pierre Melville*, 105.
37. Margaret Hinxman, "Interview with Joseph Losey," *Sunday Telegraph*, 22 February 1970.
38. Bertrand Tavernier, "À la recherche de Losey," *Positif*, no. 293/294 (July-August 1985): 28.
39. Harold Myers, "Carl Foreman's Pitch for Younger Producers Who 'Dig' Mass Taste," *Variety*, 19 November 1958.
40. Cited in Vanessa Schwartz, *It's So French!: Hollywood, Paris, and the Making of Cosmopolitan Film Culture* (Chicago: University of Chicago Press, 2007), 93.
41. Raymond Palmer, "Producer Carl Foreman to Return to Hollywood," *Los Angeles Times*, 1 February 1967.
42. Joseph Losey, "Un Américain à l'étranger," *Positif*, no. 293/294 (July-August 1985): 38.

SELECTED BIBLIOGRAPHY

ARCHIVAL SOURCES AND SPECIAL COLLECTIONS

Academy of Motion Picture Arts and Sciences (AMPAS), Margaret Herrick Library, Los Angeles
- Association of Motion Picture and Television Producers (AMPTP) Records
- Core Collection
- Ian McLellan Hunter Collection
- Paul Jarrico Collection
- Ring Lardner Jr. Collection
- Lewis Milestone Collection
- Stills Collection

Bibliothèque du Film (BIFI), Paris
- Fonds Crédit National
- Alexander Trauner Collection

Bibliothèque Nationale de France, Paris
- Inathèque
- Phonothèque

British Film Institute, London
- Clipping Files: "Blind Date," Cy Endfield, "Night and the City," Sam Wanamaker
- Carl Foreman Collection
- HUAC Collection
- Joseph Losey Collection

Columbia Center for Oral History, Columbia University, New York
- The Reminiscences of Carl Foreman, 1959.

National Archives, Washington, D.C.
- Jules Dassin File, Records of the House Un-American Activities Committee, Records of the United States House of Representatives
- Cy Endfield File, Records of the House Un-American Activities Committee, Records of the United States House of Representatives
- Carl Foreman File, Records of the House Un-American Activities Committee, Records of the United States House of Representatives

Department of Special Collections, Stanford University, Stanford, California
- Spyros P. Skouras Papers

University of California, Los Angeles, Performing Arts Special Collections
- Twentieth Century–Fox Legal Files
- Michael Wilson Papers

PUBLISHED SOURCES

Andersen, Thom. "Red Hollywood" and "Afterword." In *"Un-American" Hollywood: Politics and Film in the Blacklist Era,* edited by Frank Krutnik, Steve Neale, Brian Neve, and Peter Stanfield. New Brunswick, N.J.: Rutgers University Press, 2007.

Anhalt, Diana. *A Gathering of Fugitives: American Political Expatriates in Mexico, 1948–1965.* Santa Maria, Calif.: Archer Books, 2001.

Auerbach, Jonathan. *Dark Borders: Film Noir and American Citizenship.* Durham, N.C.: Duke University Press, 2011.

Bacher, Lutz. *Max Ophuls in the Hollywood Studios.* New Brunswick, N.J.: Rutgers University Press, 1996.

Barr, Charles, ed. *All Our Yesterdays: 90 Years of British Cinema.* London: British Film Institute, 1986.

Barron, Stephanie, ed. *Exiles and Emigrés: The Flight of European Artists from Hitler.* New York: Harry Abrams, 1997.

Barrot, Olivier. *L'Ecran français, 1943–1953: Histoire d'un journal et d'une époque.* Paris: Les Editeurs français réunis, 1979.

Barthes, Roland. *Mythologies.* Paris: Editions du Seuil, 1957.

Barzman, Norma. *The Red and the Blacklist: An Intimate Memoir of a Hollywood Expatriate.* New York: Thunder's Mouth Press/Nation Books, 2003.

Baxter, John. *The Hollywood Exiles.* New York: Taplinger, 1976.

———. *Hollywood in the Thirties.* New York: Paperback Library, 1970.

Bazin, André. "An Aesthetic of Reality: Neorealism." In *What Is Cinema?* Vol. 2. Translated by Hugh Gray. Berkeley: University of California Press, 1971.

Bernstein, Irving. *Hollywood at the Crossroads: An Economic Study of the Motion Picture Industry.* Hollywood: Hollywood A.F. of L. Film Council, 1957.

Bernstein, Walter. *Inside Out: A Memoir of the Blacklist.* New York: Da Capo Press, 2000.

Betz, Mark. *Beyond the Subtitle: Remapping European Art Cinema.* Minneapolis: University of Minnesota Press, 2009.

Biesen, Sheri Chinen. *Blackout: World War II and the Origins of Film Noir.* Baltimore: Johns Hopkins University Press, 2005.

Billard, Pierre. *L'Age Classique du Cinéma Français: Du cinema parlant à la Nouvelle Vague.* Paris: Flammarion, 1995.

Blair, Betsy. *The Memory of All That: Love and Politics in New York, Hollywood, and Paris.* New York: Alfred A. Knopf, 2003.

Bogle, Donald. *Dorothy Dandridge: A Biography.* New York: Amistad Press, 1997.

Borde, Raymond, and Etienne Chaumeton. *A Panorama of American Film Noir, 1941–1953.* Translated by Paul Hammond. San Francisco: City Lights Books, 2002.

Bordwell, David. "The Art Cinema as a Mode of Film Practice." In *Film Theory and Criticism: Introductory Readings,* edited by Leo Braudy and Marshall Cohen. 5th ed. New York: Oxford University Press, 1999.

Brook, Vincent. *Driven to Darkness: Jewish Émigré Directors and the Rise of Film Noir.* New Brunswick, N.J.: Rutgers University Press, 2009.

Brownlow, Kevin. *David Lean.* London: Richard Cohen, 1996.

Bruccoli, Matthew J., ed. *The Naked City: A Screenplay by Malvin Wald and Albert Maltz.* Carbondale: Southern Illinois University Press, 1979.

Buhle, Paul, and Dave Wagner. *Hide in Plain Sight: The Hollywood Blacklist in Film and Television, 1950–2002.* New York: Palgrave Macmillan, 2003.

———. *Radical Hollywood: The Untold Story behind America's Favorite Movies.* New York: New Press, 2002.

———. *A Very Dangerous Citizen: Abraham Polonsky and the Hollywood Left.* Berkeley: University of California Press, 2001.

Butler, Michael. "Shock Waves." *Cinema Journal* 44, no. 4 (Summer 2005): 81.

Campbell, James. *Exiled in Paris: Richard Wright, James Baldwin, Samuel Beckett, and Others on the Left Bank.* New York: Scribner, 1995.

Caute, David. *Joseph Losey: A Revenge on Life.* New York: Oxford University Press, 1994.

Ceplair, Larry. *The Marxist and the Movies: A Biography of Paul Jarrico.* Lexington: University Press of Kentucky, 2007.

Ceplair, Larry, and Steven Englund. *The Inquisition in Hollywood: Politics in the Film Community 1930–1960.* Urbana: University of Illinois Press, 2003.

Ciment, Michel. *Joseph Losey—L'Oeil du maître.* Paris: Institut Lumière/Actes Sud, 1994.

———. *Conversations with Losey.* London: Methuen, 1985.

Cole, Lester. *Hollywood Red: The Autobiography of Lester Cole.* Palo Alto, Calif.: Ramparts Press, 1981.

Cook, Bruce. *Dalton Trumbo.* New York: Charles Scribner's Sons, 1977.

Crisp, Colin. *The Classic French Cinema, 1930–1960.* Bloomington: Indiana University Press, 1993.

Custen, George F. *Twentieth Century's Fox: Darryl F. Zanuck and the Culture of Hollywood.* New York: Basic Books, 1997.

De Baecque, Antoine. *La cinéphilie: Invention d'un regard, histoire d'une culture, 1944–1968.* Paris: Fayard, 2003.

De Grazia, Victoria. *Irresistible Empire: America's Advance through Twentieth-Century Europe.* Cambridge, Mass.: Belknap Press of Harvard University Press, 2005.

De Rham, Edith. *Joseph Losey.* London: Deutsch, 1991.

Dickinson, Margaret, and Sarah Street. *Cinema and State: The Film Industry and the British Government, 1927–1984.* London: British Film Institute, 1985.

Dickos, Andrew. *Street with No Name: A History of the Classic American Film Noir.* Lexington: University Press of Kentucky, 2002.

Dmytryk, Edward. *Odd Man Out: A Memoir of the Hollywood Ten.* Carbondale: Southern Illinois University Press, 1996.

Elsaesser, Thomas. "Ethnicity, Authenticity, and Exile: A Counterfeit Trade? German Filmmakers and Hollywood." In *Home, Exile, Homeland: Film, Media, and the Politics of Place,* edited by Hamid Naficy. New York: Routledge 1999.

Erickson, Glenn. "Expressionist Doom in *Night and the City.*" In *Film Noir Reader,* edited by Alain Silver and James Ursini. New York: Limelight Editions, 1996.

Forest, Claude. "De Vichy au Quartier latin: L'âge d'or du cinéma populaire." In *CinémAction: Le Cinéma du Sam'di Soir,* no. 95, edited by Gérard Dessere and Nicholas Schmidt. Condé-sur-Noireau: Editions Corlet/Telerama, 2000.

Fraser-Cavassoni, Natasha. *Sam Spiegel: The Incredible Life and Times of Hollywood's Most Iconoclastic Producer.* New York: Simon & Schuster, 2003.

Gallagher, Catherine, and Steven Greenblatt. *Practicing New Historicism.* Chicago: University of Chicago Press, 2000.

Gardner, Colin. *Joseph Losey.* Manchester: Manchester University Press, 2004.

Gaston-Mathé, Catherine. *La Société Française au Miroir de son Cinéma: De la débâcle à la décolonisation.* Paris: Arléa-Corlet, 1996.

Gordon, Bernard. *Hollywood Exile, or How I Learned to Love the Blacklist.* Austin: University of Texas Press, 1999.

Guback, Thomas. *The International Film Industry: Western Europe and America since 1945.* Bloomington: Indiana University Press, 1969.

Guérif, François. *Le Cinéma policier français.* Paris: Editions Henri Veyrier, 1981.

Hall, Sheldon. *"Zulu": With Some Guts behind It—The Making of the Epic Movie.* Sheffield: Tomahawk Press, 2005.

Harper, Sue, and Vincent Porter. *British Cinema of the 1950s: The Decline of Deference.* Oxford: Oxford University Press, 2003.

Hedling, Erik. "Free Cinema and British Social Realism." In *The Cinema Book,* edited by Pam Cook and Mieke Bernink. 2nd ed. London: British Film Institute, 1999.

———. "Lindsay Anderson and the Development of the British Art Film." In *The British Cinema Book,* edited by Robert Murphy. London: British Film Institute, 2001.

———. "Lindsay Anderson: *Sequence* and the Rise of Auteurism in 1950s Britain." In *British Cinema of the 1950s: A Celebration,* edited by Ian MacKillop and Neil Sinyard. Manchester: Manchester University Press, 2003.

Heilbut, Anthony. *Exiled in Paradise: German Refugee Artists and Intellectuals in America from the 1930s to the Present.* Berkeley: University of California Press, 1997.

Hellman, Lillian. *Scoundrel Time.* Boston: Little, Brown, 1976.

Herman, Jan. *A Talent for Trouble: The Life of Hollywood's Most Acclaimed Director, William Wyler.* New York: G. P. Putnam's Sons, 1995.

Hirsch, Foster. *Joseph Losey.* Boston: Twayne Publishers, 1980.

Horak, Jan-Christopher. "German Exile Cinema, 1933–1950." *Film History* 8 (1996): 373–389.

Horne, Gerald. *The Final Victim of the Blacklist: John Howard Lawson, Dean of the Hollywood Ten.* Berkeley: University of California Press, 2006.

Hubert-Lacombe, Patricia. *Le Cinéma français dans la guerre froide, 1946–1956.* Paris: Editions L'Harmatton, 1996.

Humphries, Reynold. *Hollywood's Blacklists: A Political and Cultural History.* Edinburgh: Edinburgh University Press, 2010.

Jeancolas, Jean-Pierre. "From the Blum-Byrnes Agreement to the GATT Affair." In *Hollywood and Europe: Economics, Culture, National Identity, 1945–1965,* edited by Geoffrey Nowell-Smith and Steven Ricci. London: British Film Institute, 1998.

Karnow, Stanley. *Paris in the Fifties.* New York: Random House, 1997.

Knox, Mickey. *The Good, the Bad, and the Dolce Vita: The Adventures of an Actor in Hollywood, Paris, and Rome.* New York: Nation Books, 2004.

Koch, Howard. *As Time Goes By: Memoirs of a Writer.* New York: Harcourt Brace Jovanovich, 1979.

Kuisel, Richard. "The Fernandel Factor: The Rivalry between the French and American Cinema in the 1950s." *Yale French Studies* 98 (2000): 119–134.

———. *Seducing the French: The Dilemma of Americanization.* Berkeley: University of California Press, 1993.

Langdon, Jennifer E. *Caught in the Crossfire: Adrian Scott and the Politics of Americanism in 1940s Hollywood.* New York: Columbia University Press, 2008.

Lardner, Ring Jr. *I'd Hate Myself in the Morning: A Memoir.* New York: Thunder's Mouth Press/Nation Books, 2000.

Lewis, Jon. "We Do Not Ask You To Condone This: How the Blacklist Saved Hollywood." *Cinema Journal* 39, no. 2 (Winter 2000): 3–30.

MacKillop, Ian, and Neil Sinyard, eds. *British Cinema of the 1950s: A Celebration.* Manchester: Manchester University Press, 2003.

Macnab, Geoffrey. *J. Arthur Rank and the British Film Industry.* London: Routledge, 1993.

Maltby, Richard. "Made for Each Other: The Melodrama of Hollywood and the House Committee on Un-American Activities, 1947." In *Cinema, Politics, and Society in America,* edited by Philip Davies and Brian Neve. Manchester: Manchester University Press, 1981.

———. "The Politics of the Maladjusted Text." In *The Movie Book of Film Noir*, edited by Ian Cameron. London: Studio Vista, 1992.

Manfull, Helen, ed. *Additional Dialogue: Letters of Dalton Trumbo, 1942–1962*. New York: M. Evans and Company, 1970.

Mann, Denise. *Hollywood Independents: The Postwar Talent Takeover.* Minneapolis: University of Minnesota Press, 2008.

Marie, Michel. *La Nouvelle Vague: Une école artistique.* Paris: Editions Nathan, 1997.

May, Lary. "Movie Star Politics: The Screen Actor's Guild, Cultural Conversion, and the Hollywood Red Scare." In *Recasting America: Culture and Politics in the Age of Cold War*, edited by Lary May. Chicago: University of Chicago Press, 1989.

———. *The Big Tomorrow: Hollywood and the Politics of the American Way.* Chicago: University of Chicago Press, 2000.

McGilligan, Patrick, and Paul Buhle. *Tender Comrades: A Backstory of the Hollywood Blacklist.* New York: St. Martin's, 1997.

Mercouri, Melina. *Je suis née grèque.* Paris: Editions Stock, 1972.

Miller, Christopher L. *The French Atlantic Triangle: Literature and Culture of the Slave Trade.* Durham, N.C.: Duke University Press, 2007.

Milne, Tom. *Losey on Losey.* New York: Doubleday, 1968.

Murphy, Robert, ed. *The British Cinema Book.* London: British Film Institute, 2001.

———. *Realism and Tinsel: Cinema and Society in Britain 1939–1948.* London: Routledge, 1989.

———. *Sixties British Cinema.* London: British Film Institute, 1992.

———. "Under the Shadow of Hollywood." In *All Our Yesterdays: 90 Years of British Cinema*, edited by Charles Barr. London: British Film Institute, 1986.

Naficy, Hamid. *An Accented Cinema: Exilic and Diasporic Filmmaking.* Princeton, N.J.: Princeton University Press, 2001.

Naremore, James. *More than Night: Film Noir in Its Contexts.* Berkeley: University of California Press, 1998.

Navasky, Victor S. *Naming Names.* 3rd ed. New York: Hill and Wang, 2003.

Neale, Steve. "Art Cinema as Institution." *Screen* 22, no. 1 (1981): 11–40.

———. "Swashbucklers and Sitcoms, Cowboys and Crime, Nurses, Just Men, and Defenders: Blacklisted Writers and TV in the 1950s and 1960s." *Film Studies: An International Review* 7 (Winter 2005): 83–103.

Neupert, Richard. *A History of the French New Wave Cinema.* 2nd ed. Madison: University of Wisconsin Press, 2007.

Neve, Brian. "Cases in European Film Culture and the Hollywood Blacklist Diaspora." In *The Lost Decade? The 1950s in European History, Politics, Society, and Culture*, edited by Heiko Feldner, Claire Gorrara, and Kevin Passmore. Newcastle: Cambridge Scholars Publishing, 2011.

———. *Film and Politics in America: A Social Tradition.* London: Routledge, 1992.

———. "An Interview with Cy Endfield." *Film Studies: An International Review* 7, (Winter 2005): 116–127.

———. *The Many Lives of Cy Endfield.* Madison: University of Wisconsin Press, 2013.

Nogueira, Rui, ed. *Melville on Melville.* London: Secker and Warburg/British Film Institute, 1971.

North, Joseph, ed. *New Masses: An Anthology of the Rebel Thirties.* New York: International Publishers, 1969.

Nowell-Smith, Geoffrey, and Steven Ricci, eds. *Hollywood and Europe: Economics, Culture, National Identity, 1945–1965.* London: British Film Institute, 1998.

Phillips, Alastair. *Rififi.* London: I. B. Tauris, 2009.

Phillips, Gene D. *Exiles in Hollywood: Major European Film Directors in America.* Lehigh, Pa.: Lehigh University Press, 1998.

Prime, Rebecca. "Cloaked in Compromise: Jules Dassin's 'Naked' City." In *"Un-American" Hollywood: Politics and Film in the Blacklist Era,* edited by Frank Krutnik, Brian Neve, Steve Neale, and Peter Stanfield. New Brunswick, N.J.: Rutgers University Press, 2007.

Radosh, Ronald, and Allis Radosh. *Red Star over Hollywood: The Film Colony's Long Romance with the Left.* San Francisco: Encounter Books, 2005.

Reynolds, R. C. *Stage Left: The Development of the American Social Drama in the Thirties.* Troy, N.Y.: Whitston Publishing Company, 1986.

Rissient, Pierre. "Entretien avec Pierre Rissient." In *L'Univers de Joseph Losey. CinémAction,* no. 96 (3me trimestre, 2000).

Roger, Philippe. *Rêves & cauchemars américains: Les Etats-Unis au miroir de l'opinion publique française (1945–1953).* Paris: Presses Universitaires du Septentrion, 1996.

Rosendorf, Neal Moses. "'Hollywood in Madrid': American Film Producers and the Franco Regime, 1950–1970." *Historical Journal of Film, Radio, and Television* 27, no. 1 (March 2007): 77–109.

Ross, Kristin. *Fast Cars, Clean Bodies: Decolonization and the Reordering of French Culture.* Cambridge, Mass.: MIT Press, 1995.

Ross, Steven J. *Hollywood Left and Right: How Movie Stars Shaped American Politics.* New York: Oxford University Press, 2011.

Rossi, John P. "The British Reaction to McCarthyism, 1950–54." *Mid-America: An Historical Review* 70, no. 1 (1988).

Rouverol, Jean. *Refugees from Hollywood: A Journal of the Blacklist Years.* Albuquerque: University of New Mexico Press, 2000.

Ryall, Tom. *Britain and the American Cinema.* Thousand Oaks, Calif.: Sage, 2001.

Said, Edward. *Reflections on Exile and Other Essays.* Cambridge, Mass.: Harvard University Press, 2000.

Saunders, Frances Stoner. *The Cultural Cold War: The CIA and the World of Arts and Letters.* New York: New Press, 1999.

Sayre, Nora. *On the Wing: A Young American Abroad.* Washington, D.C.: Counterpoint, 2001.

Schatz, Thomas. *Old Hollywood/New Hollywood: Ritual, Art and Industry.* Ann Arbor: University of Michigan Research Press, 1983.

Schreiber, Rebecca M. *Cold War Exiles in Mexico: U.S. Dissidents and the Culture of Critical Resistance.* Minneapolis: University of Minnesota Press, 2008.

Schwartz, Nancy Lynn. *The Hollywood Writers' Wars.* New York: Knopf, 1982.

Schwartz, Vanessa R. *It's So French!: Hollywood, Paris, and the Making of Cosmopolitan Film Culture.* Chicago: University of Chicago Press, 2007.

Shandley, Robert. *Runaway Romances: Hollywood's Postwar Tour of Europe.* Philadelphia: Temple University Press, 2009.

Shaw, Tony. *British Cinema and the Cold War: The State, Propaganda, and Consensus.* London: I. B. Tauris, 2006.

———. *Hollywood's Cold War.* Edinburgh: Edinburgh University Press, 2007.

Sheen, Erica. "Un-American: Dmytryk, Rossellini, and *Christ in Concrete.*" *Film Studies: An International Review* 7 (Winter 2005): 32–42.

Smith, Jeff. "A Good Business Proposition: Dalton Trumbo, Spartacus, and the End of the Blacklist." In *Controlling Hollywood: Censorship and Regulation in the Studio Era,* edited by Matthew Bernstein. New Brunswick, N.J.: Rutgers University Press, 1999.

Sobchack, Vivian. "Lounge Time: Postwar Crises and the Chronotope of Film Noir." In *Refiguring American Film Genres: History and Theory*, edited by Nick Browne. Berkeley: University of California Press, 1998.

Stewart, Donald Ogden. *By a Stroke of Luck! An Autobiography.* New York: Paddington Press, 1975.

Stovall, Tyler. "The Fire This Time: Black American Expatriates and the Algerian War." *Yale French Studies* 98 (2000): 182–200.

———. *Paris Noir: African-Americans in the City of Light.* Boston: Houghton Mifflin, 1996.

Swann, Paul. *The Hollywood Feature Film in Postwar Britain.* London: Croom Helm, 1987.

Talbot, David, and Barbara Zheutlin. *Creative Differences: Profiles of Hollywood Dissidents.* Boston: South End Press, 1978.

Tavernier, Bertrand. *Amis Américains: Entretiens avec les grands auteurs d'Hollywood.* Lyons: Institut Lumière/Actes Sud, 1993.

Taylor, John Russell. *Strangers in Paradise: The Hollywood Emigrés 1933–1950.* London: Faber and Faber, 1983.

Vaughn, Robert. *Only Victims: A Study of Show Business Blacklisting.* New York: Limelight Editions, 1996.

Vincendeau, Ginette. *Jean-Pierre Melville: "An American in Paris."* London: British Film Institute, 2003.

———. "Noir Is Also a French Word: The French Antecedents of Film Noir." In *The Book of Film Noir*, edited by Ian Cameron. New York: Continuum, 1993.

Von Eschen, Penny M. *Satchmo Blows Up the World: Jazz Ambassadors Play the Cold War.* Cambridge, Mass.: Harvard University Press, 2004.

Vorhaus, Bernard. *Saved from Oblivion: An Autobiography.* Lanham, Md.: Scarecrow Press, 2000.

Walker, Alexander. *Hollywood, England: The British Film Industry in the Sixties.* London: Harrap, 1986.

Wall, Irwin M. *The United States and the Making of Postwar France, 1945–1954.* Cambridge: Cambridge University Press, 1991.

Wilensky, Barbara. *Sure Seaters: The Emergence of Art House Cinema.* Minneapolis: University of Minnesota Press, 2001.

Wollen, Peter. *Paris Hollywood: Writings on Film.* London: Verso, 2002.

INDEX

Note: Page numbers in *italics* indicate illustrations.

ABOUT THE AUTHOR

REBECCA PRIME is the Libman Professor of the Humanities and an assistant professor of art at Hood College, where she directs the Center for the Humanities. Her work on international film history and aesthetics has appeared in journals such as *Film History* and *Post Script* along with the anthology *"Un-American" Hollywood: Politics and Film in the Blacklist Era* and the Paris and Marseille editions of the series *World Film Locations.*